"Do not despair about India; it is like the Ganges River. Ultimately, it will find its way to the sea."

George Yeo

INDIA RISING

Fresh Hope New Fears

My diary of an Indian decade

RAVI VELLOOR

with a foreword by George Yeo

Konark Publishers Pvt Ltd
New Delhi · Seattle

Konark Publishers Pvt. Ltd
206, First Floor,
Peacock Lane, Shahpur Jat,
New Delhi-110 049.
Phone: +91-11-41055065, 65254972
e-mail: india@konarkpublishers.com
Website: www.konarkpublishers.com

Konark Publishers International
8615, 13th Ave SW,
Seattle, WA 98106
Phone: (415) 409-9988
e-mail: us@konarkpublishers.com

Indian Edition for sale in India, Pakistan, Srilanka, Bangladesh, Maldives, Nepal and Bhutan only 2016

Not for export elsewhere

First Published by Straits Times Press Pte Ltd

Photographs are the property of Singapore Press Holdings
unless otherwise stated

Cover design by Lock Hong Liang

Cataloging in Publication Data--DK
Courtesy: D.K. Agencies (P) Ltd. <docinfo@dkagencies.com>

Velloor, Ravi, 1958- author.
India rising : fresh hope new fears: my diary of an Indian decade / Ravi Velloor; with a foreword by George Yeo. -- Second edition.
pages cm
Includes index.
ISBN 9789322008741

1. India--Politics and government--21st century. 2. India--Foreign relations--21st century. 3. India--Social conditions--21st century. 4. India--Economic policy--21st century. I. Title.

DS526.7.V45 2016 DDC 954.05 23

Printed and bound at Thomson Press (India) Ltd.

For Geetika, Dhruv and Shriya

CONTENTS

IV: A DYNASTY TOTTERS

V: INDIA RISING

FOREWORD
by George Yeo

My first encounter with Ravi Velloor was at Hyderabad House in New Delhi in February 1993. He was a guest at the welcome dinner hosted by minister of state for external affairs Salman Khurshid for a Singapore delegation I led to India. Next day, we met again at a press conference I addressed at Shastri Bhawan, which houses several ministries. Ravi was then a young correspondent for the Time Inc. publication, *Asiaweek*, and I was a young minister in the Singapore Cabinet, in India to study the progress of economic reforms under prime minister PV Narasimha Rao. Ravi credits those encounters for triggering his interest in Singapore and his decision, later that year, to leave his comfortable sinecure to move to Singapore, with *The Straits Times*. I am happy to accept some responsibility, and continue to track his career with deep interest.

The period Ravi covers in *India Rising* has a personal resonance for me, because it follows a decade of assiduous nurturing of Singapore-India ties. In October 1991, finance minister Manmohan Singh and commerce minister P Chidambaram had specially flown to Singapore to explain the opening up of the Indian economy. Our two-week trip to India in early 1993, which would end in Chennai, was partly in response. We arrived in India not long after riots broke out over the dismantling of the Babri Mosque in Ayodhya the previous December. Eating dinner on the roof of the Godrej Building in Mumbai, we noticed that the streets below were eerily quiet. But we left India convinced that the reform process was serious. Young district collectors who escorted us in Mysore and Kanchipuram showed an enthusiasm for development which impressed us.

Lee Kuan Yew, then senior minister in the Singapore Cabinet, read our optimistic report with scepticism. From time to time, he would send me newspaper articles expressing doubt about India's ability to change. But he kept an open mind and constantly took in new inputs. Two years later, after Singapore's International Tech Park in Bangalore took off, he accepted that India was changing but reminded PM Goh Chok Tong to be also prepared for governmental change in India. He was prescient. Not long afterwards, a new government took charge in Karnataka. Fortunately, the new chief minister, HD Deve Gowda, flew to Kolkata to assure Goh at a Confederation of Indian Industry (CII) event of his support for the project. Lee Kuan Yew followed the ups and downs of India's development till the end. Meeting Rahul Gandhi at the Istana, Singapore's Government House, he reflected that he had known Rahul's father, grandmother and great-grandfather. No other Singaporean had the same longitudinal view of India. When he died in March 2015, PM Narendra Modi declared a day of national mourning and attended the funeral service. Singaporeans were moved to the core.

Over the years, I visited India regularly for different reasons and in different capacities. Ravi meanwhile, had moved to Bloomberg News in Singapore and at the end of 2004, was back again with *The Straits Times*, this time preparing to return to India as South Asia Bureau Chief. Our meetings grew more frequent, and often he would interview me. We would tour together frequently. Those trips included a visit to the dusty hinterland of India's Bihar state, where we were working on the revival of Nalanda University, and to the Jaffna peninsula, short weeks after Sri Lanka's long civil war ended. As fellow travellers, I would always take the opportunity to ask him questions about India and its neighbourhood. We became friends. I found his insights invaluable. He is a keen observer, not only of events but of individuals, choosing mainly to stay in the background when in company. In private conversation, though, he comes alive as a wonderful storyteller. Writing for *The Straits Times*, he opened a window into the Indian subcontinent for its readers, making the region's complexities more comprehensible for a global audience. The chapters in this book bear witness not only to his storytelling skills but also his ability to win and hold the trust and confidence of his sources at different levels of government and society.

India Rising, in some ways, is told by a person with a Singaporean eye. This is perhaps not inappropriate given Singapore's unique position. Singapore's links with India are rooted in history. The name Singapore itself is of course Sanskrit in origin. In 1819, Stamford Raffles founded Singapore as a trading post for the British East India Company. Until 1867, Singapore was governed from Kolkata, Bengal's capital. A large part of Singapore's legal and administrative inheritance came from the Raj in India. When I studied military law at Singapore's Officer Cadet School in 1973, the lecturer told us that if there ever was a lacuna in the Singapore Armed Forces Act, we should look into the Indian Army Manual for guidance. As director of Joint Operations and Planning in 1988, before settling on the design for a new Singapore Armed Forces Military Institute, I led a delegation to study the National Defence Academy in Khadakvasla, Pune. The Academy was tri-service, meaning that Army, Navy and Air Force cadets went through a common core programme before they were commissioned as officers. It was the model we wanted to adopt in Singapore.

In one conversation with Chidambaram, whom I first met in Davos in January 1993, he referred to Singapore as being almost a part of India. He did not say this in a patronising way but with a feeling I would describe as affectionate. In May 2010, my wife and I took up his longstanding invitation to visit his hometown in the Chettinad region of Tamil Nadu state. I appreciated very much his taking time off from his busy schedule as home affairs minister to accompany us for three days. Prior to that, I did not realise that the Chettiar links in Southeast Asia were so widespread and intricate, with origins possibly going back to the days of Chola involvement in Southeast Asia's China trade.

Before meeting Chidambaram in Pudukkottai, I visited the magnificent Brihadeeswarar Temple in Thanjavur built by Raja Chola I. Almost exactly a year later, I lost the elections in Singapore. Singapore's *Tamil Murasu* carried an article attributing my loss to an indiscretion – which was to enter the temple by the main gate. I should have known but no one told me.

"Singapore Sling", as the chapter on Singapore is called in this book, begins with the signing of the Comprehensive Economic Cooperation Agreement (CECA), and its longer term impact on India's economic and foreign policy. In April 2002, on an official visit to Singapore, PM Atal Bihari Vajpayee proposed to PM Goh a free trade agreement (FTA) between India and Singapore. Over breakfast with Vajpayee's disinvestment minister Arun Shourie the following morning, I told him that my officials in the Trade Ministry laughed when they heard it. Over long years, India's deeply protectionist instincts were well known to Singapore officials who are, naturally, champions of free trade. His moustache twitching, Arun looked me in the eye and said he would report my response to Vajpayee. I half regretted being so frank and ungracious with Arun but his sincerity and earnestness had caused me to drop my guard. Anyhow, it had the desired effect. Negotiations, though difficult, were serious. The original FTA became a comprehensive CECA. I took the precaution of keeping Sonia Gandhi and Manmohan Singh, then in the Opposition, briefed. CECA was only concluded in June 2005 under an Indian National Congress-led government. Ravi even then spotted the wider significance of CECA, that it was not only a bilateral trade deal but also a sign of change in India's view of international trade. When a supertanker like India makes a small change in direction, the long-term implications are huge – what we are seeing today.

My involvement with Nalanda University began with deputy PM Lal Krishna Advani's visit to Singapore in January 2004. I was his minister-in-attendance, just as I had been when PM Rao visited Singapore 10 years earlier. I knew India was looking East and proposed to Advani the promotion of Buddhist sites in India to East Asians, many of whom are Buddhists. He put me in touch with tourism minister Jagmohan, who invited me to attend the dedication of the Mahabodhi Mahavihara as a UNESCO World Heritage Site. Before the visit to the temple in Bodh Gaya, I read up on the Buddhist tourism circuit and became acquainted with the history of Nalanda. I did not know that India had such a profound influence on China over a thousand years ago and suggested to Montek Singh Ahluwalia, deputy chairman of India's Planning Commission and a close adviser to Manmohan Singh, that the revival of Nalanda should be conceptualised as an international project involving countries which the old Nalanda influenced. The past then becomes an inspiration for the future. I was honoured to be invited by the Indian government in 2007 to be a member of the Nalanda Mentor Group headed by Amartya Sen who became the founding chancellor. As Singapore's foreign minister, I helped to lobby support among the countries of the East Asia Summit for the revival of Nalanda as a secular international university. I found an enthusiastic supporter in the foreign minister of South Korea, Dr Ban Ki-moon, now United Nations (UN) secretary-general. After the leaders of the East Asian Summit gave their blessing in 2009, the Indian parliament passed the Nalanda University Act in November 2010 with unanimous support and loud acclaim from all political parties.

India Rising describes key aspects of the country's development in the last 10 years, expressing fresh hopes but also new fears under Modi. Each chapter cuts a different slice into the complex reality that is India. Like a CT scan, the slices combine to give the reader a composite sense of the unfolding Indian drama. Importantly for Asia, it also looks closely at the strategic sweet spot India has found itself in, wooed by every major power. India is too big to be ignored yet not so powerful as to be considered a threat by any of the major powers.

For the US and Japan, the rapid growth of China is threatening and therefore to be countered. Ravi describes in some detail how the US has been wooing India for years in order to help build it up as a countervailing economic and nuclear power. India plays this dynamic to its own advantage without antagonising China. The fact is that while some Indians view China as a long-term threat, very few Chinese view India in the same way. The border dispute will take time to resolve but it is not a necessary precondition for the improvement of bilateral relations. In his fascinating chapter on the Malayalees, who played leading roles in India's national security and foreign policy apparatus, Ravi underestimated the quiet achievement of Mallus like Shivshankar Menon who helped both sides gradually ratchet down the border problem as the dominant item on the bilateral agenda. I worked with Menon behind the scenes to win Chinese support for the revival of Nalanda University.

When Modi became prime minister, he surprised many of us by the brilliance of his foreign policy, keeping all external forces in dynamic balance. Knowing that his priority was to visit Japan and the US, he decided to take the Chinese president's congratulatory phone call first after he was sworn into office. The choreography of president Xi Jinping's official visit to India, beginning in Ahmedabad, and PM Modi's visit to China, beginning in Xian, was arranged by the two leaders and the two foreign ministries against a grand historical backdrop going back to the Buddhist arrival in China almost two thousand years ago. Arriving in Beijing, PM Modi and PM Li Keqiang witnessed a joint mass display of yoga and *taiji* (a Chinese martial art) at the forecourt of the Temple of Heaven, where Chinese emperors led prayers and made sacrifices for good harvests. It was a bow of two ancient peoples to each other. When India requested and China agreed to a new pilgrimage route through the Nathu La Pass to Kailash-Manasarovar, the abode of Lord Shiva in Tibet, it was symbolism suffused with meaning.

There is no danger to the US and Japan that India will get too close to China but there is also no danger that India can be made use of by others to contain China. Manmohan Singh summed it well when he said that each was too big to be contained by the other and the world is big enough for both. I therefore agree wholeheartedly with Ravi that India is now in a strategic sweet spot, courted by everyone. This can help India attract investment, export to the world and extend its global influence in all directions, including into Southeast Asia, which has always been Singapore's hope.

But India is more than just a political and economic play. India has always been a major centre of world civilisation. There is no aspect of the human condition which Indian philosophers have not reflected on and responded to. After the terrible slaughter of Kalinga, Ashoka turned to Buddhism as a better way to order society. Unlike China or Europe, India did not experience the same kind of mass killings in the last two thousand years. The tolerance, even celebration, of diversity in Indian civilisation is an important reason for India's less violent ways. For as long as India stays centred in this tradition, its contribution to the world will be much greater than just the political and economic.

Ravi's book provides valuable context for my own experiences and gives deeper meaning to that part of my life which touches India. A few months ago, the son of a former Union minister from the Congress party advised me to delete a post on my Facebook account. I had uploaded a picture of my wife and I eating *pho* (Vietnamese beef noodles) in Harvard Square. He thought it might elicit a negative response in India to my role as the new chancellor of Nalanda University. He is a good friend and certainly no extremist. I knew he meant well. I did not follow his advice of course but his nervousness troubled me.

India Rising does not baulk from analysing such tensions in Indian society today. Ravi's underlying optimism for India's future is comforting reassurance of mine.

George Yeo served as Cabinet minister in Singapore governments from 1991 to 2011, the last seven as minister for foreign affairs. He is chancellor of Nalanda University and a member of the Vatican's Council for the Economy. His book Bonsai, Banyan and the Tao *was published in 2015.*

PROLOGUE

Narendra Modi's spectacular rise to national leadership in the parliamentary elections held in the summer of 2014 was, without question, a watershed event in the history of contemporary India. In the aftermath of the communal rioting witnessed in his home state, Gujarat, a few months after he took charge as chief minister there in late 2001, few political figures in the country have presented so polarising an image. This is partly because he has never – out of conviction about his own innocence or political expediency – shown much public remorse for that ghastly event, which took 1,044 lives by official count, with three times as many Muslims dying as Hindus. Those riots had been provoked by the arson attack on a train that took the lives of 58 Hindu pilgrims returning from Ayodhya, a town in Uttar Pradesh. Had the attack happened 100 km back, when it was in Madhya Pradesh rather than in Gujarat, the world, and India, would have looked at Modi very differently.

Yet, few Indian chief ministers before him could be said to have worked so tirelessly to develop the state under his charge and to raise the welfare of every section of its people. Indeed, in Gujarat, large sections of the Muslim minority that once loathed him now vote for the man or at least have a more ambivalent attitude towards him. Beyond his initial stumble, Modi has presided over one of the most peaceful – and prosperous – eras of Gujarat, a state bordering Pakistan that is blessed with little more than an entrepreneurial spirit and having few of the natural resources of a Jharkhand or an Odisha (formerly Orissa). Indians now want him to try and use his boundless energy and forceful personality to fix the larger nation beyond

Gujarat. A quarter century after prime minister PV Narasimha Rao gave the green light to unshackle India's economy, global attention is turning once more towards the giant nation in South Asia, with its 1.2 billion people market, massive military, remarkable brainpower and, needless to say, a million wounds, mostly self-inflicted.

Laid waste in the surge towards Modi is the Indian National Congress, the party of freedom once led by Mahatma Gandhi and Pandit Jawaharlal Nehru, and now by Sonia Gandhi, the Italian-born Roman Catholic widow of Nehru's grandson, Rajiv. Ten years after she led her party and the United Progressive Alliance coalition to a stunning upset win, she surrendered power to the group she had earlier bested – Bharatiya Janata Party (BJP), now under the control of the barrel-chested Modi. Even as it remains India's only truly national party, with a support base that extends to each of the nation's districts, Congress, thanks to India's first-past-the-post system, won just 44 seats in the 543-member lower house of parliament, its worst showing on record. The dramatic vote swing – its vote share fell by 9 percentage points – was in part thanks to the five-week-long staggered polling process that accentuated the bandwagon effect towards Modi. Without the qualifying 10% of seats, Congress is in the pitiable state of not being eligible even to place one of its Members of Parliament (MPs) as Leader of the Opposition.

On the sidelines, hesitant to reach for the power that was so easily within his grasp in the 10 years of prime minister Manmohan Singh's UPA government, stands Sonia's firstborn, Rahul, the man Modi, in the campaign, sneered at as the *shehzada,* prince-in-waiting. There is a good chance now that he may never take the prime minister's seat once occupied by his father Rajiv, grandmother Indira Gandhi and great-grandfather Nehru. Indeed, he may not want to.

As Narendra Modi completes two years as prime minister, it is interesting to look back at how India came to this fork in its road. What were the political and economic mistakes the Manmohan government made that led to India's voice fading in global councils and slowed its economy, currently measured at $2.3 trillion, back to just above the pace of the 1960s and 1970s, best described by the ugly expression, "Hindu growth rate"? Have Congress and Manmohan bequeathed Modi a poisoned chalice, as many believe they have? Or is the situation more nuanced? This book examines some of the key events of the Manmohan years, the state of the nation he left behind and the circumstances that proved so fertile for Modi's rise. It ends with a look at the strategic sweet spot the nation occupies as every major world power courts it simultaneously.

In an Asia caught in rapid transition, no country is as fascinating to report on as India. Big, noisy, bulging at the seams, India's economy and society move much like the traffic on a New Delhi road – states and sections of its people advancing at varying speeds and levels of discipline. For every high horsepower engine on the road, there is the cycle rickshaw and the humanly powered pushcart slowing movement and frustrating those who seek to travel more quickly. Meanwhile, a few intrepid riders do weave ahead, often by breaking the rules of the road or fixing them to their advantage.

But behind its warts and obvious confusion – a recent writer who took a hard-eyed view titled his work *Implosion* – a pattern is discernible of an India that warrants optimism. This is the India of resilience, of improvisation, a nation of multiple ethnicities in 29 states jelling as one, even as they steadily and confidently embrace the world outside. One of the lasting memories of my reporting stint in India is of a village girl I thanked after stopping for directions up in the mountains of Ranikhet, in the hill state of Uttarakhand.

"No problem," she warbled back in a sing-song American accent clearly picked up from cable television.

Within India, once identified by its centuries-old social stratification system, the flintier edges of caste with its strict codes of inter-dining and intermarriage have dulled in a sociological sense as village folk enter towns and sit next to each other in public transport, cinemas and cafeterias. Interestingly, caste, as the 2014 "Modi election" showed, may even be losing a bit of its salience politically as a vote-aggregator as well, although every now and then politicians do attempt to use it for mass mobilisation, particularly to demand special privileges from the government for their communities. Meanwhile, new social and sexual mores are forming; the extravagance of the once-spartan nation is altering personal lives and habits. Indeed, the change extends, surprisingly, into sections of society hitherto regarded as hugely conservative.

More than anything else, there is an Indianness taking shape. This national glue, forming totally without state-directed compulsion, contrasts and occasionally coexists with BJP's contrived *Hindutva,* or Hinduness, which I have frequently attacked in print and in talks. The Indianness is backed by the large migrations of Indians across states in search of gainful employment, the spread of an English-Hindi patois, the syncretic nature of Indian culture, and the spreading acceptance of Bollywood and alien food (it is a different matter that wags are prone to say that India got its revenge for the 1962 military defeat at China's hands by murdering Chinese cuisine). As confounding as it may seem on the outside, India, as the 2014 election results showed, has begun to think as one nation. This has implications for the hitherto caste and religion-based identity politics practised by every post-Independence political group, including the Marxists.

Milovan Djilas, the Yugoslav writer and theorist, predicted a half century ago that India would not hold together and would collapse under the weight of its contradictions. Today, it is Yugoslavia that has splintered into smaller republics. Meanwhile, India's Little Republics – so-called by the colonialist Charles Metcalfe because of the self-contained nature of its half-million villages – are jelling into one large society, melded by television, cellular phones, the Internet, Bollywood, the vast railway network and of course, cricket. Seven decades after Independence, the colonial cringe is almost gone.

This book tries to chronicle that India, alongside its convulsions. It is a collection of anecdotes and observations of the significant events that marked the decade of Congress party rule under Manmohan Singh, culminating in the rise of Modi and, I believe, the terminal decline of Congress under the Gandhi family. It is built around the access that I enjoyed with some of the key decision-makers of the time. *India Rising* is targeted at the person who has a general idea of India, and perhaps is curious to know more. The reader is invited to begin anywhere, because the chapters are very nearly self-contained – quite like the traditional Indian village community that only needed to reach out of its territory for salt and matrimonial alliances.

INTRODUCTION: WRITTEN IN THE STARS

On the afternoon of May 16, 2004, I left my room at The Taj Mahal Hotel on New Delhi's Man Singh Road to visit the south Delhi home of my in-laws, where the extended family had gathered to celebrate my mother-in-law's birthday. Bloomberg News had flown me to the Indian capital to help supervise coverage of the 15th Indian parliamentary elections and after two weeks of hotel food, good as it was, I looked forward to a home-cooked meal. When I entered the house, the buzz was all about the election results that had stunningly projected the Indian National Congress party to power, a major upset for the incumbent coalition led by the Hindu nationalist Bharatiya Janata Party and its urbane prime minister, Atal Bihari Vajpayee.

The living room could have passed for the Civil Service Club, given the assortment of former bureaucrats in the throng, including my father-in-law, PN Abbi. Abbi, during his career in the Indian Administrative Service, was known to be a bold and unconventional officer. He also had a reputation for being a remarkably gifted astrologer. On this day, he was being challenged on his prediction, made weeks earlier, that while Congress would win, Sonia Gandhi would not be prime minister of India. Against every opinion poll that had predicted BJP retaining power, he had been correct on the Congress victory. With 145 seats, and coalition partners added, the party had secured more seats than the BJP, and could easily raise the required numbers to rule. But it seemed Abbi would have to concede defeat on his second forecast. Indeed, earlier that very day, Sonia had made a statement to the effect that normally, the leader of the victorious party in parliament automatically becomes prime minister. In other words, she was ready.

Service rivalries sometimes spill over into families and there was more than one person that afternoon who would not mind seeing Abbi's prediction fail. Although I had little belief in astrology, I kept quiet. I knew he could be fabulously accurate. In May 1991, while sitting in the bar of the India International Centre in New Delhi's Lodi Estate, a senior officer of the Central Bureau of Investigation (CBI) had handed him two horoscopes, without saying whose they were. After a couple of days, Abbi returned the documents to the man.

"This first here," he said, "is that of a male. It is a remarkably good one. The other is that of a woman and her stars are bad at this time. In fact, I fear widowhood approaching."

Two weeks later, a little after 9.30 pm, the phone rang in the Abbis' government bungalow on Tilak Lane. It was the CBI officer. "Prem," he said, addressing my father-in-law by his first name, "you were right. The horoscopes I showed you were Rajiv's and Sonia's. Rajiv has just been assassinated in Tamil Nadu."

I thought of that incident and another time six years later when the Indian high commissioner to Singapore had dropped in at my Upper Thomson Road home to say goodbye and also to consult Abbi, who was then visiting me, on his post-retirement future. The diplomat's bags were being packed and he was due to retire in weeks.

"Oddly, I don't see your government service ending," Abbi had said, undiplomatically adding something about his personal life that made the man flush with embarrassment.

Two weeks later, the envoy called excitedly. The Indian government, unexpectedly, had just extended the retirement age for central civil servants to 60 and he had been told to stay on in the post. He was, he revealed, happily unpacking his goods at that moment.

So I remained wary of commenting, even as several relatives turned to me, seeking my journalistic endorsement for the argument that Sonia's impending elevation to authority was only a formality. Frankly, it did look like a no-brainer to me as well.

But Abbi shook his head and looked puzzled.

"It is true that everything points to Sonia being sworn in as PM, but somehow, I don't quite see it in her horoscope."

The party broke up finally, and in the fashion of Punjabi families, the goodbyes were long. I hastened back to my hotel to follow the news.

Next day, a Monday, Delhi seemed to pause as it awaited the coronation. At Bloomberg News we followed the story of the tanking stock markets, in a swoon because of the left-of-centre orientation of the Congress party, compared with the pro-business BJP.

A day later, an online portal broke the story that Sonia was having second thoughts on taking power. No one knew why, or even whether the report was accurate. That afternoon, the Congress party met to elect a new leader and Sonia dropped her bombshell.

"Throughout these past six years that I have been in politics, one thing has been clear to me," she said. "And that is, as I often have stated, that the post of prime minister is not my aim. I was always certain that if ever I found myself in the position that I am today, I would follow my own inner voice. Today, that voice tells me I must humbly decline that post."

Instantly, pandemonium broke out in the meeting and reverberated to every corner of India. Some of the anguish and outrage displayed by the newly elected MPs looked contrived, but I could not be sure. (Certainly, two Congress MPs who seemed most upset by her decision – Renuka Chowdhury and the late Rajiv Gandhi's Doon School senior, Mani Shankar Aiyar – landed Cabinet positions in the ministerial lineup that would be announced within days.) But it was all terrific drama nevertheless.

Sonia then went to see president APJ Abdul Kalam accompanied by Dr Manmohan Singh, the scholarly Sikh who, as finance minister to prime minister Narasimha Rao, had helped dismantle the socialist-style controls on the Indian economy and set it on its current growth trajectory. I called home to congratulate my father-in-law and ask if he had spoken to Manmohan. They had been college contemporaries and fellow scholarship students in Punjab, but while they had kept up their friendship over the decades, they hadn't met for a while. Indeed, Abbi had once advised Manmohan to avoid a political career, warning it would blemish the fair name he had earned as a scholar and bureaucrat.

Rather leery about the BJP, particularly since militant Hindu hordes brought down the historic Babri Mosque in Uttar Pradesh in 1992, the 2004 parliamentary election verdict lifted my spirits. It indicated that India was returning to its centrist roots, fuelling my interest in returning to the country. India would have a Muslim president in APJ Abdul Kalam, a Sikh prime minister in Manmohan, and in Sonia, a Roman Catholic woman heading the governing coalition. I had been away from India for more than a decade and while I did visit regularly, I yearned to reconnect with the land in a fuller way. It was a good time to be back. My college contemporaries, in their mid-40s, were being appointed to key policy-making positions in the military and the bureaucracy. Politicians I had known as young men had risen to prominence in various parties. Moreover, I wanted my children, Dhruv and Shriya, to be exposed to India, and build roots there.

With that in mind I had already entered Dhruv at Doon School, a residential institution in the Himalayan valley town of Dehradun, with a tradition of social service and known to produce well-rounded men. The headmaster then was Dr Kanti Bajpai, an academic now with Singapore's Lee Kuan Yew School of Public Policy, whom I respected for his intellect and integrity. Besides, Dehradun was only five hours away from New Delhi by road, close enough for my in-laws to reach him in an emergency, my own parents having passed on.

At the time I had an offer from Singapore Press Holdings to return to its flagship paper, *The Straits Times*. The talks had begun six months earlier when associate editor Bob Ng, a mentor and lifelong friend, conveyed a message from editor-in-chief Cheong Yip Seng that I had been away from the paper too long. I laughed. Bloomberg was a fantastic company, a talent-filled organisation where you learnt something every day, and it treated its staff generously. Who'd want to leave such a firm!

Yet, there was something missing. At Bloomberg I was too focused on money and people with the most whereas journalism had to be equally about the other half, the people with the least. I had tremendous respect for Cheong, who had steered the Singapore Press Holdings' English papers ably in a political environment that refused to recognise the media as the Fourth Estate. I promised to think about it.

One afternoon the following month my phone rang. Lau Way Fong, secretary to then-*The Straits Times* editor Han Fook Kwang, asked if I'd be free to dine with her boss. We fixed a January 19 date and met at L'Angelus, a tony Spanish restaurant on Club Street. Fook Kwang ordered an expensive Merlot and we settled in for a long evening, discussing journalism, friends and the issues of the day. As we drained the last drops in the bottle he slipped the question.

"So, how about coming back? We need you back in the newsroom."

I pondered the offer. I loved *The Straits Times* and knew most of its senior staff. But I was also well-rooted at Bloomberg. On the other hand, if the paper would let me work in India, all the pieces would fit very well. Newspaper work then, before the digital media onslaught, was far less demanding than the frenetic pace of financial information services, where vast amounts of money can be made or lost on being first to break news. This meant you had the time to delve deep into issues. In Asia, no story was more fascinating to report than the Indian transition. Settling back in New Delhi was not a problem; I had excellent networks in the city. Moreover, I could drive up to Dehradun at least once a month to see Dhruv.

"I am a bit bored in Singapore, Fook Kwang," I said. "But I don't mind coming back if you'd open a bureau in India and let me work there for a few years."

This was clearly rather unexpected. Nevertheless, we parted convivially with Fook Kwang agreeing to convey my request to Cheong. A few weeks later he told me the paper was open to the idea, except that I should return to Singapore when needed and be available for key assignments around Asia. I agreed without hesitation. He then passed me over to managing editor Patrick Daniel, the man who'd eventually succeed Cheong. We met a few weeks later, our chat interrupted as Patrick took calls from TT Durai, chief executive of the National Kidney Foundation, who was suing *The Straits Times* for defamation after the paper reported that he had considered installing gold taps in his toilet. (The paper stood its ground and after sensational revelations in court, it was Durai, who ran what was Asia's most successful charity, who had to leave.)

But now that it was crunch time I went slow on the negotiations, reluctant to leave Bloomberg. *The Straits Times* foreign editor Warren Fernandez (now editor), impatient at the pace of the hiring process, took me out to lunch. Although we had shared a newsroom in the mid-1990s, I had not known him well and had considered him rather an aloof person. But there, at the Patara Restaurant in Tanglin Mall, I warmed to the man sitting across from me, earnestly discussing his vision of seeing quality writing in the paper and expanding its coverage of Asia. He didn't seem so icy after all, and I had no quarrel with anything he was saying.

On 15 September, I parked my car at News Centre, headquarters of SPH, and began my induction and orientation. By the end of the year I was in New Delhi.

The pages that follow tell of the India I witnessed and reported on, with its highs and lows, and the vast changes sweeping its society. Initially, as India's economy and clout in the world soared, my writing reflected the optimism of the day. Then, when the government began to stumble and scandals seized the day, the stories became darker. In February 2012, I was recalled to Singapore to be foreign editor of *The Straits Times* but kept in touch with developments in India. In the first half of 2014, I twice travelled to India – to cover the run-up to the election, and a month later, for the results that projected Narendra Modi to power. Subsequently, I spent more time around India working on this book.

Today, thanks to Modi's energy, charisma and love of technology, there is a sense of excitement about India all over again. Foreign direct investment into India is accelerating. At Reserve Bank of India (RBI), the central bank, Raghuram Rajan presides as governor. As former chief economist at the International Monetary Fund (IMF) and the man who so accurately predicted the 2008 global financial crisis, he lends a large measure of credibility to the Indian story. Aside from the promise of its huge market, deep questions about China's economy and the expertise available in Beijing to see through a difficult economic transformation, and a more proactive foreign policy from New Delhi, have generated interest in India once again to levels last seen when Rajiv Gandhi took power. Where corruption issues dominated the narrative about the Manmohan government, particularly in its second term, much of the criticism of Modi centres around his not moving *faster* on reform, underscoring the world's impatience for India to do more for itself and quickly. Meanwhile, New Delhi's strategic weight in the world is also rising swiftly and concepts like "Indo-Pacific" have emerged as the world attempts to grasp the significance of the Indian rise and adjust to it.

Once again, India stands at the threshold of a unique opportunity.

ABBREVIATIONS

AAP	Aam Aadmi Party
AIADMK	All India Anna Dravida Munnetra Kazhagam party
AIIMS	All India Institute of Medical Sciences
Asean	Association of Southeast Asian Nations
ATS	Anti-Terrorism Squad
BCCI	Board of Control for Cricket in India
BJP	Bharatiya Janata Party
C-in-C	Commander-in-Chief
CAG	comptroller and auditor general
CBI	Central Bureau of Investigation
CECA	Comprehensive Economic Cooperation Agreement
CEO	chief executive officer
Champs	Changi Airport Managers & Partners (Singapore)
CIA	Central Intelligence Agency (US)
CII	Confederation of Indian Industry
Congress	Indian National Congress party
CPM	Communist Party of India (Marxist)
DAE	Department of Atomic Energy
DEA	Drug Enforcement Administration (US)
DMK	Dravida Munnetra Kazhagam party
Dosco	Doon School, also used for Doon School alumni and students

DRDO	Defence Research & Development Organisation
DSE	Delhi School of Economics
FBI	Federal Bureau of Investigation (US)
FBR	fast breeder reactor
FOSS	Forum of Small States
FTA	free trade agreement
GDP	gross domestic product
IAEA	International Atomic Energy Agency
IAF	Indian Air Force
IAS	Indian Administrative Service
IMF	International Monetary Fund
IPL	Indian Premier League
ISI	Inter-Services Intelligence (Pakistan)
ISIS	Islamic State in Iraq and Syria
LTA	Land Transport Authority (Singapore)
LTTE	Liberation Tigers of Tamil Eelam, or Tamil Tigers (Sri Lanka)
MEA	Ministry of External Affairs
MP	Member of Parliament
MOD	Ministry of Defence
NAC	National Advisory Council
Nasscom	National Association of Service and Software Companies
NATO	North Atlantic Treaty Organisation
NIC	National Integration Council
NGO	non-governmental organisation
NSA	National Security Adviser
NSG	National Security Guard
OBC	Other Backward Classes
PMO	Prime Minister's Office

RAW	Research and Analysis Wing
RBI	Reserve Bank of India
RM	Raksha Mantri, the Hindi title for Defence Minister
RSS	Rashtriya Swayamsevak Sangh, a hardline Hindu outfit
RTI	Right to Information Act
SAARC	South Asian Association for Regional Cooperation
SC	Scheduled Caste
Sebi	Securities and Exchange Board of India
SPG	Special Protection Group
SRCC	Shri Ram College of Commerce
ST	Scheduled Tribe
ST Kinetics	Singapore Technologies Kinetics
TCS	Tata Consultancy Services
TULF	Tamil United Liberation Front (Sri Lanka)
UAE	United Arab Emirates
UN	United Nations
UNESCO	United Nations Educational, Scientific and Cultural Organisation
UNCTAD	United Nations Conference on Trade and Development
UP	Uttar Pradesh
UPA	United Progressive Alliance
US	United States
WTO	World Trade Organisation
YSR	YS Rajasekhara Reddy

TIMELINE

2004

May: Manmohan Singh is sworn in as India's prime minister after the Indian National Congress-led coalition upsets the incumbent government led by the Bharatiya Janata Party.

September: India, Brazil, Germany and Japan demand an expanded UN Security Council and apply for permanent seats in the Council.

December: A tsunami hits Southeast Asia and the Indian subcontinent with strong tides experienced all the way to the Somali coast. Thousands die.

2005

January: JN Dixit, India's national security adviser, dies of a massive heart attack in his home. Internal security adviser MK Narayanan is appointed in his place, the first from the police service to get that job.

April: The first bus service in 60 years opens between Srinagar, capital of Jammu & Kashmir, and Muzaffarabad in Pakistan-occupied Kashmir.

June: India and Singapore sign the landmark CECA, the most ambitious trade deal signed by New Delhi with any nation until then.

2006

February: Prime minister Manmohan Singh launches the National Rural Employment Guarantee scheme aimed at lifting millions of people from poverty, eventually to cover every rural district of India.

March: US president George W Bush and Singh sign the civilian nuclear cooperation agreement, freeing India of "nuclear apartheid". India agrees to separate its civilian and strategic nuclear facilities and accepts safeguards on its civil facilities.

November: Hu Jintao makes the first state visit by a Chinese president in a decade.

2007

February: India and Pakistan sign agreements designed to reduce the risk of nuclear war and exchange information on nuclear facilities. The agreement does not provide for detailed disclosure of nuclear activities.

March: Maoist rebels in the forests of the mostly tribal state of Chhattisgarh ambush a police post, killing 50. Manmohan Singh would later describe the Maoists as the single biggest threat to the nation's security.

May: Buoyed by the lag effects of economic policies laid by the predecessor government led by the BJP, India announces its economy grew by 9.4% in the year to March, the strongest in decades.

2008

July: Manmohan Singh's government survives a confidence vote in parliament following the withdrawal of support by Left groups, led by the Communist Party of India (Marxist) (CPM), over India's civil nuclear agreement with the US. Singh survives with help from the Samajwadi Party.

October: President George W Bush signs the nuclear deal with India.

November: Terrorists sailing in from Pakistan attack Mumbai's railway station and landmark hotels; 166 are killed. India considers a strike on Pakistan but desists.

December: India announces that the peace process with Pakistan has been "paused".

2009

January: Manmohan Singh undergoes critical "beating heart" surgery in New Delhi.

May: United Progressive Alliance (UPA) returns to power with enhanced parliamentary strength. Indian newspapers headline that "Singh is King".

June: The Ministry of Defence puts out a list of seven firms that it has blacklisted for alleged graft charges in the Ordnance Factory Board scam. The firms include Israel Military Industries and Singapore Technologies (ST) Kinetics.

September: Andhra Pradesh chief minister YS Rajasekhara Reddy, popularly known as YSR, dies in a helicopter crash.

December: New Delhi says it will allow a new state, Telangana, to be carved out of Andhra Pradesh. Street protests erupt in Andhra Pradesh as people opposed to the move clash with its supporters.

2010

May: Ajmal Kasab, the lone Pakistani gunman captured alive in the 2008 Mumbai terror attack, is sentenced to death by a Mumbai court.

September: The High Court of Allahabad rules that the disputed holy site of Ayodhya, on which the Babri Mosque once stood, should be divided between Hindus and Muslims.

October: Delhi hosts the XIX Commonwealth Games successfully after severe complaints of delays in completing civil works and the poor state of facilities.

November: The comptroller & auditor general of India tables in parliament its report on the sale of 2G electronic spectrum.

2011

April: India wins the cricket World Cup under the captaincy of Mahendra Singh Dhoni. There is national jubilation.

August: Anna Hazare, a former army driver turned social worker, stages a 12-day fasting strike in New Delhi.

November: More than a dozen people, including A Raja, the minister for telecommunications, go on trial for alleged corruption over the 2G electronic spectrum sale.

2012

July: Pranab Mukherjee, long-serving minister in Congress governments, is elected president of India, replacing Pratibha Patil, the first woman to hold the post.

August: Thirty-two people are convicted for their involvement in the 2002 communal riots in Gujarat, early in Narendra Modi's stewardship of the state. They include Maya Kodnani, a gynaecologist who served as the state's minister for women and child development at the time of the riots.

November: Ajmal Kasab, the Pakistani gunman grabbed alive during the 2008 attacks on Mumbai, is executed in a prison in Pune City.

December: Jyoti Singh, a 23-year-old physiotherapy student, is brutally attacked and raped in a moving bus in Delhi. The incident captures global attention. Flown to Singapore for emergency treatment, she dies there on December 29.

2013

September: Narendra Modi is officially announced as the BJP's candidate for prime minister.

A Delhi court sentences four men to death for their role in the Delhi rape case. Another accused, Ram Singh, died in prison during the trial.

November: The Indian Space Research Organisation successfully launches its Mars Orbiter Mission.

December: India's Supreme Court reverses a High Court decision decriminalising homosexuality, saying parliament, not courts, should decide on the matter.

2014

May: Narendra Modi leads the BJP to a landslide victory. For the first time since 1984, a single Indian party has a clear majority in the lower house of parliament.

September: China's Xi Jinping visits India, starting with a trip to Ahmedabad where he is hosted by PM Modi, before official talks in New Delhi.

India becomes the first nation to successfully reach Mars on its first attempt with the spacecraft Mangalyaan slipping into Mars' orbit after a 10-month voyage. PM Modi hails the achievement, noting that the $74 million cost of the mission made it cheaper than what it cost to film the movie *Gravity*.

2015

The anti-corruption Aam Aadmi Party (AAP) headed by Arvind Kejriwal sweeps elections to the Delhi state assembly despite vigorous campaigning by the prime minister on behalf of the BJP, dealing Modi his first electoral setback since taking charge of India.

PART I

INDIA RISING

1
Resilience Amid Despair: A Tsunami on Boxing Day

> "We need to make sure that this recovery process accomplishes more than just restoring what was there before."
>
> — Former US president Bill Clinton, speaking as UN Special Envoy for Tsunami Recovery

ON THE MORNING after Christmas Day 2004, I was on a golf course in central New Delhi with three officers from India's admiralty when a caddy mentioned that Indian Air Force chief S Krishnaswamy didn't seem to be on the course that day. This was unusual because Krishnaswamy, an ace pilot who has the distinction of having raised and led the first Electronic Warfare Squadron of the Indian Air Force (IAF), loved his 18 holes on the weekend.

As it turned out "Teacher" Krishnaswamy, days away from retirement, had good reason to deny himself his customary time out on the links. As dawn broke on Boxing Day, along the ocean floor near Indonesia's Sumatra island, deep, powerful impulses that had built up over centuries were convulsing the ground with a magnitude of 9.1 on the Richter scale, releasing energy more than 25,000 times that of the bomb which flattened Hiroshima.

Waves are meant to ripple; the swells from this undersea quake radiated. And they did so at jet speed, invisible to human eyes as they snaked below the waterline. Only close to land, as the waters got shallow and its belly began rubbing up on rocks and sand did this many-headed submarine force rear its terrifying mane, crashing into the coastline with waves taller than palm trees, sweeping ships ashore, dragging tenements inland.

The waves would be felt a few hours later all the way to Africa but it took only minutes to strike the island of Car Nicobar, and further up the chain of islands. India controls some 570 islands in the Andaman chain, of which only 40 are inhabited, including Car Nicobar, where the IAF maintains a base. Originally built as an airstrip by the Japanese during World War II, the Indians had expanded the Car Nic facility, trebling the runway's length and making it India's southernmost defence point.

In the mid-1980s New Delhi had considered developing a few islands there as a Hongkong-style free port and entrepôt centre for Indian businessmen displaced from Africa. The Defence Ministry shot it down. Instead, feeding then-prime minister Rajiv Gandhi's visions of regional dominance, and influenced by Rajiv's school chum, minister of state Arun Singh, the ministry suggested building it up as a defence outpost. Indeed, India had even briefly considered moving a squadron of Jaguar fighter-bombers to Car Nic from their base in Pune, western India. In a display of the strategic restraint that marked Indian policy right up to 2014, Rajiv gave up the idea of moving the warplanes into the base. He did so on the advice of the Ministry of External Affairs (MEA), which believed it would raise fears of Indian designs on Southeast Asia, a friendly part of the world that had generally seen India as a benign presence. But plenty of other equipment did go in, including helicopters, reconnaissance aircraft and sophisticated radars. From this vantage point, India monitored the mouth of the Strait of Malacca, logging every significant boat that passed through it, including Chinese ships, as well as air activity in the region.

But on Boxing Day in 2004, the Car Nic base stood devastated. More than 110 officers and other personnel and their families had perished. New Delhi got first news of the disaster after some pilots at the base managed to scramble into helicopters and effect lift-off, using their radio transmitters to communicate with command headquarters since much of the base systems had been destroyed. Even at that point, those on the mainland had no idea of the scale of devastation.

Around an hour later, while we were still hacking away at the turf, prime minister Manmohan Singh had tuned into the BBC and heard the first reports of a deep sea tremor in the waters off the Indonesian island of Sumatra and of huge waves lashing Southeast Asia. As the story developed it became obvious that this was no ordinary event. Two hours later, Indian television stations began to carry reports of walls of water crashing the Tamil Nadu coastline at Chennai and all the way down to the southern end of the Indian peninsula.

Odd as it may sound, it was no less than the prime minister, 72 years old at the time, who was among the first to respond in New Delhi. Manmohan asked his personal staff to contact the Cabinet secretary and other key officials for an emergency coordination meeting. Everyone responded, despite having just come through a heavy work week – Manmohan demands so much information that his staff is kept busy all the time. The exception was his national security adviser, JN "Mani" Dixit.

Snatching the opportunity of a peaceful Sunday, Dixit had left home early and was ensconced with a spiritual guru, accompanied by a retired Foreign Service colleague who had insisted on taking him there. A chain smoker and badly overweight, Dixit had begun to show telling signs of the strain of his job – people had noticed that he occasionally seemed to wheeze. A few days earlier, visiting Sri Lankan president Chandrika Kumaratunga, who had known him since his days as the Indian envoy to Colombo (they called him "the little Viceroy" down there), had voiced her worry over his health. She pressed him to go for a check-up but he had waved it away, saying he was fine.

In fact, he was not at all well. Aside from health issues, Dixit had been feeling under the gun, thanks to turf battles with the MEA then led by K Natwar Singh, as well as the bureaucrats there who resented interference from their former secretary. There were also skirmishes for influence and control within the Prime Minister's Office (PMO), particularly with internal security adviser MK Narayanan, a legendary figure in government as the former intelligence chief who had served four Indian prime ministers.

Although Narayanan was an old friend and benefactor – he had convinced former PM Narasimha Rao to name Dixit foreign secretary against the competing claims of the well-regarded CR Gharekhan – it rankled with Dixit that Narayanan usually won out. It was widely known that the former spy chief was close to the "high command", as a supreme Gandhi family loyalist, while Dixit himself had toyed with the idea of joining the BJP after retirement, something Natwar Singh, who convinced him to join Congress instead, never failed to remind him about.

Dixit had hardly settled down for his consultation with the holy figure when his cell phone buzzed. It was no less than the prime minister himself.

"Mani, where are you?" said Manmohan, sounding a little peeved as he explained the crisis. "I need you here."

Dixit promptly excused himself and left for the prime minister's residence on Race Course Road in central New Delhi. Less than a week later, he would die of a massive heart attack, but before that, the foreign secretary who had reoriented Indian policy on a host of issues (including making cosy with the generals in Myanmar that New Delhi had ignored earlier) helped set in motion a tremendous disaster relief operation, coordinating across the three service arms of the Indian military. Just as significantly, he had also convinced Manmohan that India would accept no financial aid from another nation; indeed, it should stand ready to deploy its own forces to help neighbours affected by the tsunami, and to provide money where required.

The tsunami struck India at a time when it had begun to push for a permanent seat on the UN Security Council and this was Manmohan's first opportunity as prime minister to assert to the world that the country had arrived as a major power. And he did so. In a special television broadcast that night, he said he had written to government leaders in Indonesia, Thailand, Sri Lanka and the Maldives – the arc of the tragedy – offering Indian assistance to tackle the disaster. When US president George W Bush called Manmohan, followed by Pentagon officials speaking to their military counterparts in New Delhi with offers of help and aid, they were politely told India could handle its crisis on its own. Days later, when US secretary of state Colin Powell and

UN secretary general Kofi Annan sought invitations to visit the areas in India affected by the tsunami, they were firmly turned down.

India is an ancient civilisation that has taken its knocks over the centuries, through acts of God and civil wars and at the hands of marauders. Great tragedies occur at regular intervals, sometimes in the form of a major industrial disaster like Bhopal's gas leak, at others in natural phenomena like periodic hurricanes or flooding. In some districts it is not uncommon to see floods in one part while another part suffers severe drought. Even so, I would be surprised by both the enormity of the challenge I witnessed over the next few weeks in the areas hit by the tsunami, as well as the quality of the response.

Flying to the southern Indian state of Tamil Nadu, my first stop was the village of Kasimedu in the Madras Harbour area of Chennai, the state capital. Hardship had been no stranger to this village where more than 3,000 people were crowded into 650 shanties. The tsunami had arrived with stunning speed in the lives of a people whose biggest technological leap had taken place five years earlier, when they began giving up their centuries-old wooden catamarans for fibreglass boats bought with borrowed money. These boats painted blue, pink and red, bearing the names of children, wives, parents and siblings, now lay scattered around as though carelessly flung by giant children at play. Many were perched on top of jetties, rather than alongside the pier, after being abandoned there by the waves. Dogs with giant sores limped along, too weak to run from the stones flung by naked children. Two days after the wall of water arrived, the bodies of dead children, women and men had been disposed of but dead cows lay around, their carcasses putrefying in the sun.

Down the peninsula, the worst hit district was Nagapattinam, facing the Bay of Bengal. There, 6,065 lives had been lost and the district counted 450 deaths per kilometre along a 10 km stretch of coastline. Mass graves had been dug and local residents were in terror when strange sounds, usually of gas escaping from a bloated intestine, penetrated the night. When the enormity of the disaster became evident, Tamil Nadu chief minister

Jayalalithaa Jayaram's first response was to transfer the fresh-faced J Radhakrishnan of the Indian Administrative Service from Chennai to take charge as the Nagapattinam district collector, the top government official. As I discovered in the months that followed, it would prove to be an inspired decision from a woman not known for her administrative acumen.

Leaving Tamil Nadu, I headed to Port Blair, capital of the Andaman & Nicobar islands administration. Again, the devastation was stunning but the stories from the survivors were awesomely impressive. At Hut Bay, 60 km south of Port Blair, forest worker Lakshmi Narain Rai had grabbed the family transport – a trishaw he had been trying to sell for two months – and loaded it up with his nine months pregnant wife and their six-year-old son. He then pushed the vehicle up a 10 m high hillock, the tallest spot that could be accessed on the flat island. Seven hundred others had the same idea, crowding the little patch of land left dry after the water receded, leaving a swampy mass of earth. Namita, Rai's wife, had fallen as they rushed out of their hut and now she went into labour. No doctor was available but a nursing maid offered to help. Coolly, the woman asked for a razor blade and a ball of thread. At 4.19 am, with other womenfolk holding up their saris to give her a little privacy, Namita delivered a baby boy, 20 hours after the tsunami. For three days, the newborn and his family waited on the tiny mound, with no food and only seawater to moisten their lips. Finally, an Indian Navy ship arrived and the crowd on the hill was evacuated.

A few days later I travelled further south in the island chain to Car Nicobar, hitching a ride with the IAF. Car Nicobar is a unique part of India. Deeply attached to India, despite living 1,200 km from the mainland, many of the tribals there bear Christian names (a village elder was named Aberdeen Blair) and their features resemble the people of Borneo and Myanmar. The land on which the air base stood had once belonged to a tribal chief loyal to India and the Congress party. Apparently, when the government offered to compensate him for his land he had turned down the money. Instead, he asked for a jacket worn by Jawaharlal Nehru, India's founding prime minister.

Wandering around the rubble on the devastated IAF base, I was awed by the fury of nature, visible everywhere. A radar truck was stranded on top of a building after the bridge leading to the roof collapsed. Schools were empty, the marketplace with its barber shop and meat shop was barren, like a ghost town in a Western movie. Coconut trees had their canopies sheared off. In the middle of the base was a huge depression and now it was filled with all sorts of things – an abandoned car, clothes, furniture, a boom box, a Sony Trinitron television set and a green trunk with the white lettering, "Maj N. Chakravarty, Car Nic to Tezpur".

Intrigued, I made inquiries. The story that unfolded was amazing.

Major Chakravarty, the garrison engineer of the Air Force station, had been under orders of transfer to Tezpur, an equally remote station in northeast India close to Bhutan and China. Two days before the tsunami he was sent to Chennai on "TY Duty" – Army speak for temporary assignment. When he returned to the base the day after the waves struck he found not just the station, but his life too shattered. His wife Kaveri was missing, presumed dead, his daughters Spreha and Aakansha lay lifeless in the sun, as did 27 Air Force officers and their families, and some 90 others. It was horror beyond any normal person's levels of tolerance, combined with the knowledge that if fate had struck just a few days later his family would have been safe. Chakravarty asked for a cup of tea as he absorbed the shock. Then he put his cup down and went to look for his troops. Military men are trained to absorb shocks, no doubt, but the strength and resilience Chakravarty showed was remarkable against any measure, and utterly moving.

For two days, the engineers on the base worked ceaselessly under his command, trying to save what lives they could and performing mass cremations. Then, Chakravarty boarded a military plane to Port Blair, to connect to a civilian flight for his journey to Tezpur. As he boarded the Russia-built AN-32, survivors on the base, many of whom he had led, placed an urn in his hands containing what was taken to be his wife's ashes – her body was never found. Struggling to control his emotions, Chakravarty accepted the urn and turned his back after a final salute.

The personal diary of wing commander Nitin Sathe, chief operations officer at Car Nicobar Air Force Station, revealed the pangs he and his men underwent to put the base back into some shape after the initial efforts of major Chakravarty. Arriving on New Year's Day to a situation where nights were spent in tents, water was rationed and the toilet was the open field, his first act was to commandeer all the vehicles and bicycles available for relief workers. Then he and his men got to work. Some humour helped. A superior who rained down instructions was quickly labelled "Tin Can". Why? Tin sheets make the most noise. As key government personnel and politicians descended to inspect the damage and be photographed, the diary recorded the popularity of "disaster tourism".

On January 16, after a fortnight's toil, Sathe declared a day of rest. The base held a cricket match, using a tennis ball and a piece of wood with the runway as the field. Ten days later, the officers and men held a *bada khana* or big feast, and a flypast. The officers' mess also reopened. IAF Base Car Nic was back. In April it resumed full operations, holding a mini exercise involving Jaguars and Sukhoi 30 aircraft.

My story on major Chakravarty's heroism had unexpected resonance in Singapore. Two weeks after the waves struck, the Singapore government organised a memorial service for tsunami victims addressed by prime minister Lee Hsien Loong and the envoys from India, Sri Lanka, Sweden and Indonesia. When Indian high commissioner Alok Prasad, speaking extempore, quoted from my report to mention major Chakravarty's valour, several in the audience were moist-eyed and the speech caught the attention of Lee Kuan Yew, Singapore's stern founding father, who was in the audience.

A few days after the ceremony, the Cambridge-educated Lee stopped to have a word with the eloquent Alok as he spotted the Indian envoy at the function marking the opening of Singapore's parliament.

"What language do you dream in?" he asked abruptly, taking the seasoned diplomat by surprise.

"English, I suppose..." Alok muttered, tentatively.

"Where did you go to school?"

Alok, not sure where all this was going, said he had gone to a boarding school in the northern Indian town of Dehradun.

"Ah, Doon School!" said Lee, striding away, as though that explained Alok's confident oratory.

Three months later, I returned to Nagapattinam in Tamil Nadu and caught up with Radhakrishnan, the district collector. Sitting on his front lawn and sipping from a cup of Horlicks, the former veterinary doctor showed no signs of fatigue after working 18-hour days continuously. In that period, he had supervised mass burials, treated 103,000 people preventively to ensure there was no epidemic outbreak and supervised the distribution of relief. In addition, 39,000 homes had been provided relief and 13,000 temporary shelters had been built in his district, three-quarters of them by non-governmental organisations (NGOs) that were given land and electricity. More than 400 NGOs had descended on the district. Indian officialdom tends to be suspicious of NGOs but Radhakrishnan welcomed them and accepted that they had a role. The result was rehabilitation at an exemplary pace seldom seen in India. He had also turned up at 40 weddings in the district.

Radhakrishnan had become a folk hero.

I stopped at a local orphanage. There were 52 children in the facility. I asked Gunasekaran, an 11-year-old who had lost both parents, whether he would, like his parents and forefathers, make a living from the sea.

"No," he said emphatically. "I am not afraid of the water but I want to be a collector when I grow up, so I can serve the people."

I asked Radhakrishnan where he got his energy, optimism and commitment and he told me the story of 15-year-old Nirmala, a tsunami orphan. Amid all her troubles, Nirmala had stood first in class in recent examinations, scoring 400 of a maximum 450 marks.

Tracking the child to her divorced sister's coastal shack, I discovered Nirmala to be the last of five sisters whose father had died just after she was born. Her mother had been taken by the tsunami. Most of the government's cash dole had gone to pay the debts the mother had run up for the wedding of her first daughter, who was now divorced. With another sister in college and one more still in her teens, the future was bleak without the income their mother brought in from trading fish. But Nirmala herself looked serene, soaring above her misery.

"I am studying hard so I can be a police officer one day," she told me. "One of the officers counselled us and played with us every day. He showed me the way."

I looked at the child in amazement and wondered how deep could India's resilience run if a mid-teen girl child in a rural district could face disaster with such equanimity.

It was a similar story in Car Nicobar too. The shock from the previous year's tidal wave was raw. In Nicobar district alone, 3,400 had lost their lives. But society had absorbed the blow. Yes, there was a tad more religiosity as they sang carols down at the Church of Mary Magdalene, a makeshift place of worship for the dominant Protestant faith. And the aid inflows had contributed to a rise in alcohol use. Where were the orphaned children housed? I was told there were no orphans on the islands. An orphaned child was quickly absorbed into a home in the village without any questions asked. Indeed, in Nicobarese language, no words exist for "orphan" and "widow", so secure was the net society provided.

As always, I pondered how they were preparing for the next disaster, having just come through one. It seemed, at the urging of the administration, many of the tribal people had also moved deeper into the forests, along with their pigs, goats and chickens. The area was run by Vivek Porwal, a 33-year-old from the mainland, another tireless soul. I went looking for him.

"The land by the sea is yours," I heard Porwal tell a village council, speaking earnestly. "But do not live there. I am an engineer, so let me tell you the world does not have adequate mechanisms to predict tsunamis accurately."

In the years to follow, I would see this demonstrated again and again. Indians are not the most strategic of thinkers and planners. But their capacity to withstand shocks is incredible. Where that resilience comes – whether from history, faith or genetic quality – it is hard to tell.

Maybe the steel frame of the bureaucracy is a factor as well. India's bureaucracy is much maligned, sometimes with good reason. But throughout the length and breadth of India there is also an equal amount of praiseworthy administrative talent, officers with deep convictions and commitment and a moral compass. Without question, India could not have survived as the swiftly unifying entity it is without the immense contributions of the Chakravartys, Radhakrishnans and Porwals. The corruption and the sloth that afflicts so much of India does not begin with the bureaucracy, but in the political class that they serve. When you have a sound leader who is not in the game to line his pockets, many miracles can be accomplished with the talent at hand.

My appreciation for the Indian bureaucracy was further bolstered years later, in December 2013, when I observed the disaster that unfolded after Typhoon Haiyan hit the Philippines, taking more than 5,000 lives. Even though there had been plenty of warning about the ferocity of the approaching gales, Manila had not been able to secure the people who lived in Haiyan's path. Yet only the previous month in India, when Cyclone Phailin stormed in from the Bay of Bengal to lash the Odisha coast, the death toll had been meagre by Indian standards. Fewer than 20 people died in the state. In an epic effort, Odisha state officials had proactively managed to persuade a million people to move inland. The lessons of a cyclone of similar intensity that had arrived in the Odisha area 14 years ago, taking 15,000 lives, had been well-learnt.

India's handling of the tsunami and its aftermath sent several messages to the world, particularly Southeast Asia. If there were doubts about its capabilities to project power in its area of influence, they were laid to rest when it was revealed that in the 10 days after the disaster, the IAF flew 356 sorties for relief and rescue operations to the remote Andaman & Nicobar islands, ferrying more than 1,500 tonnes of military and relief equipment. Landing ship tanks normally used in amphibious assault situations were deployed to evacuate entire islands such as tiny Chowra, where the jetty had been destroyed and the seabed profile had changed. On Car Nicobar, a mountain brigade repaired a key 11 km stretch of road within four days of landing on the remote island, helping to connect the island to a key jetty that opened the way for relief to come in by sea. As lieutenant general BS Thakur, the head of the integrated command for the islands, told me at the time, picking his words with care: "India has shown the world we have the wherewithal to stand on its own feet. We've also shown that we have the means to come to the aid of our friends in the region – if the need arises." Dixit's strategy was working.

The US military did go to Sri Lanka's help at the time, pinching India's strategic space. But New Delhi chose to ignore that development for fear of sounding churlish. Instead, it sent 10 warships with relief supplies, backed by giant Ilyushin 78 transport aircraft, to Sri Lanka, Indonesia and the Maldives. It was a deployment on a scale last witnessed during the Indian military intervention to quell the Tamil insurgency in Sri Lanka in 1987–90. It was also an unspoken message to the world that India would assert itself in the region it considered its neighbourhood.

Had Dixit, that master of realpolitik and strategy, not died so soon after the tsunami, it is an open question what follow-through measures he would have pushed for the Andamans. As the rehabilitation proceeded, lieutenant general Thakur and others in the military establishment utilised the rebuilding opportunity to plan to improve the strategic infrastructure on the islands. Plans were made to build secret facilities for drones and aircraft of the Aviation Reconnaissance Centre, a spy arm of the government. The troop carrier USS *Trenton*, which carries a complement of 400 officers and men and can land as many as 1,000 troops, was bought from the United States in 2007. Renamed *Jalashwa*, Sanskrit for hippopotamus, it was acquired with the specific purpose of beefing up amphibian landing capacity in the wake of the tsunami.

But then, as so much in India, stagnation set in after the initial rush. Once again, old worries of causing nervousness in Southeast Asia by significantly beefing up Indian military capacity in the Andamans surfaced as an excuse to delay plans. It was only several years later, when it became clear that China would challenge India in the Indian Ocean, that New Delhi stirred again. India's Ministry of Defence has now created an Integrated Command in the Andamans, combining Army, Navy and Air Force, which is now developing the command as the bedrock of its amphibious warfare capacity. Frontline reconnaissance aircraft, including the P81 Poseidon, have been infrequently spotted on the islands and plans are afoot to station submarine-hunting Dorniers in Campbell Bay, at the southern tip of the islands, where Naval Air Station Baaz's runway is being doubled to comfortably receive heavy military transport aircraft such as the C130J. At the north of the island chain, facing Myanmar, a new coastguard station is in place. Eventually, a new airfield in Mayabunder will open as well. When that is completed, India will have operational airfields in the north, centre and south of the Andaman chain, offering a unique vantage point to control all maritime activity in the strategically vital region.

What is more, negotiations are at an advanced stage with Japan for the purchase and eventual indigenous construction in India of the four-engined ShinMaywa US-2 amphibian aircraft. The US-2, which can land on water even amid heavy waves, is poised to be a force multiplier in the Andamans because it will allow India to quickly inject troops into areas where there are no landing strips on shore. That will also facilitate specialised operations, a factor bound to be noted not just in Southeast Asia but also in neighbourhood capitals such as Colombo in Sri Lanka and Male in the Maldives.

"After the initial rush, there was a slowdown but now plans are afoot for a second wave of beefing up in the islands," a top national security official told me. "We would have liked to have added the Mayabunder airfield by now, but sometimes, these delays do happen. Unfortunately, in the Indian system, politics comes into every decision. The Andaman & Nicobar islands send only a single MP to parliament. Had there been 20 MPs from the area, I am sure we would have done a lot more by now."

Today, a decade after the tsunami and with the US and India proclaiming a joint vision for Asia and the Indo-Pacific, Dixit's astute move will be remembered as the seminal event that drew global attention to India's capacity to use military force swiftly and in a benign way. At the time it drew praise not only from the US, but also from Pakistan, its testy neighbour. From the depths of despair, the nation's resilience and its developing sinews had conjured up a massive diplomatic victory.

2
Services Before Manufacturing: Bangor, Maine? No. Bangalore, India

> "After the reforms in 1991, however, one thing changed dramatically – India's software industry turned superstar. Our growth through the decade made us the poster child for the success of reforms. It was an entirely new experience for us, an industry that had so far been either reviled or ignored, and it marked the beginning of a huge change in how India viewed electronification."
>
> — Infosys CEO Nandan M Nilekani in *Imagining India*

WHITEFIELDS, BANGALORE, JUNE 2005. In the darkened upstairs hall of his villa, Arjun Kalyanpur, MD, was riveted by the scan results of the 51-year-old woman wheeled into the emergency room just before midnight at a Chicago hospital, complaining of severe abdominal pain. Rotating his computer mouse for a 360-degree view, the Yale-trained radiologist noted the large growth occupying most of the pelvis, protruding through the intestinal walls and obstructing it. A clear tumour, and detected very late.

Minutes later, the phone rang. The duty doctor in Chicago wanted a quick chat about the case. As they wound up the discussion, the Chicago man asked casually where the radiologist was located.

"Bangalore," said Dr Kalyanpur.

The man in Chicago was tired, and yawned audibly. "Bangor, Maine?" he inquired.

"No. Bangalore, India."

There was a moment's silence down the line.

Then, a yelp of disbelief: "Git out of here!"

It was daylight in the southern Indian metropolis, the country's most globalised city, and Kalyanpur, clad in casuals and flip-flops, was as fresh as any 40-year-old who had had a full night's sleep. But the scan he had examined so expertly was taken 16,000 km away at a busy American hospital on the other side of the world. Based on the Bangalore specialist's report, surgeons in Chicago would do immediate initial surgery to check whether to extract the tumour right away or wait until morning. Welcome to the frontier of knowledge process outsourcing.

India's reputation in IT rests on two pillars: code writing and computer services, and outsourced services, from simple ticketing work for airlines to high-end activity, including computer-aided design, and even healthcare. In the past two decades, no nation has figured on the outsourcing map quite as prominently as India.

Indian programmers first rose to prominence globally by helping fix the bugs for companies scared by the so-called Millennium Bug or Y2K threat – that havoc may be wreaked in computerised systems that were coded to abbreviate four-digit years as two digits, and would reset to 00 when the new millennium dawned. The threat passed without major mishaps but Indian code writers had gained global fame by then and many saw merit in outsourcing work to India, where rates were as much as a fourth that of the West. Soon, back office companies began taking on work for airline reservations, customer calls – almost any human service that could be performed remotely – hiring young, English-speaking Indians and housing them in buildings that were silent by day but came alive at night as they served customers in Britain, the US, Canada and elsewhere.

In time, more sophisticated work began to flow India's way, including, inevitably, in medicine, as information technology got matched with highly skilled medical brains. The smart lads at McKinsey, including a consultant named Manish Kejriwal who would later head the India operations of Singapore's Temasek Holdings, coined the term IT-Enabled Services or ITES to help outsourcing companies get the tax benefits India gives pure

IT companies. From Detroit to Wall Street, cost-conscious chief financial officers pushed their funds to pick the best Indian brains across the ether.

Kalyanpur, the son of a police officer, pioneered the telemedicine move in India in 2002. For American clients, his company, Teleradiology Solutions, offers round-the-clock service at a fraction of the usual specialist rates in the US. Work flows in now from more than 20 countries, with the US at the top; more than 50 hospitals across 20 American states use the service. Singapore's National Healthcare Group uses it; shaving what used to be a three-day wait for a scan report to just an hour, thus significantly improving patient care and service delivery at day clinics and hospitals.

The images arrive as electronic faxes, queuing up in a computer in the Bangalore office of the company. Whoever is free in Kalyanpur's expanding team of radiologists picks up the scan. Some scans, as that of the woman with the stomach tumour, can have as many as 460 images. Huge bandwidth is required for the purpose. Acquired at enormous expense, this allows the digitally compressed scan to download in less than two minutes.

When I visited him one morning in 2005, Kalyanpur was in his office studying the electronic films while speaking softly to an assistant who wrote down everything he was saying. The assistant, Munawar Pasha, was one of 25 who performed such tasks at the firm, and had already entered the patient's details on his computer: name, age, medical record number, the hospital she was in, the symptoms presented and whether she was an in-patient or an emergency case.

Now, saving the doctor time and the effort of typing, Pasha transcribed Kalyanpur's words. A few minutes later, the radiologist checked what Pasha had entered on the screen for accuracy. He corrected some spellings, made a few changes, then pushed a button. Within seconds, a central server in the US had received the full report and routed it to the hospital emergency ward where the patient was waiting. The time taken from start to finish: 28 minutes. That's unusual; most times, it requires less than 10 minutes.

"Increasingly, no doctor in the US is willing to wait until morning for radiology reports," Sunita Maheswari, Kalyanpur's wife and business partner, told me. "So, everyone is scrambling to find radiologists to cover the night." She said Teleradiology Solutions' accuracy rate was 99.8% versus the acceptable US rate of 96%. And the rates charged? About half to two-thirds that at a US hospital.

Teleradiology Solutions is among the companies at the front edge of the Indian outsourcing story that is now so well-known around the world, thanks to IT companies such as Tata Consultancy Services (TCS), Infosys Technologies and Wipro.

The success of Indian outsourcing owes much to Faqir Chand Kohli, an engineer now in his 90s and the founding chief executive of TCS. He sent the first Indian programmers overseas in the 1970s. But it was not until fear of the Y2K issue hit companies in the 1990s that the Indian software engineer became a global icon. Suddenly, Indian IT skills were in demand by chief information officers in all the big companies of the world, trying to protect their computer systems.

"It took us 23 years to reach one billion dollars in revenue," Nandan Nilekani, then CEO of Bangalore-based Infosys, would say in 2006. "It took us 23 months to reach the second billion." Today, even as the pace of growth has slowed, Infosys revenue exceeds $2.5 billion every quarter while TCS rules as undisputed No. 1, with annual revenue of more than $14 billion. That is less than a tenth of the overall pie owned by Indian companies.

Global companies such as Accenture and IBM are in the game as well. Sam Palmisano, when he was chairman and CEO of IBM, was one of the biggest India enthusiasts, repeatedly visiting the country. He once brought the entire IBM board to Bangalore for a staff meeting. It worked well for IBM – by 2007, the India push had improved its bottom line significantly, and the company was grabbing huge Indian contracts, beating TCS and Infosys on their own turf. IBM's global numbers too were affected positively as the Indian connection strengthened. Its research centres in Bangalore and Gurgaon, near New Delhi, have become a source for innovation in diverse fields, from telecommunications to semiconductors and software. Indeed, when Singapore's Land Transport Authority gave IBM the contract to build the core backend technology infrastructure for the next generation smart card electronic payment system, the work was farmed out to IBM's labs in Bangalore. "IBM leveraged the unique strength of the India software lab to win the LTA tender," Foong Sew Bun, IBM's chief technology officer in Singapore, told me at the time.

The Singapore connection to the Indian outsourcing story is deep, although not well-known. Cosmopolitan by culture, with an attractively cool climate, Bangalore used to be a sleepy cantonment town favoured by retirees. On a golfing holiday in 2014, Patrick Daniel, Ven Sreenivasan of *The Business Times* and I stood marvelling at Winston Churchill's unpaid bill still on display in the lobby of the colonial-era Bangalore Club. The city is home to more than a hundred technical institutes which churn out quality engineers. Bangaloreans are comfortable in English, the software language worldwide.

In the 1990s it had started to draw yuppies as the first of IT firms began to set up shop, bringing their funky lifestyles, and humour, to Bangalore. Indeed, their mood had soon infected the city. When computer companies there suffered a sales slump, several executives banded to set up an informal group called the DOS Club – DOS stood for Drown Our Sorrows, rather than Disk Operating System.

At the Non-Aligned Movement summit in 1992, India's prime minister, PV Narasimha Rao, and Singapore's prime minister, Goh Chok Tong, looking for an iconic project to highlight the growing relationship between the two nations, tossed up the idea of a business park for information technology companies. That June, Albert Hong of the Singapore design firm RSP Architects & Planners made a trip to Bangalore and came back with an upbeat assessment of the city. The following month Philip Yeo, then chairman of Singapore's Economic Development Board, travelled to the southern Indian metropolis and met top state government officials over two days. Clearances came thick and fast, and Yeo invited the Indian bureaucrats to visit his island. That was all it took; the Karnataka state officials, aiming to make their state capital India's Silicon Valley, quickly realised you could have productive capacity in a green environment.

The Singaporeans made two wise moves at the start; first, they enlisted India's Tata Group as a local partner, then they got the Karnataka state government involved in the project as well, helping ease potential problems in land acquisition, utility services and the host of other issues that confront investments in India. This would prove helpful as hydroelectric projects do not produce enough power in the summer months, and to succeed, the facility would not only need assured power supply but also strong communication links.

When Goh flagged off the Bangalore IT Park in January 1994 at Whitefields – two days after being chief guest at the Republic Day celebrations in New Delhi – India's software exports in the year to March 1993 had amounted to a mere $300 million. The country had 9,000 professionals working in the industry at the time, of which a third were in Bangalore. Today, the Kohli-inspired TCS alone employs more than 300,000 and the industry employs some 3 million across India, with Tier II cities like Thiruvananthapuram (formerly Trivandrum) and Jaipur also getting onto the IT map. Meanwhile, the Bangalore tech park has become the benchmark for dozens of similar other facilities that have sprung up across the vast nation. Bangalore itself contributes a third of Indian exports of IT and IT-enabled services.

And it's not merely about software services or call-centre operations. Time Inc for instance has put down a global in-house centre in Bangalore to provide global sourcing through processes within analytics, finance, technology, operations and shared services. With a monthly print audience of more than 120 million, the India operation provides analytics around consumer retention, sales, advertising, supply chain management and finance for more than 100 brands of parent Time Inc, including *TIME*, *People*, *Sports Illustrated*, *InStyle*, *Real Simple*, *Entertainment Weekly* and *Fortune*.

Thanks to companies such as these, India, uniquely among nations of its size and stage of development, has witnessed services far exceeding manufacturing in contributing to the economy. At about 57%, the services share of the Indian economy makes manufacturing, at 16%, pale in comparison.

Nasscom, which is the abbreviation for India's National Association of Service and Software Companies, projects that the Indian tech sector will have revenues of $350 billion by 2025. A fifth of that will come from a domestic market gathering pace with initiatives such as Digital India. But the rest will be from overseas, according to the Nasscom-McKinsey study.

Still, the report was prepared before the full extent of the emerging market slowdown led by China became known, with its knock-on effects on the world economy. Most analysts think that, between 2016 and 2018, Indian outsourcing companies are more likely to see growth in the high single digits than the double-digit expansion projected by Nasscom.

For all its vaunted successes, though, the dangers to the industry are rising. India's media, prone to bouts of great ebullience, pronounced the nation a "knowledge superpower" long before the title was earned. In fact, the country's research facilities, except in pockets, are generally quite poor. It produces far too few patents, compared with China.

And competition is rising – from China, the Philippines and elsewhere – while none of the major Indian players have scaled up their game into being full-service consultancies, which would have been the obvious route to go, given the talent that resides in India. Instead, labour arbitrage is still the competitive edge for the most part. Accenture employs a quarter-million people in India. IBM, which at its peak had more than 160,000 workers there, has now scaled back by about a quarter, partly because the software game is itself moving swiftly into robotics. IBM's own Watson supercomputer is being deployed to automate projects. Experts in the field say the big megatrend in computing, aside from the burst to cloud computing, is the trending away from labour-intensive services. With creativity increasingly front and centre of such efforts, and with the grunt work being taken on by computers, India risks being no longer the automatic choice in a field that includes Russia, Israel, the Philippines, China and even Venezuela.

Perhaps hubris played a part too in the relative decline of some companies. A senior executive at Deutsche Bank once relayed a telling instance of the differential treatment they got at two of the biggest IT companies. When he took a Deutsche board member to see S Ramadorai, then head of TCS, he found a CEO acting with immense humility. "Ramadorai listened carefully to what we had to say, then produced a notebook in which he took copious notes," he told me. "At another company in Bangalore, we got a lofty lecture on how they could help improve our banking processes."

Infosys, once considered the IT-bellwether for India, went into much turmoil for nearly a decade, in part because of its policy to reward each of its several founders with a stint as chief executive. Things slipped so much that, for a time, founding CEO NR Narayana Murthy was brought back to run the company. Fortunately for it, the decline appears to have been stemmed; Murthy steadied the ship and an outsider, Vishal Sikka, was appointed CEO in 2014.

Sikka was hired away from the German software giant SAP, where he was a member of the executive board, leading all products and driving innovation globally. The choice was wise. Infosys performance had picked up significantly by the end of 2014 and Sikka, forever insisting that Infosys leave behind "services of yesterday", has set Infosys on a path of not just organic growth but also a focus in acquiring small, innovative companies rather than dated technologies.

Indeed, Sikka's arrival has been a boost to not only Infosys, but the IT scene in India, generally. He has correctly brought some anxiety to the field, pointing out that the old focus on cost arbitrage and cost-saving must yield to true value creation and innovation.

People close to the company's thinking say the new sweep takes in artificial intelligence, robotics and automation, collaborative design and the Internet of Things, a computing concept that describes a future where everyday physical objects from cars to your refrigerator will be connected to the Net and be able to identify themselves to other devices.

It is clear that the future of India's software industry will no longer be based on cost advantage alone, but on a move to quality. Also, today's large business process outsourcing units may have to yield to specialised companies with a depth of talent in a particular area. The Indian home market itself is expanding significantly, and is tipped to accelerate from the current $74 billion, with new initiatives such as Digital India, the focus on Smart Cities, and the national E-Governance plan.

Still, there is no shortage of opportunity, even as some doomsday projections have the outsourcing phenomenon running out of steam by 2022. By that time, as much as 50 million things – from your washing machine and electric oven to your golf bag – are likely to be connected to the Internet of Things. Beyond lie the challenges of the Internet of Anything which will need a common software ecosystem capable of accommodating every kind of sensor input and operating condition.

Also, Indian software engineers have survived challenges before. No sooner had the frenzy of the Y2K bug died down, than they had to face down the dot.com bust followed by the global financial crisis six years later. Increasingly, the work done in centres like Bangalore, and even Cochin, in Kerala, has got more sophisticated. Indian companies have moved into systems integration and managing the IT infrastructure of clients. In-house, there is greater use of automation in most Indian firms, improving the bottom line. Som Mittal, who led Nasscom in the aftermath of the global financial crisis, says the nature of the game has changed dramatically. "You've done what we told you to do," he says of the large customers who do business with Indian IT firms. "Now tell us what more you could do for us."

3
Slumdog Millionaire: A Celebration of India

> "It is an Indian season. To use a phrase translated from Latin: 'Seize the day'."
>
> — Lee Kuan Yew in Mumbai, October 2007

IN LATE 2008, theatres in Canada began showing the Hollywood production *Slumdog Millionaire.* In January the next year, movie houses in the US and India followed. Set in Mumbai's slums and directed by Danny Boyle of Britain, it told the story of a young man who appears on a quiz show styled on *Who Wants to Be a Millionaire.*

Against all expectations, Jamal Mallick, the key protagonist, wins the 20 million rupees first prize, because every question put to him was somehow linked to a key event in his life. He is picked up by the police who smell a rat - how could a slum kid know all the answers? Jamal has a convincing response to that as well. Before the movie ends, he has also scooped up his childhood sweetheart, who is on the verge of being forced into prostitution.

Like *Sleepless in Seattle* and *Forrest Gump, Slumdog Millionaire* was what movie industry circles call a sleeper hit, a movie that wins terrific audiences with little promotion or marketing. Movie goers around the world, enveloped in the global economic depression, reacted warmly to *Slumdog Millionaire*'s story of hope and sense of uplift. By the time the awards were handed out on a Sunday night in Los Angeles, *Slumdog Millionaire* had grossed some $150 million, 10 times what it cost to produce.

Even the dream merchants of Bollywood could not have imagined what was to follow: *Slumdog Millionaire* was nominated for 10 Academy Awards and won eight, including Best Picture and Best Director. Two of the gold statuettes went to AR Rahman, the music maker for the movie, and Resul Pookutty, a sound technician. Rahman shared one of his awards with the lyricist, Gulzar.

Not surprisingly, Indians went into raptures. In the eight decades that Academy Awards had been handed out before *Slumdog*, only two Indians – the late Satyajit Ray for Lifetime Achievement and Bhanu Athaiya for Best Costume Design in the movie *Gandhi* – had won Oscars before. So, there was plenty of cause for celebration.

But the success of the Rahman-Gulzar-Pookutty trio carried a significance far beyond the rising acceptance of the sounds of India by a global audience, or recognition for its gifted technicians. Indeed, it was a victory for the very idea of India, the rich tapestry of its syncretic culture and the rise of a common popular culture spanning the nation. Rahman and Pookutty, such big names in Hindi cinema lately, are rooted in southern India, which has a tradition of chafing at domination from the Hindi-speaking north.

Slumdog Millionaire itself is a sort of testament to a more sophisticated Western appreciation of this vast and teeming nation as a land of resilience, hope and increasingly, opportunity. It showed how much the West had journeyed to recognising the merits of India. Eighty years before, around the time the first Oscars were being handed out, an American writer named Katherine Mayo had just published the book *Mother India*.

Mayo had been a supporter of the Asian Exclusion Acts, racist legislation that sought to restrict immigration from Asia and Africa into the US in favour of whites from Europe. *Mother India* painted a picture of despair, an India steeped in child marriage, mistreated widows and abysmal hygiene. Mahatma Gandhi famously called the book "the report of a drain inspector".

Slumdog Millionaire did not go easy on India's squalor or its social tensions. Indeed, there were flashbacks to the 1992 communal riots of Mumbai. But it used these as bricks to build a staircase leading to sunshine, and thus, eliminated the insult and eased the injury. And so, Indians grabbed this Hollywood movie as their own.

Beyond the claims to recognition of a good drama, backed by excellent acting and wonderful music, the world had good reason to celebrate India's arrival on the stage. Rising income levels and the unsatiated thirst for consumer goods and travel had begun to tell on the bottom lines of companies from Paris to Singapore and Sydney. At the highest levels, the Indian super rich lived another life altogether. After years of hiding their wealth, now they too felt free to display extreme ostentation.

"Whether for Hermes fashion or Mirage jet fighter planes, India is rapidly emerging as a critical market for us," a senior European diplomat told me a few months after *Slumdog Millionaire* appeared. "I went to a wedding in one of those farmhouses in south Delhi the other night and all the women who turned up went back carrying Louis Vuitton bags as return gifts. Five such weddings, and it begins to show up on the bottom lines of companies."

The celebratory – indeed, near-triumphalist – mood in India had been palpable for a few years. Perhaps the most telling example of this was the way, in January 2005, the nation went berserk over the performance of an 18-year-old girl from Hyderabad at the Australian Open tennis championships. For the record, Sania Mirza's third round duel with the American tennis legend Serena Williams, who went on to win the title, ended in a 1-6, 4-6 defeat for the teenager, ranked 166 in the world, 159 places behind the American.

But never before had the vanquished looked so much like a victor. Despite the loss, there was national exultation over her performance. Her former coach, CGK Bhupathy, predicted a Top 10 ranking for his former ward, a forecast that was accepted uncritically (she peaked at World No. 27 in 2007, though is currently ranked No. 1 in women's doubles). Even prime minister Manmohan sent along a note of congratulations. The media went into a Sania frenzy and newspapers carried huge advertisements with Sania as poster person for the government's Save the Girl Child campaign.

To be sure, much of the adulation was due to the photogenic looks that made her the No. 2 crowd favourite at the tournament, behind Maria Sharapova. At 168 cm, Sania was then a smiling, oval face above a shapely frame on her way to womanhood. Her habit of half closing an eye while responding to questions on television, and her on-court tendency to tuck her tongue into her left cheek, gave her innocence an unwittingly pagan appeal that had India in thrall.

The Indian reaction to the Sania phenomenon also underscored the growing celebration of Western-style individual achievement, not to speak of consumerism, that has been evident since economic liberalisation of the 1990s threw the field open to individual enterprise. Sania represented a new generation of Indians raised with no memories of colonial rule – confident in themselves and with a hunger and will to succeed against the best in the world. And she was a contrast to the days when Indians at the peak of their form somehow failed at the finish line for want of a killer instinct. At the height of his tennis career, Vijay Amritraj said that if what it took to be No. 1 was to act like John McEnroe, a player notorious for his petulance, he did not mind not being in that slot. Today, Amritraj draws his fame not from being a champion, but the man who talks to champions as a sports anchor.

In 1991, faced with a balance of payments crisis and in hock to the IMF, prime minister PV Narasimha Rao, a dour polyglot from the southern Indian state of Andhra Pradesh, ordered his finance minister, Dr Manmohan Singh, to take steps to dismantle India's state-controlled economy, also called the licence-permit Raj because of the myriad regulations choking growth. The nation's entrepreneurial sinews were unleashed. To be wealthy, and show it, was no longer a matter of embarrassment. The world began to sit up and take notice that the world's greatest frontier market was opening up and rich pickings awaited.

The beauty industry was first off the mark. In late 1994, Sushmita Sen, the daughter of an Indian Air Force wing commander, was chosen as Miss

Universe at a pageant held in Manila, Philippines, the first Indian to wear the crown. Weeks later, the woman who placed second to Sen in the Miss India contest, Aishwarya Rai, was picked as Miss World in Sun City, South Africa.

For a time, as Hollywood looked for a quality Indian brand, just as it reached out to East Asia by casting the Malaysian-Chinese beauty Michelle Yeoh in a Bond movie, it fixed on Rai, whom Julia Roberts once called "the world's most beautiful woman". With a *Time* magazine cover to her name, an appearance on the *David Letterman Show* and an interview on *60 Minutes*, Ash was a brand ambassador for the L'Oreal group and Swatch group's Longines brand. While she did act in a Hollywood movie, *Pink Panther 2*, where she was cast as a villainous temptress, she became a major star at home, eventually marrying Abhishek Bachchan, the only son of the Bollywood legend Amitabh Bachchan.

Even as Indians embraced the world, the world was embracing them. Hotels around Asia began to cater to the Indian traveller, including Hindi movies in their pay television systems and putting *tandoori* dishes on the room service menu. On the Star Cruise liners that ply from Singapore, a corner of the huge buffet began to be set aside for Jain cuisine, which caters to the vegetarians of that Hindu sub-caste, many of whom are wealthy businessmen.

In other directions too India was making waves around the world. Nano, the people's car, as it was called, was launched by the Tata Group in 2008 to much excitement worldwide. I was fortunate to have an early glimpse of it when the Tata Group brought it to the Taj Mansingh Hotel in New Delhi for Singapore's prime minister, Goh Chok Tong, to take a look. The tall Goh – he is about 1.9 m – sat in the cabin and pronounced it roomy. Billed as the cheapest automobile on wheels, it caught global attention for the engineering that made such a low-cost car possible – it was priced at 100,000 rupees, or $2,500 at the time – and held the promise of doing for India what Henry Ford's Model T did for America. Suzuki Motor's Maruti 800, until then the cheapest on the road, went for double that price.

Nano became a sensation globally. John Elliott, at the time correspondent for *Fortune*, said his blog entry on Nano chalked up more than 21,000 hits in less than two days. In contrast, his entry on the hugely successful Reliance Power IPO, the largest offered by an Asian company, got less than 2,000 hits over a week. Climate change gurus worried about the prospect of a million Nanos on India's roads every year. The *Hindustan Times* headlined it "Small Wonder".

India's well-to-do fretted about domestic help turning up for work in Nanos, rather than cycles and motor scooters. It wasn't to be; Nano performed unspectacularly on the market, thanks to its "low cost" label and Tata would admit later that it made marketing mistakes. It has now been relaunched as a more classy product, another indication of the way Indians think and behave.

That year, 2008, came India's biggest moment on the global sporting stage when a 25-year-old shooter named Abhinav Bindra brought the nation its first Olympic gold medal in an individual event. When his name was called out in the Beijing stadium, Bindra accepted his victory with a Zen-like detachment. No fist-pumping à la Tiger Woods or a Michael Jordan high-five. Just a bemused expression playing on his face as though he was watching someone else on the podium. Until that day, India's most celebrated sportspeople had been athletes who had narrowly missed bronze medals at the Olympics, "The Flying Sikh" Milkha Singh for the 400 metres at Rome in 1960 and PT Usha, who lost by 1/100th of a second in the 400-metre hurdles at Los Angeles in 1984. Usha, in fact, had been erroneously declared third before the announcement was withdrawn.

In the excitement over Bindra's win, some of the larger questions were forgotten. Why were more medals not being won by a nation with over a billion people and a military of 1.3 million, where diet, discipline and spare time ought not to be an issue? Why were much smaller countries and more recent entrants to the Olympic Games doing better even as India had participated in every Olympics since at least 1900? The previous time India had won an Olympics gold was in 1980 and that was in a team event, field hockey, always considered the national sport until cricket overwhelmed it. In 2008, the hockey team did not even qualify.

And the hype, at the time, was everywhere. The IMF and others had begun to refer to India as a "growth engine" for the world. Indian companies were buying up iconic Western firms. Arcelor Steel was bought by the Mittals. The Corus Group and Jaguar Land Rover were bought by the Tata Group. Germany's Betapharm was snapped up by the Indian generic drugs maker Dr Reddy's Laboratories. Singapore's Sembawang Engineering & Construction became a fully owned subsidiary of India's Punj Lloyd and Videocon bought South Korea's Daewoo Electronics.

Despite worry that Tata may have overpaid for Corus, a gush of nationalism flowed. The former colony was now picking up a crown jewel of its former colonial master. Newspapers chronicled with glee that a century ago, British administrator Frederick Upcott had sneered at Tata's audacious proposal to make steel to British Railways' specifications and vowed to eat every pound of the metal Tata succeeded in making. Others noted that the Corus buy vaulted Tata Steel to 268 in global company rankings, just below Coca Cola Corp. "Forget your old fears about Coca-colonisation," one wrote. "The era of Tata-colonialism is at hand."

The benchmark index, Sensex, rode up to the 21,000 levels from 14,000, a 50% increase, in less than a year.

And Indian professionals had started to gain recognition worldwide as top-flight managers. Indra Nooyi of Chennai (formerly Madras) was given charge of Pepsico in 2001. Shantanu Narayen was elevated to the top of Adobe in 2001, when he was just 41 years old. But no Indian was as prominent abroad as Rajat Gupta, the Kolkata-born engineer who would run McKinsey from 1994 to 2003 and sit on the boards of some of the bluest chips of Wall Street, including Goldman Sachs. Sadly, his career would end in ignominy after another India-born professional, the New York prosecutor Preet Bharara, nailed him in an insider trading scandal. Likewise, Dr Reddy's would take losses on the Betapharm acquisition and Tata would have to downsize Corus. But at the time the party was in full swing.

It is amazing how perceptions can change once the jaundice is removed from the eye. Three years after *Slumdog Millionaire*'s release, *The New York Times* published a story on Mumbai's Dharavi, which it described as one of the world's most infamous slums and a cliché for Indian misery. Jim Yardley, the reporter, went on to describe the incredible industry and entrepreneurship of the million or so working on a triangle of land barely two-thirds the size of New York's Central Park. He estimated that Dharavi's economic output may be as much as a billion dollars a year. The headline for his piece – "In One Slum, Misery, Work, Politics and Hope" – said it all.

And yet there was more to *Slumdog Millionaire* than a story of hope and upliftment. By their very persona and social background, the musicians, Rahman and Pookutty, also sent subliminal messages that resonated not just across India but even into Pakistan, which was built on the theory that the subcontinent's Muslims needed a separate homeland because Hindu and Muslim societies were "two nations".

Pookutty, the youngest of eight siblings, was born into a Muslim family in Kollam district of Kerala, a part of India that got Islam around the same time as its birth in the Middle East. Now a Mumbai resident, his infant children were cared for by a Hindu neighbour while he travelled to Los Angeles for the awards ceremony.

Rahman, celebrated as the Mozart of Madras, was an even more interesting figure as a convert from Hinduism. He is a Sufi Muslim, believing in a strain of the faith that draws on universalism and a mystical tradition.

The widespread popularity across India of Rahman, unabashedly devout and deeply proud of his country, lent its 165 million Muslims a sense of security at a time when sections of the Hindu right wing were prone to question their loyalty and patriotism. And yet he was not the only Muslim to do India proud. Rahman takes his place alongside other Muslims, including Shah Rukh Khan and Aamir Khan of Bollywood, the tennis star, Sania Mirza, and the cricketing brothers, Yusuf and Irfan Pathan.

Indeed, it was ironical that Rahman should have been called Dilip Kumar at birth, a name given by his Hindu parents. Seven decades ago, when the handsome Mohammed Yusuf Khan was cast in his first movie, the director, thinking that Indian audiences may not take to a leading star with a Muslim name, gave him the screen name Dilip Kumar. Born in Peshawar, now part of Pakistan, Khan would go on to become Hindi cinema's most acclaimed male actor. In December 2015, at 93 years and nearing the end of his life, Dilip Kumar was awarded India's Padma Vibhushan, the second highest civilian award.

I wrote in 2009 that for all the celebrations, Indians and their leaders would do well to remind themselves that while *Slumdog Millionaire* was shining, their own nation had a long way to travel before it too could bask in the sunshine. For many children, including some who featured in the movie, the early years are too often a Dickensian morass. India's 2001 census noted that some 13 million poor kids were trapped in child labour in India, with girls the more vulnerable. One of two Indian girls aged 6–18 had never stepped into a school.

The dramatic scene in *Slumdog Millionaire* of gangs blinding children to be more effective beggars is not an exaggeration. It is known to happen.

"While the movie does a good job depicting the realities of slum life to a large extent, there are many more challenges these children are up against," Dr Jayakumar Christian, National Director of World Vision India, an NGO which works with children and communities across 150 locations in India, told me at the time. "Moviegoers should realise that poverty in India is a clear and present challenge for children in India – but there are tangible ways people can make a difference."

To India's credit, by the time the next census was done a decade later, the number had dropped to 4.35 million in child labour amid a total child population of 260 million.

PART II

TRIUMPHS, A BLUNDER AND A DISASTER

4
Singapore Sling: The Merlion and the Elephant

> "The Singapore relationship is so strong that it is our foremost external partner in the world. Singapore has helped us enormously in dealing with globalisation and understanding it."
>
> — Tarun Das

NEW DELHI, JUNE 2005. At 1.30 am on June 30, a bleary-eyed Soh Tze Bian, senior state counsel at the Singapore Attorney-General's Chambers, was looking for a taxi outside New Delhi's Ministry of Industry and Commerce. The searing, dry summer heat had seen temperatures rise to 44 degrees Celsius, and thanks to the pre-monsoon showers that had brought a measure of relief to the Indian capital, the weather had turned sticky and uncomfortable. It was not unlike a wet Singapore afternoon.

Singapore's prime minister, Lee Hsien Loong, had arrived in the Indian capital four hours earlier with his foreign minister, George Yeo, and trade and industry minister Lim Hng Kiang. Accompanying them was Ho Ching, Lee's wife, who runs the powerful state investment company Temasek Holdings. Lee and his Indian counterpart, Manmohan Singh, were due to sign the Comprehensive Economic Cooperation Agreement (CECA) at 7.45 pm that day, but the two sides were still deliberating over the fine print in the financial services part of the agreement. At 8.55 am, as Lee left his hotel for the formal welcome ceremony, Soh was looking for a vehicle to take his team back for a final scrub of the draft.

Few countries can match India when it rolls out the pageantry, and the ceremony in the magnificent forecourt of the presidential palace that day was impressive with its cavalry and tall, turbaned soldiers of the President's Bodyguard. Shortly after the ceremonial welcome was completed, Manmohan, meeting me in his South Block office for an interview, mused that Goh Chok Tong had been the first head of government to visit India since he had taken office the previous May. Subsequently, Manmohan noted, he had met Lee, the new Singapore prime minister and son of the island state's founding father, in Laos and Jakarta.

I looked around Manmohan's office as this wise old man spoke to me. The table was bare except for a single blue file. A box of pens supplemented the Cross ballpoint that rode in his breast pocket. There were fewer books on his shelves than had been there when some of his predecessors held the same office, I recalled, even though few of them shared his academic distinction. This was a man who felt he needed to prove nothing about his intellect.

"Singapore has consistently been bullish on India's reform process ever since it started and we appreciate this endorsement," Manmohan went on, jerking me back from my brief reverie. "CECA is a symbol of our commitment to liberalise the economy. With CECA, Singapore can act as a window to India – an India which is just beginning to realise its immense growth potential. We have a common vision and understanding of economic and security issues."

As he spoke, Soh, sitting in the Indian Commerce Ministry, had signed off on the documents. Four hours before the official ceremony involving the two prime ministers, Singapore and India had an agreed full text comprising some 740 pages, the document weighing in excess of 2 kg. Never before had Singapore negotiated such a free trade agreement with a developing nation, much less one in South Asia. For India, it was the most wide-ranging and complex economic agreement ever envisaged. And it gave Singapore an improved double taxation avoidance treaty by which companies registered on the island enjoy the benefits of zero capital gains tax in India. Only strategically vital Mauritius, in the Indian Ocean, had enjoyed that privilege before and Indian Finance Ministry officials had actually been trying to close that tax loophole for years. Manmohan had intervened personally to give Singapore the same privilege, in the process packing off a recalcitrant officer to another job in order to smooth the way.

CECA was a game-changer in the evolving Singapore-India relationship, which had lifted in the 1960s, then cooled in the 1980s, and thanks to Goh and his foreign minister, Yeo, was soaring once again. On the Indian end, Narasimha Rao, after he ordered then-finance minister Manmohan Singh to unchain the Indian economy in 1991, had identified Singapore as a key launch pad for his Look East Policy.

The response from Singapore had been warm and positive in every way – the island state had long spotted India's potential and had been impatient for it to fulfil its tryst with destiny. This impatience – and Singapore founding father Lee Kuan Yew's candour in conveying his disappointment – had contributed to a mild frost in ties since 1983 because the advice had been poorly received by Indira Gandhi, K Natwar Singh, the long-serving Indian diplomat and politician, told me. India was at that time close to the Soviet Union, which had underwritten its security since 1971. According to Natwar Singh (who claimed to have witnessed one frosty exchange between Gandhi and the older Lee), PN Haksar, a left-leaning aide to Mrs Gandhi, had also contributed to sour ties by projecting Singapore as a lackey of the United States. Besides, Lee's enthusiastic championing of China's prospects in the wake of its 1978 reforms had caused some angst in New Delhi.

With Lee having handed the reins to Goh Chok Tong in late 1990, India sensed the time was right to power up the relationship. This it did with a master stroke – inviting Goh as chief guest of the 1994 Republic Day parade, a spectacular show of pomp and power that is held every January 26. The move was loaded with meaning and it paid off. As he departed for India, Goh spoke of hoping to spark off a "mild India fever" in Singapore. The comment resonated around the world and particularly in India, which received it with delirious joy.

Three years into India's economic liberalisation programme, Goh's words were the first significant endorsement from an international leader. So chuffed was India that some Indian newspaper editorials even suggested that Singapore might want to consider investing its entire investible reserves in their country. Goh would not know it at the time but he would spark a bigger fever in India about Singapore.

Rao himself would travel to Singapore in late 1994 and outline his vision for Indian engagement with East Asia at a Singapore Lecture organised by the Institute of Southeast Asian Studies. Lee Kuan Yew, chairing the lecture, would add his own valuable endorsement; Rao's moves to liberalise India's economy, Lee declared, could potentially have as much impact on his nation's destiny as Deng Xiaoping's decision in 1978 to open China to foreign investment.

Coming from Lee, who had been sceptical of India for some years, this was considered high praise. Lee patched up whatever hard feelings remained with New Delhi by subsequently proclaiming at a Jawaharlal Nehru Lecture in the Indian capital that he had been happy to change his view on India. Sonia Gandhi, chairing that lecture, responded that India had listened carefully to his words, "*even* when you were critical of us".

Still, compared with Singapore's swift reflexes, things move slowly in India. George Yeo, who was minister for trade and industry before he became foreign minister in August 2004, had noted the slow progress of negotiations at the World Trade Organisation (WTO) and decided by 2001 that Singapore could not possibly wait for the WTO to finish its work in order to gain entry into the promising Indian market. It would have to strike its own, independent trade deal with the South Asian giant, and the sooner the better. It was a brilliant, strategic move and immediately endorsed by Goh. Then, as the wider relationship progressed, the ambition of what was meant to be a mere trade deal widened to cover services, investments, sharing information and a host of other issues.

For its part, India found the island state a surprisingly welcoming place. In 1993, when Tarun Das, the guiding force behind the Confederation of

Indian Industry lobby group, brought a delegation to Singapore to promote the India story, he found Goh impressively attentive. Not only that, the Singapore leader quickly put together a team of local industry captains to meet the CII delegation over dinner. Since then, CII has made an annual pilgrimage to Singapore and even has a branch office on the island.

On the strategic front, too, there had been much movement. New Delhi noted with gratitude that Singapore had backed India's entry into the Association of Southeast Asian Nations (Asean) as a sectoral dialogue partner, then pushed for full dialogue partnership. It had midwifed India's entry into the Asean Regional Forum and the East Asia Summit, against the objections of some states. Besides, Singapore's strategic proximity to the US was another factor in the Indian calculus, with New Delhi itself inching closer to Washington DC every day. In April 2002, the two sides convened a joint study group and agreed to expand the agreement beyond trade.

The story of how CECA was clinched is a saga of tenacity, patience and, ultimately, compromise on both sides. Initially slated for completion in 11 months, the negotiations ran on for two full years and clocked 13 rounds of meetings. At some points, as many as 40 officers from each side, in groups of six to 10, held parallel discussions. The complications of negotiating a treaty with such a wide scope, plus a government change in New Delhi that saw the installation of a new finance minister and central bank governor, prolonged the negotiations. Throughout, then-trade minister Yeo kept encouraging his troops. Heng Swee Keat, managing director of the Monetary Authority of Singapore at the time and now minister for finance, told me that Yeo would often liken India to the Ganges River: "Do not despair; ultimately it will find its way to the sea."

The original deadline for CECA, April 2004, was thus missed. Negotiations began in earnest only the following month, with the freshly installed Manmohan Singh government in charge of India. By mid-May the following year, CECA had finally been scrubbed up into an acceptable shape and the Indian Cabinet had endorsed an early draft of the accord. The trickiest part of the negotiations had centred on an annex on telecommunications, and the finer details of a financial services and enhanced double taxation avoidance agreement. Much time was also spent on working out the rules of origin, with New Delhi insisting on a minimum "Singapore-added" component for goods the island would send to India. Finally, Indian industry, key sections of which had been leery of the accord, came around to backing CECA.

If trade-driven Singapore had its reasons for pushing for CECA, Manmohan had his own too, and it is indicative of the political canniness he is capable of. According to senior sources in the Indian government, he had seen CECA as the thin edge of the wedge to prise open the Indian economy. "It is like Archimedes and the lever. You give some to the Singaporeans and before you know it, every other significant nation will start asking for the same and it will be tough to say 'no'," a top official in the Commerce Ministry confided to me.

With many of his key liberalisation measures blocked by the Opposition and resistance from within his own party, Manmohan was using CECA as a lever to kickstart a second round of reform, having authored the first round in 1991 as finance minister.

And he did have good reason to use a bit of subterfuge.

A few months later, when I met Prakash Karat, boss of the CPM party, he was at his inflexible best. Sitting in front of a portrait of Che Guevara, dressed in a short-sleeved shirt and chinos, Karat insisted that the "consensus on liberalisation and economic reform is a very superficial one". "At the ground level, the people have not really accepted this, as was clear from the last election. Nobody would have imagined the BJP doing badly because of its economic policies, but we were clear that it would. You cannot talk about economic growth in GDP terms."

As the head of a party that lent crucial parliamentary support to Manmohan without participating in his government, Karat was a very powerful voice at the time, one that almost managed to stymie India's pathbreaking civil nuclear agreement with the US. But Manmohan had sneaked CECA through nevertheless, and right under Karat's nose.

Indians, who tend to be loquacious, and Singaporeans, who are known to be extremely business-like, learnt something of each other in their prolonged contact over the CECA negotiations, which set the stage for many tight, personal friendships. After the Singapore experience, the Indian Commerce Ministry prepared a limited-circulation document on negotiating strategy. At the wedding of Indian commerce minister Kamal Nath's daughter a few months later, the guest list included both Yeo and his successor at the Singapore Trade Ministry, Lim Hng Kiang.

Indian ministers, too, learnt to adjust to Singapore's famous matter-of-fact approach. P Chidambaram, who ran the Finance Ministry and was himself a man known not to waste a moment, once was taken aback when a Singapore minister called on him some months before the deal was locked down. With barely a friendly preamble, the Singaporean began the meeting saying: "We have three problems with CECA ..."

But Singaporeans also would learn to loosen up with the Indians. At a celebratory post-CECA dinner hosted by Kamal Nath, the level of banter was infectious to all in the room.

"We have a small present for you," Nath said at the end of his speech, presenting a huge parcel to Lim.

"I am glad that my officials had the foresight to prepare an equally small present," Lim responded, handing over his own huge gift.

The high-fives over a successful CECA had barely died down when a serious wrinkle appeared in the bilateral relationship.

On September 3, 2005, a Saturday, *The Straits Times* carried my report that Singapore's Changi Airport Managers & Partners (Champs) may pull out of a consortium bidding to manage airports being privatised in New Delhi and Mumbai. According to the upgrade plan, overseas and Indian private companies would have been allowed to buy 74% of the two airports and manage them for 30 years. State-run Airports Authority of India was to hold the remainder. My sources had told me that Bharti Telecom boss Sunil Bharti Mittal, who was leading the consortium in an effort to diversify from telecoms into infrastructure projects, had returned from Singapore on Thursday night after a frantic bid to save the consortium. But Champs had determined that the performance deliverables demanded by the Indian government were hard to meet, and it did not want to risk damaging its reputation. It was unfortunate, because the Bharti-led consortium had been regarded as a cinch for the project, thanks to Champs' role in the joint venture. It was well-known that the Indian government, preparing the city for the 2010 Commonwealth Games, was very keen to hand the Delhi Airport project to Singapore. Indeed, aware of this, the third partner, DLF, had switched sides to join Mittal.

When my story broke it was received with disbelief, particularly in India. Mittal was in thick with the Singaporeans and carried a lot of clout. His Bharti Telecom, which goes under the Airtel brand, had consistently delivered high returns for Singapore Telecommunications, which then owned about a third of the Indian company. Indeed, in India's high circles Mittal was often referred to as "Singapore's son-in-law".

For a few days, Bharti continued to maintain that the joint venture was on. But 10 days after my report, it announced bitterly that it was pulling out of a bid for Delhi Airport because "we cannot proceed without the commitment of Changi, as it is an essential qualification criteria to have an airport operator participate in the bidding process". "Bharti is dismayed at this development."

I felt sorry for Mittal, whom I had befriended in 1992, when I was a correspondent for the Hongkong-based magazine *Asiaweek*. He used to make push-button telephones and answering machines branded Beetel at the time, played squash to keep fit and also happened to be the son of a prominent Congress party figure. In an India where shoddy was acceptable, the fine quality of his products – which sat on my office table – tickled my curiosity and led me to seek him out. After spending a convivial afternoon with him in his modest office in New Delhi's Nehru Place commercial district, I had profiled him as an entrepreneur worth watching. Within a decade he had emerged as a shining star on the Indian business firmament after having built up India's top cell phone service provider.

The Delhi Airport project finally went to a consortium in which Malaysian Airports was a partner. Present at the inauguration, I could not help feeling sad that Singapore had lost an opportunity to plant its flag on the Indian capital's most prominent infrastructure building, what could have been a shining red dot on the forehead of Mother India. Today, Delhi Airport's efficiency levels match or exceed Changi's in several aspects, including luggage delivery.

Still, there were good reasons for Champs to be cautious. In the 1990s Singapore Airlines and the Tata Group of India had applied to set up a joint venture domestic airline. Domestic pressure on the civil aviation minister from a private Indian airline killed the project. A year later Tata and Singapore teamed up to bid for the new airport in Bangalore, along with Raytheon of the United States. Again it ran into difficulties and the project, after an eight-year delay, finally went to Siemens of Germany.

Champs' decision caused severe consternation in official circles in India and some wondered whether there was a pattern to all this. Four years earlier, the Indian government led by Atal Bihari Vajpayee, Manmohan's predecessor, had offered Singapore Airlines a 49% stake in Air India, the national carrier. SIA backed off after doing due diligence. The Singapore carrier was having a rough time with its investment in Air New Zealand and the civil aviation environment was not conducive – SwissAir had just gone under because of its overseas investments. A little later, Delhi Airport's modernisation was offered to Singapore on a government-to-government basis but again Singapore baulked, preferring to bid in an open international tender to avoid allegations of sweetheart deals that could be planted on India's aggressive media.

Now, there were dark hints in New Delhi that the last-minute pullout was because Singapore was reluctant to see high quality air facilities take shape in India, lest it affect its own hub status. A delegation of young Indian parliamentarians visiting Singapore a few weeks later would visit the port and housing estates – but pointedly decline a tour of Changi Airport.

In all fairness to Champs, the Indian government had revised the tender conditions some weeks previously, putting excessive performance obligations exclusively on the foreign partners in the projects. They were to guarantee not just project deadlines, but revenue yields as well. Also, as Goh Chok Tong told *The Hindu* newspaper later, Champs did not receive in writing the indemnity agreement that Bharti had offered it. Champs' decision, he said, "was to the greatest of disappointment of ourselves, and me in particular".

Even Lee senior weighed in on the dispute with a critical comment against the home side: "I think we should learn to take more risks."

But India served up its share of surprises as well. Perhaps the most embarrassing for Singapore was the blacklisting in 2009 of the defence firm Singapore Technologies Kinetics over unproven suspicions of bribery to win defence orders. (This story is told in Chapter 12.) There had also been the shock of the Mumbai attacks the previous year which caused the death of a young woman lawyer from Singapore, the first time a Singaporean had died in a terrorist attack. (See Chapter 7.) There were questions whether the Indian authorities had done enough to save her life.

While the suspicions were understandable given the circumstances, nothing underscored Singapore's attitude towards India like the interest it took in midwifing the project to revive Nalanda University. Singapore's involvement in Nalanda was triggered when Indian president APJ Abdul Kalam mentioned his interest in seeing the ancient place of learning revived, during a visit to the island in February 2006. The following month Rahul Gandhi, in his debut speech in India's parliament, called for India to be developed as a global hub for education, noting that Nalanda and Vikramshila had been the Harvard and Cambridge of their day.

Yeo, who considers himself a Taoist and is known for the broad sweep of his vision, saw Nalanda as offering an avenue for multiracial, multi-ethnic Asia to ponder its common heritage – "not only a celebration of the past, but also an inspiration for the future of Asia and the world". Unlike the pain and politics associated with the interactions of Islam, Christianity and Judaism, the Buddhist message had been one of compassion and peace, and

Yeo knew that as India and China, the key tectonic plates of Asia, began to rub up against each other it would be useful to have such an enterprise to diffuse tensions.

Yeo also saw early that for the project to succeed, and gain international credibility, it had to be a truly multinational enterprise. Japan, for instance, would probably have been happy to underwrite the entire enterprise but that could have put off China and South Korea, because of their testy ties with pre-World War II Japan. The effort was to enlist the common support of several nations. His global contacts pushed the project along, even as it went through several stumbles thanks to bureaucratic infighting in India, disquiet over the selection of its first vice chancellor and bureaucratic foot-dragging.

Sadly for Nalanda, Yeo stepped down as foreign minister after a shock electoral defeat in 2011, when his team was ousted from its constituency in a voter backlash against the ruling People's Action Party. While he remained an influential voice and stayed on the advisory panel of the university and the governing board led by Nobel laureate Amartya Sen, the project has never been quite the same after his departure from government. A grateful India bestowed him the Padma Bhushan civilian award in the 2012 Republic Day honours, and in 2015, requested Yeo to succeed Sen as head of the Nalanda advisory board when the economist quit, complaining of government interference. Yeo took the job after persuading Sen to remain on the board.

Singapore's widening footprint across the face of India is emblematic of the tiny city-state's ability to punch above its weight and be the benchmark that even the largest nations tick their boxes against. For many Indians, the island state is the destination of choice for their first "foreign trip" and, upon their return, the template by which they judge civic services and administration at home. Indeed you could spot a bit of Singapore in every corner of India. In remote Port Blair, capital of the Indian part of the Andaman & Nicobar islands, I once followed an arrow on the wall of a small store near the main bazaar that pointed to a flight of stairs. Beneath, a legend promised "Singapore-style shopping". Similar boards can be spotted across India, including in the highland town of Thekkady in Kerala and in Bangalore's Majestic Circle area in Karnataka. Developers launching new projects promise "Singapore-style living" with condominiums named after residential estates in Singapore. In Chennai's modest neighbourhood of KK Nagar, named after former chief minister Muthuvel Karunanidhi, a three-storey block on a tiny plot of land, Green Peace Maplewood, is reminiscent of a condominium called Maplewoods along Singapore's Bukit Timah Road.

When new office buildings or factories are built, the model is frequently a Singapore-designed facility. For this, much thanks is owed to the iconic International Tech Park Bangalore built in the mid-1990s. For risk-averse Singapore, starting work on the project in 1993 was a huge leap of faith. Whitefields, the suburb where it is located, was then a leafy edge of the Garden City, as Bangalore used to be called, an area where the rich maintained farmhouses and palm trees were the tallest objects in view. Today, a transformed Whitefields is home to offices of many of the world's biggest multinationals. "Bangalored", the verb increasingly used to describe job losses in the West to outsourcing firms out East, began here.

"Singapore was the first to prove that these things were doable in India and the footprint they have is a lasting one in terms of sound business practices, processes and very strict adherence to quality and design controls," Rajan Viswanath, head of property management for the Embassy Golflinks Software Park, a 4.6 million square foot facility in Bangalore, told me. "They set the passion for large office-recreation-residential facilities and set the benchmark for what was world-class in India."

Ascendas, the company that built the first International Tech Park in Bangalore, went on to build several more business parks in southern India. Today, it is confidently venturing beyond the south of the country, having entered Maharashtra state and Haryana to the north. Other firms from the island have picked up so much work around the country that to plot them on a map would make it look like a red rash has spread over the face of India.

The early Bangalore tech park initiative has led to massive spinoffs elsewhere. Every day, thousands of India's air travellers look down at their food trays and spot the Singapore Airlines golden bird logo, thanks to a food catering joint venture between Singapore's SATS and the Tata Group. When India freed up rail container movement to private players, Singapore-owned Gateway Distriparks, chaired by Gopinath Pillai, was the first company awarded a licence. And, as India allows its citizens to keep more of their money overseas, Singapore has emerged as the private banking centre of choice.

Today, Indians are among the most visible expatriate groups on the island, particularly in the banking industry. At DBS Group, Southeast Asia's top lender, the St Stephen's College-educated Piyush Gupta presides, having powered it to record profits. Gunit Chadha heads Deutsche Bank in the region. ANZ Bank's head of retail for the region, Sanjoy Sen, is headquartered on the island and the bank's Singapore head, Vishnu Shahaney, is of Indian origin. At Royal Bank of Scotland, Rohit Sawhney heads global transaction services for the Asia Pacific from Singapore. The list is long.

Tata and Singapore Airlines finally managed to get a joint venture airline up and running when Vistara began flight operations in January 2015, some 17 years after the first plans were laid. Connectivity between the two countries has leapfrogged. Today, 440 flights a week link Singapore and Indian cities, and every few months a new Indian airport comes on the air map. Meanwhile, defence ties, which began with Anti Submarine Warfare exercises in 1994, have flowered. Singapore is the only foreign nation allowed to conduct air, artillery and infantry training exercises on Indian soil. In late 2015, the two upgraded ties to the level of a full strategic partnership, with much emphasis on defence, including the joint development of weapons.

The scaffolding for all this is, no doubt, hardworking diplomacy sustained by close contacts across the Indian political and economic spectrum. I got a sense of the deep inroads Singapore had made into the political establishment when I visited Chandrababu Naidu, now chief minister of Andhra Pradesh, at his Jubilee Hills home in Hyderabad, the state capital. Naidu had lost power in 2004 and was sitting on the Opposition benches then. Dr K Anji Reddy, the pharmaceuticals tycoon and a close friend, had fixed up the meeting and we drove there in his car.

Naidu smiled when I expressed surprise at spotting a book on Changi Airport among the pile on his table. Although he was no longer in charge of the state, he was keeping a close watch on the modern airport being built for Hyderabad and was clearly comparing it with Singapore. In a nation notorious for project delays, the Hyderabad airport project was on time. A Singapore company was in charge of landscaping the facility.

"After I was voted out of office, Singapore invited me over as a Lee Kuan Yew Fellow," he told me. "Your PM and senior minister told me it doesn't matter whether you are in power or out of it. We see you as a lifelong friend. How can I forget that?" In 2014 Naidu was voted back to power in Andhra Pradesh, now a rump state which stands poised to lose Hyderabad to the newly formed Telangana state. Sure enough, he turned to Singapore to do the central planning for the city.

Likewise, Narendra Modi's special fondness for Singapore stems in part from the fact that the island did not treat him as a pariah when he was in the international doghouse after the 2002 communal riots in Gujarat, where he was a newly installed chief minister at the time. Even before Modi was cleared of wrongdoing by multiple investigations, Singapore leaders, recognising the potential in this development-minded leader, had built bridges with him. In January 2006, less than four years after the communal violence, I accompanied senior minister Goh Chok Tong to Ahmedabad. Goh sat through a Gujarat government presentation on plans to redevelop the Sabarmati riverfront into a strip of condominium projects, recreation areas and housing for the poor. When the Gujarat officials had finished, he looked them in the eye.

"Politicians like to always talk of the poor," he said. "The fact is, you are probably better off preserving the real estate value here and using some of the money to build better housing for the poor elsewhere." The officials took careful note.

A few days later, in Kolkata, Goh addressed the annual Partnership Summit of the CII. There, he spoke of how glad he was at having read the

India story early. His early interest in India, he said, had been kindled by the large gap he spotted between the country's potential and output. This had led him to the firm conclusion that the country was underperforming. That perception had been bolstered watching the Indian talent among Singapore's ministers, doctors, lawyers and economists. "I formed my faith in India on the basis that it has talent that has not been maximised."

He also said he had drawn a great deal of satisfaction from having persuaded Lee Kuan Yew to believe in the India story. When Goh started taking interest in India, Lee laughed but did not discourage him, saying it boded well for Singapore's ties with India. "To be able to convert him to believe in India gives me tremendous personal satisfaction that my faith in India has been justified." The CII crowd, mostly industrialists, clapped rapturously.

Lee Kuan Yew, who moved from enthusiasm to disappointment to a renewed faith in India, died in March 2015. Not one given to display emotion publicly, he would have been surprised at the reaction in India to his passing. The Indian tricolour was lowered to half-mast in his honour, and a day of mourning was declared. In Tamil Nadu, the principal source of Indian immigrants to Singapore, parts of the state saw street processions taken out in his memory. Modi, now prime minister, flew to Singapore for the state funeral service.

Goh Chok Tong and George Yeo continue to enjoy remarkable goodwill in India. Indeed, Goh feels vastly comfortable with the cold-eyed Modi, who regards the lanky Singaporean as something of a mentor. When he met Modi in New Delhi just after the 2014 elections that had projected him to national power, Goh caused the usually stern Indian leader to break out into a guffaw.

"You are moving so fast I can feel the earth shake," he told the Indian leader.

5
The US and India: The Eagle Has Landed

> "How can we not afford to join each other, on a global scale, to support opportunity and prosperity and justice and dignity and freedom and democracy?"
>
> — US Secretary of State Condoleezza Rice in New Delhi, June 2007

NEW DELHI, MARCH 2006. The blue and white Boeing 747 of the American president, shaped like a dolphin, landed smoothly in the late evening light and turned towards the technical area of New Delhi's Indira Gandhi International Airport, rolling to a stop with its portside front door almost perfectly aligned with the lush red carpet unfurled on the tarmac. There was the usual flurry of activity before George W Bush and his wife, Laura, emerged from Air Force One. Surprised to see Manmohan Singh breaking protocol to personally receive him at the airport, Bush began happily waving from the top of the ramp. As he was introduced to the officials on the ground, Stephen Hadley, his national security adviser (NSA), touched his arm and pointed to the trim figure of his Indian counterpart, MK Narayanan, standing just behind secretary of state Condoleezza Rice.

Bush reached around to Narayanan and whispered, loud enough for the people around to hear: "I want that deal."

That deal was the US-India civil nuclear agreement of 2006. Inked during the visit, it marked the coming of age of ties between the world's biggest democracies. With a flourish of their pens, Bush and Manmohan agreed in effect to end what the Indians complained was the "nuclear apartheid" practised against their nation. The joint statement effectively recognised India, which had signed neither the Nuclear Non-Proliferation Treaty nor the Comprehensive Test Ban Treaty, as a nuclear weapons state worthy of getting "the same benefits and advantages as other such states". America would help develop the Indian civilian nuclear industry and work to pass legislation that would allow its companies to export nuclear fuel and technology to India, including in the critical area of the disposal of nuclear waste and the reprocessing of spent fuel. And it would use its leverage with the Nuclear Suppliers Group to lean on other countries to help India get access to uranium. This would cut the cost of procuring uranium by a third.

In turn, India would split its integrated nuclear programme by separating the energy programme from weapons production. The civil facilities would be put under the safeguards imposed by the International Atomic Energy Agency (IAEA). On the strategic facilities required for its weapons programme, there would, effectively, be no questions asked although no uranium sold for the civil facilities could be diverted for military use. The US had not wished to allow more than four of India's 22 nuclear power reactors for strategic uses. India managed to keep eight away from inspection, including two fast breeder research reactors in southern India.

India would also agree to not conduct nuclear testing and to not proliferate enrichment and reprocessing technologies. But it did not do this anyway, and Manmohan's predecessor government had forsworn the tests unilaterally, so this was no concession. After a so-called 123 Agreement was signed by the Indians, the US would also strive to get its Congress to approve the sale to India of high-level technologies as well as civilian technology that had military implications.

On the long flight down to New Delhi, Hadley had conducted an extended phone conversation with Narayanan. While Shyam Saran, the former Indian foreign secretary, was the key negotiator of the accord on behalf of the Ministry of External Affairs, Narayanan was critical in the negotiations because he spoke for the Department of Atomic Energy (DAE). The DAE was filled with US sceptics, including its chief at the time, Anil Kakodkar. They had good reason to mistrust the Americans, who decades earlier reneged on a contract to continuously supply fuel to the Tarapur Atomic Power Station in Mumbai and imposed further sanctions after India conducted multiple nuclear tests in 1998.

Faced with obstacles to access all levels of nuclear high technology, the dedicated DAE scientists had built up the Indian programme almost on their own while their counterparts at the Indian Space Research Organisation and the Defence Research & Development Organisation worked on delivery systems. The DAE folk were particularly proud of the fast breeder technology they had developed, essential to tapping the vast thorium reserves of the nation for the nuclear fuel cycle. India has a quarter of the known reserves of thorium while its indigenous sources of uranium are critically poor. Now, they feared the Americans would attempt to stifle the fast breeder programme.

Narayanan, initially sceptical of the deal and defensive in outlook after long years of intelligence work, had become an enthusiastic convert for the nuclear accord. Hadley and he had become good friends over the past year and Narayanan was grateful to the American official for his help in negotiating the various interest groups in Washington, including at the State Department, that were hostile to the accord. Unknown to the world, Hadley had also arranged for his counterparts from Britain and France to guide the former Indian spy chief through the intricacies of the nuclear game. They were only too ready and willing, particularly the French. As they tutored Narayanan on the best way to stop India's military interests from being compromised by the concessions that diplomacy may seek to extract, some of the meetings were held in secret in Munich, Germany. Narayanan would often disappear for days. Except for prime minister Manmohan and his principal secretary TKA Nair, others in the PMO would not know where Narayanan was. It was clear that the Western alliance, fearful of China's rise, had picked India as one of their own for the future and was midwifing a deal that would be in India's best strategic interests, even if that could not be told to the broader world. Instead, the Bush administration projected the deal as a key part of its non-proliferation agenda.

Two days before Bush arrived in New Delhi, Manmohan, timing his words so the US president would have enough time to mull over his response, had told India's parliament that India would not put the key breeder reactor programme on the list of civil facilities, subject to international inspections. "Our strategic nuclear programme will not be compromised in any way," he said. "In deciding the contours of our separation plan, we have taken into account our current and future strategic needs consistent with our nuclear doctrine."

The agreement was signed in the evening of March 2. The moment it was done, one of India's biggest backstage supporters, Mohamed ElBaradei, head of the IAEA, released a statement he had clearly been itching to put out. He called the agreement a "milestone, timely for ongoing efforts to consolidate the non-proliferation regime". Equally critically, Japan, the only nation in the world to suffer nuclear attack, also came out in support. Shinzo Abe, Japan's government spokesman at the time and now its prime minister, could hardly hide his excitement.

"It is wrong to discuss the Indian nuclear issue and that of North Korea on the same level," he said, countering those who argued that the deal would set a poor example for other states that had not signed the Nuclear Non-Proliferation Treaty and the Comprehensive Test Ban Treaty. "India is a country that shares the values of freedom, democracy, basic human rights and the rule of law with the United States and Japan." Abe, planning his ascent to prime minister, could already see the pieces falling into place in the years to come.

Even so, the follow-up negotiations would prove tough. A particular sticking point was the indigenously developed fast breeder reactor (FBR), which India considered a civilian programme, yet wanted it kept off IAEA safeguards. FBRs reprocess spent fuel, ultimately leading to more fuel. The US understandably insisted that if FBRs were part of the civil programme, they should come under safeguards. But Saran insisted there could be no scrutiny, because of the proprietary nature of the technology. Finally, they struck a compromise: FBRs could remain outside safeguards as long as they did not use imported fuel.

Another issue cropped up when it came to personnel. Under the separation plan, nuclear facilities and material meant for strategic purposes could be kept away from the civil programme. But what of the scientists involved? Washington was insisting on a division of personnel as well, warning that Indian reluctance on the matter could prove a deal breaker. At one point, Saran exploded: "This is not possible. In any case, how do you intend to enforce it? Are you going to ask us to put electronic tags on our people?" The US quietly took the issue off the table.

The deal with the Republican president was all the more remarkable because Indians have traditionally favoured Democratic presidents in the White House, partly because they tended to be more generous with aid and grants. But times had changed and they had prayed for a George W Bush victory in the 2001 American polls. There were many reasons for this. Indian-Americans, perhaps the most affluent immigrant community in the US, were increasingly shifting support to the Republican Party. As they formed an important vote bank and source of political funding, their influcncc had begun to tell on bilateral ties.

The move to win over America had begun with Indira Gandhi. After getting on the wrong side of Richard Nixon, she had sufficiently charmed Ronald Reagan at a meeting in Mexico in 1981 to set up a summit with him in 1982 that produced a Science and Technology Initiative, the first breakthrough with a Republican administration. Reagan kept up his interest in India, even sending his vice president, George Bush Sr, to Houston to accompany Rajiv Gandhi, Indira's son and successor, when the young Indian leader toured the Johnson Space Centre in 1985.

When Vishwanath Pratap Singh, after ousting Rajiv, led India between 1989 and 1990, he accepted an American proposal to set up a steering committee on defence. Chandra Shekhar, who briefly succeeded him with

Congress party backing, allowed US warplanes overflight and refuelling facilities during the first Gulf War. Then Israel, a key US ally, was allowed to open an embassy in New Delhi. Tel Aviv and New Delhi have kept much of their relationship under wraps, and still do, but in Washington, the Indian and Israeli lobbies had begun to work very closely.

All this played into the India-US relationship. With the Soviet Union's collapse, New Delhi had done some nifty about-turns in foreign policy. Conservative US interests were warmed by India's move to mute its traditional support for the Palestinian cause. Only strong domestic pressure had kept India from sending its troops to join the US and British forces in Iraq, where the coalition toppled India's old ally, Saddam Hussein.

Besides, New Delhi saw the Republicans as more willing to stand up to China. This fitted better with New Delhi's insecurities about its northern neighbour, compared to the more nuanced approach of Bill Clinton and his first secretary of state, Madeleine Albright. At the MEA, officials were often contemptuous of Albright and frequently referred to her as "half-bright", especially after she declined to make a formal declaration that China had transferred nuclear weapons technology to Pakistan. But Clinton would turn into an enthusiastic India-backer in his second term, and when his wife, Hillary, entered politics through the US Senate, critics often derided her as the "Senator from Punjab".

When George W Bush prepared his run for the presidency, India was already primed for him. Indian ambassador Naresh Chandra twice visited Bush at his Crawford, Texas ranch. Behind the scenes, Henry Kissinger, Nixon's secretary of state who had initiated the famous US opening to China in 1972, had begun advising New Delhi, and it was he who told India to build bridges with Condi Rice, at the time a Stanford University professor. The early gambit proved mighty useful when Bush hired Rice as NSA and later, kept her on as secretary of state. With Nicholas Burns by her side as under secretary of state during the crucial 2005 to 2008 years, Rice proved to be very positive for India. In January 2000, a year before she was appointed to government, Rice authored an important essay in *Foreign Affairs* magazine urging that the US should pay "closer attention to India's role in the regional balance in Asia" and that Washington should assist in the effort. For this, India would need high technology and easy access to nuclear fuel. With that in mind, the Bush administration initiated the "Next Steps in Strategic Partnership" with the Vajpayee government in New Delhi.

Meanwhile, the conventional militaries were also pressing for a closer relationship. India, which depended on Russia for two-thirds of its defence supplies, was desperately looking to diversify its weapons purchases. After the Soviet collapse, the Russians, going through deep internal turmoil, were not the most reliable of suppliers. Delays and cost escalations were endemic and particularly told on the Indian Air Force, where too many planes were going down in peacetime because of faulty spares. The US, looking to build influence as well as tap into India's growing appetite for military equipment, was a willing partner.

And in the background lurked the China factor.

When Indian military delegations went over to the US, they found themselves getting fabulous welcomes. The Indians would be shown around bases, the latest gadgetry on offer, and dined ceremonially. They were told the short cuts to the US establishment's procedures that would help Washington put arms supplies to India on a fast track. Then the strategic briefings would start. At the outset would be expressions of regret that three decades of US sanctions had kept General Dynamics, Lockheed and others out of the world's most lucrative arms market. Within minutes, though, whether at the US State Department or the Pentagon, the subject would turn to Beijing.

"What do you guys plan to do about China?"

A ranking officer told me after one such visit that the Indians were constantly taken aback at the wariness about China that resided in the sole superpower. "Perhaps fear is a better word," he told me. "The US trepidation about China, I would say, seems to surpass our own."

It was clear that containing China, or at least curbing its excessive ambitions, was seen as a job not to be accomplished alone. To corral the dragon would take the sinews of large Asian nations in its periphery and there was none with more potential than India, even if it was the weaker of the two for the moment. Nuclear energy was essential both for India's power-short economy as well as to help it build a credible deterrent that could simultaneously take on both China and its ally, Pakistan.

Thus, when Indian and US negotiators sat down in early 2006 to discuss the agenda for George W Bush's trip to New Delhi, the centrepiece of the summit was the agreement on civilian nuclear cooperation.

Yet, there were many within India – even recognised China sceptics – who looked upon the negotiations with a great deal of suspicion. Among those was my classmate, Brahma Chellaney, a respected analyst and China baiter, who was a strident critic of the separation plan and worried that the deal was designed to ensure that India stayed close to America indefinitely. Within the MEA, just as in the US Department of State, there were wells of deep suspicion. Indeed, as the negotiations progressed, some senior officials in India were deliberately kept out of the loop as the key desk officer for America, joint secretary S Jaishankar – later India's envoy to Singapore, China, Washington and now foreign secretary – worked with Shyam Saran and Narayanan to move the deal forward. Besides, DAE disdain for the US ran deep. Thus, in February 2006, when France and India agreed to work towards nuclear cooperation, New Delhi, seeking to make a point that India would never compromise on its military nuclear programme, pointedly got DAE chief Kakodkar, its top atomic energy scientist, to ink the agreement with the French foreign minister.

But if many in government were sceptical, wider India was enthralled by the US embrace. From outside the establishment, K Subrahmanyam, the doyen of Indian strategic analysts, added his firm support for the deal. As he told me once, there was no reason to pooh-pooh American intentions. The US wanted a balance of power in Asia as China grows rapidly. "What is happening," said Subrahmanyam, who died in 2011, "parallels the Nixon initiative to China in 1972."

Subrahmanyam's firm backing for the deal helped ease Narayanan's concerns. The two, recognised for their brilliance from the start, had advanced in government together and been friends for five decades. When Jaishankar, Subrahmanyam's middle son, was choosing between an academic career and one in the civil service, it was to Narayanan that his father had sent him for counsel. The old bonds helped; Narayanan would often brush aside those who sought to whisper in his ear that Jaishankar, in putting the deal together, was acting too much in favour of the Americans.

Manmohan, meanwhile, was taking his own big gamble at home. Unflinching Left opposition to the developing strategic relationship, exemplified by the civil nuclear accord, had left the coalition floundering. Many senior Congress figures were also sceptical and worried that the Left might pull the plug on a government that had barely crossed the two-year mark. Left backing could not be ignored; with 59 seats in parliament, they lent critical support. Without their backing, the government would be 20 short of a majority in the powerful Lok Sabha, the lower house of parliament, which at the time had 541 MPs. The Marxists, led by the rigid Prakash Karat, had ordered the government to not negotiate special safeguards with the IAEA to bring the nuclear deal to fruition. The government said it would not renegotiate the deal even as it sought to buy time with an offer to set up a special committee to examine the implications of the US Hyde Act, which gave India, a non-signatory to the Nuclear Non-Proliferation Treaty, special access to the global nuclear trade. The committee was also to look at the bilateral 123 Agreement between Washington and New Delhi, which would help implement the Hyde Act.

It was an unenviable position for Manmohan to be in. When he went before his Congress party's working committee to explain the agreement, he was asked what would happen if the deal did not go through. "The prime minister will have to resign, I suppose," he said.

He was taking a calculated gamble. Earlier, he had needled the Left in a newspaper interview, daring them to withdraw parliamentary support. "I told them to do whatever they want to do. If they want to withdraw support, so be it," he told the Kolkata daily, *The Telegraph*, choosing to place his remarks where the powerful West Bengal wing of the CPM, which had testy ties with CPM boss Karat, would gain most resonance. For all that bluster, the Left knew they too were taking a risk. In the Left bastions of West Bengal and Kerala, public opinion was largely for the deal. Indeed, the severe miscalculation into which Karat drove the Left would make it pay a heavy price in both states in the state and national elections to come.

By the summer of 2008, things had got to a head in New Delhi. The Left was sticking to its position that it would withdraw parliamentary support if the government moved further on the agreement. A joint panel of the ruling coalition and Left allies came up with no solutions. News leaks from the PMO were indicating that Manmohan had told the Congress party boss that should the deal be further stymied for fear of the Left, the damage to his credibility would be intolerably severe. That would make it impossible for him to attend the Group of Eight summit the following month, or even continue as premier. The latter was probably a ruse. Those who worked closely with Manmohan say he had no intention to quit office over the deal but it helped to put out word that he was prepared for that sacrifice. With Bush to leave the White House in a few months, and his successor's support for the deal not to be taken for granted, New Delhi did not have much time to lose. Ultimately, Sonia relented, and gave Manmohan the go-ahead. UPA, led by Congress, was ready to take on the Left, never mind the critical support it got in parliament from Left MPs. Several Left MPs, including some from the CPM itself, were wavering. But Karat, who has never fought a regular election in his life, was unrelenting.

With Left support gone, Manmohan and Sonia reached out to the Samajwadi, or Socialist, Party of Uttar Pradesh, led by the backward caste strongman Mulayam Singh Yadav. Narayanan, the NSA, was sent to negotiate – ostensibly to clear "doubts" about the nuclear deal. As a former intelligence chief, Narayanan probably also had plenty of levers to pull. Indian politicians are notorious for their indiscretions. With 39 Samajwadi Party MPs now voting for UPA, the rest was easy. Manmohan was home and dry. A confidence vote on his government was carried 275 to 256.

Karat and his party would pay heavily for their actions. The CPM came across as churlish, even anti-national. It fast began losing support. Today, the CPM is a mess in Kerala and has lost control of populous West Bengal, a state it dominated for three decades. Subsequent by-elections showed the CPM was third in the vote count in Bengal, behind the regional All India Trinamool Congress, which ousted the Marxists, and surprisingly, the BJP. The Red revolution in India started with the election of the world's first democratically elected communist government in Kerala in 1957. Now, with the fruits of economic reforms trickling down to the middle and lower classes, the concept of class struggles and aggressive union actions, strikes and shutdowns no longer resonated with India's youth. The way events have played out, Karat may well have the dubious honour of denting the Red influence in India. That would be a sad thing; given India's massive inequalities, the nation needs strong voices to speak up for the marginalised.

But then, Indian communists have always been on the wrong side of history. In 1942, the communists, then undivided, opposed the Congress party's Quit India Resolution against British Rule. When Independence came five years later, they called it a false dawn. By proclaiming US imperialism a bigger danger than the BJP's communalism, Karat further damaged the CPM by aligning himself with the BJP to oppose the nuclear deal, thus fatally eroding the CPM's credibility.

If there is growing consensus on the widening ties with the US in India, there is also bipartisan backing for the India account in Washington. Bush would be succeeded in the White House by Barack Obama, the first African-American president of the US. Like Clinton before him, Obama's initial priorities would be settling the relationship with China.

Obama, coming immediately after the super-enthusiastic George W Bush, was initially looked at with unease. New Delhi remembered then-Senator Obama's attempts to dilute Bush's nuclear accord by introducing language unfavourable to India. As president, Obama made a landmark Asia speech in Tokyo that did not include a single reference to India. In Beijing, he spoke about the US and China working together "to promote peace and stability in South Asia", India's backyard. India affected disdain to hide worries about the direction of this president who was also a gifted orator. Just as in the 1950s when John Foster Dulles was called "Dull, duller, Dulles" and Madeleine Albright had been dismissed as "Half-bright" in the Indian national capital in the 1990s, Obama began to be referred to as Oblahblah.

India did not figure greatly in Obama's early calculations because there was enough going on at home to keep the American president preoccupied. With the big chill of the global economic crisis, the US was suffering its worst economic crisis in living memory. As ambassador Robert Blackwill, who had moved to RAND Corporation, put it: "It is not clear the Obama administration has the same preoccupation with the rise of China's power and India's role in containing it. Rather, the administration is focused on US-China economic relations, or the G-2 as some call it."

Hillary Clinton, the new secretary of state, had travelled to Beijing just weeks after taking charge at Foggy Bottom, Washington DC. To quell some of those misgivings, Clinton flew down to New Delhi shortly after the Indian election in 2009 that retained Manmohan in office. She went back promising to "broaden and deepen the relationship".

Over the next five years, the US would be good on its word. In 2009, Manmohan and his wife, Gursharan Kaur, were hosted at the White House as Obama's first state visitors. The US president himself visited India in November 2010, starting in Mumbai, scene of the 2008 terror outrage, and staying in the historic Taj Mahal Palace & Tower hotel, which was nearly destroyed in the attack.

In early 2014, as it became clear that Narendra Modi had the best chance of emerging as prime minister, the US, which had barred him from entering the country in the wake of the 2002 Gujarat communal riots, mended fences with him. It lifted the nine-year-old visa ban and Modi received US ambassador Nancy Powell at his residence, the meeting lasting 75 minutes. Modi, who has been cleared of wrongdoing by every investigation that followed the riots, has shown no trace of animosity towards the US. In fact, he has gone out of his way to befriend Obama. Modi's attitude charged up the relationship, which had taken a dive after the US, in December 2013, arrested India's deputy consul general in New York on charges that she had lied on her housekeeper's visa application, and strip-searched her as if she were a common criminal. The Indian government reduced security outside the US embassy in New Delhi in retaliation.

With Modi installed in New Delhi, Obama made a rare repeat visit to India as president, this time as chief guest at the 2015 Republic Day parade, the same honour given to Singapore's Goh Chok Tong in 1994 as India and Singapore ties warmed. And just as the Comprehensive Economic Cooperation Agreement had transformed India-Singapore ties, so too would the civil nuclear agreement improve relations with America. The announcement of the US-India Joint Strategic Vision for the Asia-Pacific and Indian Ocean Region during the visit spoke of building on their partnership "from Africa to East Asia". In a clear signal to East Asia, where China has claimed almost all of the South China Sea, it spoke of the "importance of safeguarding maritime security and ensuring freedom of navigation and overflight throughout the region, *especially* [emphasis added] in the South China Sea".

There was no longer any ambiguity about which way India, a founding member and pillar of the Non-Aligned Movement, was heading. The American eagle had landed in India.

There is little question that the definitive move on India had come from George W Bush. More than any president before him, he had spotted India's potential, admiring its democratic instincts, tolerant society and entrepreneurial energy. As he told his wife Laura: "Do you know? Millions and millions of Muslims, and yet not a single Al-Qaeda!" It was his firm conviction and a desire to help Manmohan that had contributed most to the blossoming relationship.

History will probably record that Bush arrived in India at a time when his popularity at home was at its lowest. In India, though, approval for the US and its leader had never been higher. The 2005 Pew Global

Attitudes survey found 71% of Indians had a favourable view of the US and 54% admired Bush's handling of world affairs. Thanks to Bush, India and Pakistan would never again be bracketed together. The new clubbing would be China and India, a linkage that New Delhi preferred and that fitted better with its ambitions. Incredibly, these were nations that, for decades, had been perceived as being on opposite sides of the Cold War.

It takes a unique kind of individual to push through a deal simply because he thought it should be done. Bush accomplished that, and by doing so, he set the contours of a relationship between the US and India that will define global politics in the first half of the 21st century. Equally, Manmohan showed great courage to stand his ground with the doubting Thomases of his government and party to push the accord through. It stands to his credit that he was even prepared to give up his post to push the deal through. It is India's tragedy that he seemed to lose that tough, idealistic edge as the years wore on. The nuclear deal was never fully operationalised because India passed legislation that put intolerable and excessive liabilities on suppliers in the event of a nuclear accident. Although Modi has sought to change the laws to make them more investment-friendly, it is still a work in progress. But that has not overly affected the strengthening relationship.

Today, US missions in India process more H-1B (for persons in special occupations) and L visas (for intracompany transferees) than missions in any other country, with Indians receiving 69% of all H visas and 30% of L visas. More than 130,000 Indian students were enrolled in US universities in the 2014–15 academic year, a 29% increase from the previous 12 months. The US conducts more military exercises with India than any other power. Trade, once memorably described by US envoy Blackwill as "flat as a *chapati*", is growing steadily. The partnership is moving to third countries; the two are drawing several African states into their joint training programmes. As Shivshankar Menon, who succeeded Narayanan as NSA, once put it, India and the US used to look at each other across the European landmass. But now, they look at each other across the Pacific and a different perspective of emerging transnational and global threats draws the two together.

Bush once said "the partnership between the US and India has the power to transform the world". It is too soon to say whether his words will come true in a global context. India is capable of exciting and disappointing its backers in equal measure. But certainly, in Asia, the relationship is proving transformational and impacting every nation in the region.

6
Style and Scandal: Diplomatic Blunder Tharoor

"I am not sure we want a strong secretary general."

— John Bolton, former US ambassador to the UN, writing in his memoirs about why Condoleezza Rice advised him to quash Shashi Tharoor's nomination for UN secretary-general

AMID THE DIPLOMATIC successes of Manmohan Singh in his first term, there was at least one instance where he stumbled significantly. India lost much diplomatic traction, and focus on its bid for a UN Security Council seat, with his ill-considered backing of Shashi Tharoor, a UN under-secretary-general who was close to UN boss Kofi Annan, and sought to be his successor, apparently with his blessings.

Tharoor, a brilliant student who got his PhD degree from Tuft University's Fletcher School of Diplomacy at age 22, had been a charismatic figure at University of Delhi's St Stephen's College in the 1970s, where he had a rock star following for his looks, brilliant academic performance and renown as a champion debater. Throughout his student life he had one ambition – to be secretary-general of the world body. This dream he chased by joining the UN after university. Early on in his career he was posted to head the UN Refugee office in Singapore, during the Vietnamese boat people crisis. His twin sons were born on the island and Singapore, always respectful of intelligent minds, took to the bright and handsome Indian with a flair for literature and oratory. His first wife, Tilottama Mukherji, known to friends as Minu, contributed frequently to *The Straits Times*, then and now Southeast Asia's leading newspaper.

Tharoor's ambitions could have been realised if merit alone was the criterion for the top UN job. It isn't. What is more, the post has always gone to figures from smaller nations, starting with Trygve Lie of Norway, the first UN secretary-general. It also rotates between the continents. Now, as Tharoor's career peaked, it coincided with Asia's opportunity to have a UN chief to replace Annan, who was from Ghana, Africa. Armed with his vast credentials of being a UN insider and the highly sympathetic biography of Jawaharlal Nehru that he had authored, Tharoor, in April 2006, sought an appointment with Manmohan to press for New Delhi's backing of his candidacy. Well into his 70s then, Manmohan, whose three children are all girls, took to the well-spoken Tharoor, probably seeing in the urbane, intellectual and well-mannered Tharoor the son he may have wished for.

Manmohan was charmed, but also careful. Something like this, he told Tharoor, would need Sonia Gandhi's blessing. Secondly, he was wary of Beijing. What was the guarantee that China would back him?

Tharoor said he would suss out Chinese thinking on the subject. He then flew to Beijing where he called on foreign minister Li Zhaoxing and revealed his interest. Inscrutable though he was, the Chinese leader seemed positive to Tharoor's eager ears, even as he promised nothing concrete. "We've said that we are for an Asian to head the UN," Li responded, picking his words carefully. "China itself has no candidate for the job."

Tharoor took that as endorsement enough and reported back to Manmohan, who checked with his top aides. There seemed to be few objections; principal secretary TKA Nair and national security adviser MK Narayanan, neither schooled in the higher intricacies of global diplomacy – Mani Dixit would never have allowed it – seemed to like the idea. It helped that, like Tharoor himself, they were from the state of Kerala. A meeting with Sonia Gandhi was arranged and Tharoor duly showed up at her door, carrying a copy of his elegantly written biography of Nehru. Not fully aware of the wider consequences of what India was about to do, Sonia went along as well. Tharoor now had India's backing.

Within the Indian foreign office, however, this was all received with plain fury. Foreign secretary Shyam Saran and his seasoned diplomats knew the bid simply would not fly. UN secretaries-general have all come from small states. What is more, the country would have to expend valuable goodwill and effort in what they knew was a futile endeavour at a time when it was making desperate attempts to get accepted as a UN Security Council member.

At Manmohan's instructions, the Ministry of External Affairs had tapped the US, Britain and France, and all three had advised India to not put up its hand. The US had made known its preference for a South Korean and its dislike of Annan was well-known, a sentiment that would rub off on anyone seen to be too close to him, as Tharoor indisputably had been. In fact, John Bolton, the US ambassador to the UN, firmly declined to get Tharoor an appointment to see secretary of state Condi Rice. Uncomfortably for New Delhi, Ban Ki-moon, the South Korean diplomat who had Washington's backing, was an old friend of India's. He had passed over an opportunity to serve in the US and had chosen the Indian capital as his first career posting, back in 1972, and later served as the desk officer for South Asia in Seoul. Ban's daughter was married to an Indian. Meanwhile, the Association of Southeast Asian Nations, or Asean, had its own candidate and Sri Lanka offered Jayantha Dhanapala, a seasoned diplomat noted for his handling of the arms control talks.

But Tharoor was adamant he would stand as an independent if India did not back him. What is more, the PMO knew that the next shot for an Asian would come round only after 40 years since the job moves from continent to continent and an incumbent usually holds office for a decade.

While I had been aware of Tharoor's plans for several months, I had no idea that New Delhi had moved so far along to push its own candidate until a Sri Lankan delegation arrived in New Delhi to seek backing for Dhanapala. Certain of India's support – New Delhi and Colombo were enjoying a honeymoon period, thanks to India's firm support for Colombo's war on the Tamil Tigers – the visitors were taken aback to find a prime minister who cleared his throat and looked the other way when they presented their case.

Puzzled, they pushed one more time.

"I am afraid we may have our own person," came the response finally, as the visitors sat back stunned, not sure they were hearing right.

To the credit of the Indian Foreign Service, once Tharoor was announced as India's candidate, its officers went full tilt to rustle up support for him. In conversation with me a few months later, a Bangladeshi diplomat posted to the UN headquarters marvelled at the way Nirupam Sen, the permanent representative of India to the UN, had performed.

"Everyone knew Nirupam was angered by this stupid move by New Delhi and the waste of diplomatic time it involved," he told me. "But you could not see it in the way he went about his job. Once a decision was taken, Indian diplomats went all out to lobby for their man."

I later learnt that Manmohan, afraid of angering his foreign secretary, had not even kept the MEA informed of his decision to back Tharoor. Instead, instructions had been issued to the permanent representative of India to the UN in New York directly, bypassing his civil service boss. Manmohan, early in his tenure, was still calling the shots, a quality that would desert him so mysteriously in his second term in office.

In the event, Tharoor lost the race in a series of straw polls meant to find a candidate by consensus. After the first straw poll went against him, he called Nicholas Burns, then at the US State Department, to suggest that the US would jeopardise its budding strategic relationship with India if it stopped his bid. An irritated Burns telephoned his Indian counterpart, Saran, to stress that US unwillingness to back Tharoor had nothing to do with bilateral ties. Saran said little but his response confirmed to Burns that New Delhi had no such apprehension. The State Department then called in Indian journalists based in Washington DC and repeated the message in a private briefing.

An indication of China's attitude to Tharoor, if any was needed, was the fact that it was usually the Chinese envoy who briefed the media after every round that went against Tharoor.

Surely, Tharoor, so familiar with the UN's workings, knew from the start that his chances were dim. Even in the days immediately following New Delhi's announcement, I sensed that he was working on Plan B. After a meeting with him in his government-paid suite at the Hotel Imperial, we left together in his state-provided limousine as he headed out to call on rail minister Lalu Prasad Yadav, followed by a meeting with BJP's Arun Jaitley, now Modi's finance minister. When I put the question to him, Tharoor reacted angrily, insisting that he was fully committed to the UN race and denying any other motive.

Some weeks later, as part of his global tour to drum up support for his candidacy, he showed up in Singapore, spending several days on the island where he addressed gatherings, gave interviews and got photographed in the local press playing cricket. At one public lecture, K Kesavapany, a veteran Singapore diplomat now retired, rose to remind him that Singapore's support was committed to the Asean candidate, Surakiart Sathirathai. Indeed, Vanu Gopala Menon, permanent representative of Singapore to the UN, had privately advised Tharoor that he was wasting his time. Still, Singapore saw nothing wrong in allowing Tharoor to present his case at the Forum of Small States (FOSS), a body that it had helped midwife in 1992 and now grown to more than 110 nations. But Menon, chair of FOSS at the time, was careful to extend the same privilege to South Korea's Ban and Sri Lanka's Dhanapala.

Poor Tharoor. Having taken on Ban Ki-moon, even suggesting to the media that the Koreans were spending too freely to ensure Ban's success, he had a hard time reconciling to the idea that his UN career, to which he was devoted from his early days, was coming to an end. He went to see the man who had bested him and made his request.

"I am surprised you want to stay on, Shashi," came Ban's diplomatic response.

Tharoor hung around in his own office for a few days, then sought out Vijay Nambiar, the experienced and well-liked Indian diplomat who had been picked by Ban's predecessor, Kofi Annan, to be the UN chief's chef de cabinet.

"I think you should realise that Ban doesn't want you here, Shashi," the able Nambiar told him gently, yet not mincing words.

At that point, Tharoor announced to the media that he had resigned from the UN. The Wikipedia entry on Tharoor is more sympathetic to the man, saying that he "withdrew his candidacy and declined Ban's invitation to remain in service beyond the expiry of his term as secretary-general".

Sure enough, Plan B went into operation. Tharoor set up domicile in the Gulf emirate of Dubai, as the head of Afras Ventures, a company set up with the avowed purpose of channelling foreign investments into India. Used to a tax-free existence as a UN employee, the emirate's friendlier tax regime may have been a factor in his thinking. The Gulf states also teem with Keralans – or Malayalees, as the people of the southwestern Indian province are called. Famous migrants for a century, the Keralans, or Malayalees, are also immensely attached to their home. Dubai would hence also link Tharoor directly to Kerala, his home state in India.

In 2009, against stiff resistance from the Kerala state unit of the Congress party, Tharoor secured a party ticket to stand for parliament from Thiruvananthapuram, the state capital of Kerala. The constituency was carefully chosen. Tharoor's home district, Palakkad, is way to the north of Kerala, but the Marxists were entrenched in Palakkad; Thiruvananthapuram's high literacy level and its record of having elected outsiders in the past made it a sensible choice.

Tharoor was at his best during the campaign, shedding his Western suits for the tunic and sarongs popular in Kerala, even modifying his Malayalam accent from his native Malabar sound to the Travancore twang popular in southern Kerala. At his request, Sonia Gandhi dropped in to address a rally in his constituency and, buoyed by the support of admiring women – Kerala is the only Indian state where the gender ratio favours the fairer sex – the elegant diplomat turned politician won by a thumping majority of close to 100,000 votes.

Manmohan, eager to have modern-minded people in Cabinet, accommodated him as a minister of state in the MEA, where some bureaucrats, senior to Tharoor at University of Delhi's St Stephen's College, now had to do his bidding and knock on his door before entering.

It was a job Tharoor took to with aplomb. With his wit, charm, articulate nature and global contacts, Tharoor was a celebrity politician, gaining more news column inches and television time than senior Cabinet ministers. By then he had parted from his second wife, a Canadian and fellow UN worker, and was increasingly seen with Sunanda Pushkar, an attractive Kashmiri woman he had met in Dubai and who, like him, married twice before. The two became fixtures on the social circuit.

Then, a bombshell tweet from Lalit Modi, the businessman who ran the Indian Premier League (IPL) cricket tournament, exposed a murky deal that allegedly bestowed a huge sum of money on his fiancée, Pushkar. The widely accepted inference was that it was a payoff for Tharoor's intervention to get a cricket franchise for a group of businessmen. Tharoor insisted to the last that he was innocent, and went on NDTV 24x7 television to tell presenter Barkha Dutt that he had no intention of quitting his junior ministerial post over the issue. Next day, April 18, eleven months after he was given the ministry, Manmohan summoned him to the prime minister's home late in the evening and told him he had to leave. Tharoor emerged, and told the press he'd resigned.

For the next two-and-a-half years, he stayed on the sidelines, marrying Pushkar in his ancestral home in Kerala, assuring friends that he would soon be back in Cabinet. Then, in October 2012, with the cricket controversy having faded against the backdrop of far more dramatic scandals, he was invited back to the ministry, this time as junior minister for human resources, chiefly, education.

Tharoor is never too far from controversy, but this time the circumstances would be lethal. In January 2014, Pushkar was found dead in the expensive hotel suite they had moved into while their government bungalow was being renovated. Hotel staff had heard the pair having mighty arguments for several hours. Pushkar had even grabbed Tharoor's Twitter handle and sent out several tweets meant to embarrass him. She had also told a newspaper reporter shortly before her death that she would soon "out" his corruption.

A few months after her tragic death under strange circumstances, journalist Nalini Singh, sister of BJP notable and former Ramon Magsaysay Award-winning writer Arun Shourie, gave sworn testimony to a court in New Delhi that Pushkar had confided in her about Tharoor's plans to marry Pakistani journalist Mehr Tarar after extracting a divorce from Pushkar. That account was backed up by another well-known Indian writer and socialite, Shobhaa De, who was chummy with the Tharoor spouse.

"The sort of damaging information she was privy to, would have made a lot of powerful people very uncomfortable had she chosen to go public with it," De wrote in her blog. Later, De revealed in *Mumbai Mirror* that Pushkar, hurt at her husband's complete indifference to her condition, may have even planned to contest against him in Thiruvananthapuram.

Tharoor is surely made of Teflon. Despite the scandal, he retained his seat in the 2014 election, albeit with a much slimmer margin – the nearly 100,000 in 2009 had slid to less than 15,000. But his victory was remarkable because it came even as his party, Congress, was decimated through most of the country. For every 10 candidates the party fielded, just one would make it to the powerful lower house, and Tharoor would be one of those 44 Congress MPs, the lowest representation on record for the party that had brought freedom to India.

Tharoor gets to keep his sumptuous government bungalow in central New Delhi until 2019, and deservedly so, perhaps. His parliamentary interventions are brilliant. Not many Indian MPs nurse their constituencies so assiduously – in Tharoor's case, travelling the long distance to the tip of the subcontinent, attending weddings and appearing at college functions. In the dreary, chummy environment of Indian politics, no one else in the Congress party lights up the landscape so much as Tharoor.

In January 2015, almost a full year after Pushkar died, Delhi Police announced that they were registering a case of murder after concluding through autopsy reports that she had died of poisoning. Ever since the government changed, Tharoor had been aware that he was under scrutiny over the death, even though he was not around Pushkar when she died. His manservant, Narayan Singh, had been roughed up by police detectives and he suspected his phone was tapped.

In his home state, Kerala, the Opposition bayed for his blood while senior Congress party figures stayed silent. In the six months prior, he had tried to mend fences with the BJP, which was now in power, and with prime minister Narendra Modi, its unquestioned supremo. He had readily accepted Modi's invitation to join his Clean India campaign and written what some considered a too-laudatory article on Modi in *Huffington Post*, days after India's new leader took office.

If the BJP or its prime minister considered that reason enough to go soft on Tharoor, there is little evidence of it. Delhi Police has been asked to do a meticulous, thorough investigation of the murder with specific instructions to conduct a fair probe and only indict people against whom there seemed a watertight case. Tharoor has not been indicted and he has cooperated fully with police investigations, declining to comment on the matter to media until the police have finished their job. His journey across life continues to light up column inches and bump up television ratings in India.

7
Pakistan: Demons Inside the Demon

> "Regardless of what may be desirable, the army will continue to set the limits on what is possible in Pakistan."
>
> — Stephen P Cohen in *The Idea of Pakistan*

MUMBAI, NOVEMBER 2008. KL Prasad, joint commissioner of police in charge of law and order in the city of Mumbai, seldom left his office before the departure of his boss, police commissioner Abdul Ghafoor. November 26 had been an unusually busy day and Prasad, reputed across the police force in the state of Maharashtra for his efficiency and integrity, was a weary man as night approached. At 8 pm he had spoken to a junior colleague, Ashok Kamte, additional commissioner of police and the No. 2 in the Anti Terrorists Squad. Kamte had been feeling under the gun from the hardline Hindu outfits, Shiv Sena and Bajrang Dal, over his tough policing, and had come to Prasad for counsel and help. The senior man had obliged, placing calls to key figures in the twin outfits, asking them to lay off this fine officer, whose grandfather had been the first Indian to lead the Maharashtra state police force.

The politicians had laughed and told him not to worry.

"We know he is a good fellow," a senior leader in Shiv Sena, which has ruled Mumbai and Maharashtra off and on over the past quarter of a century, had told Prasad. "But this is the way politics is played, so tell him it is not personal."

Prasad had relayed that assurance to Kamte and had sent him on his way. He had also advised Kamte to take a few days leave since the prime minister was to be in town that Sunday for a ceremony marking the construction of the Mumbai Metro Rail. Kamte would be needed to make sure nothing went wrong.

He looked at his watch. It was almost 9 pm. So much for planning to go home early. The yard in front of the historic stone structure that was the headquarters of Mumbai Police was empty. Summoning his official driver, Prasad got into his Tata Indigo sedan and was home in a quarter of an hour.

At the same time as Prasad was leaving his office, over at the small fishermen's colony in Colaba, South Mumbai, the sounds of traffic punctured the inky night. Still, it was quieter than usual because much of the attention in the shanty homes as well as the expensive residences nearby was on a one-day international cricket fixture in the eastern state of Odisha where the national side was playing England and the Indian stars Suresh Raina and Rohit Sharma were at their punishing best. Along the waterfront, the million lights of Mumbai's famed Queen's Necklace promenade glittered.

Approaching the fishermen's village, guided by hand-held Global Positioning System (GPS) devices, the 10 Pakistani men sent to attack Mumbai were taut as the string on a drawn bow, keen to afflict maximum damage on the vast metropolis before the inevitable death that would follow – for some, sooner than the rest. The youngest was 18, the oldest only 25. They carried China-made rucksacks with English markings that read "Change the Tide". Each of them had been issued AK-47 assault rifles, pistols, plenty of ammunition and grenades – as well as raisins, almonds and walnuts, which were easy to preserve and light to carry, and even when taken in small quantities, were tremendous sources of nourishment. Army commandos going into jungles are issued similar rations. Coming off the inflatable black and yellow dinghy in pairs, they moved like the trained commandos they were. Most people around did not give them a second thought. Only one bystander, a steward at the Taj Mahal Palace & Tower hotel, named Bharat Tamore, thought the gang looked out of place and raised a challenge. He was met with a brusque response from Ismail Khan, the team leader: "We've had a rough day. Shut up and get out of the way."

Less than an hour later the young men headed in pairs for the famed Taj hotel, the Oberoi Trident Hotel, a Jewish chabad house, Leopold Cafe and the Chhatrapati Shivaji Railway Terminus, where the attacks would begin.

Most nights Prasad's first act upon reaching his apartment on Malabar Hill would be to have a quick shower. It helped him unwind. But today, too tired to freshen up, he simply removed his shoes, washed his hands and sat down for dinner. At 9.45 pm his residential land line trilled. On the other end was Henry, a handyman who often came to his house to fix things.

"Sir," said Henry, his voice quivering. "There is some firing going on Leopold Cafe in Colaba."

Gang fights among Mumbai's underworld are not unknown and Prasad was not overly concerned. "What are you doing in Leopold, Henry?" he asked, mildly amused that the handyman should be in this chic café late in the evening.

"It is my birthday today, sir. You've forgotten," came the mild reproach.

Prasad laughed, wished Henry many happy returns and placed the receiver down. On his cell phone he located the number for the additional commissioner of police for south Mumbai, Dr K Venkatesham.

"Venky, there is some firing going on in Colaba. Lock down entire South Bombay. We must catch the buggers," he ordered. "Put *naka bandi* all over, up to Mahim."

Confident that *naka bandi* – police roadblocks and checkpoints – would nab the gangsters, Prasad returned to his meal. The phone trilled almost immediately. Once again it was Henry, voice shaking, as a series of shots from repeater weapons crackled in the background.

The sounds were the handiwork of Abu Soheb and Abu Umar, the pair assigned to attack Leopold Cafe. They had alighted from a taxi, stopped on the road to chat on cell phones, and suitably instructed, entered the trendy cafe.

"Can you hear the firing, sir?"

Probing Henry over the land line, Prasad was dialling Venkatesham from his cell phone with his other hand. This was bigger, much bigger, than anything Mumbai Police had known.

"Venky, this is not a normal incident. Ordinary gangs do not do continuous firing," Prasad was getting anxious now. "This is serious. Rush!"

He then looked for the number of Vishwas Nangre Patil, deputy commissioner of police for zone 1, which covered all the expensive hotels in South Mumbai. In his haste, Prasad pressed on zone 10 in his contact list, which appeared ahead of Zone 1. That DCP was also a Patil and the man was mystified.

"What firing in my zone, sir? Everything is quiet here."

Prasad, recognising his error, cursed and cut the line.

The Chhatrapati Shivaji Railway Terminus in downtown Mumbai is used by hundreds of thousands of people every day. Ismail and the lad named Ajmal Kasab headed to the terminus, knowing a rich harvest of lives waited for them. Calmly firing from the hip, they killed 58 people there and left more than a hundred people wounded. Then, surprised by the spirited response from a thin, poorly equipped police force present at the station, they exited the place and emerged on the road, looking to commandeer a vehicle. A Toyota Qualis minivan was approaching with sirens on. Kasab and Ismail, taking cover in the narrow lane, sprayed the police vehicle with bullets from their AK-47s, mortally wounding six of its seven occupants. Unknown to them, they had wiped off the top terror fighters of the metropolis, including Kamte, who had just been consoled by Prasad, as well as Kamte's boss, ATS chief Hemant Karkare. They died because they were carrying big weapons and it was difficult for them to react from inside the vehicle. This had given Kasab and Ismail, hiding behind a roadside bush, the advantage. Karkare had been wearing a bulletproof vest and sections of the Indian media would later say that the poor quality of the vest was responsible for his death. In truth, the slug entered an area of his body that the vest did not protect, and that had proved lethal.

Overjoyed at their kill, Kasab rushed towards the Qualis and reached for Kamte's AK-47, also extracting two magazines from his person. Then the duo pulled the bodies off the front seat and rode the Qualis back into the street. Abandoning the vehicle 3 km away, they grabbed a Skoda Laura and drove it into a police block. A firefight followed and Ismail lay dead. One constable grabbed Kasab, and was given a full blast of bullets in his chest. But others closed in and beat the lad into submission. India had its first captive, only barely alive, but alive. In the weeks that followed, Kasab would prove to be a mine of information and reveal every detail of the complicated operation, enabling New Delhi to get insights into the operations of the Pakistani deep state and its principal irregular combat arm, the Lashkar-e-Taiba.

Prasad meanwhile was still working the phones. He called police commissioner Ghafoor, briefing him on the situation and what steps had been taken so far. Then he reached out to his friend, the joint commissioner of police (crime) Rakesh Maria, whose fame was built on hunting down the perpetrators of the blasts that rocked Mumbai in 1993, months after Hindu zealots razed the historic Babri Mosque in Uttar Pradesh.

Maria, who lived next door, had heard as well.

"My car has gone out, Prasad. Pick me up as you leave."

At the Oberoi Trident Hotel in South Mumbai's seafront, Jai Arya, executive vice president at Bank of New York's Singapore operations, and his wife, Rohini, were dining at the Kandahar Restaurant. Visiting Mumbai, their guests that night were Ashok Kapur and his wife, Madhu. Ashok, who is my wife's cousin, was chairman and co-founder of Yes! Bank, the Mumbai headquartered lender. Earlier, Ashok had led Rabobank's Singapore operations and we were frequent visitors at his Mount Echo Park bungalow, where Ashok would be at his avuncular best, pressing drinks and food on his younger relatives.

Suddenly, the sounds of what appeared to be firecrackers exploding could be heard from the lobby below. The four diners felt no particular alarm. Firecrackers are common at Indian celebrations, although it was unusual for the Oberoi to allow them indoors. From that moment on things changed swiftly. A grenade exploded as the terrorists made their way towards the restaurant on the first floor. Arya and the others fled through the kitchens, making their way to the top floors. But then firing began above them and they scrambled downstairs again, locking themselves into a mattress cupboard on a middle floor.

There, trembling, they stood with three others, bodies pressed against each other and unable to sit for even a moment. For the next 14 hours, bombs went off regularly in their hearing, punctuated by screams. A terrorist taking cover blew out the lights, robbing the tiny space of the little illumination it got through the bottom of the door. Water began flooding in as the firefight triggered fire alarms.

When security forces rescued them after noon the following day, the stairs were strewn with BlackBerrys, glass shards and handbags. I was outside the building when Jai Arya and Rohini walked out after their ordeal. They looked like zombies. Madhu had managed to escape from the hotel the previous night but Ashok, who had run upstairs, was missing. He had been killed on the stairs.

In the same restaurant with the Aryas and Kapurs, but at another table, was Lo Hwei Yen, a 28-year-old Singaporean lawyer on her first trip to Mumbai. Like others there that night, she had fled the place when the shooting started. She had made her way to the rooftop, then descended a few floors and been captured. Initially, the terrorists said they did not intend to harm women. She was allowed to make some contact with her family through a text message. Later, the attackers changed their minds, ordered by their handlers in Pakistan to execute every hostage.

"We found her in the corridor on the 17th floor and there were two other dead women on the same level," a senior hotel executive told me, when I talked my way into the hotel, then under a security clampdown, two days later.

Was there a chance she may have died in friendly fire when the National Security Guard stormed the hotel?

"No chance," he said. "She was shot in the head from close range."

Lo became the first Singaporean to be killed in a terrorist attack, plunging the tiny island into sadness.

Meanwhile, Prasad and Maria headed back to the commissionerate, both on the phone continuously. Prasad, by habit, kept a copy of his *Standard Operating Procedures* in the back of his car, often taking a quick glance at the book on the way home from work. It was a relatively fresh manual, published only in 2006. After his own copy was worn out, he had borrowed Karkare's manual a month back and he knew the drill. His own job was to man the control room at Police HQ and that was where the pair headed.

There was total bedlam now across Mumbai. Television stations had picked up the news and had come alive to the seriousness of the attacks that had begun three hours earlier. The deaths of the ATS chief and his deputy had contributed to the sense of panic enveloping Mumbai. Now, a concerned AN Roy, director general of police for Maharashtra, was on the line. DCP Nangre Patil, who had gone to the Taj Mahal Palace & Tower hotel, was not contactable. Mumbai Police had already lost three of its finest officers. Now another star officer was missing. Roy was deeply concerned.

"OK, sir," Prasad responded. "I will go to the Taj in five minutes. Let me inform the CP." It was 1.40 am on Thursday. There wasn't time to mourn for his batch mate Karkare, or Kamte, who had served two postings under him.

Fortunately, it turned out that Nangre Patil was safe. He had traded fire with the terrorists, then withdrawn when he ran out of ammunition. Prasad entered the Chambers, the exclusive area of the hotel used by guests to conduct business meetings. Scared hotel guests were huddled there in small groups. In batches of 10, he extricated several people. And so it went until the next morning when MARCOS, the Indian Navy's commando outfit, took charge of the operation, holding the fort until the National Security Guard (NSG), based in the outskirts of New Delhi, arrived to complete the job.

The final count was 166 dead and more than 300 wounded.

Mumbai, which collects a third of the income tax paid in all of India, is the business capital of India. It is the home of the rich and the famous, including Dilip Shangvi and Mukesh Ambani, India's richest men, and Amitabh Bachchan, the most popular Bollywood star of all time. Politicians rule in New Delhi, and Mumbai rules the politicians. As India's principal gateway to the world, home to its central bank and top lenders, headquarters of its main stock exchanges and, most important of all, Bollywood, Mumbai has been a favoured target for those seeking to rattle India. With frightening regularity, the city has been attacked time and time again. In March 1993, four months after Hindu zealots razed the Babri mosque in Uttar Pradesh, Mumbai suffered its worst attack in history. Terrorists set off 13 coordinated explosions, killing some 260 people in various parts of the metropolis. In August 2003, three explosions in South Mumbai claimed more than 40 lives. Three years later, a series of bombs placed in commuter trains caused more than 200 deaths. Every time it has been attacked, the great city's get-up-and-go spirit has reasserted itself.

Indian intelligence agencies, increasingly coordinating well with MI5, CIA and Mossad, as well as a slew of other intelligence outfits, had learnt as early as August 2006 that the Lashkar-e-Taiba had been making preparations for a strike on Mumbai. Indeed, intelligence had indicated that several top hotels were targets. Subsequently, another two dozen alerts had come their way, all pointing to Mumbai. Three of them specifically talked of suicide squads and a dozen alerts had spoken of the possibility of multiple targets.

Although the warnings did get some attention, several times key dates had been mentioned and had passed without incident. At one point, the Taj Mahal Palace & Tower hotel, the iconic structure whose blazing turrets became the globally recognised image of the Mumbai attack, had significantly stepped up security. But this had been allowed to wilt for fear of inconveniencing the great and the good who passed through its doors.

That would prove to be a huge mistake. In the crowd that entered and departed was an American of Pakistani origin, David Coleman Headley, a 6-foot-2 figure with a gigolo-like frame. His name in Pakistan was Dawood Saleem Gilani, and his father, estranged from his American mother, was the head of Pakistan's public broadcaster. He has been described aptly as "half Gilani, half Armani". Indeed, one of his eyes was blue, the other brown.

Like many on either side of the India-Pakistan border, he too had heard at his dinner table the horrific tales of the 1947 Partition and the massacres of the time. Now, he was not only "casing the joint" for Lashkar-e-Taiba, as the Americans would call it, he was also working for the US government as a clandestine informant for the US Drug Enforcement Administration (DEA), which had busted him and was now trying to see if he could be of use as a mole in the heroin trail of which Pakistan was a key centre, thanks to its proximity to the poppy fields of Afghanistan. The DEA was often infuriated with Headley, whom they found notoriously undisciplined and difficult to control, but some of the information he gave them was first-rate, so they put up with him. One of his wives had grown terrified of his *jihadi* friendships and had gone to the US consulate to complain. She was given a hearing and sent away. Headley continued to operate.

Over multiple visits to Mumbai, Headley did the reconnaissance for the mission, identifying and videographing key sites and various details, including access points. Kasab and his nine friends had been instructed on the sites to attack based on feedback from Headley. Who knows what could have been prevented if those warnings about Headley, and the tip-offs of the strike to come, had been heeded.

Too busy with my assignment, I had no time to visit the Kapur home in Mumbai to offer my condolences to Madhu. Instead, I paid my respects to Ashok's body after gaining access to the JJ Hospital's Morgue in Byculla, where it lay before it could be claimed after the autopsy. The global media had been alerted to the bodies at JJ Hospital Morgue but had been penned away outside the gate. Once I dropped Prasad's name, the authorities not only let me and my colleague, P Jayaram, into the morgue, one tired policeman even got us tea.

"Sir, it is not a pleasant sight inside. Are you sure you will be able to stomach it?"

The mortuary, which had never had to deal with so many bodies – more than half of the 166 dead were brought there – was a nightmare. Bodies were strewn about. Some were washed down with water to keep them from deteriorating too rapidly. In the main hall, bodies lay scattered. In the adjoining room, four of the young terrorists lay dead, some with eyes open. One, whom I recognised later from pictures was Abdul Rehman "Bada", had taken a bullet in the eye. They looked like ordinary kids, these young men sent out on a suicide mission.

Then, I turned to look for Lo Hwei Yen. The 28-year-old lawyer, like the other victims, had been reduced to a number. In Lo's case, that was 791/125, according to the mortuary's record.

My editors in Singapore had pressed me to get precise details of her death, and where she had been shot. But, approaching the corner, I realised the slender body I was pointed to was unclothed. Not wishing to look at a naked woman's body without her permission, even in death, I turned around quickly. I asked to see the post-mortem report. Finally, a doctor yielded and allowed me to see it. It read: "Fracture of skull with abdominal injury. Firearm injury."

Not far from Lo lay a huge man on the floor, in the dress of a Jewish rabbi. His face was soot-black from the explosion that probably killed him and he was one of the few that were clothed – his sect forbids post-mortems on the dead. Others had faces smashed beyond recognition.

Lo Hwei Yen's death would shock and sadden Singapore, which had never before lost a life in a terrorist incident. The young lawyer had travelled to Mumbai for just a night, to deliver a speech on the global credit crunch. To her bad luck, she had been checked into the Oberoi Trident Hotel. Taken hostage, the attackers had ordered her to pass a message that the Indian authorities refrain from storming the Oberoi hotel or else they would harm her. A little while after that message was passed, Lo was executed. The world outside would not know about it until two days later; indeed, Lo's husband, accompanied by Singapore diplomats including high commissioner Calvin Eu, would wait outside the hotel for two days, holding up a placard with "Singapore" scrawled on it.

It was a rare moment of tension between Singapore and India as the island state anxiously waited for word on Lo's safety. Subrahmanyam Jaishankar, the well-regarded Indian high commissioner, was good friends with S Premjith, head of the Southern Asia and Sub Saharan division in the Singapore Ministry of Foreign Affairs. But now the tension between the two was palpable. Slightly nasal in normal times, Premjith's voice coming over the telephone relayed anger and frustration as the hours wore on and Jaishankar could provide no word about Lo's safety. Unbeknown to both diplomats, Lo had been dead for a long time.

Later, India would hand out copies of cell phone intercepts, details of markings on seized grenades, tailoring labels on clothes found in the vessel that brought the terrorists to Mumbai, and the interrogation report of the lone gunman captured alive. The details were handed out to friendly governments to establish its case of Pakistani culpability and, in Singapore's case, to prove that there was very little that could have been done to save the young woman's life.

Three months later, the Pakistan government published the results of its preliminary investigation, after India handed over a dossier that included cell phone records, phone intercepts, details of weapons recovered and other data linking several Pakistanis to the outrage. The material put out by Rehman Malik, the top Interior Ministry official, revealed to the world the extensive global network that Lashkar-e-Taiba operates and the frightening prospect of an outfit as deadly and committed to its cause as Al-Qaeda.

For instance, a Thuraya satellite phone used during the attack had a number that was issued in the Middle East. The Internet Protocol address of an e-mail sent to the media after the attack was traced to a proxy server in Russia. The investigation threads even included Austria and Italy, and the US city of Houston, Texas. A man based in Spain used the Voice Over Internet Protocol platform to link up with the Mumbai attackers. He paid for the connection and five other subscriber identity module (SIM) cards in Italy. This was no ordinary terror group at work. Clearly, it had the backing of a bigger power, one possibly with offices around the world.

At the time India welcomed the investigations as a "positive step" by Pakistan. New Delhi figured that Lashkar-e-Taiba, raised and funded by Pakistan's Inter-Services Intelligence (ISI) to weaken India's grip on Kashmir, may have outgrown its former master. Indian intelligence estimated that it had a foothold in 21 countries. MK Narayanan, the NSA, called it "as big and omnipotent as Al-Qaeda and its most visible manifestation". But today, seven years after the event, top Indian officials say they have no doubt whatsoever that the hit on Mumbai was planned by the Pakistani deep state and cleared at the topmost levels of the Pakistani establishment.

It is now an all-too familiar saying that most countries have armies but in Pakistan, the army has a country. There is little indication that things will change. Benazir Bhutto, who was assassinated in Rawalpindi, the national capital, while campaigning to return to power, was tutored in the realities of Pakistan's power structure in 1989, days after being elected prime minister for the first time. At her very first meeting with the Army and intelligence chief, she was clearly told by the generals where she stood. Several critical matters, including the military-run nuclear programme, were off-limits to the prime minister, she was informed. Angered, Bhutto left for her home city of Karachi to sulk in silence for a few days. Bhutto was wasting her time being upset. Since the days of Ayub Khan, the country's first military dictator, the Pakistan Army has regarded itself as the arbiter of the nation's destiny.

As the Manmohan Singh government considered its response to the terror strike on Mumbai, many options were discussed, including a military counterstrike on the country. But, although intelligence agencies already had transcripts of conversations between the terrorists and their handlers, they were not sure initially how far up the Pakistani chain it went, and whether it was a rogue operation. Pakistan's early response, emanating from the office of prime minister Yousuf Raza Gilani, was to offer to send the ISI chief Ahmad Shuja Pasha, to visit India. Washington and London, aware of the anger in New Delhi, worried about the reaction from India. US secretary of state Condi Rice was in London that week. She called for Islamabad to cooperate fully, demanding that it follow the evidence "wherever it leads" and for "complete, absolute, total transparency and cooperation". As people gathered in public squares across India in an unprecedented outpouring of grief and rage, president George W Bush ordered her to fly to New Delhi while sending admiral Michael Mullen, chairman of the Joint Chiefs of Staff, to Islamabad.

Pakistan's president Asif Ali Zardari, the late Bhutto's husband, appeared equally shaken by the developments and was probably unaware of the extent of Pakistani involvement – the establishment simply did not trust him. He too vowed to cooperate after a phone conversation with Manmohan. While he probably was not aware of the strike before it took place, he was fully alive to the consequences and had spoken to a host of other world leaders to draw attention to the deteriorating situation with India.

A week after the attack, Manmohan called in his NSA, Narayanan, and Narayanan's predecessor in the BJP government, Brajesh Mishra. Both were known hawks on Pakistan. Fortunately, both advocated restraint. With Pakistan in the global doghouse – Madeleine Albright, no particular friend of India, had just described the country as "an international migraine" – the last thing they wanted to hand Islamabad was a moral victory and global sympathy that an Indian attack might trigger. There was always the other, longer option, which was indeed considered over the following weeks. This was to work on Pakistan's many fault lines and splinter the nation into three or more pieces. Pakistan is a nation where the official language, Urdu, is not the local tongue in any of its four provinces. Punjabi is spoken in Punjab, the most populous province; Sindhi is spoken in Sindh, Balochi in Balochistan and Pashto in Khyber Pakhtunkhwa. But that line of approach was put aside as well, the Indians judging that the instability would then become uncontrollable.

Pakistan was tottering anyway. Extremism, once confined to the frontier areas, had reached deep into the heartland. The Pakistani Taleban were boasting that they would be in power in Islamabad within two years. The same group had also said they would sink their differences with the Pakistan military and fight alongside them should India attack. It was decided that the cheaper option was to keep Pakistan's fault lines ticking but not push it over the edge. Just the previous year, Pakistan had recorded more than 1,400 terror incidents and 2008 was no improvement.

"You face one Mumbai. Pakistan is facing Mumbais every day," the Pakistani columnist and parliamentarian Ayaz Amir pointed out repeatedly to Indian television channels.

As the dust settled, New Delhi began to see through the fog and was amazed at the perfidy. Ajmal Kasab, the lone Pakistani gunman captured alive, had begun to squeal and the agencies had a clear picture of how the gunmen had been recruited and who trained them. New Delhi and Washington gave Islamabad 48 hours to act, or face the consequences. It was only then that the Pakistani authorities picked up Zaki-ur-Rehman Lakhvi, Lashkar-e-Taiba's military commander. Foreign minister Pranab Mukherjee had already begun to hint at the Pakistani hand. Indeed, his counterpart, visiting New Delhi, had been quietly advised to go home. Pakistan began to backtrack on its offer to send the spy chief, first offering to send a less senior officer, then dropping the idea altogether. Things were back to square one.

Less than three years after the attack on Mumbai, Pakistan would suffer its biggest international embarrassment on the night of May 2, 2011 when US Special Forces crossing the border by helicopter landed clandestinely in the garrison town of Abbottabad and killed Osama bin Laden inside a safe house not far from the Pakistan Military Academy. They even ferreted away his body, which, after identification procedures, was dumped into the sea from aboard the aircraft carrier USS *Carl Vinson*.

Until that night, and even subsequently, Pakistan had strenuously denied it had any knowledge of the Al-Qaeda leader's presence in the country. The official explanation in Pakistan was that Osama escaped being noticed because of a colossal "intelligence failure". But Pakistan's intelligence services are well-known for their efficiency and many found it impossible to believe that Osama had found a secure house specifically designed to prevent electronic eavesdropping of its premises and lived there for six years without being known to at least some high-ups in the establishment. The head of ISI when Osama moved to Abbottabad was no less than General Ashfaq Kayani, who later succeeded Pervez Musharraf as Army chief. The man who succeeded Kayani as ISI chief was lieutenant general Nadeem Taj, a Musharraf loyalist who was previously commandant of the Abbottabad military academy.

India would rub home the point. Meeting his US counterpart, Janet Napolitano, P Chidambaram, then India's home affairs minister, described Pakistan as the "global epicentre of terrorism". "The vast infrastructure of terrorism in Pakistan has for long flourished as an instrument of state policy," he would tell Napolitano. "Today, different terrorist groups, operating from the safe havens in Pakistan, are becoming increasingly fused, the society in Pakistan has become increasingly radicalised, its economy has weakened, and the state structure in Pakistan has become fragile."

All of it was true.

The great tragedy of India-Pakistan relations was that just over three years before the attack on Mumbai, things had never looked rosier between the two. In April 2005, about 500 foreign correspondents had descended on the Kashmir Valley for the inauguration of the first bus service to ply between Muzaffarabad, in Pakistan-held Kashmir, and Srinagar, capital of the Indian state of Jammu & Kashmir. The peace process had been on for 14 months and India thought it had found in Musharraf a Pakistani leader who, finally, had the military's backing to negotiate a settlement. After all, Musharraf was himself of the military. Not surprisingly, on both sides there were powerful interests aligned against the rapprochement as well.

Indian and Pakistani engineers had worked hard to clear the route of landmines. A disused bridge that connected the divided territories had been repaired and its paint changed from the Indian tricolour to a neutral white by the Indian government. To scare off potential passengers, Kashmiri separatists had published the names and addresses of people who had registered for the journey. Armed insurgents blew up the Tourism Reception

Centre in downtown Srinagar, setting the green-roofed building ablaze, in the hope of killing bus passengers they thought, wrongly as it turned out, had been housed there. The bus service was meant to run only once a fortnight and carry no more than 30 passengers, but the excitement was the equivalent of opening the Channel Tunnel from England to continental Europe. Manmohan and Sonia both went to Srinagar for the inauguration, Manmohan exulting in this "caravan of peace", as he described it.

A few days later, when Musharraf showed up in New Delhi to watch an India-Pakistan cricket fixture, the euphoria was still high. "The two leaders ... determined that the peace process was now irreversible," a joint statement enthused.

India's move in the previous months to ease the visa regime for Pakistani academics, elderly and businessmen, Manmohan's vision of a border being "mere lines on paper", were all bearing fruit. Over the next two years, backchannel activity to improve the relationship was frenetic, cloaked in great secrecy. A three-stage peace plan on Kashmir was drawn up, starting with freeing up travel and trade along the Line of Control, just as in the old days before the Partition. A second step would see stronger self-government by Kashmiris. The hope was that as the peace process moved forward both nations would be able to withdraw the troops they had lined up against each other, paying heavy costs – a massive security and economic windfall.

If only things were so simple when it came to the two, divided at birth. Within two years, the peace initiatives would fizzle out, first because of resistance within India, then because of Musharraf's weakening grip on Pakistan. Things were back to where they were.

This was not a surprise. India-Pakistan relations had been bedevilled from the start. India had been slow to pay out cash assets owed to Pakistan after the Partition, and only settled with its new neighbour after Mahatma Gandhi, then aged 78, threatened a fast days before he was assassinated in January 1948. In October 1947, just two months after they won independence, Pakistani irregulars entered Kashmir dressed as tribesmen and almost made it to the state capital Srinagar. Having stopped to plunder and rape, including at a Christian nunnery, they were delayed in marching to the state capital by a day – giving New Delhi just enough time to secure from the Hindu maharaja unqualified accession to India. New Delhi quickly landed troops and ammunition in the Kashmir Valley. Since then, Kashmir has been a bone stuck in their mutual throats, one unwilling to give up its claims to the province, the other unwilling to loosen its increasingly militarised grip.

Alongside this was a parallel and in some ways, related, issue – the sharing of Himalayan river waters that are a lifeline to Pakistan. The Indus and its five main tributaries rise in India before flowing into Pakistan, traversing east to west. While the Indus and the Jhelum enter Pakistani territory quickly, others such as the Beas, Sutlej and Ravi have a long run in India before flowing into Pakistan, giving India a potential stranglehold on Islamabad. Indeed, in April 1948, India, angered by the Pakistani attempt to send infiltrators to destabilise the Valley, had blocked the Ravi and Sutlej, threatening a drought on the wealthy farmers of West Punjab, now in Pakistan. New Delhi, then looking to irrigate the grain fields of northern India, had also just begun to build the Bhakra Nangal dam on the Sutlej River.

The water issue was settled with World Bank intervention, which gave waters of three rivers exclusively for Pakistan's use while three other rivers were given to India. But Pakistan's sense of vulnerability has never ceased even though India has an impeccable record on upholding the Indus Water Treaty of 1960, which fixed the sharing of the rivers. The dozens of projects it is building along the rivers whose waters are given to Pakistan, it fears, can be used as dams to turn off the spigot, threatening the very existence of Pakistan. Moreover, with China contemplating diverting the waters of key rivers that flow from Tibet into India, a threat to India's northeastern states, there is increased fear that this will give India the perfect excuse to do the same with Pakistan, China's "all-weather friend".

These experiences have clouded bilateral ties and set the stage for the enduring discord between the two nations. Indeed, Pakistanis are often baffled when they see the level of trust India enjoys around the world as a restrained and honourable player on the global stage. For instance, Stephen Cohen, the noted American scholar of South Asian militaries, begins the first chapter of his book, *Arming Without Aiming: India's Military Modernization*, with the words "One of the most remarkable attributes of India as an independent nation has been its longstanding restraint in military strategy." Such assessments enrage Pakistanis.

Cohen and his co-author, Sunil Dasgupta, go on to note that following India's greatest strategic success, the victory over Pakistan in 1971, which occurred in reaction to millions of refugees crossing into India to escape the Pakistan Army's pogrom in East Pakistan, New Delhi did not press its military superiority in the west to settle the Kashmir problem.

From its birth, Pakistan has coveted control of all of the Kashmir Valley, which it feels was snatched from it by the sleight of hand of the British bureaucrat who drew the line on the map, as well as a Hindu maharaja who initially sought independence for the state, then unfairly opted to join India. By the logic of Partition – contiguous Muslim areas would be attached to Pakistan – the Muslim-majority valley should have been Pakistan's. But it did not happen that way, and with the maharaja's accession to India, New Delhi quickly made sure that the province stayed in its grasp. The theoretical explanation then was that it was essential to show the world that the two-nation theory – that Hindus and Muslims are separate "nations", hence the creation of Pakistan – was wrong, and that the two communities could indeed live as one.

Today, regardless of its keenness to show the two-nation theory is flawed, New Delhi will not yield simply because it does not have to. It has the power and wherewithal to hold Kashmir for as long as it is necessary. On the other hand, it sees Pakistan as weak and weakening.

A nation of moderate Muslims for the most part, Pakistan began to slide when it actively supported the Central Intelligence Agency's (CIA's) plans to arm and train radical fighters to overturn the Soviet occupation of Afghanistan. The Saudi nobleman, Osama bin Laden, a devout Sunni

Muslim and Arsenal Football Club fan, was a creation of that era. When that war ended, the fighters remained, particularly in the frontier city and surroundings of Peshawar, spreading their violent creed.

Pakistan's sense of wretchedness with the US began in the summer of 1999 during the Kargil War, when Bill Clinton unequivocally turned towards India after summoning Nawaz Sharif to Washington for a dressing-down. Clinton had also invited Vajpayee, but the latter curtly refused, saying he saw no reason to talk until Pakistan had vacated the mountain heights it had occupied. That this turn to India happened so soon after the sanctions the US imposed on India following the 1998 nuclear tests, stunned Islamabad.

Since then, and particularly from 2002, the steadily improving US-India relationship was watched with growing alarm and anxiety by Islamabad. When the Twin Towers went down in 2001 and America had decided to go to war with the Taleban, Richard Armitage, a deputy secretary of state, had threatened Musharraf that "we will bomb you into the Stone Age" if he did not cooperate. This elicited the swift, but reluctant, about-turn in Pakistan's policy of backing those terrorist groups.

All this feeds into the Pakistani anger against India and its sense of victimhood as well as frustration at its own lack of muscle. To deflect attention from its own internal misery, it was essential to periodically target an external threat, and India, with which it had a rich history of animosity, was just the right target.

Pakistan has also been watching with despair – much like India does with China to some degree – as its larger neighbour's economy pulls away in size, while its own remains mired in a sea of internal conflict, crumbling infrastructure and capital flight. This, aside from the tragedy of bottling up the tremendous talent that resides in the country – Pakistan could easily have gained from the outsourcing boom, for instance – imposes a wretched cost in terms of defence spending, merely to retain an element of strategic parity. And, as the parity slips in conventional military terms, it needs to reach for the nuclear option to keep India in check, along with periodic testing of ever more sophisticated delivery systems built with the assistance of North Korea and China.

There are other demons that many Pakistanis – and Indians – have to live down. Take two hawks, Zaki-ur-Rehman Lakhvi, military commander of the Lashkar-e-Taiba, the terror group behind the Mumbai attack, and the group's founder, Hafiz Mohammed Saeed, a firebrand religious scholar. Before the emergence of the Islamic State in Iraq and Syria (ISIS), Lashkar-e-Taiba ranked with Al-Qaeda as the most dreaded terror outfit, although its focus is India and Israel. In its initial avatar, it was meant to be a force of non-state actors raised to loosen India's grip on Jammu & Kashmir. The US and India say it operates today under the guise of a charity named Jamaat-ud-Dawa, which runs schools, dispensaries and five big hospitals. Saeed moves around with impunity inside Pakistan although the US has put a $10 billion bounty on his head. Lakhvi is nominally in prison, where he is treated like a royal.

What drives people like Saeed and why is the Pakistani establishment so reluctant to rein him in, covering itself with explanations that it cannot act until there is tangible proof against the man? And how much hatred could you harbour for the people of your neighbouring country, who, essentially are ethnic brothers?

In an interview to a Karachi daily Saeed once gave a hint of the memories that tear at his soul. His family's roots were in the Indian state of Haryana, once a part of undivided Punjab. With Punjab aflame in the communal frenzies of Partition, his father, Kamaluddin, a farmer, decided it was time to migrate to the new country named Pakistan. Fearful of travelling by rail and road because of the massacres taking place along these systems, the family moved on foot, taking four months to cross the yet-to-be-closed border and reaching Pakistan in March 1948. By then, 36 members of Kamaluddin's extended family had been slain. Saeed himself was born near the town of Lyallpur, now called Faisalabad, a few months later. As he puts it, had his birth come a few months earlier, who knows if he'd have survived?

It took time for Kamaluddin to get the 15 acres of land that Pakistan gave him in lieu of the property he'd left behind. Meanwhile, a one-room tenement was the family abode, a far cry from the comfortable existence they had known in India. Perhaps to exorcise the memories, and perhaps as a thanksgiving, his devout mother opened a madrasah. Saeed, the eldest of five siblings, remembers being thrashed just twice in his early years – each time for forgetting to say his prayers. Today, Saeed's Jamaat-ud-Dawah operates 170 madrasahs across Pakistan.

Saeed holds double Masters degrees – in Arabic and Islamic studies – both from the prestigious Lahore University. The turning point in his life was a 1981 scholarship he won to Saudi Arabia's King Saud University. There his principal influence was the Grand Mufti Sheikh Abdul Aziz bin Baz, whose pupils included another man who would in later years have another huge American bounty on his head, under the Reward for Justice programme. That man was Osama.

There is the slimmest chance that the Pakistani military may have covertly helped the US bring Osama to justice. But Saeed is another case because he represents the ideological core on which Pakistan was founded – the two-nation theory. At best, he can be reined, as Islamabad seems to have done. Likewise, there are enough Hindu nationalist hotheads in India, including those that fire-bombed the weekly train service to Pakistan in February 2007 and killed more than 60 people. They too operate under the guise of social work and charity.

The savage strike on Mumbai, and the bombing of Islamabad's Marriott Hotel a few months earlier, underscored to deep-thinking Pakistanis the helplessness of the Pakistani state and how things were spinning out of control right under their noses. The Marriott bombing, according to some people in the heart of the Pakistani establishment, was perpetrated on the orders of the ISI because it wanted to destroy the high-tech snooping gadgetry the Americans had installed on the hotel's fifth floor, an area that was out of bounds for everyone else. The hotel's owner, Sadruddin Hashwani, was to suffer another blow the following June when militants said to be allied to a little-known group called Fidayeen-e-Islam fought their way through the gates of the Pearl Continental Hotel, located in one of the most secure areas of Peshawar, capital of the Khyber Pakhtunkhwa province.

Having killed the security guard at the gate, they drove in a truck filled with explosives and blasted the place down. Hashwani had reportedly been in talks to sell the property to the US to be used as the consulate. In all three cases, unable to confront either India or the US directly, there was deep suspicion that the establishment turned to the deep state to effect its strategic purpose.

For India, the shock of Mumbai had its after-effects. The federal home affairs minister and the home affairs minister in Maharashtra state lost their jobs. With the efficient Chidambaram now installed as home affairs minister of India, the security apparatus and intelligence agencies were significantly upgraded. Dozens of terror cells were smashed in the months that followed. India went through 2009 without suffering a single terror attack.

For Pakistan, however, the cycle of violence has not ended although there has been improvement lately. In December 2014, six years after Mumbai, it would suffer its most tragic terrorist attack to date. More than half a dozen gunmen from the Tehreek-e-Taleban Pakistan would enter the Army Public School in Peshawar, capital of Khyber Pakhtunkhwa province, and gun down schoolchildren sitting their exams. Of the 145 slain, fully 132 were schoolchildren, many the wards of senior military staff. Some were as young as eight years old. Experts drew parallels with the Beslan school hostage crisis in the Russian Federation's North Ossetia-Alania region that took place in 2004. Pakistani special forces killed the attackers, who turned out to be Arabs, Afghans and Chechens.

Pakistanis took note that the attack took place on December 16, the date that their country was split in two, with the hived off former East Pakistan emerging as the new state of Bangladesh, thanks to covert Indian assistance. Some in Pakistan saw more than mere coincidence in the date and wondered if the massacre was retribution for the attack on Mumbai six years earlier. But many more saw it as one more example of how badly their nation, dominated by its Army-led establishment, had gone wrong.

A few years after the Mumbai attack, former Pakistan Army chief Jehangir Karamat, now a leading figure on the seminar circuit, was visiting New Delhi for a strategic affairs conference and sought a meeting with LK Advani, who had served as deputy prime minister in the Vajpayee Cabinet. Advani, who was born in Pakistan's Sindh province before the Partition, received the visitor with every courtesy, even making sure that his wife and daughter were around to welcome the distinguished Pakistani general.

The talk soon turned to the 2008 terror attacks on Mumbai. Advani pointed to the evidence of the Pakistani deep state's hand – the recruitment of the terrorists from the countryside, their indoctrination, and finally, expert commando training. Until the Pakistani media had themselves gone to the village and confirmed Kasab's identity by talking to his father, the Islamabad establishment had continued to maintain its posture of denial.

Karamat steadfastly denied that the Pakistani Army had actively supported the terror strike.

Advani smiled. Then he looked the Pakistani gentleman-soldier in the eye.

"If you insist that this was not the work of the deep state and also that your government knew nothing of the detailed preparations that went into this attack on your soil, then it is clear that Pakistan does not have a state," he said, shocking his visitor with the directness of his remark and its incontestable logic.

8
Vengeance in Sri Lanka

> "Politically speaking, former prime minister Rajiv Gandhi was killed and India can never forgive the LTTE for it. However, as a person I do not have any grudges against Prabhakaran and do not hate him."
>
> — Priyanka Gandhi on the stump in her brother's constituency in April 2009, a month before the death of Velupillai Prabhakaran, the founder of the Liberation Tigers of Tamil Eelam

AS 2009 APPROACHED, matters were once again coming to a boil in a key neighbour, Sri Lanka, which lies at the southern tip of the subcontinent. During a visit to the teardrop-shaped island in August 2008 my sources in the Sri Lankan military told me they were sure they were entering the final lap of the 25-year conflict. Diplomats stationed in Colombo were sceptical; they had heard this many times over the past years. But my Army friends in Colombo were dead sure, as they explained the strategy, plotting the movements of formations on maps. Based on those inputs, *The Straits Times* reported on August 13: "After 70,000 deaths and years of despondency, there is a glimmer of hope that the Sri Lankan Army's recent battlefield successes might presage an end to the civil war in the north of the island. Troops have fought their way into Tamil Tiger strongholds. The feared fighters are said to have lost two-thirds of their strength. Their supply lines from sympathisers in India have been crimped by a vigilant New Delhi working in tandem with Colombo."

This was welcome news. If Velupillai Prabhakaran, the fearsome chieftain of the Liberation Tigers of Tamil Eelam (LTTE), could be vanquished, the island could hope for renewed prosperity. With all its troubles, the Sri Lankan economy had been growing by more than 6% annually in recent years. In the Heritage Foundation's Index of Economic Freedom, Sri Lanka outscored every other South Asian economy, including India, Pakistan and Bangladesh. Yet, its gross domestic product (GDP) size was small at $28 billion and it suffered some of the worst inflation in Asia. The IMF's public information notice on Sri Lanka that year said its economic outlook depended "critically" on an end to the war. The country, once considered a potential rival to Singapore, was on its knees.

In the 1980s, New Delhi had got involved in the long-running ethnic tensions between the Sinhala majority of the island, which is mostly Buddhist, and the small but influential Tamil community, which is chiefly Hindu and has deep ethnic ties with millions of Tamils just across the water, in India's Tamil Nadu state. The rising majoritarian politics of the dominant Sinhala had seen the island once called Ceylon renamed Sri Lanka. Shortly after Independence from Britain, successive governments began promoting pro-Sinhala policies, leading to fury among Tamils, who, though only 12% of the population, were generally better educated and had dominated the administration. Still, communal ties held through the 1970s. The municipal district of national capital Colombo, for instance, had a Tamil majority.

Thanks in part to the deep friendship between the Nehru-Gandhi clan and the Bandaranaikes, the first family of Sri Lankan politics – Sirimavo Bandaranaike was the world's first elected woman leader when she became prime minister of Ceylon in 1960 – the two nations had good ties for decades. A touch of humility from the smaller neighbour helped; when Indira Gandhi visited Colombo, Bandaranaike moved out of her official residence, Temple Trees, so the Indian premier could be safely housed in it herself. India, caught up with hostile Pakistan on its western flank and not-too-friendly China on the east, spent most of its defence expenditure protecting the two frontiers and was grateful to leave its southern borders unguarded. Things changed when the nationalist, Junius Richard Jayewardene of the United National Party, rose to power in Sri Lanka in 1977.

JR, as he was known, quickly set about changing the island's policies. A believer in free enterprise, he unshackled the economy from its socialist moorings, allowed *Voice of America* to set up a broadcasting transmitter on the northern tip of the island, facing India, and handed over three oil tank farms in the strategic Indian Ocean harbour of Trincomalee to a company suspected to be a front for the CIA in the US.

This was enough to set off insecurities in New Delhi, where Indira Gandhi had returned to power in 1980. Her response was to order India's external intelligence outfit, the Research and Analysis Wing (RAW), to arm and train the island's Tamil rebels to put pressure on Colombo. Several Tamil groups with acronyms like PLOTE, TELO, EROS and EPRLF thus gained from India's covert help.

There was another group that also accepted India's help, but at the same time kept a wary distance from it. It was the fiercest, deadliest and most committed of the Tamil groups, the LTTE, or simply, the Tamil Tigers. Its leader, Velupillai Prabhakaran, was a squat, mustachioed man whose whose blooding had taken place in 1975 when Prabhakaran assassinated the mayor of Jaffna, Alfred Duriappah, as he emerged from a Hindu temple after offering prayers, although he was a Christian himself.

Older by nearly four decades, JR had a mildly patronising attitude towards Rajiv Gandhi – he had known Rajiv's grandfather, Jawaharlal Nehru, and corresponded with him – which did not sit well with the young Indian leader, who came to power after his mother's assassination in October 1984. Never too interested in statecraft until his younger brother's death in a plane crash in 1980 caused his mother to turn to him for support, forcing him to leave his civil pilot's job, Rajiv was a trusting, good-natured soul who cared deeply for the plight of Tamils. Now, as the violence in Sri Lanka escalated, Rajiv intervened. In the late summer of 1985, he forced JR to agree to peace talks with the Tamil groups, which he organised in Thimphu, with the help of his friend, Bhutan's King Jigme Singye Wangchuck. (Quite by chance I was then the only foreign journalist allowed into Bhutan since I had an interview with the King fixed up earlier and got most of my information from a Sri Lankan intelligence officer who had the room next to mine in my Thimphu hotel.) Two rounds of talks failed, because JR's representatives would not budge from their offer of district development councils while the Tamils sought a clear federal alternative. Piqued by the failure of the talks, Rajiv would order the deportation from India of Prabhakaran's key adviser, Anton Balasingham, a British citizen, allowing him back into India only after Balasingham sent emissaries to Rajiv, thus setting up one of the first major ruffles between him and the Tamil Tigers.

Outfoxed by JR, India watched with alarm as the Sri Lankan military moved on Jaffna, applying a security tourniquet on the district and choking even civil supplies. In June 1987, as the humanitarian crisis widened over Jaffna, Rajiv acted; five Indian Air Force AN-32 transporters were loaded up with food and oil in the southern Indian city of Bangalore, then, escorted by Mirage 2000 fighters, the planes entered Sri Lankan airspace without authorisation and relief-bombed Jaffna. Allowed to be a passenger in the cockpit of the mission commander's plane, I marvelled at the sight of the parachutes attached to the supply boxes opening like mushrooms after free-falling from the hatch of the Russian-made transport aircraft. The drop target was a large public ground in Jaffna and few of the boxes landed where they were intended. But India, and Rajiv, had sent an unmistakable message to Sri Lanka and JR. On July 29, 1987, the two signed the Indo-Sri Lanka Accord, with Colombo agreeing to grant devolution of power to the provinces, and to withdraw its army, and the Tamil Tigers agreeing to disarm and hand over their weapons to the Indian Peace-Keeping Force, which soon arrived to enforce the peace.

Aware of Prabhakaran's unease with the peace accord, and his clear unwillingness to trust Colombo, Rajiv had him flown to New Delhi for talks and kept him virtually a prisoner at the Ashok Hotel, until the Tiger supremo appeared to endorse the accord. A warm-hearted man, Rajiv was merely looking for an effective solution. He had no desire to see the Tiger chieftain harmed, or particularly disadvantaged. Indeed, he felt he could trust Prabhakaran. Seated in the drawing room of his official residence in New Delhi as they wrapped up their discussions, Rajiv had called for his personal bulletproof vest.

"You will need this," he told Prabhakaran, handing over the kevlar vest. Four years later, the LTTE assassinated Rajiv Gandhi while he campaigned in Tamil Nadu for the 1991 parliamentary polls. It was revenge for the indignity Prabhakaran had suffered at his hands, and for Rajiv's decision to send in Indian troops to enforce the peace accord. Rajiv had been genuinely sympathetic to Tamil grievances. To lower his guard, the Tigers had sent peace emissaries to him. But Prabhakaran was a man who had not hesitated to wipe out even prominent Tamils who stood up for the cause, if they came in his way.

One of them was the barrister Appapillai Amirthalingam, secretary-general of the Tamil United Liberation Front (TULF). Amirthalingam had incurred Prabhakaran's wrath by standing for a negotiated settlement on the ethnic tangle and asking for the Indian peacekeepers to stay longer on the island. His murder, two years before the Tiger got Rajiv, was vintage LTTE, executed with deep cunning. Two Tiger youths had befriended a senior TULF man, frequently showing up at his door to seek "advice". On a day that Amirthalingam was in the senior TULF man's house, the two came visiting again. They accepted tea from their host's wife, then shot the host dead along with their target, Amirthalingam.

When the LTTE's history is written, two events will stand out as watershed moments that would shift the ground from under Asia's deadliest militant group. In its immediate neighbourhood, LTTE's strategic blunder was to assassinate Rajiv Gandhi, whose family is deeply popular in Tamil Nadu. The group lost tremendous goodwill in the southern Indian state, home to 60 million Tamils, after that outrage. This also set the Indian government against the group forever.

The other event, over which it had little control, was the September 11,

2001 terror attacks on the United States by Al-Qaeda. Suddenly, sympathy for all forms of militancy vanished around the world and Colombo used the moment to press diplomatically and succeeded in getting several nations to label the Tigers a terrorist group. When Sonia Gandhi's Congress unexpectedly came to power in 2004, Prabhakaran would have known that for the next five years he could expect no help, or even sympathy, from New Delhi. The straws had been in the wind a long time.

In early 1993, when the Congress leader, PV Narasimha Rao, was India's prime minister, and Sonia was still in mourning, the Indian Navy and Coast Guard had sunk an LTTE boat in international waters. It was suspected to be carrying arms to Jaffna, supplied and loaded up in Phuket. More than the arms, the Tigers mourned the loss in that sinking of their former military commander of Jaffna, the dreaded Sathasivam Krishnakumar, known to all as "Kittu", along with eight other senior Tiger cadres. Kittu's legend within LTTE had been exceeded only by that of the outfit's boss, Prabhakaran. And it was not the only ship that the Indians would help put down, feeding intelligence to Sri Lanka about a host of other shipments that it learnt about from signals intercepts, aerial surveillance and its own contacts in the arms bazaars.

Soon, things began changing on the ground as well. Sri Lanka's military was steadily building up its sinews, at great cost to the national exchequer. Arms from India and other nations were pouring in. At first, India was shy to acknowledge its role in the build-up, describing its decision to install military radars and send helicopters as putting in "defensive equipment". Still, for a long time, there were no clear battlefield victories. Diplomats in Colombo had convinced themselves that neither side was powerful enough to inflict convincing damage upon the other. It was a stalemate.

It was against this backdrop that Sri Lanka elected Mahinda Rajapaksa, a cheery politician from the Sinhala heartland, as the president of the republic in late 2005. His rise to national leadership, and particularly his decision to appoint his brother, Gotabhaya, as the all-powerful defence secretary, would cause the decisive turn in the war.

Gotabhaya, or Gotha as he is known around Sri Lanka, was a former lieutenant colonel in the Sri Lankan Army who had emigrated to the US after early retirement, returning to the island after his older brother became president. In early 2006, shortly after he took charge as defence secretary, Gotha submitted a long list of expensive war equipment he wanted to purchase. Many, including the president, were surprised. Gotha's response was simple: "All of you will start with hopes of talking peace with the Tigers," he told them. "When you realise it is futile, you will come to me. I cannot wait until that moment. I need all this now to be fully prepared."

Prabhakaran, whose world view was limited, failed to see the world had changed around him. But his organisation had grown so big, with networks around the world, that he may well have felt secure in his hideout. In March 2007, the Tigers had stunned Sri Lanka by bombing an air force base in Colombo. Flying low over the coastline, using no lights, they dropped their ordnance and flew away. The IAF-supplied Indra radar had failed to spot the approaching aircraft for the simple reason that they had been turned off at night to save power – no one could have imagined the Tigers had night flying capability. In the event, three people on the base died and no aircraft was hit, a far cry from the devastating attack on the base in 2001 when the Tigers blew up six civilian jets and more than a dozen military planes in a guerilla operation. This time, the Sri Lankans quickly determined that the Tigers had been using light trainers, but the nation's shock was evident as it contemplated the implications of a suspected "Tiger Air Force" – the first rebel outfit in the world to claim such a facility. Two months later, they bombed a fuel storage facility and refinery, as Sri Lankans sat in their homes on a Sunday morning watching the national side in the World Cup cricket final against Australia.

Sri Lankan intelligence suggested the Tigers had got flight training in South Africa and acquired Czech-designed Zlin aircraft. Army chief Sarath Fonseka described the Tiger air capability as a "joke" and likened it to lobbing a grenade while riding a swing. He was hiding a worry; the Sri Lankan military sends ships with as many as 1,500 soldiers at a time from Trincomalee to Kankesanthurai Port, near Jaffna, capital of the north. Fonseka could not afford a kamikaze-style attack on one of the troopships. India was worried even more at the prospect of an Air Force, however primitive, in the hands of a non-state actor. Manmohan Singh had been stressing nuclear power and the last thing New Delhi wanted was the Tigers doing a contract job for a hostile power, or deciding to attack one of the nuclear installations along the Tamil Nadu coast.

By April 2007, the Norwegian-brokered ceasefire agreement was effectively dead. By then, the LTTE had violated the agreement 3,830 times and the Sri Lankan government 351 times. The Sri Lanka Monitoring Mission had stopped issuing rulings on ceasefire violations because they were proving to be too many. Mahinda, who had no particular animus against Tamils, was convinced that there was no point trying a conciliatory approach to the ethnic crisis. What's more, the Tigers had targeted no less than Fonseka in a suicide attack that badly wounded the general, needing him to be airlifted to Singapore, where he spent weeks in hospital. In early January the following year, Colombo was taking the fight to the enemy. The Air Force, now equipped with MiG-27 bombers, struck rebel bases and the government closed the highway providing the only land link between Sri Lanka's south and Tamil rebel-held areas in the north. A few days later, Colombo announced officially that the ceasefire was over, the Cabinet spokesman adding with calculated impudence: "In the future, due to change of situations, if the Tigers decide to lay down their arms and come to talks, the government can reconsider."

Led by Fonseka, the Army was showing great morale, advancing in the face of heavy casualties. The Tigers were also losing the propaganda war; no less than 37 nations had listed the LTTE as a terrorist outfit. New Delhi watched with cold eyes. When Japanese diplomat Yasushi Akashi, appointed by Tokyo to attempt to mediate a peaceful resolution to the Sri Lankan conflict, pressed Narayanan for a more sympathetic Indian attitude towards Prabhakaran, he was brushed aside. "Have you ever seen his eyes?" Narayanan asked Akashi. "I have."

By January 2009, the Tigers had suffered their biggest setback when the town of Kilinochchi fell to the advancing Sri Lankan Army. Troops also captured part of the highly strategic Elephant Pass, a causeway linking the northern Jaffna peninsula to the mainland. Soon, Mullaitivu, where the Tigers had their main military facilities, would fall as well. When Sri Lankan troops arrived in each spot they had managed to clear, surprises awaited them. Troops found Tippmann A-5 guns capable of firing chemicals, 120mm cannon and thermobaric weapons that create a two-stage explosion with the blast sucking all the air out of the area. One vital discovery was an "undersea craft" still under construction.

As a hostile India choked their supply routes and stopped Tamil Tiger cadres wounded in battle from being treated on the mainland, Tamil Tigers showed their anger on Tamilnet, the website associated with LTTE. "The Indian establishment run by Sonia's Congress is waging its own proxy war in the island of Sri Lanka, concurrent to Colombo's war against Tamil nationalism," an article on the site said. "This time the war is not going to be confined to the island of Sri Lanka, but will be fought involving Tamil Nadu too." New Delhi responded by upping security along the Tamil Nadu coastline and ordered airfields and a nuclear power plant at Kalpakkam on the Tamil Nadu coast to be put on heightened security.

But the Tigers had made a bad mistake. Not learning from their earlier war with the Indian Peace-Keeping Force two decades earlier, the guerillas tried to fight like a conventional army, and were mauled. It was one of many strategic blunders by Prabhakaran as his 26 years of militancy approached its end. By the end of April 2009, the war was almost over. Hemmed into an area about twice that of New York's Central Park, a far cry from the 15,000 sq km of territory it once controlled in Sri Lanka's north and east (the Tigers even had their own version of courts and district administration), the rebel outfit was now calling for a ceasefire. That was the last thing Colombo was prepared to consider. Indeed, earlier in the month, they had released Norway from its role as mediator in the ethnic conflict. The Rajapaksas never had much time for the Norwegians, believing them to be partial to the

Tigers. Meanwhile, there were grave shortages of food, water and medicine as the Tigers, cruelly, used 150,000 civilians as human shields against the onslaught. There were babies with shattered knees, women whose eyes had been hit by blast fragments and teenagers who died from shock. Shocked by the unfolding disaster and facing domestic pressure – pro-Tamil rallies were held on the streets of London and Paris – world leaders, including Australian premier Kevin Rudd and British premier Gordon Brown, tried to speak to Mahinda. They were told he was not available. "I could not talk to them as I was busy with the New Year festivities. I ask them not to talk about a ceasefire or a pause in military operations," the president said.

The war would have ended at least two weeks sooner had not India's politics intervened. Tamil Nadu, with 39 parliamentary seats, was second only to Andhra Pradesh among the South Indian states, key to Congress fortunes. It was to vote on May 13, the last of five voting days in the staggered polls. Congress was contesting 16 seats, leaving the rest for its partner, Dravida Munnetra Kazhagam (DMK). Worried that the state might react badly to seeing their ethnic brothers slaughtered across the water with Indian help, Manmohan despatched Narayanan and foreign secretary Shivshankar Menon to press for a suspension of the military action pending the end of voting. Colombo, on the brink of annihilating the Tigers and grateful to New Delhi for its assistance, was ready to help. It declared its ties with New Delhi to be at an "all-time high".

Then came one of those great farces that only India, and particularly movie-crazy Tamil Nadu, could have scripted. Early on the morning of Monday, April 28, the state's chief minister, Muthuvel Karunanidhi, who was allied with Manmohan's government in New Delhi, got up from his bed and ordered his driver to take him to the Marina, facing the Bay of Bengal. He then announced a "fast unto death" to protest against the killings of Tamils by Sri Lankan security forces. Television cameramen were woken up from their slumber to record the Tamil politician coming to the rescue of his brethren across the Palk Strait. "I thought I should sacrifice my life to the Sri Lankan government, just as hundreds of Sri Lankan Tamils have done.

Let me become another victim of Mahinda Rajapaksa's war," he said, as party workers, city elders and movie personalities gathered around him, as he was resting on a cot, fanned by two portable air-conditioners. Manmohan and home minister Chidambaram urged him to call off the fast, voicing concern for his health.

The drama was played perfectly; a few hours after the fast began, the Sri Lankan government ordered a halt to the artillery and air strikes after a meeting of its security council. Shortly thereafter, Karunanidhi, 85 years old then, accepted a glass of milk to end his fast and claimed victory.

Dayanidhi Maran, Karunanidhi's nephew and a former Cabinet minister in the Manmohan government, gave his uncle full marks for pressuring Colombo on behalf of Tamils. "When Jayalalithaa goes on fast, no one bothers," he proclaimed, referring to the DMK party nemesis, Jayalalithaa Jayaram, erstwhile chief minister and head of the rival All India Anna Dravida Munnetra Kazhagam (AIADMK), who had reversed opposition to the Tigers and demanded that India help achieve an independent Tamil Eelam in Sri Lanka. "When Karunanidhi goes on fast, people react immediately."

Manmohan's government in New Delhi quickly also sought to share credit for the ceasefire. "It means a cessation for hostilities," Chidambaram, who was himself contesting for Tamil Nadu's Sivaganga seat on his Congress party ticket, told the media. What he did not say publicly was that the previous night, after Narayanan and Menon had reported back on their talks, he had tipped off Karunanidhi about Colombo's willingness to accommodate the Indian government's pleas for a temporary adjustment to the war strategy.

"There is constant discussion between our two governments," PM Amza, Sri Lanka's deputy high commissioner and the head of its consulate in Chennai, capital of Tamil Nadu, confided to me that week. "Where we can, we try to help each other. This was one of those cases."

For a few days, the Sri Lankan air strikes stopped and the artillery fell silent. Then, once the last vote in Tamil Nadu was cast, Mahinda left for an overseas trip, leaving a simple order for the military: finish the job before the next government is installed in New Delhi. The artillery strikes began and the infantry moved in for the kill. After 70,000 deaths in battles, suicide attacks and assassinations, Sri Lanka's quarter century of civil war was over. Major General Kamal Gunaratne, the security forces commander of the Wanni area, told me the Sri Lankan Army had lost 6,000 soldiers in the last 18 months of the war alone, with another 27,000 wounded, many critically. Also to be counted among the dead were the 1,248 Indian soldiers and their former prime minister, felled for attempting to broker peace on the island.

Towards the end, Prabhakaran's struggle for the Tamils looked increasingly like a massive joke, especially when the rebels held thousands of Tamils hostage and fired at those seeking to flee to safety. Like Kim Jong Il in a food-short North Korea, pictures of the chubby Prabhakaran and his older son, Charles Anthony, contrasted sharply with the weary, starved look of his cadres and the people he was supposedly protecting.

The Prabhakaran legend was so impressive that it was always believed that if the troops were to ever discover his body, it would be with a cyanide capsule in his mouth or a self-inflicted bullet wound to the head. It was also assumed that loyal cadres would burn his body before the troops reached him. After all, this was the man who had taught the Tigers to perfect the cult of the woman suicide bomber.

Nothing of the sort happened. Cornered in a Mullaitivu lagoon, Prabhakaran sought to stay alive till the very last, attempting a final breakout with the aid of 60 Tiger fighters. His son, Charles Anthony, was dead by then. His daughter, Duwaraka, who had joined the Tigers, had been killed a few days earlier. Tragically, his 12-year-old son Balachandran seems to have been among the last to die, killed execution-style, underscoring the military's determination to root out the Prabhakaran cult root and branch. The child's body was found with five bullets in it, all delivered from close range.

Prabhakaran himself was found with his eyes wide open in death. A portion of his head seemed to have been lopped off as though someone had taken an axe to it. Some of his last hours had been with Pottu Amman, the

LTTE intelligence chief who masterminded the Rajiv Gandhi assassination 18 years ago that month. Pottu Amman's body, believed to be in the lagoon, was never identified. The following week, when Gotabhaya Rajapaksa, the Sri Lankan defence secretary, travelled to New Delhi to thank India for its assistance, there were many high-fives all round, but deep-thinking Indian officials were already worried of the trajectory Sri Lanka would take post-war. Without the pressure point of the Tamil issue, many in New Delhi felt, Sri Lanka would have less and less reason to be mindful of Indian strategic concerns in the neighbourhood, particularly against a China that was pressing in, with huge pockets and a fast-increasing military might. For that moment, though, no one cared. A fiend who had eliminated so many Sri Lankans, including dozens of prominent people from his own Tamil community, as well as one of the most promising Indian leaders, had been rubbed out. For now, that was cause for celebration.

The dysfunctional diarchy. Manmohan Singh, as head of government, and Sonia Gandhi, as head of the ruling coalition, had a somewhat tense but mutually respectful relationship. Singh, nevertheless, completed a full ten years in power, in part because the Gandhis felt comfortable with him at the helm of government. (Photo: Ravi Raveendran)

Nalanda University chancellor and former foreign minister of Singapore, George Yeo, with Amartya Sen. (Photo: Ravi Raveendran)

Tamil Nadu street procession mourning the death of Singapore's founding prime minister, Lee Kuan Yew in March 2015. (Photo: Ravi Raveendran)

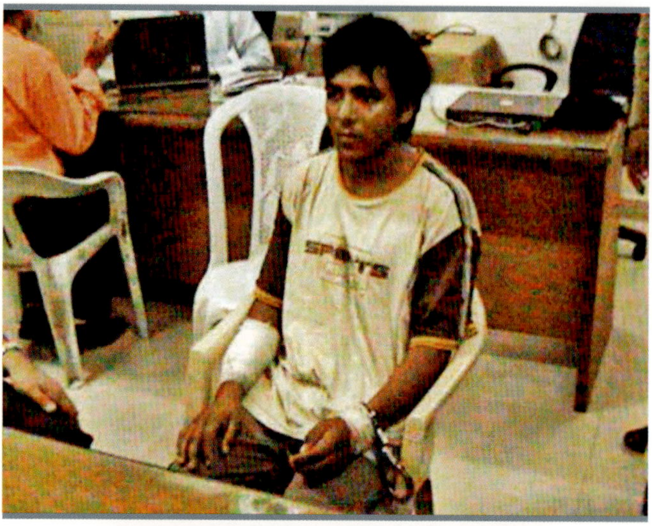

(Top) Mohammed Ajmal Kasab, the lone surviving member of the 10-man group that attacked several Mumbai landmarks, at an undisclosed location under police custody in this undated video grab shown by CNN IBN Television. (Photo: Ravi Raveendran)

(Bottom) KL Prasad, joint commissioner in charge of law and order, led the police action against the terror attacks on Mumbai until the National Security Guard flew in from New Delhi. (Photo: Ravi Raveendran)

Shashi Tharoor with his glamorous wife Sunanda Pushkar who was found dead in January 2014.
(Photo: Ravi Raveendran)

MK Narayanan (foreground), the powerful spymaster turned national security adviser, with Shivshankar Menon, his successor.
(Photo: Ravi Raveendran)

Vinod Rai, the comptroller and auditor-general, who set the cat among the pigeons with his devastating reports on government malfeasance. (Photo: Ravi Raveendran)

Troops of India's paramilitary Border Security Force dressed in ceremonial uniform march past on India's Republic Day. (Photo: Ministry of Defence, New Delhi)

Indian industrialist Ratan Tata shows off the Nano, billed as the world's cheapest car. (Photo: Ravi Raveendran)

Muslims at prayer in India. India's minorities have been a worried lot since the BJP returned to power in 2014. (Photo: Ravi Raveendran)

South Asian bonhomie. Modi made the unprecedented gesture of inviting leaders from around the Indian subcontinent to his swearing-in. Every nation responded, plus a few more.

Obama and Modi during a rare second visit to India by a serving US president. Modi's monogrammed suit would later be slammed by India's media. (Photo: Ravi Raveendran)

Singapore's Goh Chok Tong with Modi in September 2014. "You are moving so fast I can feel the earth shake," Goh told India's leader. (Photo: Prime Minister's Office, India)

Sonia Gandhi with her children, Rahul and Priyanka, at Rajiv Gandhi's funeral. Rajiv was killed by a Tamil Tiger woman suicide bomber while campaigning to return to office.
(Photo: Ravi Raveendran)

Honour, above all. India's navy chief, admiral DK Joshi, with his eventual successor, vice admiral Robin Dhowan, in the background. Joshi became a national hero after resigning his post to take moral responsibility for a string of accidents involving navy ships. The admiral's display of integrity, and little effort by the government to convince him to withdraw the resignation, would reflect poorly on Manmohan Singh and his defence minister, AK Antony.
(Photo: Press Information Bureau, Government of India)

AFGHANISTAN
Pakistan-occupied Kashmir
JAMMU & KASHMIR
Srinagar (Summer)
Jammu (Winter)
CHINA
PAKISTAN
HIMACHAL PRADESH
Shimla
PUNJAB
Chandigarh
Dehradun
UTTARAKHAND
HARYANA
NEW DELHI
Gurgaon
NEPAL
SIKKIM
Gangtok
BHUTAN
ARUNACHAL PRADESH
Itanagar
Jaipur
Lucknow
Ayodhya
RAJASTHAN
UTTAR PRADESH
Patna
BIHAR
Dispur
ASSAM
NAGALAND
Kohima
Shillong
Imphal
MANIPUR
BANGLADESH
Agartala
TRIPURA
Aizawl
MIZORAM
Gandhinagar
GUJARAT
Bhopal
MADHYA PRADESH
JHARKHAND
Ranchi
WEST BENGAL
Kolkata
CHHATTIS-GARH
Raipur
MYANMAR
Bhubaneshwar
ODISHA (ORISSA)
MAHARASHTRA
Mumbai
TELANGANA
Hyderabad
Bay of Bengal
Arabian Sea
INDIA
KARNATAKA
Panaji
GOA
ANDHRA PRADESH
Bangalore
Chennai
Andaman Islands
Andaman Sea
TAMIL NADU
KERALA
Cochin
Thiruvananthapuram
Nicobar Islands
SRI LANKA
INDIAN OCEAN

PART III

THE SLIDE BEGINS

9
An Unexpected Re-election

> "I would be the first person to admit that we could have done more."
>
> — Manmohan Singh, in May 2010

ON JANUARY 24, 2009, while Indians prepared to celebrate Republic Day, Manmohan Singh was driven to the All India Institute of Medical Sciences (AIIMS), hours after lunching with his wife and two daughters (a third daughter lives in the US). Waiting for him was Srinath Reddy, head of the cardiology unit at AIIMS, who had flown down an expert heart surgeon from Mumbai to lead the critical and complicated surgery that awaited the 76-year-old Manmohan the next day. There had been some criticism of Reddy's decision to go for heart surgery over angioplasty and even in his choice of Ramakanta Panda, the principal surgeon. But Manmohan, who had had his first bypass operation in Britain in 1990 and an angioplasty in 2003, had full confidence in Reddy and had endorsed his opinion that surgery assured a better quality of life. Despite the obvious risks involved, he had taken less than five minutes to make up his mind.

Beating heart surgery is one of the most complicated heart operations. Unlike in typical bypass operations, where the patient is put on a heart-lung machine, Manmohan's heart was kept working while Panda and his team operated to repair the organ. It was the first time this procedure was done at AIIMS, India's premier research hospital, but Panda was an expert and had one of the lowest failure rates for heart surgeons in India. Manmohan could not have been in better hands. Still, because it was repeat bypass surgery, doctors had to work painstakingly on the tissue beneath the breastbone before entering the heart, which had five bypasses. Four were arterial grafts that came from the chest and arm of the prime minister, while one was a vein from his leg. The operation, which began at 8.45 am, took 11 hours.

News of the complicated surgery travelled across the vast land and raised anxiety in every corner. On the day, millions of Indians sat glued to television sets waiting for updates on Manmohan's condition – radio was no longer the principal medium for breaking news. As the surgeons toiled, the anxieties increased. Prayers were said in Sikh gurudwaras, Hindu temples, mosques and churches. At the end of the day, when the doctors announced success, it was as though the entire nation let out a collective sigh of relief.

Manmohan had often been the butt of ridicule from his political opponents, particularly the BJP. Jokes about his lack of effectiveness were many, some reducing him to a caricature. But on that day millions of Indians realised what this decent, humble, and above all, honest man meant to them and their nation. And they would carry that sentiment to the voting booth when elections to fill the 15th Lok Sabha or lower house of parliament, began in mid-April.

India's democracy sometimes delivers surprises that befuddle even the most expert pollsters. In 2004, with the ruling BJP going full throttle with their triumphalist India Shining campaign, few expected Congress to do so well or to see the Vajpayee coalition toppled. Yet, it had turned out so. The BJP people would have their hopes raised for the 2009 polls, only to have them crash all over again. The BJP's optimism rose because, perhaps not all of India, but certainly voters in the national capital seemed to have started showing their misgivings about Congress midway through the United Progressive Alliance's (UPA's) first term. Civic polls in Delhi held in April 2007 showed big wins for the BJP, which won 164 of the 272 municipal wards, riding on a wave of popular resentment against the demolition of illegal buildings. Building laws in the national capital are breached by almost everyone, leading to construction beyond permitted heights and limits, vast encroachments and illegal glazing of balconies to expand floor space. The Municipal Corporation of Delhi was forced to tear down the illegal structures after the High Court of Delhi, acting on public interest petitions, ordered the administration to perform its duty. While Delhi voters had unique reasons for turning against Congress, the results were further affirmation of a trend that saw the BJP and allies deliver a stunning blow to Congress in municipal polls in Mumbai, held two months earlier. "The civic polls were the quarter-finals," enthused Harsh Vardhan, president of the BJP's Delhi unit. "The Delhi state assembly elections in 2008 will be the semi-finals and the 2009 general election will be the finals."

It was not to be. The 714 million eligible to vote in the 2009 polls amounted to a number higher than the combined populations of the European Union and the United States. They went to the polls at the height of summer and the verdict they delivered was resounding by the standards of the day. Against all expectations, Congress, written off by pollsters as a lame duck, was returned with an enhanced mandate.

The seeds for the victory were sown the previous February, when finance minister Chidambaram presented the annual budget to the nation. The headline news was that the loans of 40 million farmers would be forgiven. Ignoring the strict fiscal norms of his previous years, Chidambaram said the government would pay off loans amounting to 600 billion rupees owed to banks and cooperatives by small and medium farmers. Banks had been ordered to cancel the loans by June 30. After that, farmers would be eligible for fresh loans. A programme that guarantees willing workers employment for at least 100 days a year would be extended to all 596 rural districts of India. "In doing all these, we are discharging the deep debt owed to our farmers by the people of India," the Harvard Business School graduate and tax lawyer told parliament.

The measure was clearly aimed at the 30% of India's billion plus population that live directly off the land, a crucial vote bank. There was good reason to consider the debt cancellation. Since 2004, when Congress unexpectedly got power, thousands of poor farmers under pressure to repay loans, often taken at usurious interest rates from moneylenders, had taken their own lives. A bit of pump priming was also helpful for the economy. In the December 2007 quarter, as the thrust from the Vajpayee government's policies began to ease, economic growth had slowed to 8.4%, from 9.1% in the same period a year ago. The loan waivers sent ripples of shock through Opposition ranks. Just the previous month, the BJP had said that if it came to power, it would waive all farm loans, including those taken from non-bank sources. Of course, the twin measures of loan waiver and a larger job guarantee programme would hurt India's credit culture and distort the employment market in later years, but the results for the UPA, in electoral terms, proved sensational. Indeed, it convinced many in Congress that the road to retaining power lay in ever-bigger sops in the name of protecting the poor and underprivileged.

Meanwhile, with blood flowing freely into his heart after the blockages were removed, Manmohan was a new man, frequently checking with his doctors when he could return to work. As he recovered at home from the surgery, finance minister Pranab Mukherjee presented an interim national budget. He announced that spending on the national job guarantee plan that had touched 41 million households in the past year would continue. So, too, funding for rural infrastructure and a national mission to provide free midday meals to poor schoolchildren, the biggest such effort by any country. By then, thanks to the slow-moving bureaucracy, millions of farmers had just started gaining from the loan waiver announced by Manmohan the previous year. In a nation where 40% of the people live on less than $2 a day, the electoral ground had been well-watered.

Voters also had an interesting choice as they prepared to exercise their franchise; re-elect the government of the 76-year-old Manmohan or choose the alternative, a BJP-led coalition that would, in all likelihood, be headed by the even older Lal Krishna Advani, impatiently waiting for Vajpayee to step aside. But the 81-year-old Advani, whose campaign for a temple to the God Rama had galvanised the BJP in an earlier era, was no longer the charismatic figure he once was. Indeed, he was seen as a divisive personality. If he had been cast early as the BJP's candidate for prime minister, it was only because influential sections of the party wanted to checkmate the chances of the ambitious chief minister of Gujarat state, Narendra Modi. Opponents and allies took note. In the eastern state of Odisha, the Biju Janata Dal broke its 11-year alliance with the BJP, a mighty setback. Then, Congress stitched up an alliance with the All India Trinamool Congress of West Bengal that had splintered from it in the past and allied with the BJP. In an election in which alliances were going to play a major role in determining the complexion of the government, the BJP-led National Democratic Alliance was disintegrating.

For all that, Congress expected to get no more than 150 of its own MPs into the 543-seat lower house of parliament. It had good reason to moderate its expectations; in Bihar, its top ally, Lalu Prasad Yadav, had made a deal with a rival that would see their parties contest 37 of the 40 seats in the state, leaving a mere 3 for Congress. In next-door Uttar Pradesh, which sends 80 MPs to New Delhi and is electorally the richest state in India, the Samajwadi Party announced it would field 75 candidates, leaving just 5 for Congress. Even as Congress insisted it would go ahead and contest more seats, 150 seemed a tough ask. Indeed, a poll for the magazine, *India Today*, forecast that the Congress-led UPA would get between 191 and 200 seats, fewer than the 234 it had garnered five years earlier.

But some shifts were taking place on the ground. Travelling around the country before the polls, one could not help noticing that Muslims, who formed a Congress vote bank that had slipped away after the Narasimha Rao government failed to protect the Babri Mosque from demolition at the hands of Hindu zealots, were trickling back to the party. Manmohan's benign personality was clearly an asset; another was that the growth spurt the BJP had left behind, although it had begun to ebb, had helped improve lives across the board, including those of people in the Muslim community. Congress was reaping credit for what the BJP had sown. As Advani criss-crossed Uttar Pradesh, his attacks on Manmohan were relentless and often personal. Everywhere, he painted Manmohan as a weakling, "the weakest prime minister" who took orders from the woman who ran Congress.

Yet, Manmohan's image did not appear to suffer too greatly from the jibes. If anything, it exalted him in people's eyes as someone who would not stoop to personal attacks against his opponents. In Sultanpur, which adjoins the Gandhi family's bailiwick of Rae Bareli and Amethi, Mohammed Ansari, a dressmaker who was on home leave from Dubai, said he was surprised to see the change of attitude among his fellow Muslims. "At least in my village, the wind is blowing towards Congress," he told me. "It wasn't that way the last time I was here two years ago."

The southern states, which account for 129 of the lower house's 543 seats, thus became even more crucial for Congress, and nowhere more important than Andhra Pradesh, the largest of them, which sends 42 MPs to New Delhi. In the 2004 polls, Congress and its allies had won 36 of the Andhra Pradesh seats, helping it ride to power. At first glance, it appeared that a repeat performance would not be easy because a measure of anti-incumbency is endemic in politics.

In Hyderabad, chief minister YSR Reddy, who died in a helicopter crash a few months later, confided to me that Congress had another problem – Rahul Gandhi's utter lack of charisma. The Gandhi family always had a spectacular following in southern India but Rahul, now leading the charge, was leaving people cold. Reddy's men had to gather people by the truckload with bribes – money and alcohol for men, money and saris for women – and ferry them to the rallies.

"The high command orders me to ensure that Rahul's rallies are a success," Reddy complained. "But what to do, the moment he starts speaking people get restless or get up to leave."

Still, travelling in the Andhra Pradesh hinterland offered a lesson in the ways the Indian voter makes up his mind. At Mahbubnagar, about 100 km from the state capital of Hyderabad in the Telangana region, I stopped to chat with a bunch of people discussing the coming election. One man who gave his name as Prabhakara Rao told me why his vote was for

Congress. He had a single reason – Service 108, the emergency ambulance service started four years earlier by Andhra Pradesh and increasingly being emulated nationwide. Initially founded by a trust backed by Ramalinga Raju, the software mogul, it had been taken over by the government run by YSR Reddy after Raju was thrown in jail for massive corporate fraud. The ambulance service had been renamed Rajiv Gandhi Ambulance Service and the late prime minister's face was on every vehicle. Service 108, dialled for free, had in the few years since its launch saved an estimated 44,000 lives in Andhra Pradesh alone.

"I know several people who owe their lives to 108," Rao said. "It is the biggest gift Congress delivered to us."

Could I be hearing right? But in the town of Shadabad, Chand Pasha, who made a living renting out bicycles, also gave me the same reason. "My 23-year-old nephew was involved in a traffic accident four months ago," he said. "He died after eight days, but thanks to 108, I have the satisfaction of knowing I got him medical attention promptly. The rest was in God's hands." Pasha had one more inducement to vote Congress: a 10,000 rupee bank loan had been cancelled, thanks to the loan waiver scheme.

The underground betting market also leant towards a victory for the Congress-led coalition, midway through the polling process. But they were projecting no more than 142 seats for Congress and about 15 seats fewer for the BJP. Still, the *satta* market, as it is called, carried uncommon respect in the country for its accurate predictions. The previous year it had accurately predicted that Manmohan would win the trust vote in parliament over the nuclear deal with the US. Likewise, the bookies had correctly predicted that *Slumdog Millionaire* would win the Academy Award for Best Picture.

Based on these and other insights from the ground, I ventured to suggest that despite the opinion polls predicting a middling result for the Congress party, it had the upper hand. Thus, my report in *The Straits Times* on April 16, 2009 said: "No major communal issue darkens the horizon and India, although affected by the global recession, is still expanding. Besides, with inflation as measured by the wholesale price index at a 30-

year low, opposition parties have not had much ammunition to attack the government. With little sign of anti-incumbency sentiment, Congress may well emerge as the party with the most seats."

Still, the results, when they came in May, delivered a massive surprise for Congress on the upside. Its individual tally in the lower house jumped to 206, an increase of 61 seats from the previous Lok Sabha. Indeed, its share of the vote had risen by more than 2 percentage points, while the BJP's had dipped by 3.4 percentage points and it was poorer by 22 seats. Incredibly, Congress won 21 seats in Uttar Pradesh, just two behind the dominant Samajwadi Party. In Andhra Pradesh, it took 33 of the 42 seats. In Tamil Nadu next door, where Karunanidhi had staged his fasting strike just before the poll, the Congress-DMK-Viduthalai Chiruthaigal Katchi alliance bagged no fewer than 27 of the 39 seats. The Manmohan government, against all expectations, had returned stronger than before. The UPA led by Congress was more than 100 seats ahead of the BJP-led National Democratic Alliance.

Perhaps no one was more surprised than Manmohan himself. Just two months earlier, he and his wife had scouted around central New Delhi for the home they would live in upon retirement – former prime ministers and presidents are given large government bungalows until their death. Gursharan Kaur had found the house best suited to her taste was the one occupied by close family friends, Montek Singh Ahluwalia and his wife, Isher Judge, both top economists. She had even identified her choice of prayer room in the bungalow. Then came the unexpected political windfall and another five years in power.

It was the BJP's worst showing in 20 years. Congress could now easily dominate the coalition it was leading after arranging for support from another dozen MPs for a majority in the House. Financial markets cheered the news as they looked forward to a burst of policy initiatives and reform measures from a government that had gained political strength.

Before the polls, Sonia Gandhi had explicitly stated that Manmohan Singh would remain prime minister if Congress retained power. And certainly, in northern India, if not elsewhere, the strong vote owed a lot to the respect, goodwill and affection people had for Manmohan personally.

Of course, the high command of Congress – essentially the mother and son – interpreted it differently. Neither side was off the mark. In 2009, Rahul's star had been shining at its brightest. It was his idea to go it alone in Uttar Pradesh, after seat adjustment talks with allies failed. Congress had improved its tally in the country's politically most vital state from 9 in 2004 to 21 in 2009. While his charisma was suspect, none could doubt his energy. Indeed, *Yahoo! India News* voted Rahul the top online newsmaker of 2009. "Some of the key stories for Rahul to be the top newsmaker for the year included pulling up the sagging fortunes of the Congress party in Uttar Pradesh, tirelessly working towards making Congress a youth-oriented party and repudiating Manmohan's offer to take a seat in Cabinet amongst others," the Internet company said. Even the mainstream media seemed to be in Rahul's thrall. A headline in the *Mail Today* tabloid screamed "Ra-Ra Rahul" while it was "Rise and Surprise of Rahul" for *The Times of India*.

Manmohan himself appeared bashful of taking credit, and instead sought to put the spotlight on the mother and son, saying voters had "expressed faith in Congress, in the visionary leadership of Sonia Gandhi and the sustained hard work by youth leader Rahul".

Yet, it was clear that in Sonia's assessment another factor had delivered the vote: the massive sops given out to voters in the form of loan waivers, job guarantees and more, as Naresh Chandra Saxena, who served on her National Advisory Council (NAC), explained to me. It would convince her that this was the way to go, setting up confrontations with Manmohan in the second term as she pushed several populist schemes, including a food subsidy programme, while Manmohan kept a worried eye on the worsening fiscal situation of the country. This would fundamentally affect the Gandhi-Manmohan relationship in the second term, although both worked to ensure that it would not become a full-scale rupture.

In the highly readable *The Accidental Prime Minister*, Sanjaya Baru gives much of the credit for the party's showing to Manmohan's image as a clean and sincere leader. Certainly, in the initial weeks after the rousing victory, Manmohan also seemed to think that way. What's more, there was no "common minimum programme" agreed with coalition partners or the Left parties to crimp his initiatives. Five years earlier, when the UPA came to power, stock markets had plunged so swiftly that trading had to be halted for a period. This time, the key index soared by a fifth as investors warmed to the prospects of a stable administration. The economy, whose size now comfortably exceeded a trillion dollars, was showing remarkable resilience, having ended the financial year to March 31 with 6.7% growth, although this was down from 9% in the previous year. In the euphoria few cared to notice that the cancelled farm loans had hurt the credit culture and public finances, and pushed the budget deficit to more than 6% of GDP, exposing it to the threat of cuts to its credit rating.

Baru captures the self-confidence Manmohan exuded when the former media adviser called on him after the UPA's stunning return to power: "His normal posture was restrained and formal; he sat straight, with his hands resting on the arm of a chair or on his lap, much as he might do in a conversation with a visiting dignitary," Baru writes. "But now, as we spoke of the election result, and much else, he was supremely at ease, reclining with his right leg on his outstretched left, the right ankle resting on the knee of the left. It was a posture that exuded confidence, and suggested that he felt, at this moment, the master of all he surveyed."

Too bad it was not to last. Manmohan's delusions, if that is the best way to describe his feelings, were quickly put to rest by Sonia, who imposed her writ on the composition of the post-election Cabinet. Manmohan, unable or unwilling to stand up to her, caved in promptly. Among those he was forced to accept in Cabinet, and that too in the key portfolio of communication and information technology, was the Tamil Nadu politician Andimuthu Raja, from the UPA's key coalition partner, DMK.

Many events would contribute to the swift unravelling of his power and the UPA's decline in the months to come.

Sonia would return to lead the policy-oriented NAC a few months later. It was clear that she wanted to have her say in economic policy, while allowing Manmohan to focus on external policy. In its earlier avatar, in UPA-1, the NAC had pushed for two key pieces of legislation – the Right to Information (RTI) Act, a path-breaking piece of legislation that has helped curb corruption and brought more accountability to India's teeming bureaucracy, and the rural employment guarantee scheme. Both pieces of legislation were well meant but would have several adverse effects. The RTI would paralyse a bureaucracy that was sluggish to begin with, since bureaucrats would often push away files with a "Let's discuss" note, afraid that any decision would come to haunt them later. But it was lauded as a political master stroke at the time.

"Sonia has a genuine interest in policy," Saxena, a reputed administrator and policy expert, told me when the NAC-II was announced. "She also realises that this is the only way she can stay in power and that this is in the long-term interest of her family."

That was the intellectual explanation. The practical one came to me from Mahesh Rangarajan, one of India's finest analysts of Congress party politics. "There have been rising murmurs that the government is losing touch with the people and the party will suffer for it," Rangarajan told me at the time with great prescience. "There have also been reports planted in the media of how Manmohan, after successfully holding on to power in the election, is increasingly assertive on issues. I see this as the beginning of the end of Manmohan Singh's control over government."

It is hard to put a precise date to when things started sliding for the government itself, but some events a few months apart stand out as significant punctuation marks. One was something over which Manmohan had no control.

On the morning of September 2, Andhra Pradesh's YSR Reddy boarded a Bell 430 helicopter in state capital Hyderabad to fly to Chittoor in the south of the state. A medical doctor by training, Reddy was a committed grassroots worker and was on a whistle-stop tour to check on development projects. With him was his principal secretary and head of security along with the pilots, one of them an Indian Air Force wing commander on secondment. Forty minutes later, buffeted by gusting monsoon winds and blinded by dense rain, the pilot either lost control of the craft or steered it into a hillside. All on board perished. YSR's body would be taken for autopsy in the town of Kurnool by the same ambulance service that had proved such a vote-getter for him.

It was a huge blow for Congress. YSR had not only been a staunch Congressman, he had also been an effective one – keeping a firm grip on Andhra Pradesh, the south's biggest electoral prize. What's more, he was also incredibly well-funded by the state's thriving entrepreneurs and this helped fill the national coffers of Congress. From that moment on, the state would begin to slip from Congress' hands.

Within weeks, YSR's son and wife would be rebuffed by Sonia when they staked a claim for the son to succeed the father as chief minister. A few months later, when the son planned a series of condolence meetings across the state to mourn his father's passing, he was expressly forbidden from doing so, the high command fearing, correctly, that this was a ploy to drum up a political wave. Jagan Mohan Reddy went ahead, nevertheless. Then, when the younger Reddy refused to come to heel, he was arrested on corruption charges by the Central Bureau of Investigation, which is supervised by the Ministry of Home Affairs in New Delhi. The concatenation of events would help carry the state into Opposition hands when Andhra Pradesh voted next, providing a boost for Narendra Modi's national campaign. Jagan Mohan Reddy's breakaway party, YSR Congress, is the principal Opposition in Andhra Pradesh state, now run by the regional Telegu Desam Party. Sonia's Congress is nowhere in the picture in the state that had once been so resolutely in its corner.

10
Slaying the "Mallu" Mafia: A Coup in the PMO

> "In a bureaucratic culture dominated by North Indian Hindi speakers, this Keralite lock on the PM's inner bureaucratic circle represents something of an anomaly, which could in the long term create new fault lines around the prime minister."
>
> — US ambassador David Mulford in a leaked US diplomatic cable from New Delhi in 2005, put out by Wikileaks

AS HE SETTLED into his second term, Pakistan was still much on Manmohan Singh's mind, notwithstanding the shock of the previous year when Mumbai had been attacked and brought to a near standstill for three days. In his first term, he had come close to clinching a deal with Pervez Musharraf, Pakistan's military ruler, for a series of mutual steps on the thorny topic of Kashmir that held the promise of leading to a wider settlement of their many issues. However, Pakistan's internal dynamics rapidly changed and so did things in India. Now, with a renewed and stronger mandate, Manmohan wanted to give peace with Pakistan one more shot. "When can I go to Pakistan?" was a frequent question that he put to the Afghanistan-Pakistan-Iran division of the Ministry of External Affairs.

Born in Gah, a village in the outback area of the Punjab, he had been, like millions others, displaced by the Partition of India, which came with Independence from British Rule in 1947. When the subcontinent was cleaved to create Pakistan, the line drawn by Cyril Radcliffe, a British lawyer flown down for the purpose of drawing up the boundaries of the new state, ran through the heart of Punjab. Hindus and Sikhs, like Manmohan, travelled south to India and met hundreds of thousands going the other way to the new, or soon to be, Pakistan, created as a homeland for the Muslims of India. Naturally, great violence ensued, violence that the British may not have minded; theirs was, after all, a policy of divide and rule. Indeed, there is firm evidence that the communal violence which tore across India arrived last in the North West Frontier Province (now called Khyber Pakhtunkhwa) and the Punjab, places where Muslims dominated. There is equally credible evidence that the communal fires raged worst in districts where the administration was led by British officers of the Raj.

Although Punjab was among the last of the northern Indian provinces to go up in flames, when the violence finally erupted there it did so with frightening intensity. In pre-Partition Punjab, Muslims outnumbered Hindus and Sikhs and now they turned on their brothers with immense ferocity. They were met with fierce resistance and an equal savagery. Like countless others, Manmohan's family had suffered too.

Most of the Partition generation of Punjabis have passed on, but a few remain, like Manmohan, with mixed feelings about the land they left behind. My wife's grandmother, who died in New Delhi in June 2015, just short of her 102nd birthday, was born in the Punjab that now belongs to Pakistan. Some years ago, when I offered to take her across the border – getting a Pakistan visa is a near-impossible task for Indian tourists – she demurred. What's left behind is best left behind, she told me. And when I described her little cottage in the hill station of Murree and her last home in Lahore – in Krishna Nagar, now called Islampura and a part of prime minister Nawaz Sharif's constituency – she changed the subject. It is a good guess that like her, Manmohan also has mixed feelings about the land he left behind. There were happy memories and clearly some very painful ones.

But more than sentimentality, he had two good reasons to attempt a lasting settlement with the nettlesome neighbour, envisioning a future not unlike the manner in which Germany and France coexist today. The first was that peace with Pakistan would be a huge fillip to the South Asian economy in every respect – lowered defence spending, increased trade and tourism, even a salutary effect on communal tensions. Besides, who knew what the combined talent pool could achieve, when Pakistan's own skilled hands were added.

The other reason, and this can only be guessed, was that making peace with Pakistan would seal his historical role, even more than the civil nuclear deal he had cut with the US – perhaps even lead to a Nobel Peace prize. After all, few conflicts have been so bitter, or so bloody. Manmohan loved collecting awards, listing even the most minor ones in his curriculum vitae.

Yet, as long as the confident, articulate MK Narayanan was at the PMO, he could be counted on to be the sceptic that stood in the way. Narayanan would not hear of normalising ties with Pakistan until Islamabad put a cap on the terror nodules it funded to keep India off balance. After decades in intelligence, the NSA, like others of his ilk, had a fundamental suspicion and distrust of the neighbour. The Mumbai attack, which had blemished Narayanan's reputation – after all, he coordinated the nation's intelligence apparatus – had only hardened his outlook. Manmohan had immense respect for the NSA. His integrity was unimpeachable, his grasp on intelligence and national affairs unquestionable. But Narayanan also had a puckish sense of humour and Manmohan probably suspected he was sometimes the target of the NSA's mirth and that he didn't always get Narayanan's full respect.

In all that, Narayanan was a complete contrast to Shivshankar Menon. For one thing, the foreign secretary did not seem to harbour firm prejudices. Cerebral and soft-spoken, the Scindia School and St Stephen's College-educated Menon, who had been his nation's envoy to Israel, Sri Lanka, China and Pakistan, was a favourite with Manmohan. He had passed over a dozen officers to appoint Menon foreign secretary three years earlier, when he still retained an occasional bold streak and could assert himself. Menon had not only been an excellent foreign secretary, he had proven his personal loyalty to Manmohan as well. In June 2009, at a meeting with his Pakistani counterpart, Yousuf Raza Gilani, on the sidelines of the Non-Aligned

Movement summit in Sharm-el-Sheikh, Egypt, Manmohan had yielded to Pakistani pressure and instructed his foreign secretary to include a line in the joint statement that seemed to suggest that Pakistan was aware of Indian involvement in the insurgency in Balochistan, a Pakistani province bordering Iran. Since Manmohan had given Menon the instructions in the presence of the Pakistani leader, there was little the bureaucrat, who would have instantly guessed at the furore that would erupt at home, could do to contradict his boss. The line that was announced in the joint statement seemed innocuous to all except those who quickly surmised its import: "Prime Minister Gilani mentioned that Pakistan has some information on threats in Balochistan and other areas."

When news of the Indian "concession" travelled home the predictable uproar followed. India had always claimed it kept its hands off the insurgency wracking Balochistan and now, here was Manmohan seeming to acknowledge it, however elliptically. Even the Congress party would not back its prime minister. At this point, Menon had stepped in, taking the blame upon himself by calling it a "drafting error". That deflected public anger, no doubt putting Manmohan, who abhorred criticism, in Menon's debt.

Menon had superb credentials in many other ways, coming from a long line of distinguished diplomats and public servants. His great-grandfather, Sir C Sankaran Nair, had been president of the Indian National Congress in 1897. Menon himself was the third generation from his family to have risen to the post of foreign secretary – his grandfather and uncle, both named KPS Menon – had been foreign secretaries before him. His own father, PN Menon, had been from the Foreign Service, dying relatively young while posted to Belgrade as ambassador during the time that Yugoslavia was a key pole in the Non-Aligned Movement. Menon's father-in-law, Ram Sathe, had been foreign secretary as well.

The line of distinguished public servants in his family did not end there. His paternal grandfather, Dr KCKE Raja, was the first Indian to be appointed director-general of Health Services in 1947. Upon retirement,

Raja was tasked to raise the All India Institute of Medical Sciences, India's top research hospital, where Manmohan would have his heart surgery five decades later. Raja's reputation was so immense that New Zealand, which provided the seed funds for the AIIMS, had insisted on his being retained to oversee the project. Menon thus had both pedigree and panache and wore both without being in your face. It was commonly said in the PMO that the two MEA officials Manmohan liked most were Menon and his predecessor, Shyam Saran, who had been drafted, in retirement, to help complete the negotiations on the nuclear deal.

"When Shyam enters the room, the PM's eyes light up," a senior figure in the government told me once. "When Shankar walks in, his whole face lights up."

Now, as the elegant Menon prepared to retire at the end of July, Manmohan, reluctant to see him leave, pondered whether to extend his foreign secretary's tenure by a year or more. But Menon suggested that he would not want to stay on, since it would upset the career paths of those waiting to succeed him. Nirupama Rao, another China hand, was ready and would miss her turn if he continued. There had been controversy enough when he was appointed, with several officers senior to him resigning, angered at being overlooked. Now, Menon did not want to fuel Foreign Service angst by overstaying and holding up the prospects of those junior to him. Manmohan asked Menon what he intended to do next. The diplomat, picking his words carefully as ever, said he would take a break and consider his options, perhaps even accepting a lecturing position for a while.

"Don't agree on anything without telling me first," Manmohan instructed. They understood each other perfectly. Menon wanted nothing less than the NSA's job; Manmohan's task was to find a way to give it to him.

That moment would not be long in coming. Narayanan's turf battles with the hard-driving Minister for Home Affairs P Chidambaram had weakened his standing in New Delhi. They had been friends for years. Narayanan, as Intelligence Bureau chief, had rescued the rising Chidambaram out of a pickle or two with Rajiv Gandhi. Now, the Harvard-educated

Chidambaram, unquestionably one of the finest ministers in Manmohan's Cabinet, was nevertheless seeking to assert his ministerial authority over the bureaucrat. Chidambaram became more demanding after his visit to the National Counterterrorism Center in Washington DC in November 2009. He began making speeches and issuing press statements expressing his desire to consolidate all intelligence, internal security and counterterrorism functions under a single entity that reported to him, rather than to the NSA.

At the same time, Manmohan had probably also received hints that Narayanan's ties with the Gandhi household were not as strong as they were cranked up to be, or had worn a bit thin lately. The talk in New Delhi's salons was that Narayanan had offended powerful people close to the Congress high command by doing a favour to an influential Indian expatriate business family as a quid pro quo for their role in smoothing things at the White House over the nuclear accord. This had denied the Gandhi family satrap some influence-peddling of his own, and he was fuming, saying the old gumshoe was getting too big for his boots.

Three months later, when Menon ended his rest and briefed Manmohan on his future plans, Manmohan told him to wait to be made NSA. But there was still the issue of how to deal with Narayanan, who clearly loved his job and wasn't likely to let go without a fight. Not only had Narayanan to be pushed out, he had to be given a billet that would keep him sufficiently tied down. A state governorship was the best way out. Governors are figureheads but there are enough ceremonial happenings in any given week to keep them busy. Besides, they need the president's permission to leave their stations and cannot come to New Delhi at will. It was the perfect solution.

Manmohan, who hated confrontations, pondered how to break the news to the confident former spycatcher. He picked his moment one afternoon when Narayanan was briefing him after a secret trip to Tokyo. Japanese PM Yukio Hatoyama had conveyed to Manmohan that he intended to skip their annual summit because he was running a lame duck government. But Manmohan, mindful that Beijing might well interpret it as an apparent weakening of the nascent Japan-India strategic bond, wanted Hatoyama to come nevertheless. Narayanan was despatched to convince him to make the trip. To everyone's surprise, the former policeman succeeded in the delicate diplomatic mission. Hatoyama would come after all. Manmohan smiled at the news, obviously pleased.

The talk turned to northern Punjab state, which had witnessed Sikh separatism in the 1980s, an insurgency that had been violently put down by the Indian Army and later, Punjab Police. The NSA expressed his worries about latent stirrings among Sikh separatist elements. Manmohan instructed him to have a word with the provincial chief minister, Prakash Singh Badal. Narayanan was reluctant to place that call. In turn, he suggested that it would be better for Manmohan, a fellow Sikh from Punjab, to have that conversation. Manmohan nodded in agreement and ended the meeting.

As he walked out, he stopped at the door, turned around and sought to score from a distance. "Maybe you should go as governor in Punjab."

Before the mystified Narayanan could react, the prime minister had vanished from view.

A few weeks later, at another meeting between the prime minister and his NSA, the talk turned to Bangladesh, which borders India's West Bengal state. Again, Manmohan instructed Narayanan to fix the matter and said he should also have a word with Mamata Banerjee, the West Bengal chief minister. Leaving the meeting, Manmohan again stopped at the door.

"Maybe you should be governor of West Bengal," he said, and briskly made for the exit.

At that moment, Narayanan knew his long tenure in New Delhi spanning five decades was coming to a close. He went home and told his wife, Padmini, known to all as "Ammu", that something was afoot.

Still, when the announcement came in mid-January 2010 as a press release from the presidential palace late on a Saturday night, the Narayanans received it with shock and anger. The shock was the more severe because only a few months earlier, when Congress had surprised everyone by returning to power with stronger numbers, Narayanan had asked Manmohan if he should expect any changes in his role. The lease on his apartment in

Chennai, rented out to a software company, was coming up for renewal and if he were to retire, that would be the home he would return to. If he was not staying, he would not renew the lease. Manmohan had told him his services continued to be needed in New Delhi. Thus assured, Narayanan had renewed the tenancy and focused on his work.

According to people close to the couple, there was also a sense of betrayal that Shivshankar Menon had kept them out of the loop about his private chats with the prime minister, which clearly had taken place over several weeks. The Menons and the Narayanans went back decades. Narayanan's mother and Menon's paternal grandmother had been fast friends in New Delhi in the 1950s, often spending afternoons playing on the carom board and arguing about the score. Menon himself had been Narayanan's ward during his salad days at University of Delhi's St Stephen's College, when Narayanan was a rising star in the intelligence establishment. Perhaps Menon hesitated because he knew how much Narayanan liked the NSA position and would have fought to keep it.

The Pakistani and Chinese establishments welcomed the change in New Delhi, diplomatic sources told me at the time. Leaked US diplomatic cables also suggest that the US was not unhappy to see the new NSA, even as it had grown comfortable with Narayanan. "His tenure as Foreign Secretary, serving under then-external affairs minister Pranab Mukherjee, coincided with an unprecedented transformation in India's relationship with the United States, despite Menon having never served in or spent considerable time in the United States," read a January 22 cable from the mission. "He sees the strategic value of the U.S.-India relationship, but is not reflexively pro-American. He took a hard line on a variety of issues over the course of the civil nuclear cooperation agreement negotiations, including at a critical moment during the Nuclear Suppliers Group (NSG) deliberations, but also skillfully piloted critical decisions through the Indian bureaucracy. He expressed surprise that the FBI role in the investigation into the 26/11 Mumbai attacks did not generate more controversy, but thus reassured, later advocated a more robust cooperative relationship on counterterrorism.

Whatever his personal views, Menon is now invested in the success of the U.S.-India relationship and will be a formidable advocate for the relationship working directly under Prime Minister Singh."

Narayanan's departure to Kolkata, the West Bengal capital, marked not just the seeing off of a powerful bureaucrat but also a whittling down of the clout of the Malayalee gang, the latest regional cabal to have enormous influence in the upper echelons of the Indian government.

Malayalees get their name from Malayalam, the language of Kerala, India's most literate and socially advanced state. For this reason, they are often referred to as Mallus and the Indian media quickly tagged them Mallu mafia. In truth, almost every Congress government has been linked to purported cabals supposedly controlling the PMO. In Indira Gandhi's time, a Kashmiri "mafia" headed by the redoubtable diplomat PN Haksar held sway in her initial years in power. The head of RAW, the external intelligence arm that played so critical a role in dividing Pakistan and the emergence in 1971 of East Pakistan as the new nation of Bangladesh, was Rameshwar Nath Kao, also a Kashmiri. A bunch of intellectualised bureaucrats, this Kashmiri mafia was noted for a Left-leaning ideology and a deep belief in central planning. Educated at University of Allahabad – which was when he came into contact with the Nehru-Gandhis – as well as the London School of Economics, Haksar was never a communist as the Americans, particularly the Nixon administration, portrayed him to be. But he certainly had an anti-American streak in him. Haksar's influence in the PMO and the foreign office, then headed by TN Kaul, another Kashmiri, saw the Indira government tilt towards the Soviet Union, even if she herself, as recent research shows, had a more balanced view of the world.

After Haksar moved to the Planning Commission, another Kashmiri, PN Dhar, was appointed principal secretary to Mrs Gandhi, serving during her unpopular Emergency Rule between 1975 and 1977 – the only time democratic rights were suspended in free India. In her last stint in power though, from 1980 until her death in 1984, the Kashmir mafia had lost influence and she had picked a "Mallu" – PC Alexander – to be her principal secretary.

Likewise, in Rajiv Gandhi's time, the government was supposedly dominated by the "Doon mafia", a reference to the alumni of the boarding school in the Himalayan foothills where Rajiv had his secondary school education. Unlike the Kashmiri mafia of his mother's time, Rajiv's Doon School alumni, or Doscos, had few suspicions of private enterprise, and ranged from wealthy industrialists to bureaucrats, echoing the student intake of that great secondary school. The Doon mafia's influence endured, in muted fashion, during the Manmohan government as well, with Cabinet minister Kamal Nath and ministers of state Jyotiraditya Scindia and Jitin Prasada being its alumni.

In Manmohan Singh's first term, it was the Mallu mafia that dominated New Delhi. The key members of the Mallu mafia comprised a triumvirate of the principal secretary, TKA Nair, national security adviser JN Dixit and then-internal security adviser Narayanan. All had the rank of minister of state.

Beyond the PMO, the Mallu mafia also extended to Sonia Gandhi's household, where her key aides – PP Madhavan and Vincent George – were Malayalees. In the president's office, the top bureaucrat was another Malayalee, Christy Fernandes. The head of India's external intelligence agency, RAW, was Hormis Tharakan, a Malayalee. Mallus also held assorted slots in the higher bureaucracy. Despite their ominous label, the Mallus were generally recognised as a bunch of efficient individuals, combining deep loyalty with high levels of integrity and a prodigious capacity for hard work. Still, they were hardly a cohesive group. In my knowledge, the only time the top Mallus met socially in a substantial number was when civil aviation secretary Madhavan Nambiar organised a dinner at his home in early 2009, which was attended by Narayanan, Nair, home secretary Gopal Krishna Pillai and Shivshankar Menon along with their wives. Only the spouses of the last two were non-Malayalees.

The higher bureaucracy in India is dominated by the Indian Administrative Service. Ordinarily, Nair, who is from the 1963 batch of the service, should have been the natural leader of the pack because of his position, IAS pedigree and constant access to the prime minister. But he was junior in the civil service to both Dixit and particularly Narayanan, and did not have the personality to dominate either man. Besides, Nair was disadvantaged by the knowledge that he had not been Manmohan's first choice as principal secretary. That was Montek Singh Ahluwalia, a fellow economist and a Sikh. Montek, as all of India's inner circle refers to him, was highly regarded in international circles and was a key member of the IMF's self-evaluation group in the aftermath of the Asian financial crisis. At Davos, where the great and the good gather every year, he stands out and is known to almost every notable by his first name. He also knew his boss's mind, the kind of papers that tickled his imagination and was a sounding board for the scholarly Manmohan. His wife, economist Isher Judge Ahluwalia, was close to Gursharan Kaur, Manmohan's wife. But perceptions matter. Manmohan was told it would be politically unwise to have another Sikh in that critical office, and so, Ahluwalia was steered towards the Planning Commission, where he was deputy chairman with the rank of Cabinet minister.

The brilliant Dixit dominated in the initial months, partly because Narayanan was shuttling between New Delhi and Chennai, where Ammu Narayanan was caring for his aged mother. Both men had known each other for over four decades. When Dixit's name was considered for foreign secretary, prime minister Narasimha Rao had concerns about the man and initially had tilted towards CR Gharekhan to hold that office. But Narayanan had persuaded Rao to go for Dixit. Just after the 2004 election, when Manmohan was putting together his PMO, Narayanan, Sonia's nominee, had his pick of positions. Instead, he had suggested Dixit for NSA, himself taking the more modest internal security portfolio as he travelled back and forth to Chennai.

Still, despite the old ties, the two had soon begun to feud over turf. Dixit could not impose his will on Narayanan, and frequently felt outflanked. The pressure of the job also told on him. Sri Lanka's Chandrika Kumaratunga, visiting New Delhi in late 2004, was startled to see how poor Dixit looked as he sat near her at an official dinner.

"Mani," she told him, using Dixit's nickname, "you look terrible. Please see a doctor."

Dixit had waved it aside, insisting he was fine. A few weeks later, he was dead, felled by a massive heart attack. The NSA job migrated to Narayanan, who thereafter had been unchallenged in power and influence. Since he had initially been the Congress high command's nominee, Manmohan was known to be wary of the man, yet began to find him immensely useful. Most nights, Manmohan's last act of the day before turning in was to call Narayanan to check all was right with the nation and the world. Manmohan would find the NSA at his desk even at that late hour. Many of his former intelligence colleagues admired the way Narayanan had shed his spycatcher past and picked up a real knack for global affairs, flitting around the world, helping stitch up the nuclear deal. He had also been a big help to Manmohan in shoring up support for the ruling coalition after the Left parties ended their support and almost succeeded in toppling Manmohan. The scientists of the DAE seemed to trust him. Within the PMO, none, not even Manmohan, had his breadth of experience, institutional knowledge, or depth of contacts across the political and bureaucratic spectrum.

History has a knack of repeating itself, particularly in New Delhi. Observers of the Congress party's contemporary fortunes think the late Rajiv Gandhi's prime ministership started unravelling on January 20, 1987, the day he announced at a press conference that he was planning to replace his foreign secretary, AP Venkateswaran. The announcement was made casually, while responding to a question from a Pakistani journalist about a potential prime ministerial visit to his country.

"That's why you will soon be talking to a new foreign secretary," Rajiv had said, when questioned about an apparent contradiction between his words and those of his top diplomat.

Angered by the young man's impudence and crassness, Venkateswaran, a largely competent but blunt man who had been in the post just 10 months, resigned that very day. The young and untested prime minister – he was 42 at the time and not yet halfway into his tenure – walked into a fusillade of criticism over his impetuous nature, while Venkateswaran was hailed as a national hero who had not hesitated to speak truth to power.

While there was much to sympathise with Venkat, as he was known to friends and colleagues, the Indian Foreign Service officer was also capable of superciliousness and had made it untenable for Rajiv to let him stay on in the job. In private, he had often been patronising towards his political master. Once, summoned to discuss the application of a Foreign Service junior for permission to marry a foreign woman – Indian government rules at the time frowned upon it – Venkateswaran blew his top at the prime minister for not having sent the note back to the officer with instructions to follow proper channels and write first to the head of the Foreign Service, which was himself.

Rajiv, not big on protocol, did not quite understand the foreign secretary's outrage. That had angered Venkateswaran further.

"I would not have declined permission if he had asked me, Prime Minister," said Venkateswaran icily. "But don't you think he had the audacity to write you directly because your own wife is a foreigner?"

Venkateswaran had clearly gone too far with Rajiv Gandhi. Rajiv, whose intellect was considerably thinner than the older man's, was stunned and hurt at the obvious lack of respect from his bureaucratic underling. On the other hand, there was no denying that Venkateswaran had his uses; he had just organised a hugely successful visit by Soviet Union leader Mikhail Gorbachev, and delivered another big score by getting the United States to permit the sale and use of the Cray supercomputer, billed as a monsoon forecasting aid but in reality needed for India's strategic nuclear programme.

Rajiv let it go that time. Not too long after that he had summoned the foreign secretary to his residence on an urgent matter on a weekend. Venkateswaran had shown up smelling of alcohol, and on his way out, had tripped over the doorway. Rajiv, who was not known to drink, was pushed beyond the limits of his tolerance. He had turned that day to a friend and vowed to soon get himself a new foreign secretary. It was unfortunate that he chose a public forum to humiliate Venkateswaran. From that moment,

India's media would become unsparing of the handsome and well-meaning Gandhi, seeing him only as a high-handed princeling.

Twenty-three years after Rajiv's blunder, Manmohan, in a manner of speaking, had his own Venkateswaran moment in January 2010 when he put Narayanan out to grass by banishing him to the governor's mansion in West Bengal. As his government unravelled and was paralysed by scandal after scandal, the PMO lurched around like a skiff caught in a storm.

Fifteen months after Narayanan was banished to West Bengal, TKA Nair, the remaining pillar of the Mallu edifice in PMO, was moved out as well. The Gandhi family, alarmed at the government's precipitous slide, introduced its own nominee, Pulok Chatterji, as Manmohan's principal secretary. Nair, defanged but still the prime minister's man, was retained in PMO, as an adviser.

Both PMO and Congress could have used the services of the sure-footed Narayanan, if not his counsel, to control the damage and reach out to influential sections of the political class and media. A classic case was Andhra Pradesh, the biggest of the southern Indian states. There, when Congress badly bungled the succession after the death of its popular state chief minister, YSR Reddy, Narayanan's influence with the Reddy family – YSR respectfully always addressed him as "Narayanan-sir" – could have prevented the messy fallout from Sonia's refusal to allow YSR's controversial young son to succeed his father. Today, Andhra Pradesh, which sends 42 MPs to parliament, has been split into Telangana and the rump state of Andhra Pradesh. In what was once its southern bastion during YSR's time, Congress stands decimated.

As for Menon, his tenure as NSA did not quite end on the high note on which he had finished as foreign secretary. Tasked with three priorities – getting the civil nuclear deal with the US off the ground, normalising ties with neighbours, and improving cyber security – he failed to move the Indian establishment on the first count and had only limited success on the other two.

Colleagues in the MEA, who had long regarded him with admiration, were disappointed that once in the PMO, Menon seemed to have lost his lustre. He was too cautious, too much of a politician, they said. The military brass scoffed at an NSA quick to take out a little black notebook to jot down their demands, then seemed incapable of effecting a solution to the problems they took to him, particularly when it came to confronting the all too cautious defence minister, AK Antony. Neighbouring nations looked askance at an NSA who not only could not deliver on his promises, but also made about-turns. Sri Lanka, which faced deep criticism for its violent ending of the Tamil separatist war, was a case in point.

"Shankar Menon called me in March 2013 just before the UN human rights vote in Geneva and promised Indian support," Gotabhaya Rajapaksa, the Sri Lankan president's brother and defence secretary, told me. "He also said to let him know which countries seemed likely to vote against Sri Lanka so he could use Indian influence to stay their hand. When the vote came, we were most surprised to see India voting against us!"

Perplexed, Gotabhaya sought an explanation. It turned out that Minister for Home Affairs Chidambaram, whose political base is Tamil Nadu, had gone to Sonia Gandhi and pressed for the negative vote to assuage public opinion in his state, which has close ethnic ties to Sri Lanka's Tamil-dominated north. Unable to say no to the high command, Manmohan's PMO had simply keeled over and complied.

Towards the end of his tenure, Menon's credibility with his boss too would suffer. This was particularly evident after a serious Chinese incursion into the Ladakh region of Jammu & Kashmir state in April 2013, called the Depsang Incident. More than 30 Chinese troops penetrated some 20 km into what India considers its territory in the Depsang Valley, and stayed for three weeks. It was one of the most serious provocations on the uncharted border and nearly brought the two nations into a confrontation as India mobilised its own forces in response.

Menon suffered because he had always seemed more sanguine about China than other senior establishment figures, once dismissing talk of a Chinese "string of pearls" strategy in the Indian Ocean by calling a pearl necklace a "pretty poor murder weapon". As the evidence mounts of a Chinese push into the Indian Ocean, its ingress into India's strategic neighbourhood, and its unflinching support for Pakistan to keep India off balance, Manmohan may have wondered whether it would have been wiser to have retained the former policeman as his NSA, or handed the job to Shyam Saran instead.

11
Scamland India Speeds the Unravelling

> "There is zero loss to government from the 2G spectrum allocation."
>
> — Kapil Sibal

EARLY ON JANUARY 7, 2009, my cell phone rang and a familiar Singapore number displayed. It was Lai Kwok Kin, founder-director of the Singapore investor relations company, WeR1 Consultants. Lai and I had been friends for more than two decades - he had edited, and personally delivered my curriculum vitae to the editors of *The Straits Times* in April 1993 - and I responded with pleasure. He revealed that he was speaking from Hyderabad.

This itself did not surprise me; Lai is a Singaporean who has travelled in India more than most Indians would have. Whether it is the pepper trade of Kerala or the *kumbh mela* Hindu festival in Allahabad, Lai is curious, has visited the place or knows something about it, traits acquired during more than a decade's work for Reuters where he was a star correspondent in Asia, covering, among other big events, the Tiananmen Square revolt of 1989. There was unusual excitement in his voice.

"I am here in Hyderabad for a Satyam matter," he said. "What are your plans for the morning? I cannot tell you more at this point, but it would be worth your while to wait by the phone."

What followed a few hours later would rock India, dragging down the benchmark Sensex index and denting the rupee. Ramalinga Raju, founder and CEO of Satyam Computer Services, India's fourth biggest software company at the time, admitted that he had been cooking the books for years to show profits fatter than the actual numbers. In a letter to stock exchanges and Securities and Exchange Board of India (Sebi), the regulator, he accepted sole responsibility for the fraud, which amounted to misstating more than $1 billion of profit. He admitted that Satyam, which had 185 clients on the Fortune 500 list, had a balance sheet stuffed with "fictitious assets" and "non-existent" cash.

Satyam at the time had 53,000 employees, operated in 40 countries and had the largest presence of Indian software companies in Singapore. Clients, some of whom had been Satyam's clients for years, included Nestlé, General Electric and Qantas. Its proclivity to occupy tony addresses was legendary; in Australia, when the American giant, IBM, vacated prime office space downtown and moved to an area with lower rental, Satyam moved in to occupy the place it had vacated.

In an unprecedented show of contrition, Raju said he had tried to conceal the gaps and to plug them, including by attempting to inject the assets of two real estate companies linked to his family. However, the bid had failed the previous month under shareholder pressure.

"Every attempt made to eliminate the gap failed," said the 54-year-old Raju, who insisted that neither he nor his family had profited a rupee from the wrongdoing. "I am now prepared to subject myself to the laws of the land and to face the consequences."

Satyam (ironically, the name means "truth" in Sanskrit) was set up in 1987 with 20 employees as the quiet and understated Raju – so calm that Hyderabad society referred to him as the "man with the Mona Lisa smile" – sensed the opportunity in outsourced code writing. Within no time business was booming. Andhra Pradesh, of which Hyderabad is the capital, has one of the largest pools of skilled manpower. Satyam would prove a doughty competitor, pricing its services so aggressively that it seemed prepared to accept wafer-thin margins in order to attract customers. But once he sold shares to the Indian public in 1992 and on the New York Stock Exchange in 2001, pressure mounted to deliver high performance. And so he started to cook the books. According to Sebi, the regulator, from April 2003 through September 2008, more than 7,500 fake invoices were created. The orders were used to illustrate the origin of the company's ballooning bank balances. Satyam was declaring ever-growing bank balances in a number of local and international banks when the accounts' balances were in fact little changed. Oddly, PriceWaterhouseCoopers, the Satyam auditor, seemed to have no clue about the goings-on.

The news could not have come at a worse time for India. Word of the biggest accounting fraud by an Indian company reinforced the poor sentiment that had seeped in the previous year and led to a drain of $13 billion from the stock markets. India had also yet to recover from the shock of the Mumbai terror attack. On top of everything, the effects of the global financial crisis had begun to tell on the economy, which had at first seemed to be relatively insulated from that crisis.

When Virender Aggarwal, Satyam's hard-charging head of Asia Pacific, Middle East and Africa, got wind of the company's plight, his first instinct was to call Indian high commissioner S Jaishankar. The envoy to Singapore, now India's foreign secretary, caught the drift immediately and realised its global consequences – every Indian outsourcing company would come under negative scrutiny. Jaishankar quickly placed a call to Montek Singh Ahluwalia, the head of India's Planning Commission.

A former senior official with the IMF, Ahluwalia, a respected economist with a global view, was also prime minister Manmohan Singh's closest confidante in government. Ahluwalia quickly put into place a damage control operation in New Delhi. The government immediately barred Satyam's board from holding a scheduled meeting and said it would itself appoint 10 new directors, who would meet within a week. Ahluwalia's swift reaction – he immediately set up a task force to rescue the company and repair the damage – would eventually save the day for the Indian software industry's reputation.

But larger questions lurked behind the collapse of Satyam, and they fed back into the Congress party. At the time, one of the biggest financiers of Congress coffers was the Andhra Pradesh chief minister YS Rajasekhara Reddy, known to all as YSR. Corrupt but efficient, YSR had an iron grip on his state, which he ruled like a monarch, taking care only to pledge unquestioned fealty to the Gandhi family. His housing schemes for the disadvantaged were named after Indira Gandhi. A statewide ambulance service, styled along the 911 service, was a huge hit and contributed to his re-election in 2009. The ambulance service, now copied all over India, had been Raju's brainchild.

What Raju did not tell the world was that, on the evening before the day he confessed, he had called on YSR and briefed him on the company's plight. Raju and YSR were close; Raju's real estate firm, Maytas, which is Satyam spelt backward, had profited from several sweetheart deals bestowed by the YSR government. And Maytas, run by Raju's sons, controlled a considerable land bank in Hyderabad. The arrangements were so cosy that the previous September, E Sreedharan, the legendary railway engineer who also fathered the Delhi Metro Rail Corp, the Indian capital's showcase infrastructure project, had referred to the Maytas deal with the Andhra Pradesh government as a "scandal".

"Making available 120 hectares of prime land to BOT (build, operate and transfer) developer for commercial exploitation is like selling the family silver," he had charged. Despite Sreedharan's massive reputation, neither New Delhi, then run by the Manmohan government, nor Andhra Pradesh, run by Raju's friend, YSR, took note of the objection. In Hyderabad, everyone knew why. But then, that was the way Andhra Pradesh was run at the time.

The Satyam brouhaha did not affect Manmohan's government much. In the public mind, it was not associated with official-level corruption and was seen more as a case of an individual's ambition and greed leading him astray. The first scandal that stuck in the throat of Indians revolved around the 19th Commonwealth Games, the biggest sporting event the nation had hosted to date. Due to be held between October 3 and 14, 2010, the Games were scheduled to draw more than 70 nations and territories. The early stirrings of a controversy over the Games came in the manner of fears that the security arrangements were sloppy and inadequate. This was raising concern in countries such as Britain which were actively collaborating in the US war on terror in Afghanistan. The worries were not unfounded. Mumbai had been attacked by Pakistani terrorists the previous year. In March 2009 the Sri Lankan cricket team had also been attacked inside their tour bus in the Pakistani city of Lahore, leaving some of the visitors wounded and forcing them to cancel their tour to return to Colombo. Around the same time, Indian Minister for Home Affairs Chidambaram had said he would not be able to ensure security for the Indian Premier League cricket series because it clashed with the national elections. That led organisers, at short notice, to move the venue to South Africa. At the end of December 2009, 10 months before the Games were to open, Britain's *Daily Telegraph* quoted unnamed Whitehall sources saying there was "virtually no chance" that Britain would send a team to New Delhi. The *Daily Telegraph* report was a red herring; there was no way the Foreign and Commonwealth Office would lose the opportunity to see the Union Jack fly in the capital of India, the former jewel in the British Crown. But it served to draw attention to the shortcomings of the Games organisers.

To understand how Indians tend to be so last-minute in things, compared with the methodical way the Orientals operate for instance, you have to go for a big fat northern Indian wedding. The venues are booked months in advance but the last-minute scramble never ceases. Wedding homes are painted over, rooms lined up in guest houses, jewellery and clothes bought right up to the last day. Ultimately, though, things do move more or less to plan. There is dancing, much food, and at the end of it the bride weeps dutifully at leaving her parental home and everyone goes up for a good night's rest.

The Games were no different. With less than two weeks to the event, there were questions about whether it would go through at all. Leaking toilets, exposed electrical wires and construction debris littered the Games Village on the Yamuna riverbank. The New Zealand team, among the most vocal critics, were given fresh quarters after chef de mission David Currie lodged a strong protest. Commonwealth Games Federation chief Michael Fennell called the Village "seriously compromised". Adding to the embarrassment, a pedestrian bridge connecting the main stadium to a car park collapsed, injuring 27 people. The heaviest monsoon rains in three decades and the tight security thrown around the venues did not help matters.

Had the Games been away from the Indian capital, with its concentration of national and international media, it would have escaped the bad notice it got. But Indian newspapers and electronic media, angered over being misled by organisers that the facilities were near-perfect, were unsparing. Some described the Games as "falling apart" while others ran headlines such as "The Con Games" and "Shambolic Games".

Like a wart left unchecked, the Games emerged as a bigger and bigger scandal as the months progressed. The Indian Olympic Association, the organiser, had a total disconnect with the Delhi government, the implementing machinery. It also kept out the Ministry of Sports, leaving successive sports ministers sullen and ambivalent about the Games. The irony was that Delhi had seven years to prepare. Things should have moved smoothly since the Congress party was in power at both the federal and the Delhi state levels. And the Indian Olympic Association was led by a Congress MP. In 1982, when India hosted the Asian Games without a hitch, Indira Gandhi had been in power and her son, Rajiv, then an MP, took charge of the preparations, working with a handpicked team of officials. This time, the Gandhis kept a cool and deliberate distance from the Games.

In the end, though, the event passed without incident and the arrangements were even praised. "Delhi, you have delivered a truly exceptional Games, and above all, a wonderful experience for us all," Fennell gushed. The Punjabi wedding had indeed been pulled off.

Still, the mishandling of the Games and talk of widespread corruption in Games projects sealed a rising conviction in the minds of many Indians that Manmohan's government was in disarray, just 17 months into his second term. Suresh Kalmadi, the head of the Games organising committee who shouldered much of the blame, had a spectacular falling out with Sheila

Dikshit, the Delhi chief minister. Dikshit had said that a week before the Games, when she checked out the Village, she had discovered that 63 of the 75 lifts were not working. "The corruption charges are disturbing." Kalmadi countered that Dikshit should have reflected on the corruption in her own departments – while the Games committee had an operating budget of 16.2 billion rupees, the Delhi government's outlay for the infrastructure development had been 160 billion rupees. "We don't want to be scapegoats anymore," Kalmadi thundered.

The stench of corruption, always present in New Delhi, became all-pervasive. Over-invoicing was the norm with almost everything related to the Games. Some senior business figures in New Delhi told me they shied away from bidding for contracts for fear that in years to come they would be hauled into court for participating in the rigging of the various deals. It just wasn't worth the hassle, never mind the windfall gains to be made – and shared.

"The Games fiasco seals the deal on Singh's lack of effectiveness as PM," the analyst, Mahesh Rangarajan, ever on target, told me. "They are not going to throw him overboard, but he is emasculated."

Besieged by a deteriorating external environment as ties with Pakistan and China remained rocky, unsure how to tackle the popular revolt against Indian rule in the Kashmir Valley, and threatened by a Maoist menace tearing at the hinterland of the sprawling nation, Manmohan was groping for solutions. The close ties with the US that had been the hallmark of his foreign policy had also come slightly unglued with Barack Obama preoccupied with fixing the US economy and his own re-election. And now the event that Manmohan had said was meant to show India "rapidly marching ahead with confidence" was being held up as one that showed up everything that was wrong with India – slow decision-making, lack of consensus on important issues, widespread corruption and poor execution.

It wasn't just Manmohan who had suffered a knock to his reputation. India itself, a member of the G-20, the world's second fastest growing major economy with aspirations for a permanent seat on the UN Security Council, was deeply embarrassed. "We used to call Pakistan a failed state," one senior government figure told me at the time. "Now the worry is that we too will be put in the same category – albeit one with impressive economic growth."

And yet the bad news was only starting. In April came scandal laced with a little titillation. It involved cricket, the colonial game, and now the subcontinent's favourite sport, controlled from Mumbai, India's business capital and home of the Board of Control for Cricket in India (BCCI). The cricket board's pride and joy was the IPL, a mix of money, glamour and political power. India's richest man then, Mukesh Ambani, was an IPL team owner and so too was Vijay Mallya, who at the time ran the world's biggest whisky empire. BCCI chief N Srinivasan owned a team himself, the Chennai Super Kings, even though he was the game's regulator. Other team owners included movie stars Shah Rukh Khan and Preity Zinta. It was a party everyone sought to crash. Lalit Modi, a canny entrepreneur and head of the IPL cricket series, had vaulted the league, in just three years, into one of the world's richest sporting extravaganzas. At the time it was valued at 150 billion rupees, and rising by the day. Television viewership was doubling with every year – it passed 22 million rupees a day in 2009 – and with that rose the values of individual cricket franchises.

But Lalit, then only 46 years old and already recognised as a business genius, also controlled the league tightly, even seeking to decide who got the franchises. In this, he had a falling out with Shashi Tharoor, the flashy minister of state for external affairs and one-time aspirant for the post of UN secretary-general. Lalit revealed on Twitter that the winning bid for one of two new successful franchises that would take the number of participating teams to 10 had gone to a consortium headed by Rendezvous Sports World. It then appeared that the promoters of Rendezvous had given part of the stake franchise to a Dubai-based woman named Sunanda Pushkar. That equity was valued at several million dollars. In no time, India's alert journalists had identified Pushkar as the woman seen with Tharoor in recent months.

Tharoor swiftly denied he was a beneficiary, but the taint would not go away. Pushkar quickly offered to return the "sweat equity" as she called it, and Tharoor insisted he had only been "mentoring" the consortium, and even then, only to steer the franchise to Kochi, the bustling port city in his home state of Kerala. Despite Tharoor's protestations of innocence, the BJP attacked him, its spokesmen describing Pushkar as a "parking lot or parking bay [sic]" for Tharoor. On April 22, Manmohan met Sonia for nearly an hour. Late at night, Tharoor was summoned to Manmohan's house and told he had to go. In fury, the government rounded on Lalit Modi for exposing the scandal. He was suspended as chairman and commissioner of IPL and nearly two dozen charges of improper dealings were laid against him. His woes would not end there. He was also bounced out of BCCI, the body that governs the sport that he had powered into a billion dollar operation. Tharoor became the first minister in the UPA-2 government to be forced out on corruption charges. Sadly for him, and for Manmohan, who had taken such an interest in this intellectual-politician, he would not be the last.

Within a year of his remarkable return to power, Manmohan was on the ropes. The first setback had come in the ministry formation itself, when Manmohan was unable to keep tainted communication and information technology minister Raja out of the Cabinet. The compulsions of coalition politics – Raja was from DMK, the Congress party's biggest coalition partner – stayed the prime minister's hand. Manmohan could not even move him to another portfolio. The fiasco over the controversial joint statement in Sharm-el-Sheikh after talks with Pakistan was a big stumble. With even his Congress party keeping a stony silence on the issue, Manmohan was left high and dry. On the economic front, inflation was running rampant, reflecting poorly on Manmohan's reputation even as an economist.

Yet the bigger scandals were only brewing, and some of them were a legacy of decisions from his first term. In May, when the government completed the auction of its 3G mobile phone spectrum, it made a $14.6 billion windfall, nearly twice the amount projected in the annual budget. The success of the 3G auction focused attention all over again on the sale of the spectrum for 2G licences two years earlier, at what suddenly looked like throwaway prices. The 2G licences issued between December 2007 and January 2008 earned the government less than $3 billion. The comptroller and auditor general (CAG), who probed the sale, estimated that Raja's arbitrary methods in issuing licences may have cost the Treasury as much as 1.76 trillion rupees (about $40 billion then) in revenue. Ignoring expert advice from the finance and law ministries to auction the licences, Raja had gone for a "first come, first served" method. It was said that cronies of the telecom minister were making windfall gains. One example cited in the CAG report involved a prominent real estate firm, which got a licence in 2007, apparently in violation of the company's own articles of association. This firm paid just 16 billion rupees for the licence and, within no time, had flipped a controlling two-thirds stake to a European group for a 62 billion rupee windfall.

Raja's defence was that under his watch, phone connections in the country had risen from 300 million to 700 million, while call rates on mobile services had dropped to a quarter of the previous rate. And then, there was his clinching argument: he had kept the PMO informed at every stage of the licensing process. Subramaniam Swamy, a maverick politician known to expose many a scandal, had written to the prime minister seeking permission to prosecute Raja – in India, ministers can only be sued if the prime minister permits it, and he has a three-month window to grant or decline the permission – but Manmohan had sat on the file for 16 months. Swamy then went to the Supreme Court, which roundly criticised Manmohan, saying his actions, or lack of, were "troubling". Ultimately, the Supreme Court cancelled most of the licences.

Raja was finally forced out in November 2010 but by then it was more or less all over for the Manmohan government. In a trenchant editorial that summed up the situation, the financial daily, *Mint*, said: "India is fast turning into a corrupt oligarchy with bleak economic and political prospects. Raja may have caused immense damage in the telecom sector, but don't be surprised if he looks like an angel when bigger scams break out." The editorial would turn out to be prescient.

Manmohan, upright and honest, would end his decade in power noted not for the good he did for India but for all its blights, particularly the odium of having presided over possibly the most corrupt period in its history.

To be fair, the decay had been building up over the decades, starting with Nehru's time. From the first election after Independence, moneybags had begun to supplant freedom fighters in grabbing tickets to parliament and state assemblies, PS Krishnan, a highly respected bureaucrat from the 1956 batch of the IAS told me, as he sketched out the decades. Nehru had largely ignored the corruption of political figures like Pratap Singh Kairon of Punjab and Bijayanandra, or "Biju", Patnaik of Odisha because he saw them as robust men who could deliver results. The rot spread during the time of Indira Gandhi, Nehru's daughter. V Krishnamurthy, a legendary figure in the Indian public sector – he headed Bharat Heavy Electricals, Steel Authority of India and Maruti Udyog in turn – said Indira had demanded of the chiefs of state-run companies that they help supply party funds by raking off the top of inflated contracts. "Mrs Gandhi used to say, 'I don't want corruption to seep to the levels of the police inspector, so I want you fellows to provide me the money in a way that the commoner doesn't see or is affected by it,'" Krishnamurthy told me once.

Naturally, not all the money so skimmed reached the party. To buy the silence and cooperation of ministers and bureaucrats, everyone got a slice in descending order. This found their way into foreign bank accounts in tax havens, many opened in the names of family pets or cattle. Global Financial Integrity, a Washington-based advocacy group, estimated that in the 40 years since 1948, some $462 billion in illicit money flowed out of India, amounting to twice the external debt of $230 billion. Between 2004 and 2008, $19 billion flowed out of India every year.

The sobering aside to the scandals was how much the scale of the alleged corruption had changed over the years. More than three decades earlier, Raja's party boss, Muthuvel Karunanidhi, then chief minister of Tamil Nadu, had faced prosecution over a bribe of 100,000 rupees for a pipeline contract. The scandal over the payoffs linked to the purchase of artillery from Bofors AB, which cost Rajiv Gandhi his prime ministership in 1989, involved 640 million rupees. Now, the loss to the government over the 2G spectrum sales supervised by Raja was being touted at as much as 1.76 trillion rupees.

And it wasn't just the politicians and the bureaucracy. The decay had spread to India's most hallowed institutions, the military and the judiciary. In February 2011, lieutenant general PK Rath, a three-star general who was formerly deputy chief of the Army, was found guilty of corruption in a land deal. His seniority and pension was reduced days before his retirement (the decision was reversed in 2014 by the Armed Forces Tribunal). The Army chief he served, Deepak Kapoor, was only doing slightly better in retirement. His name featured on the list of people awarded apartments at concessionary rates at a high-rise in Mumbai's most expensive district, which was initially meant for war widows and veterans of the 1999 Kargil conflict with Pakistan. Also on the list of beneficiaries was the former Indian Navy chief, admiral Madhvendra Singh.

Indians had always looked upon the judiciary as an island in a sea of corruptibility. But even here, dark spots had appeared. In September 2010, Shanti Bhushan, a legal luminary and former law minister, intervened in a Supreme Court case and filed an affidavit saying he believed eight of the 16 previous chief justices of India had been "definitely corrupt".

Overseas Indians, always the pride and joy of the home country, were also doing their share to dent India's reputation. In October 2011, Rajat Gupta, the iconic management guru and former head of McKinsey & Co, was arrested and charged with six counts of insider trading in the biggest such scandal to hit corporate America. Just two years earlier, Gupta, an alumnus of the Indian Institute of Technology and Harvard Business School, was toasted as one of the faces of New India – a whiz from a middle-class background who rose to global fame as the head of 8,000 consultants at McKinsey. The US Securities and Exchange Commission charged him with illegally tipping off a brilliant Sri Lankan-born fund manager named Raj Rajaratnam, on the internal discussions of Procter & Gamble and Goldman Sachs, on whose boards he sat. Gupta denied every allegation but in July 2012, the Federal District Court of Manhattan found him guilty for conspiracy and securities fraud. The case was built largely on circumstantial evidence.

Gupta, who had stepped down as head and was now senior partner emeritus at McKinsey, was the biggest name of the 70-odd Wall Street figures prosecuted by Preet Bharara, the US Attorney in Manhattan, who, like Gupta, was an emigre from India. A year later, Dominic Barton, then head of McKinsey, told Vikram Khanna, my colleague at Singapore's *The Business Times*, that the firm had sent a director to tell Gupta that he could no longer identify himself with the firm or use any of its facilities. It was a sad end to a spectacular career, marked with several stellar contributions both to his land of adoption and the land of his birth.

By the time 2011 rolled around, Manmohan's stewardship of India had gone lame. The government was wilting. Maoist violence claimed 998 lives in 2010 alone. From the boast of imminent double-digit expansion, the talk was of a return of the hated "Hindu rate of growth", the term used to describe a rate of expansion that had stagnated at 3.5% or less in the first decades after Independence. Food inflation was running at close to 15%, a huge tax on the third of India that lived in poverty. Investors who had pumped a record $28 billion into Indian financial markets in 2010 were now pulling their money out. Agriculture productivity was lagging way behind industrial productivity because of the state's unwillingness to countenance reform, for fear of political repercussions. The Mumbai Sensex was the world's worst performing index after Cairo's benchmark. Investors were pulling money out of India and Indians themselves were finding better investment prospects overseas, rather than at home. Outward foreign direct investment was nearly a third more than inward flows, rare for an economy at its stage of development.

The tragedy was that 2011 marked the 20th anniversary of Manmohan's market opening reforms that placed India firmly on the global stage, or as the Confederation of Indian Industry's Tarun Das put it, "the fall of India's Berlin Wall". Oddly enough, both the government and the Congress party were cool to the anniversary, as though they did not wish to be reminded about it. One reason was that it was Narasimha Rao who presided over that period. Sonia had come to detest the man before his death, forcing him out of the party leadership. The other reason was that Congress was worried that the poorer sections of India did not appreciate the reforms, and indeed, might be resentful of the changes they brought. Hence, celebration of the reforms would dilute its common man image.

Even the industry titans who had gained most from reform were in a phase of deep introspection. Ratan Tata, India's most respected industry figure, was voicing fears that India could "degenerate into that banana republic kind of atmosphere unless necessary parts of government play their part in upholding the law". Foreign policy pundits worried about the impact on India's security. Brahma Chellaney, who is one of India's top strategic affairs experts, put it this way: "When the head is rotten and putrid, the body cannot be healthy. India's ability to secure its interests is being undermined by the deterioration of the state."

Manmohan's response to all this bordered on the pathetic. Speaking to a group of select television editors in his home in a rare appearance before media, he sought to explain his predicament in what he called the "coalition dharma". "In coalition politics, one has to tolerate a lot or risk going in for elections every six months. Some compromises have to be made in running a coalition government and those issues have to be viewed against a context in which no single party has emerged that can rule by itself."

His explanation was received with scorn. The Commonwealth Games fiasco could not be blamed on coalition politics, nor the Army housing estate scandal in which most beneficiaries were linked to Congress. But many Indians would have picked up on the message about single-party rule, and act decisively in the next general election. What's more, when they looked around, not all was bad. Surprisingly, many Opposition-ruled states appeared to be doing well. BJP states were being held up as a beacon of efficiency and good government, including Madhya Pradesh and the mostly tribal Chhattisgarh. And of course, there was Gujarat, run by Narendra Modi.

12
Dodgy Defence: India Sinks Yet Another Navy Chief

"The worst defence minister ever."

— Headline of an *India Today* magazine special report in March 2014

ON THE MORNING of February 26, 2014, admiral Devendra Kumar Joshi was in his Rajaji Road bungalow scanning the morning newspapers when he got first word – signal, in navy parlance – of an accident on board the submarine, *Sindhuratna*, while it was being put through trials in the Arabian Sea. It was the second accident on a Kilo Class sub in eight months for a navy that had been going through an unprecedented and breathless expansion for the past decade.

As he digested the news, he thought back on a 40-year naval career where he had excelled in every command. The first of those commands was on a guided missile Corvette, his second a guided missile Destroyer, and his sailing days had ended on a high, on the aircraft carrier *Viraat*. As his career progressed and he won his third star, he had been appointed CINCAN, or Commander-in-Chief of the Andaman & Nicobar Command. After that, he was what in the Navy is known as C-in-C (West), short for Commander-in-Chief, Western Naval Command, the No. 1 strike arm of the Indian Navy which focuses on threats from the Arabian Sea, chiefly Pakistan.

Joshi, the son of a top forest conservator with roots among the hill folk of the lower Himalayas – the Army's Kumaon Regiment, which comprises men drawn from these parts, is the highest decorated – was the first in seven generations of his family to choose the Navy or even the military, as a career. He was also the first to rise so high from the Indian Naval Academy in Kochi, which has since relocated to Goa; previous chiefs had all come through the National Defence Academy near Pune. To the surprise of his peers, "Joe" had always managed to speak truth to power, and gotten away with it. An impressive list of decorations had come his way, testimony to his professionalism, patriotism and integrity.

As his career progressed, and particularly in his last decade as he moved from two-star to three, and finally, four-star admiral, the very top of the chain, his dwellings had been more and more impressive. In Port Blair, capital of the Andaman & Nicobar islands, he had a commanding view of the sea from his hilltop bungalow. In Mumbai, the C-in-C's home had been a heritage property sitting on acres of priceless real estate next to the Taj Mahal Palace hotel in Colaba. Now at the apex of his service career, he was ensconced in the sumptuous bungalow in central New Delhi earmarked for the Chief of Naval Staff. Not bad for the boy from the Garhwal mountains, where a modest cottage, his retirement home, had been ready for a few months. Joshi pulled on his pipe as his mind ticked over. It was to be the start of a momentous day.

A little after he reached his office two hours later, the vice chief of the Navy, vice admiral Robin Dhowan, came to brief him on the accident at sea. While the submarine was underwater, there had been a fire, three decks above where the submarine batteries – initially thought of as the equipment that had malfunctioned – were located. To save the men trapped in the chamber, the sub's commanding officer had bravely entered the place but, in his haste, had forgotten the standard operating procedure of donning a gas mask. In seconds, the fumes had overwhelmed the man and he now lay gasping for life in a Mumbai hospital where a Navy helicopter had ferried him from the stricken submarine. Two officers were dead and several sailors were injured. It was just awful. "You have to brief the RM, sir," Dhowan told him, using the abbreviation for Raksha Mantri, or defence minister.

Joshi nodded, and dismissed his deputy. Unknown to Dhowan at the time, the chief's mind was already made up. Strict observance of standard operating procedures is imperative in any high technology environment, and it was clear, even without the routine board of inquiry that would doubtless follow, that the submarine's officers had been imprudent, even as they had shown exemplary courage. In the past year, Joshi had ordered nearly a dozen officers stripped of their command over a series of accidents, some trivial, as he sought to crack down on indiscipline and poor leadership.

Not having fought a real war in more than four decades, military standards had been slipping, including that in the Navy. In early 2008, the troop landing ship, *Jalashwa*, the former USS *Trenton* acquired only the previous year, had suffered an accident at sea, with the loss of five lives. In January 2011, 18 months before Joshi was elevated as chief, the frigate *Vindhyagiri* had slammed into a box carrier at the mouth of Bombay Harbour, and sunk to the ocean floor. A year into his charge, *Sindhurakshak*, a Kilo Class submarine that was being loaded up with torpedoes and missiles for a regular patrol mission off Karachi, suffered fatal explosions and sank at the pier of the naval docks, embarrassing the armed forces. Eighteen people died in the *Sindhurakshak*, which had just returned from an expensive refit in Russia, meant to prolong its service life. Those in the Navy knew that poor observance of missile handling protocols had caused the blast. There had also been a series of smaller incidents, including a fire on board the aircraft carrier, *Viraat*.

As much as he had tried to defend the service from criticism, Joshi knew that the buck rested on his desk. While no service chief would admit it, backroom duels to seek parity with the civil service – promotions to the level of commander today are timescale-bound with merit-based promotions only kicking in for selections for captain and higher – had worked against the quality of officers in each of the services. The aggravation had been mounting after a series of pinpricks from the Ministry of Defence (MOD): the previous November, he had been stung by defence minister AK Antony's comment at a naval commanders meeting, that the Navy ought not to "fritter away valuable national resources". Senior ministry bureaucrats had worked in that line to slight the forthright naval chief, knowing an alert media would pick it up and go to town with it after the series of accidents involving naval assets.

Some of the "accidents" were trivial, and in some cases, the fault, if any, had to be laid at the door of the government, not the Navy. For instance, in early February, the landing ship tank, *Airawat*, a frontline warship used to land troops on beachheads, suffered damage to its propellers because of inadequate dredging of the Visakhapatnam harbour. The plain-spoken Joshi had not helped his cause by staying aloof from journalists – indeed, there were official instructions from his office to the Navy to avoid contact with a top correspondent from a television news channel known for its aggressive and sensationalist reporting style. The defence correspondent of *The Indian Express*, who had run a series of negative stories on the Navy, had not been invited to that year's Navy Day soirée. Just days before, the paper had run a big story listing the naval accidents. With little sympathy for the Navy chief, the media thus feasted on every misfortune suffered by the Navy, sometimes failing to add perspective by comparing it with the service record of the other arms, particularly IAF, which had a longer list of expensive accidents.

What's more, Joshi knew full well that Antony would not have dared to use phrases like "fritter away resources" with the Army chief. Indeed, Antony had abjectly swallowed a series of provocations from general VK Singh, who had even moved the Supreme Court to take on the MOD, which had resisted his attempt to alter his official date of birth in a poorly disguised effort to delay his retirement.

The Navy, despite the swift expansion in recent times, is the smallest of the services, and with its assets based along the coastline, it poses little threat from any rogue action against the civilian government. That made it easier to bully, and it had been bullied before. In 1998, the Atal Bihari Vajpayee government had fired admiral Vishnu Bhagwat after the Navy chief, widely regarded as a visionary officer whose impact on the force continues to be felt to this day, had refused to heed the government's prodding on the appointment of the deputy chief of naval staff. The three-star admiral, although well-regarded within the service, had earned Bhagwat's ire by enlisting the support of the Akali Dal party, a coalition ally of Vajpayee's BJP, to push his case. Bhagwat had other quirks that had also irritated the government – he once engaged a visiting head of state in conversation when all he was supposed to do was line up with his fellow service chiefs to shake her hand. Unlike Bhagwat though, Joshi could never be faulted on protocol, or for pushing himself to the forefront.

All these factors played in Joshi's mind as he contemplated the step he was about to take and weighed its consequences. On the one hand, he still had 18 months left to finish his tenure in a national capital where bureaucrats and military wheels cling on to office until the last day, hoping to be extended in service or be thrown crumbs like a post-retirement governorship or ambassadorial posting. His daughters, Pallavi and Purba, had not been settled yet. There was also the strain he would put on his wife, Chitra, if he decided to leave suddenly. Yet his entire training pointed him in another direction. In his junior years as a midshipman and lieutenant, he had seen heroic captains protect their juniors from the wrath of senior brass. When a particularly tough admiral cracked the whip, the captain would step in to take the blame for the younger men's lapses. The Navy knew that if youngsters didn't make mistakes, they would never learn. That is how his seniors had raised him in the service. Too honest to ignore the wider circumstances, he knew it was time to go.

Joshi asked his secretary to connect him to Chitra, who just then was preparing to receive more than 200 wives of retired senior naval officers at a lunch she was hosting in the Navy House garden. He described the situation, explained the need to take moral responsibility, and added a final word – do not speak to anyone about this until the official announcement is made. Late that night, the women who had enjoyed Chitra Joshi's hospitality that pleasant afternoon would marvel at this no-nonsense woman's composure, – she was smiling through the afternoon as she looked after her guests, even as her mind was in torment for her husband and the step he was taking.

Joshi next summoned Jayashree, the woman who had served as personal secretary to four Navy chiefs, and dictated a three-paragraph letter of resignation. Ignoring her tears and her entreaties that previous chiefs had gone through worse without quitting, he ordered her to type it up and make copies. A few minutes later, he walked into defence minister AK Antony's room and briefed him on the accident. At the end of the briefing, Joshi took out the letter and handed it to the minister, who sat back stunned, as though Joshi had struck him.

"You don't have to do this, Admiral," Antony whispered.

What followed in the next few hours would seal Antony's reputation as India's "Worst defence minister ever", the headline of a special report on Antony's record in the March 17 edition of *India Today*, the nation's most widely read news weekly. Joshi's resignation letter sped through the bureaucracy and the PMO. President Pranab Mukherjee, himself a former defence minister and now the nation's titular commander-in-chief, was informed. There was no attempt to convince the gallant and upright officer to withdraw his resignation. Yet, eight years earlier, when Mukherjee himself held the defence portfolio, then Navy chief Arun Prakash had offered to quit over a far more serious issue – the War Room Leak scandal where Prakash's nephew, a former naval officer, was accused of illegally procuring naval secrets, including details of plans to make Scorpene submarines, on behalf of arms companies. At the time, Mukherjee and then-national security adviser MK Narayanan had firmly rejected the offer, saying Prakash had no culpability in the matter and should continue. Indeed, vice admiral Sureesh "Faggy" Mehta, then deputy chief of naval staff and the officer directly in charge of the War Room, suffered no damage to his career, eventually succeeding Prakash when the latter was superannuated.

Joshi's resignation, and its hasty acceptance, would have been justified if the poor record on accidents was unique to the Navy. According to MOD figures given to parliament, no less than 28 planes and 14 helicopters of the IAF had crashed since the start of 2011, by no means a small number. Half the IAF crashes involved MiG aircraft and the causes were depressingly similar to the Navy's accident record; outdated equipment, poor quality of spares and fuel, and, of course, human error.

Yet, the Navy chief was left spinning in the wind. Many people in top positions simply looked away. Shivshankar Menon, the NSA, did not ask Joshi to see him nor did he pick up the telephone for a farewell chat, either on the day of the resignation itself or in the weeks to come. Instead, the Indian government moved with unseemly – and unusual – alacrity to accept the resignation. It was almost as though there was widespread relief that the defence bureaucracy, and the minister, could find someone willing to shoulder the blame for everything that had gone wrong with the services under Antony's charge – the poor preparedness of the forces, slow acquisitions caused by indecision, cancellation of contracts and whimsical blacklisting of defence contractors over the tiniest suspicion that they may have paid speed money or kickbacks.

And indeed, the stagnation and rot under Antony had been severe during the seven years and seven months he served as defence minister, the longest any single person had held that position in post-Independence India. The reasons for the stagnation and ministerial inertia were many, but two took particular importance. First, India's bureaucrats as a class had turned immensely cautious since 2005 when the Manmohan government passed the Right to Information Act on Sonia Gandhi's prodding. RTI significantly relaxed the Official Secrets Act and enabled any citizen to petition for documents after paying a paltry fee. Scared of the consequences, bureaucrats simply kept files pending with notes such as "Please discuss" and "Needs further examination". Secondly, in the MOD, things were made worse by Antony's abhorrence of scandal. At the slightest hint, sometimes from rumours started by an arms contractor who had lost a bid to a rival, that grease money had been paid for a contract, Antony would stall the acquisition or even seek to blacklist the supplier.

The most egregious case was the blacklisting of seven vendor firms, including Singapore Technologies Kinetics and Israel Military Industries, after Sudipto Ghosh, the head of India's Ordinance Factory Board, was nabbed by the CBI on corruption charges. ST Kinetics had been in the shortlist to supply ultralight howitzers, which were badly needed by the Indian Army to bolster its defence on both the Chinese and Pakistani frontiers. The mainstay of India's artillery, cannons made by Bofors AB – so controversial when they were purchased in the mid-1980s that it caused Rajiv Gandhi's government to stall – were on their last legs and needed urgent replacement. The Indian Army had loved ST Kinetics' Pegasus gun after it had conducted field trials. It was just the weapon needed on the China border. Yet, Antony would not relent or accept ST Kinetics' denials that it had participated in bribery. The Singapore company, keen to get its first big defence contract in India, offered to open its books for inspection by the Indian authorities. Antony did not take up the offer. To clear its name, ST Kinetics filed a suit against the Ministry of Defence in the Delhi High Court, hiring Harish Salve, India's most expensive lawyer, to represent it. That judgment has not yet been delivered. The howitzer deal finally went to British defence company BAE Systems in February 2016.

It wasn't weapons purchases alone. As any strategic thinker knows, one way to bolster defence is by showing you have powerful friends willing to come to your aid in a crisis. That is defence diplomacy. Richard Nixon rattled India in 1971, when India was at war with Pakistan, by ordering the Seventh Fleet to sail into the Bay of Bengal. But even defence diplomacy suffered because of Antony's morbid fear of irritating China, especially when it came to multilateral exercises. In 2007, the first time the Navy announced plans to hold Exercise Malabar with the US and other friendly navies in the Bay of Bengal, Antony hit the roof, recalled a three-star admiral, now retired. Left parties led by the CPM, always sympathetic to China, were supporting the Manmohan government in New Delhi at the time. Coming from Kerala, where the principal opposition to the Congress party came from the CPM, Antony was hugely sensitive to their politics. CPM chief Prakash Karat was threatening to march from Kolkata to Vishakhapatnam, the Bay of Bengal port city that is home to the Eastern Fleet, if Exercise Malabar went through. Antony was shaken.

"Malabar is an area in Kerala, which is off the Arabian Sea coast. How can we hold Exercise Malabar on the other side of the peninsula, in the Bay of Bengal?" he demanded of admiral Mehta. "Have you thought through how the Chinese are going to react to all this?"

Mehta stood his ground. He countered that Exercise Malabar 2007 was too far gone in the planning to be pulled back and Antony had to relent. And thus, the exercise went through. Joined by the American carrier, USS *Kitty Hawk*, the US, Japanese, Australian and Singapore navies participated in the exercise with the Indian Navy between September 4 and 9 in a vast stretch of sea from Vishakhapatnam to the Andaman Islands. On the deck of the Indian carrier, *Viraat*, stood vice admiral Raman Prem Suthan, the C-in-C of the Eastern Command, who, as defence adviser in the Indian High Commission in Singapore in 1994, had initiated the joint Anti Submarine Warfare exercises between India and Singapore that would turn into a close strategic embrace. Now the Singapore Navy was in a strategically significant exercise with the Indians. Suthan was pleased.

What explains Antony's behaviour? As he increasingly took on the tag of "Saint Antony", particularly in Manmohan's second term, some saw lurking ambition in the diminutive figure from Kerala. Perhaps he secretly longed to be prime minister. Antony had stood in for Manmohan at the January 2009 Republic Day parade, when the prime minister was recuperating after tricky heart surgery, and he seemed to have enjoyed the moment. Given the prime minister's thin skin, there was a good chance that the man, fearful of losing his own reputation for probity amid the scandals that engulfed his second term, might quit office abruptly. Should that come to pass, who more politically acceptable in a time of widespread scandal than super-clean Antony, never mind that he did not speak the national language, Hindi, or that his English was not easy to follow? Hence, the more defence contractors blacklisted for seedy doings, the better for him.

What about his soft-gloved approach to general VK Singh, the Army chief? Antony's troubles with general Singh would not end with the Supreme Court chiding the general into withdrawing his case against the government. In March 2012, as he prepared to demit office, India's media seized upon the startling leak of a letter the soldier had addressed to the prime minister, detailing the woeful state of the military's preparedness. The Army's tanks had run out of ammunition, the air defence was 97% obsolete and the infantry was short of critical equipment, general Singh complained. The letter went on to say that "the state of the major (fighting) arms, i.e. Mechanised Forces, Artillery, Air Defence, Infantry and Special Forces, as well as the Engineers and Signals, is indeed alarming". Blaming the "hollowness" in the system as a result of the procedural encumbrances for procurement, general Singh's letter went on to request the prime minister to pass suitable directions to enhance the preparedness of the Army. It was the nadir of military-civil relations.

The vitiated atmosphere in New Delhi between the military and the civilian administration was probably best exemplified by a news report in *The Indian Express* in April 2012, which suggested that in January that year, on the night that general Singh approached the Supreme Court over the issue of his age, the establishment had been spooked by the mysterious movement of two Army units towards the national capital.

India, unlike neighbouring Pakistan and Bangladesh, or other significant Asian nations such as Myanmar, Thailand and Indonesia, has never been under military rule. The forces have been professional from the start. Soldiers have never emerged from the barracks except at the command of the civil administration. *The Indian Express* report said a unit of mechanised infantry left its base in Mathura, a town southwest of New Delhi, and advanced towards the capital in what the paper described as a "non-notified" movement. At the same time, another unit of parachute commandos, stationed further south in Agra, had also begun to move towards New Delhi. Alarmed, New Delhi put out a terror alert and ordered all vehicles on the highway to be stopped for checking, a tactic meant to delay traffic. The report went on to say that defence secretary Shashi Kant Sharma, then visiting Malaysia, rushed back to New Delhi and demanded an explanation from the Army. He was told that this was routine training to test preparedness for the Army to move quickly in foggy conditions. Not satisfied, the defence secretary nevertheless ordered the troops to be sent back.

The Indian Express report carried the bylines of its then editor in chief, Shekhar Gupta, and two other top writers, Pranab Dhal Samanta and Ritu Sarin. The report could not be dismissed lightly. Sarin, particularly, was renowned for her diligent fact-checking. Moreover, it was widely whispered in military circles that general Singh had packed several key appointments with officers from his own regiment, the Rajputs. Since loyalties run deep in the Army, the suggestion was that general Singh had enough senior officers around him who would follow instructions unquestioningly, should he have wanted to do mischief.

Even so, the story did not make sense on two counts, as a serving chief of staff, who is no friend of general Singh's, explained to me at the time.

Firstly, if general Singh had been trying to pressure New Delhi over the issue of his age, he had chosen the wrong time – the matter had gone to the Supreme Court and was well out of the hands of the civilian establishment. Surely, he wasn't attempting to spook the judges! Secondly, if general Singh needed to sound a warning rattle, he didn't need to move troops from so far away. There were plenty of infantry and mechanised units already in the capital, preparing for the Republic Day parade on January 26.

Publicly, Antony dismissed the speculation that followed the report, describing the movements as a "routine training exercise". He then waited for general Singh to retire, choosing not to confront the Army chief while he still held the post. In those final months of his tenure, the general prepared his launch into politics, giving media interviews critical of the administration and building up his base among the warrior caste of Rajputs. It was as though he was taunting the civilian administration to fire him.

Admiral Bhagwat had been fired over issues far less severe, but the Congress-led government would handle general Singh with kid gloves. It did not have the nerve to call the soldier's bluff, or warn him to stop leaking to the media. On the sidelines of the annual Shangri-La Dialogue in Singapore that year, I asked Antony why he had been so timid around general Singh.

"Don't you think that was the least painful way to deal with the nuisance?" he responded. Perhaps the course he adopted was indeed the right one at the time, although there were many who thought he should have made a firmer point.

The informed opinion was divided on the issue, but a year later, Antony's response to another incident left the nation and its entire armed forces heavily incensed. This was the brutal killing of five Indian soldiers along the Line of Control with Pakistan, authorised at the highest levels of the Pakistani Army, as reliable Pakistani sources told me later. The bodies of the soldiers from India's Bihar Regiment had been beheaded when rescue parties along the Line found them on the morning of August 6, 2013. It was an act of barbarity calculated to shock the Indians. The Indian Army issued a statement through its Northern Command in Jammu that the ambush on the Indians had been carried out by members of the Pakistani Border Action Team, aided by the Pakistani Army. That statement was hurriedly withdrawn a few hours later on orders from New Delhi. Antony went before parliament the following day to say that "20 heavily armed terrorists along with persons in Pakistani Army uniform" were responsible for the killings.

The phrasing appeared deliberately vague in order to offer the Pakistanis an element of deniability. To most Indians, it appeared that their defence minister simply did not have the nerve to confront his enemy. There could not have been a bigger let-down for the forces.

In the event, a high-ranking delegation of the BJP met prime minister Manmohan Singh to register their protest over Antony's soft approach. Cornered, Antony went before both houses of parliament to issue a fresh statement clarifying that a specialist group of the Pakistani Army was involved in the attack and that ties with Islamabad would be reviewed. He justified his earlier statement by saying that the incident had happened early in the day and he had not wished to "jump to conclusions".

It is possible that Antony, already under pressure from aggressive Chinese patrolling along that disputed frontier, didn't want to open a tricky second, Pakistani, front. Also, Nawaz Sharif had just been elected prime minister and New Delhi may have wanted to keep open nascent peace initiatives with a Pakistani leader who seemed to want to improve ties, even as his military remained deeply suspicious of India and would have liked to thwart any conciliatory moves. Whatever the reason, it was one more nail in Antony's reputation as the premier guardian of India's national security.

On March 5, 2014, hours before India's Election Commission announced the national general election and new conduct rules, Antony had the MOD issue an 11,000-word statement on his record in office. Starting with the fact that he had served seven and a half years in the post and thus was the longest-serving defence minister in free India, it went on to talk of the planes and ships that had been added to the forces. Even the induction of a robot that would detect and defuse explosives found a mention. The release failed to mention that the IAF's fighting squadrons had dropped from the required 44 to a mere 32 squadrons as he left office, that every one of the 70 and more strategic road projects on the China border was behind schedule, and that most of the submarines in the Indian Navy had reached the end of their operational life and only six were really serviceable. For a nation that had set its sights on strategic parity with China, it was a pitiable record. China, for instance, has more than 50 submarines in active service.

Antony's signal failing was that he was overawed – and overwhelmed – by the civilian bureaucracy. Unlike Mukherjee, who was wise to the wiles of the bureaucrats and knew how to assert himself, Antony was far less successful in curbing their manipulative ways. India's biggest curse, where defence preparedness goes, is the excessive civilian dominance over military planning. In fact, parallel bureaucracies in the defence forces and the MOD complicate matters because of a lack of confidence in one another.

A year after his retirement, Joshi himself, in a rare public outburst, lashed out at this, complaining about the "dysfunctional and inefficient business model that we have". In this model, said Joshi to NDTV 24x7 television's Nitin Gokhale, professional competence, domain expertise, accountability, responsibility and authority reside in separate silos, in different locations. While professional competence, accountability and responsibility are with the service, that is not the case with authority. "And by authority, I mean really the power to approve something. For example, change of submarine batteries, or for commencing refits and repairs of ships or aircraft – the service does not have that empowerment. Where there is authority, there is no accountability. And where there is responsibility, there is no authority," Joshi concluded bitterly.

That is a real pity. In my interactions with the higher command across the three sword arms of the Indian military, I have always found the military men better informed, more globally aware, more amenable to trying new things, and strategically more acute than their counterparts in the civil service who dominate the MOD. Yet, in India, the bureaucrats rule. Ministers are unable to check them because, for the most part, they are poorly informed and often have little experience in military matters when handed the portfolio. Even better if the minister is corrupt; the bureaucracy, with its ability to leak, has a real handle on the man. Antony was not corrupt. He was just inept.

Before he finally left office, Antony had one more significant move to make – the appointment of a new Navy chief to replace Joshi, the man who had fallen on his own sword after the submarine accident and upset the succession plans in the Navy. Antony had to draw from a list of four contending vice admirals – vice chief Robin Dhowan and the commanders-in-chief of the Western, Eastern and Southern Naval Commands. The admiral who was most senior and hence, next in line, appeared to be Shekhar Sinha, a naval aviator who was C-in-C of the Mumbai-based Western Command. But both submarine accidents had fallen in the Western fleet. Since Sinha, unlike Joshi, had not offered to quit, it was difficult to morally justify his elevation. The vice admiral groomed to succeed Joshi was Satish Soni in the Kochi-based Southern Command, but he was the most junior of the four and elevating him would have risked the resignations of the three who were overlooked.

Complicating all this was one more issue: Dhowan, though vice chief and regarded as a hard slogger in the military, had never led a command – indeed, he had declined Joshi's offer to lead Eastern Command after Shekhar Sinha, nominally his senior, insisted on getting the prestigious Western Command. Dhowan, preparing for retirement, had chosen to stay on in headquarters as a largely toothless vice chief (in the Indian Navy, the deputy chief, not the vice chief is in operational command of the force). New Delhi was his hometown after all. The decision to stay back was fortuitous, for had he gone to the Western Command, as he desired, the two major submarine accidents would have been his responsibility.

On the afternoon of April 16, Dhowan, who had not occupied the Navy chief's office even as he had been officiating in the role, got a telephone call from defence secretary RK Mathur.

"Admiral, I hear good things about you," said the veteran bureaucrat.

"Thank you, sir," said Dhowan, and after a few pleasantries, placed the receiver down.

That evening, Dhowan conveyed to his wife Minu that his appointment as Navy chief appeared to have been cleared. Elated, his wife said she was going to scramble eggs. A fine cook who often shoos away her platoon of orderlies to cook up a meal for the family herself, Minu had vowed to not touch eggs until her husband had been elevated to the job he had coveted throughout his service life.

"Not so fast," Dhowan told her. "Wait for the official announcement."

Leaving home next morning, Dhowan carried an extra uniform shirt in a suit bag. On the shirt's shoulders were the regalia of a four-star admiral.

Just before noon, a middle-ranking MOD bureaucrat walked into his office with the order of appointment.

Dhowan changed into the new shirt. He then called his staff officer, who appeared not to have noticed his superior's enhanced rank, and asked him to walk with him into Joshi's old office.

"You may congratulate your new chief," he said, taking the chair that Joshi had vacated.

Sadly for Dhowan and India, the spate of naval accidents would not abate. In the six months to December 2014, the Navy would suffer another four accidents, the worst of which was the sinking of a Torpedo Recovery Vessel off Vishakhapatnam, with loss of lives. Returning from a routine assignment, she had experienced flooding in her steering gear compartment and went down within an hour. Dhowan would prove an efficient Navy chief. Still, the Navy's cup of woe continues to runneth over.

13
The China Factor: Enter the Dragon

"There is a new assertiveness among the Chinese. It is difficult to tell which way it will go. So, it's important to be prepared. China would like to keep India in low-level equilibrium."

— Manmohan Singh, in September 2010

ADDU CITY, MALDIVES, November 2011. On the morning of November 8, I walked into the dining room of the Equatorial Village Hotel on Gan, a once secret World War II base for the British Royal Air Force, located south of the equator in Addu Atoll of the Maldives. As the designated media hotel for the 17th summit of the South Asian Association for Regional Cooperation (SAARC), meeting in nearby Addu City, it was filled with journalists from around the subcontinent putting in a hearty breakfast before a long day's toil. Not surprisingly, they seemed to have clustered by nationality. Indians, who were most numerous, were at two or three large tables. Some Sri Lankan and Nepali journalists had joined them. Pakistanis were huddled together.

In one corner, alone at his table, sat a man with Chinese features. Intrigued, I poured a cup of coffee from the buffet and, ignoring the beckoning calls of my Indian and Pakistani friends, walked over to the Chinese fellow, asking if he would mind sharing his table. He gestured to an empty seat and I sat down and introduced myself.

It turned out he was a junior Chinese diplomat from the embassy in Colombo, Sri Lanka. As we chatted, he let slip with a grin that in Male, capital of the Maldives, the Chinese were opening a brand new embassy building that day with the Maldivian foreign minister as chief guest at the inauguration.

Forget SAARC and its declarations that lead to nowhere. This was the story of the day! As India, South Asia's dominant power, was sitting down with its fellow nations for a summit, here was the China dragon at its door, audaciously opening a huge diplomatic mission in its backyard, the timing clearly meant as a cheeky challenge to New Delhi. Having confirmed the scoop and alerted my Singapore desk, I mentioned it to two friends – Ali Rafeeq of the popular Maldivian portal, *Haveeru*, and Amal Jayasinghe, the distinguished Sri Lankan journalist and long-serving bureau chief of Agence France-Presse for Sri Lanka and the Maldives. It was a quid pro quo for several favours Amal had done me over the years.

In no time, thanks to Amal, whose report was quickly followed up by the Associated Press and other wires, it had become a global story as well. No longer was the story about South Asian nations. It was about regional Big Power rivalry in India's backyard.

As it turned out, it wasn't just the embassy inauguration that week that the Chinese would pull off to show their increasing muscle in South Asia. At the summit, China, which had observer status, would propose that the association consider holding a SAARC Plus One meeting with China as a regular fixture of future meetings, just as Asean held its regular Plus One with China. Even more hilariously, as summit guests departed from Gan Airport, Chinese officials were at the facility, thrusting into the hands of departing delegates a booklet that detailed China's benevolent moves in each of the South Asian states.

Most Pakistanis took the book, so too some Sri Lankans. Indian delegates simply dropped their copies on the floor.

Beijing's gambit didn't really pay off. The final SAARC declaration was not conducive to China. Like the Shanghai Cooperation Organisation meeting which mentioned that the institutionalisation process of the body be first strengthened before expansion of the multilateral institution, the

SAARC meeting echoed the same sentiments.

Two months later, I stood on the floor of a factory situated amid the mustard fields of India's Haryana state for an unexpected New Year treat offered by a friend – the opportunity to see the production of the launch vehicles for the Agni range of ballistic missiles. Named after the Hindu God of Fire, the Agni range of medium to intercontinental nuclear-capable missiles are India's top security guarantor against China. Before me was the blackened trailer of the Agni IV, a 3,500 km range missile tested around the time of the SAARC meeting and now back for repairs. The longer trailer for the three-stage Agni V, a missile that reportedly can travel more than 6,000 km, was being readied in another corner.

India's missiles not only have stationary bases, they are also moved around on rail tracks and roads, to avoid detection. The trailers can be loaded on to a goods train, which can stop in the middle of nowhere for the trailers to be disembarked in less than 20 minutes, then left to roam in the countryside before reconnecting with the rail system, hundreds of miles away. My friend, a partner in the firm making the trailers, pointed to the three dozen or so shiny metal wheels on the vehicle, a contraption so long yet engineered to manoeuvre easily through narrow village roads.

"We went to Wheels India first," he said, naming a company based in southern India. "But it quoted too high and its delivery schedules were slow. So we've been ordering from China. The quality is fine and there is never a delay. On-time delivery is important when you are struggling to cope with the rush of orders we are getting from the DRDO."

India's Defence Research & Development Organisation, or DRDO, had been commissioning missiles at a frenetic pace over the past year as India's strategic command poured the rockets into Eastern India, particularly across Arunachal Pradesh, a state bordering Tibet that is claimed in its entirety by China. Having neglected these and other neighbouring states for decades, New Delhi had become acutely aware of the need to match the airfields and smooth roads along the border areas that Beijing was rapidly building on its side.

Besides, India had not bought new artillery for decades, exposing a key gap in its defence. To compensate for its lack of strategic planning, New Delhi's response had been to send in Sukhoi fighter bomber squadrons to the China-facing Eastern theatre and to build up missile batteries that could be used in a stand-off battle, risking fewer human lives. Some of the missiles were mounted on trailers like these that could roam the countryside. With Indian firms unable to supply fast enough, well, why not ask China to fill the demand! If the practical-minded Chinese had guessed the use to which the wheels were being put, they did not seem to care.

The twin examples underscore the complexity of ties between Asia's two tectonic plates. In 1948, Nehru, in a fit of post-colonial idealism, pushed for China to be given a UN Security Council seat when it had been offered to India first. For a short while, in the mid-1950s, the slogan was "Hindi-Chini bhai bhai" – Indians and Chinese are brothers. But both were already jockeying for influence and the geopolitical reality had been significantly altered in October 1950, when China invaded and annexed Tibet, thereby presenting India with the stark new reality of having the dragon at its door. This altered things substantially for India because Tibet, through the millennia, had never had any quarrel with it. Indeed, as the historian Ramachandra Guha notes, Tibet and China had sent separate, independent delegations to the Asian Relations Conference in 1947. But all that was no longer relevant. From 1950 onwards, the Himalayas as a secure frontier could not be taken for granted.

The two big boulders of Asia, which share thousands of kilometres of boundary, meet at three broad points – in the west, they meet in India's northernmost state of Jammu & Kashmir in the Buddhist-dominated area of Ladakh. In the middle, or central sector, they meet across the states of Himachal Pradesh and Uttarakhand. And they meet in the east, along Arunachal Pradesh, a sparsely populated state with an area of 90,000 sq km. The border here was drawn along the 900 km McMahon Line, following the crest of the Himalayas, under a treaty Britain signed with Tibet in 1914.

In Chinese thinking, it was an unequal, unfair, colonially imposed line, drawn at a time "when China was weak". But for the Indians it was a key defence line. For this reason, it steadily sought to increase its grip on Arunachal Pradesh, designating the area as Northeast Frontier Agency in 1955, declaring it a Union (federal) Territory in 1972, and ultimately giving it full statehood in 1987.

Civilisational friends for millennia, the two Asian giants had a dip in their ties from the mid-1950s after Jawaharlal Nehru seemed to have patronised Zhou Enlai at the Afro Asian Relations Conference in Bandung, Indonesia. Four years after Bandung, in 1959, a young Dalai Lama was spirited into India as he fled Tibet, thus setting up a perennial sore in the relationship that lasts to this day. Then came the 1962 border war, which went badly for an India that was totally unprepared.

India had accepted Chinese sovereignty over Tibet far too readily. Then, when issues over the unsettled border began to surface, it began a suicidal "Forward Policy" of moving its border posts further up the undemarcated line. Pressured by MPs, Nehru had boasted in parliament that he'd ordered his troops to "throw the Chinese out". Instead, the reverse happened. India got a bloody nose.

The Chinese forces, having delivered the blow, went back to their positions in the eastern sector. In the northwest, they held on to a strategic piece of territory at the top of India's map called the Aksai Chin, which they hold to this day, gaining more territory ceded to it by Islamabad after its own invasion of Kashmir, half of which Pakistan holds still.

India had got the shock of its life. Its self-esteem took a huge beating and the idealism of Nehru's external policy and pronouncements began to look naive. Yet, the Chinese may have done Indians an unintended favour. It was also a war that would unite a still-young India as never before. Shedding their cultural and ethnic differences, Indians stood as one nation for the first time. More than 2,000 km away from the fighting, women in the southernmost parts of India would stand in line to donate their most cherished possession – the gold chain worn to signify marriage – to contribute to the war effort.

The defeat crushed Nehru, who died less than two years later. By then, India had begun a swift build-up of its armed forces that would prove useful three years later, when it faced attack from Pakistan. Thus, by 1971, when the next war with Pakistan took place, India had become the dominant power of the subcontinent. With this newfound muscle, it cleaved Pakistan in two, thus helping to midwife the birth of Bangladesh as an independent nation from the remnants of former East Pakistan. The Pakistanis had hastened their own vivisection by trampling on its Bengali-speaking eastern wing, then committing vast atrocities on its people. When the unrest matured sufficiently, India took advantage.

By then, India also had a credible atomic plan in place. In 1974, it held its first atomic weapon test in the Rajasthan desert, disingenuously announcing it as a "peaceful nuclear explosion". The codename for the blast was Smiling Buddha. It also had a rocketry programme with the twin objectives of using space for development purposes, such as communication, as well as building a missile programme. Both objectives have been met. APJ Abdul Kalam, a former rocket scientist with DRDO, became a folk hero and was elevated to the national presidency. Creditably for India, some of its top rocket scientists today are women.

The Henderson-Brooks report, the official Indian analysis of the 1962 China war, remains a classified document to this day, nearly six decades after the conflict ended. Although leaked versions of the report are available on the Internet, the lack of publication of a correct assessment of the conflict and its triggers has denied Indians the opportunity to have a proper debate on the war. For this reason, and also because in the years prior to the conflict Nehru had spoken frequently of "Hindi-Chini bhai bhai", the sense of betrayal was huge on India's side, and has persisted.

From India's perspective, the Chinese are sly and treacherous, never to be trusted. Indeed, Indians from the northeastern states often get poor treatment even in New Delhi, the national capital, because of their Chinese features. In China, on the other hand, the war with India is hardly discussed, having taken place around the time of the Great Leap Forward. It is as though the conflict, since it occurred during a period of great tumult on the mainland, is an embarrassing family secret that is best not mentioned.

Relations thus remained frozen for nearly two decades until Rajiv Gandhi, four years after his landslide victory in the elections that followed the assassination of his mother, made a landmark trip to China in December 1988. There in Beijing, China's transformational leader, Deng Xiaoping, received him with a handshake that lasted a long three minutes. A notable upshot of the visit was that the two agreed on some key points. The most important was to normalise and develop bilateral relations and try to resolve the boundary dispute, while ruling out the use of force to change the status quo along the Line of Actual Control. They also agreed to set up a Joint Working Group to ensure peace on the border as well as make recommendations for a border settlement within a time frame. The Indian foreign secretary and the Chinese vice minister for international affairs would lead the talks for the respective sides.

Ties began to creep forward from that point. Over the next five years, the Joint Working Group held six meetings, each time moving things forward an inch. Defence ministers exchanged visits. Consulates reopened in Shanghai and Mumbai.

A hiccup came in 1998, shortly after India tested a series of nuclear bombs, when defence minister George Fernandes declared candidly that the tests had been necessary in view of the massive number of weapons with China, "India's Number 1 threat". But slowly, the relationship grew. Trade contacts opened. From less than a billion dollars a year, two-way trade jumped to $10 billion in 2004 and leapt towards the $100 billion mark in no time. This worked well, particularly for China, since the trade balance was overwhelmingly in its favour. Indeed, because Chinese imports were so cheap, many small enterprises in India, weighed down by labour, power and other infrastructure issues, shut down and their owners began importing goods from China by the containerload.

In the background, however, the relationship was changing by the day. Three years after the Rajiv-Deng meeting, India was in the throes of an economic crisis and prime minister Narasimha Rao, in hock to the IMF, agreed to follow its instructions and throw the economy open. China, meanwhile, was already into the second decade of its reforms. As its economic sinews built up rapidly, the gap between the two widened. India's own reforms, which started in 1991, would pump up growth, but China's economy outpaced India's for all but one of the next 20 years. With every passing year, from a position of rough equality, the economic weight moved towards Beijing. All concerned knew only too well that there was very little India could do to enforce its claim on the border beyond hoping that the dragon would not be too demanding, too forceful – or too impatient.

This was the situation when I arrived for my posting in New Delhi. It was an India that was about to play a trump card – a significantly upgraded relationship with America. Not long after I began my assignment, US secretary of state Condi Rice, on a swing through the region, told Manmohan Singh that US president George W Bush was committed to help India "become a major power in the 21st century" and move the relationship into "new and substantially more complex areas".

The dynamics in South Asia, indeed, in wider Asia, were about to change all over again.

No two nations were more wary of the unfolding relationship and its implications for the Asian power balance than Pakistan and China. When Chinese premier Wen Jiabao, whom the Indians always seemed to like, arrived in India that April, he called the visit his "most important agenda item for 2005". There was hope that it could set the stage for a settlement of the thorny border issue without involving an exchange of people, or "settled populations". On the sidelines of the Asean summit in Laos the previous year, Wen had told Manmohan: "When we shake hands, the whole world will be watching." Following that, the two had held their first "strategic dialogue" in January 2005.

But, when pressed for an endorsement of India's bid for a permanent seat on the UN Security Council, the Chinese were evasive, saying a lot and yet saying nothing. At a press conference that followed the talks, Wen merely repeated the formulation offered in the joint statement – "China fully understands and supports the Indian aspirations to play an even bigger role in international affairs, including the UN."

Still, India's media had never seemed so optimistic about the relationship. "At the gates of heavenly peace? Nearly" said the *Hindustan Times* daily, New Delhi's top-selling English mast. Across town, the main business paper, *The Economic Times,* carried the China-related stories under a theme borrowed from the title of kungfu legend Bruce Lee's movie: Enter the Dragon!

Despite the outward bonhomie, it was business as usual for the two backstage. Wen came to India after agreeing to sell four frigates to Pakistan at cheap rates, as well as announcing a joint fighter aircraft programme with Islamabad, with which it declares an "all-weather friendship". And on the day he arrived, the Indian defence minister, Pranab Mukherjee, was in the southern port of Kochi inaugurating the construction of India's first homebuilt aircraft carrier. China hadn't yet declared its Indian Ocean ambitions but the Indians were already well on their way.

After the US-India civil nuclear agreement was signed later that year, China took stock of the situation and was clearly discomfited by what was developing. A few days after Bush left town, having sealed the deal, national security adviser MK Narayanan, the designated special representative for border talks with China, received his counterpart, Dai Bingguo. It was India's turn to host and New Delhi sought to make a special statement through the choice of venue, Kumarakom, a canal-lined resort in the southern state of Kerala.

The venue was calculated to convey the centuries-old connection between Asia's oldest civilisations, which was marked by peace until the dispute over the boundary erupted into the brief 1962 war. The lagoon was specked with Chinese-style fishing nets. The evening cultural programme featured the Kalari fight, the ancient martial art of Kerala. According to some accounts, Buddhist monks travelling from Kerala to China in the 6th century had carried with them the skills that evolved into the Shaolin

Chuan. Of course, Shaolin monks deny the connection is that strong.

India went into the talks hopeful that efforts to settle the border would pick up pace. Wen and Manmohan had agreed to speed up work on the border settlement, having agreed earlier on the guiding principles to settle the border, which included a clause seen as key to India's interests – that any accord would not disturb "settled populations". This really meant that the ground situation would be the most likely basis for a deal.

The Chinese, past masters at negotiations, were giving nothing away in a hurry. After a lot of stalling and promises to "get back to you after discussions" with military officials on the border and his own foreign office, Dai went home. The Chinese were buying time.

Beijing was still optimistic that India, whose commitment to a non-aligned approach to global politics it had judged to be sincere and deep-seated, could be prevented from drawing too close to any Western alliance. Arriving in India shortly after Wen's trip, Chinese princeling Bo Xilai, at the time minister for commerce, but has since been purged and stripped of all power, suggested that Indian participation in the Chinese growth story was more than about good economics.

Sketching out the cultural connections in a speech to businessmen in New Delhi, he noted that Chinese households had long been familiar with *Journey to the West*, the story of a Tang dynasty monk who travelled to get the authentic Buddhist sutra.

"That journey to the West," Bo said to his audience passionately, "was to India." Likewise, 600 years ago, admiral Zheng He travelled around the world and visited India no less than seven times, yet was never accused of a single misdeed against the country. "We welcome you to take a share of our market. It is something we also want emotionally," Bo said to applause.

At the time, the gambit of waiting seemed to have paid off for Beijing. As the excitement of the US-India civil nuclear agreement faded after the initial hoopla, and there was no sign of the massive strategic warming between the two that was widely expected, the Chinese relaxed. They no longer needed to be placatory towards India. Visiting India at the end of

2006, there was a visible lack of bonhomie between president Hu Jintao and Manmohan. Too many suspicions remained. China would not permit India a consulate in Lhasa, the Tibetan capital. Instead, it only agreed to host one in Guangzhou. India agreed to allow China a consulate in Kolkata, but said, rather surprisingly, that it could not have jurisdiction over the nearby northeastern states that border China and Myanmar. The two described the talks variously as "cordial, open and constructive" and "friendly and candid". Neither called it warm.

Backstage, things were cool. Just ahead of Hu's visit, India had requested a meeting of the special representatives tasked to negotiate the border. It was told that Dai, China's representative, was caught up with a crisis over North Korea and could not come. India had already signalled that there was little likelihood of it agreeing to China's keen demand for a free trade agreement. The year 2006 had been designated India China Friendship Year. If anything, the two Asian giants drifted further apart.

Not surprisingly, things got worse in 2007. Beijing shifted from its agreed position on the framework of a border agreement, one key principle of which was that there would be no transfer of populated areas in any eventual exchange of territory. Beijing informed New Delhi that this understanding did not cover the Tawang Valley in Arunachal Pradesh, an area sacred to Buddhists. With the Beijing Olympics approaching, China had become even more sensitive about Tibet.

Beijing clearly felt it could not let go of Tawang. The sixth Dalai Lama was born in the valley and in 1959, the present Dalai Lama, 14th in the chain, had entered India through Tawang as he fled Tibet. The Chinese and Indian leadership have a deal to meet in summit once a year. That year, shortly before Hu Jintao's visit to New Delhi, Sun Yuxi, the Chinese ambassador to New Delhi, gave a television interview that soured the ground. He reiterated his country's claim to all of Arunachal Pradesh, particularly Tawang. New Delhi saw it as the Chinese shifting the goalposts again.

It was a pattern that the Indians would come to expect before every key bilateral meeting, an aggressive statement of claim or a forceful patrolling of the boundary, the People's Liberation Army troops often pushing way deeper than the normal patrolling and staying longer.

Having fought its last full-scale war three decades earlier, India's military modernisation had suffered some neglect. The improving geostrategic climate had also contributed to a sense of complacency in defence planning. While this held across the services, it was particularly severe in the Army, whose artillery was outdated and ammunition reserves were barely enough for five days of a full-blown conflict. Also, India's border infrastructure was poor. On the other side, the Chinese had smooth-as-glass highways running up to the border, facilitating rapid military movement when necessary.

India knew it had little choice but to beef up its defences in Arunachal Pradesh. Army chief JJ Singh, who had twice served in Arunachal Pradesh as a junior officer, and had recently retired, was sent to the state as governor. Manmohan Singh himself, in a rare sign of strategic assertiveness, decided to visit the state. Plans were made to upgrade several military airfields and build several strategic roads.

More importantly, perhaps, India began sending missile squadrons into Arunachal Pradesh, clearly indicating that while it may be disadvantaged in infrastructure, it would turn any battle for territory into a missile war, given the logistical constraints its troops may face. Work on building an arsenal of the Agni IV, the intermediate range missile with a range of upwards of 6,500 km, was speeded up. The Indians figured that just as the US sat down to negotiate with China after it built intercontinental missiles capable of hitting the west coast of the US, Beijing would talk seriously with New Delhi once its missiles could hit every major populated area of China.

As these words were being written, India had initiated building 73 border roads totalling nearly 4,000 km, the work expected to be completed by 2017. Should a settlement be reached at some point and trade ties take off, these roads could well be the arteries of a new relationship with China. For the moment, though, that looks a distant dream.

Aggressive Chinese patrolling on the border came to notice in 2008. China also ratcheted up the claims over Tawang. Even so, India's Army and paramilitary commanders on the borders were told to make no threatening moves.

"The Chinese have been a little more assertive in all the areas that are treated as disputed," Narayanan told me in an interview in August 2008. "They have been careful not to intrude into any area which, by their very careful assessment, does not fall within what they regard as their area." As for Tawang, Narayanan said, this "is an area with substantial settled populations". "Not a small number too. It flies in the face of guiding principles and political parameters for China to demand it. But both of us are committed to maintaining peace along the border."

It was clear New Delhi was anxious to avoid confrontation at any cost.

Alongside the aggressive patrolling, India was also troubled by China's refusal to grant proper visas to Indians from troubled Jammu & Kashmir state. The Indians demanded that China stamp the visa on passports, while the Chinese agreed only to stapled visa sheets. China also began making references to India's northernmost state as "India-controlled Kashmir". The new way of stamping visas for Kashmiris came after China refused visas to people from Arunachal Pradesh, saying they do not require visas as they are "Chinese" anyway.

Then, in July 2010, it denied a visa to lieutenant general BS Jaswal, the Northern Army commander, whose territorial responsibility covers all of Jammu & Kashmir, a region claimed in part by Pakistan. Jaswal was to lead a military delegation for a five-day visit to China, signalling the resumption of military contacts between the Asian giants.

New Delhi saw this as Beijing dropping its traditional neutral stance on Kashmir, thus tilting towards Pakistan, which it calls its "all-weather friend". India responded by cancelling the visits of two Chinese military officers, surprising those who had become used to a softer approach from the Manmohan government. New Delhi also followed up with more blunt language, telling the Chinese it expected to see the same sensitivity as India had shown China on the issue of Tibet and Taiwan. This came at a meeting in November 2008 that foreign minister SM Krishna held in Wuhan, Hubei with his counterpart from China, Yang Jiechi. The meeting took place on the sidelines of a trilateral meeting that included Russia. The Indians held Yang in poor regard, unlike the respect they have for Dai, whom they consider an honourable man. That made delivering the tough message a lot easier, one senior Indian official told me at the time.

Not surprisingly, the tough Indian stance was taken a week after Barack Obama, who replaced Bush in the White House, left India after his first visit to the country.

It is hard to say why the Chinese decided to spook the Army general's visit, except that it was all part of the move to pressure India on Kashmir. It took a year of diplomacy before the visit took place, and India downgraded the delegation to one led by a two-star general who headed counterterrorism operations, while making sure that the officer was drawn from the same command as Jaswal's. By then, the Chinese embassy had resumed regular visas to Indians from Kashmir. Some of it was accomplished by India asserting its traditional, centrist line in foreign policy. It had even sought membership of the Shanghai Cooperation Organisation, a body that looks suspiciously on any expansion of US, or North Atlantic Treaty Organisation (NATO), military presence in Asia.

But, having probed and sensed weakness, China would continue its pinpricks. One of the most serious, which came to be called the Depsang Incident, came in the Ladakh region of Jammu & Kashmir in April 2013. More than 30 Chinese troops penetrated some 20 km into what India considers its territory in the Depsang Valley, and stayed for three weeks. It nearly forced a confrontation as India mobilised its own forces in response.

That pattern would continue throughout Manmohan's tenure and until Narendra Modi took charge of India in late May 2014. In September, the new Indian leader hosted Xi Jinping in his home state of Gujarat for six hours, before the two flew to New Delhi for official talks. Before his president arrived in India, China's consul-general in Mumbai had talked of bilateral deals worth $100 billion to be signed between the two. Eventually, the figure given out was less than a quarter of that.

Clearly, something had gone wrong during the visit, and this was it. Shortly before Xi arriving in India, about 1,000 Chinese troops had crossed into an area of Ladakh called Chumur, triggering Indian mobilisation. The two were now staring at each other from a close distance, always a dangerous thing when both are heavily armed.

It was not the first time that China had used the gambit before a key meeting with the Indian leadership, but this time the Chinese had to deal with a new leader. Modi, eager to build personal rapport with Xi, saved the issue for the official talks next day.

A cold-eyed Modi confronted Xi: What were you doing in Chumur? Were you trying to send me some sort of message?

The Chinese leader, who also heads the Central Military Commission, suggested that if intrusions had taken place, they had not been authorised by Beijing. The troops did withdraw subsequently under Indian pressure but Modi has since carried a feeling that Xi was not as trustworthy as he'd thought.

The pity is that the border issue could have been settled for all time when Zhou Enlai visited India in 1960 and offered a package deal whereby India could keep Arunachal Pradesh if it would concede the Aksai Chin area of Kashmir to China. At the time, the Indians haughtily turned it down. Zhou was given a stiff lecture by Morarji Desai, finance minister in Nehru's Cabinet, who went on to become prime minister in 1977 after the disastrous Emergency Rule of Indira Gandhi.

Today, the unsettled border is the principal factor contributing to the lukewarm nature of the relationship that prevents a flowering of economic ties that could benefit all Asia. While there has been no firing in the area for more than two decades, it is a brittle peace. At the Nathu La Pass, 50 km above Sikkim's capital of Gangtok, a state which joined India in 1975, border trade at the roof of the world is at a virtual standstill. No sophisticated items pass through and the only acceptable currency of exchange is the American dollar. In 2014, India sent less than $3 million worth of goods through the pass into Tibet, according to figures published by *The Economic Times*.

The other bone in China's throat, and the reason for its intense claim over Tawang, is related to the Dalai Lama, whose presence in India since 1959 is resented by Beijing. Deeply revered, received by global leaders around the world – Barack Obama, after avoiding meeting His Holiness during two of his visits to the US, appeared at the National Prayer Breakfast with him in early 2015 – the Dalai Lama is the red rag to the Chinese bull. Possessing a unique charisma – "not all Tibetans are good people" was his humorous response to a fellow air passenger who watched with incredulity as he ate a beef steak – His Holiness has a massive following around the world. In the US, two big fans are Democrat leader Nancy Pelosi and actor Richard Gere. China frequently accuses him of fomenting discord in his homeland.

The Dalai Lama, eyes twinkling all the time, of course denies it – "they can examine my pulse, my urine, my stool – my everything," he offered, after Wen Jiabao accused the Dalai Lama clique of instigating unrest in Tibet ahead of the 2008 Beijing Olympics.

India, without question, uses the Dalai Lama as a pressure point on China, although his salience in that role diminishes with time. New Delhi, after yielding the Tibet card in negotiations with China early in the game, is now trying to reel some of it back. When the Chinese increased the pressure on India after the Beijing Olympics, New Delhi encouraged the Dalai Lama to visit Tawang monastery in Arunachal Pradesh. "The Dalai Lama is free to go anywhere in India," foreign minister SM Krishna said at the time. "He is only not expected to comment on political developments." The foreign secretary then, Nirupama Rao, also made a very public visit to His Holiness at the time. But Beijing knows time is on its side. Besides, fewer and fewer nations are willing to invite the Dalai Lama. His Holiness's last days will be spent in India. Although there is a substantial ethnic Tibetan population in India, it is doubtful whether the old fervour for a free Tibet can live on if the Dalai Lama were not around. That will reduce one key chip in India's hand.

But India may not need the Tibet option by then. The strategic equation was levelled significantly in 2008, and more decisively four years later, when India successfully tested the Agni III and Agni V range of missiles. Agni III, which has a range of 3,000 to 4,000 km, can be mounted on rail wagons to escape easy detection, and reach every major Chinese city when fired from northeastern India. Designed for conventional and nuclear warheads, it travels at more than 4 km a second and takes less than 13 minutes to reach its target. Agni V is the upgraded, more accurate version, built to travel 5,500 km although some accounts give it a range of 8,000 km. India deliberately understates the range so as not to trigger undue alarm. Agni V is now being inducted into the forces and future versions of the missile may have as many as 10 warheads with independent targets, making it a very potent weapon. Surprising as it may sound, India's rocketry is pretty good, and in some cases, more advanced than China's.

Both also have sea denial capacities that are growing by the day. India is also building a series of five nuclear-powered submarines meant to complete the nuclear triad – weapons based underwater that can be launched close to enemy shores, thus reducing the time it takes to deliver their payloads. However, India does not feel the need to match China weapon for weapon. As Vishnu Bhagwat, a former Indian Navy chief, once explained to me, the strategy is to ensure just enough strength "that your knuckles don't crackle when the other guy shakes your hand."

Bolstered by the fast-expanding US relationship, India has been pushing back repeatedly. When China demanded that nations boycott the Nobel Peace Prize ceremony for jailed Chinese dissident Liu Xiaobao, it was politely told that India would not accede to the request. While top level officials were more circumspect, more often than not it was the gung-ho junior officers who were standing up to China. In this case, Sandeep Chakravarty, the director for the East Asia Division, who ranks just below the joint secretary in charge, was at lunch when he was told about the Chinese démarche. He instructed the desk officer to not touch the file until he returned. Back in office, he laid down "on file" several reasons why India should not agree. Once that was down on paper, it was difficult for people higher up the chain to put down a contrary view, without appearing to be squeamish on record. And so, the Indian ambassador went for the function, joining representatives of more than 40 other nations.

Likewise, in January 2014, a few months before the historic national election, it permitted Lobsang Sangay, the Tibetan "prime minister in exile", to visit Tawang. China policy did not change after the government change in India. If anything, it got more firm. Few could have missed the significance of Sangay's presence at Modi's oath-taking ceremony in May 2014, alongside leaders of the South Asian nations. The Tibetan exile government runs, in the Indian hill town of Dharamsala in Himachal Pradesh, a "parliament", a Department of Home, a Cabinet office, an International Relations Department and even an Election Commission.

But even the Dalai Lama is not immortal and he is into his 80s now. The Tibet card will dwindle in importance once he has passed, and for China, it is but a waiting game. It will most certainly not recognise any Dalai Lama that it has not itself selected.

India's view of China is of a general wariness but India has also vacillated from time to time until it arrived at its current perception – that, while Beijing generally has no significant aggressive designs, Beijing wants to see India bottled up in its South Asian neighbourhood. Here too, the Indians ruefully say, Beijing wants to have a say. Hence, the little diversion in the Maldives while the SAARC was meeting.

Other South Asian nations have sought to take advantage of this by playing off Indian insecurities. Sometimes they fail, and pay a price. Sri Lanka's Mahinda Rajapaksa tried to convince India to buy into his dream project of developing Hambantota, his bailiwick in the southern tip of Sri Lanka, into a port and airport hub rivalling Colombo, the national capital. When India didn't bite, he turned to China, which was only too willing to assist. The facilities have been built but with Mahinda out of power, thanks to a nudge from Indian intelligence agencies – or so the belief goes in Colombo – the project has run out of steam.

In January 2010, when India offered to print machine-readable passports for the Nepal government at $4 a booklet, Kathmandu pointed out that a Chinese company had offered to do it for half the amount. An

Indian official responded that the price quoted was already at a discount to cost. But when the Nepalese persisted in trying to bargain down the price, he responded that Kathmandu was welcome to give the contract to China.

"But what about data security?" the Nepalese asked.

"That is your problem," was the Indian response. Ultimately, the contract went to India.

While China has a mildly patronising attitude towards Indian ambitions of Big Power status – no surprise, given it now has an economy four times India's – it also keeps an eye on India's strengths in key pockets. For instance, it has always studied India's outsourcing model carefully, as it seeks to build up its own services sector. Services constitute a tad less than half of China's GDP whereas in India, that number is nearly 10 percentage points higher, rare for a developing country.

In 2004, no less than 150 software delegations visited India. When Wen Jiabao came in early 2005, he visited Bangalore and pronounced China and India the "twin pagodas", referring to their mutual strengths in IT manufacturing and IT services.

Chinese interest in Indian software firms was so intense at one time that Satyam Computer Services, the Hyderabad-based company that nearly shut down over a scam, was given rent-free office space for three years in the Shanghai Pudong Software Park. In turn, Satyam and other Indian outsourcing majors such as Tata Consultancy Services found a fine talent pool there of fast learners who were not only diligent but displayed great clarity of thought. Satyam once took a bunch of young Chinese engineers to Hyderabad for a six-month attachment and found they scored well enough against their Indian counterparts.

Now, with Chinese companies like Huawei and Taiwan's Foxconn planning to set up major manufacturing operations in India, the twin pagodas that Wen talked about could slowly turn into a reality. Foxconn has announced it may invest up to $5 billion for research and manufacturing in India by 2020. Little surprise there; Indians snapped up no less than 140 million smartphones in 2014.

Indians and Chinese are fairly compatible in the work place. On the factory floor of Orind Refractories in northeastern Liaoning province, China's rust belt, I stopped to talk to a 32-year-old packaging manager named Cheng Wei. "Many Chinese are in key positions here and the management invites us in too for important meetings," Cheng told me, explaining why she had stayed with the company for eight years. "Japanese and Korean bosses tend to not mix too much. On the other hand, we mix well with Indians."

Orind Special Refractories, promoted by an Indian from Kolkata, had reached China in search of the critical fused magnesite required for high quality refractories, the special bricks that line the furnaces of steel mills. It was the precursor to dozens more Indian companies that have since set up manufacturing in China, the most significant being the Tata-owned Jaguar Land Rover, which had never produced its cars outside of England before.

It's not just in manufacturing, but in white-collar jobs like programming as well that Indians and Chinese seem to have good working relationships. Girija Pande, who was then Singapore-based chairman of TCS for the Asia Pacific, once arranged for me to visit one of the TCS facilities in Hangzhou. There, I found rows and rows of Chinese working with Indian supervisors.

Their work quality was just as good as Indians', I was told, and the two nationalities meshed well. There were only mild cultural differences; Chinese programmers tend to treat their jobs like any industrial shift and would put their tools down come the appointed hour. In contrast, an Indian programmer, if he had an unsolved problem, would linger at his desk for hours until he had the solution.

Like every other nation, India is now chasing the Chinese tourism dollar, eager to get a slice of the high-spending Chinaman. In the spring of 2014, it unleashed a tourism promotion campaign in 12 Chinese cities with the theme, "Glimpses of India". But the interest is still one-way, partly on account of the bad press India has been getting on women's safety. India, next door to China, gets only a tenth of the Chinese tourists who go to France, for instance. In 2014, only some 200,000 Chinese visited India but nearly five times that number went the other way, to see China.

Needless to say, there is much ignorance about China within India. Baba Ling, proprietor of the popular Nanking restaurant in New Delhi's Vasant Kunj area, once told me of how he had to confront angry Sikhs who had thronged his outlet. They were angry that Ling had insulted their faith by naming his restaurant after Nanki, elder sister of Guru Nanak, founder of Sikhism. Ling had a hard time explaining that Nanking was the name of the Ming dynasty capital of China.

Still, curiosity about China is growing in India, particularly among those who have already visited Europe and the US. What they see in China leaves many in stunned disbelief.

Some years ago, flying from New Delhi to Shanghai on a China Eastern Airlines flight, I heard an Indian woman with a Prada handbag sniff at the quality of the aircraft and the onboard service. "This is no better than our Shatabdi Express," she said, referring to the run-down inter-city express trains that link India's state capitals to New Delhi.

Then, as she entered the glittering terminal building at Shanghai Pudong International Airport, I heard her gasp in amazement: "Good God, where have we arrived!"

For all the strategic rivalry between the two, some of which perhaps lives more in New Delhi's mind than in America-focused Beijing's, China shows no embarrassment in acknowledging its cultural debt to India. A lot of the civilisational contacts recorded between, for instance, Nalanda and China, are a result of the Chinese royal monk Xuan Zang's 17-year trip to India, during which he spent much time in Nalanda. Those travels to India formed the basis for the 16th century novel by Wu Cheng'en, *Journey to the West*, still popular in China. The west here refers to India.

The Chinese-style building at Nalanda called Xuan Zang Memorial Hall was built by several dozen artisans from China, who worked through frequent brownouts, coping with unfamiliar food and living conditions. The results of their sincere efforts were breathtaking when I visited there last. The entrance to the 50 acre compound had an elaborate, antique gate from Shanghai. At the other corner hung a 3.6 tonne bell with Chinese markings.

Xuan Zang's statue itself is carved in black marble, a stack of books on his back denoting the works he brought back to China, a fly whisk in one hand and an umbrella in the other, a lantern hanging from his headgear to light the way at night. When Chinese foreign minister Li Zhaoxing inaugurated the facility in 2007, he expressed the "hope that the Chinese can learn from the great spirit of Xuan Zang, who travelled a great distance to India amid great hardship to learn from the Indian people".

Likewise, China's debt for the Buddhism it received from India is exemplified in the White Horse Temple in Luoyang, built in the Ming dynasty and refurbished again in 2008 under a Sino-Indian cultural project. The horses were the animals that ferried the two monks on their long journey to China and the two men were honoured in death by being buried in the temple's first courtyard. Theirs are the only graves there.

How will their strategic rivalry play out? Will India and China go to war at any point? The stakes are simply too high for both not to manage their relations properly, but perhaps, even more for China. Even a five-day ground war – which is about all that nations of its size could possibly afford before the war spins out of control – will set them back years. India has little chance of prevailing. For China, there is little to gain from entering a conflict whose end result cannot be predicted, especially if there are sides to the India-US strategic partnership that have not been placed in public view. Besides, it would also distract it from its principal strategic goal, which is strategic parity with the US.

Talking to officials from the Chinese government and the People's Liberation Army during a visit to China in May 2015 organised by the East West Center of Hawaii, I did not get the impression that the Chinese were overly concerned about India. Indeed, they had only warm words for it, while recognising that the border issue was a thorn in the relationship. They also seemed to be confident that India would stay its centrist course in foreign policy and not align too closely with either Japan or the US. On the other hand, a Japanese colleague in our delegation of Jefferson Fellows was often embarrassed by the vehemence of the remarks directed against his nation.

Asia's two most ancient civilisations are not fated to live in rivalry. Unlike Japan, which borrowed the Chinese script and a good part of its philosophical system, then took the mainland by surprise by defeating it in war in 1894–95, there is no historical grievance in China against India. Instead, most Chinese avoid talking of the 1962 border war, partly because it happened around a turbulent period in China's history, the Great Leap Forward. That said, a mild condescension towards India and a proclivity to regard it as a lesser power is undeniable. I once heard Fu Ying, when she was the Chinese vice foreign minister, describe India as "well-behaved".

Still, there is little question that the Chinese also know that India is the only nation that can truly challenge its dominance over Asia, even if they are loath to concede it. After the May 1998 nuclear tests, which India arranged surreptitiously, escaping the attention of US spy satellites, it was China that took the lead in drafting the UN Security Council Resolution 1172 that condemned the tests. And for all its talk of appreciating India's desire to play a larger role in global affairs, it is unlikely to back a permanent seat for India in the UN Security Council, especially if it comes with veto powers. In the Chinese mind, there can only be one tiger on top of a mountain.

The developing India-US-Japan relationship is the game changer in this scenario because there is no knowing where it may lead; the last thing Beijing wants on its doorstep is an Asian version of NATO. It is in China's interest, even more than India's, to settle the border quickly and thus remove a powerful magnet driving the India-US partnership, which extends to Tokyo and increasingly, Australia. More and more, the talk is of an "Indo-Pacific" region and China is the stuffing in this sandwich.

To break out of that vice it needs a neutral India. If Xi Jinping is serious about his vision of an Asian security concept in which Asians alone determine their destiny, China will need to start treating India as an equal. As the Chinese economy slows, and India's accelerates from its lower base, China will also need access to the vast Indian market for its goods and services. Convincing New Delhi to sign on to its belt and road project would bring benefits to both.

The question now is whether Beijing will see it in its interest to have a fair settlement of the border and move on, or think the other way – that it has the power to stand its ground and gain nothing from doing a deal, especially with an India that is ever more firmly in the US camp. That is a judgment only Beijing can make.

Whatever happens in the decade ahead, one thing is clear: the two are not going to carve each other's names on trees. But as long as the wariness is kept in check, and the contacts build, there will be a healthy exchange between the two civilisational powers. For now, that should be good enough for Asia.

PART IV

A DYNASTY TOTTERS

14
Three Men Who Rocked the Dynasty: Anna Hazare, Arvind Kejriwal, Vinod Rai

Not Just an Accountant.

— Title of the autobiography by Vinod Rai, comptroller and auditor general of India, whose office exposed scandal after scandal in the Manmohan Singh government

RAMLILA GROUNDS, NEW Delhi, August 2011. Could this be the French Revolution with Indian characteristics? The shoeless ones pouring in from the Indian hinterland to support the 74-year-old staging a protest fast on an elevated platform was indicative of a nation so sickened by its effete and corrupt power elite that they would clutch at anything. Hope for them was represented by the aged man reclining on bolsters, clad in white homespun and with a cotton cap on his head. Every time he stirred a cry went up in the crowd: "*Inquilab, inquilab*!"

Long live the revolution.

Declining all food and accepting only water for sustenance, Kisan Baburao Hazare, popularly known as Anna Hazare, had held India in thrall as he steadfastly demanded that the government accept his version of an anti-corruption bill, and his alone, and have it passed quickly by parliament. The plank on which he built his campaign was to have a Lokpal, or national ombudsman, with enough powers to scrutinise the work of the prime minister, Supreme Court judges and sitting MPs. Hazare's ombudsman would also have supervisory power over the CBI, the national white-collar crime-buster that reports to the Ministry of Home Affairs and is a powerful tool in the hands of the government to nail not just the corrupt, but also the politically inconvenient.

No government will agree to give over so much power to a single individual or office, and Manmohan Singh's administration too had initially ignored his demands. That was met by Hazare with a short fasting strike in April 2011 in his home state of Maharashtra and New Delhi responded by inviting Hazare and other civil society activists to discuss the proposed Lokpal Bill. Nine meetings were held and Manmohan's government said yes to 34 of the 40 clauses listed in the "People's Lokpal Bill". When that did not satisfy Hazare he announced a bigger fast, to be held in New Delhi this time. Congress spokesmen then began attacking the spartan Hazare's character, calling him corrupt and likening his supporters to a gang of hoodlums. Then he was offered humiliating conditions for his fast to be permitted in a public place, with restrictions on both the number of people allowed to attend and the number of days he could fast. When he said he would ignore the restrictions and fast for as long as he chose to, he was briefly thrown into jail.

That ignited an India sickened by corruption. In Mumbai, the city's famed *dabbawalas* – runners who pick up and deliver lunch boxes from homes to offices – held their first strike in 120 years in support of Hazare. Candlelight vigils were held in cities across the nation. Thousands of poor Indians travelled to New Delhi to camp outside the prison gates, the peaceful nature of their protests seeming to give them a moral authority that left the government bewildered.

It was with that level of swelling public support that Hazare had walked out of Delhi's maximum security Tihar Jail to the huge fairground in central New Delhi, even as the government struggled to contain what would evolve to be a national uprising. The support cut across the traditional divisions of class, caste and age groups. Thousands of Indians got their hair shorn and went about wearing T-shirts emblazoned with the words I AM ANNA.

Having first engaged, then threatened, and finally, arrested Hazare, only to see the old fellow's popularity climb, Manmohan's government had run out of ideas to tackle the phenomenon.

The ample wind in Hazare's sails was fanned to a large extent by an unlikely hero who held, at that point, the unexciting portfolio of comptroller and auditor general, or as the nation knew him, CAG. Slim, white-haired and with a chiselled jawline, the tennis-playing Vinod Rai had been educated at University of Delhi's Hindu College and the Delhi School of Economics (DSE), where his lecturers included Dr Manmohan Singh. (His classes, apparently, were not particularly popular with DSE students, Rai told me.)

Inducted into the elite Indian Administrative Service in 1972 – government service being the cherished ambition of the young in pre-liberalisation India with its limited opportunities – he had spent his entire working life in the bureaucracy. Early on he had been picked for Nagaland, a remote tribal-dominated state in India's northeast, but ended up assigned to southern Kerala, where for some years he was the popular and well-regarded administrator of my home district, Thrissur, formerly Trichur. Within the bureaucracy he had risen to the post of secretary for finance in New Delhi and was regarded in those circles as a "sound" officer, which generally translates as a reliable pair of hands that can be trusted to not "rock the boat".

In January 2008, short months before his superannuation at age 60, Rai was appointed by finance minister P Chidambaram as the CAG, a post he would hold until he turned 65.

Protected by the Constitution, Rai, who as a senior bureaucrat had watched with dismay the rot spreading through the political-bureaucratic-business nexus, infused a new vigour into the office of the CAG. His 2014 biography, *Not Just an Accountant – The Diary of the Nation's Conscience Keeper*, sums up the attitude he brought to his job as India's auditor. The Manmohan government would rue its decision to appoint him.

On November 16, 2010, Rai had presented to parliament the "Performance Audit Report on the Issue of Licences and Allocation of 2G Spectrum". Simply put, the CAG held that the mishandling and the bending of guidelines for allocating the scarce electronics spectrum to telecom companies may have cost the exchequer as much as 1.76 trillion rupees, or about $40 billion at the time, in potential revenue. At a press conference later, CAG officials, using PowerPoint presentations, detailed the suppression of facts, use of fictitious papers and the throwaway prices at which spectrum was allocated to new players. The CAG's investigators said they had based their projections on the auction of 3G spectrum in 2010.

The CAG's decision to present these findings based on presumptive loss was controversial – audit is, after all, a certainty. But it did not matter, for as leaks of taped conversations between the telecom minister, a key influence peddler, and business leaders involved in the bidding surfaced, it was clear that there had indeed been a massive fiddle.

Telecommunications is dear to Indians. They had emerged from decades of having to wait for a telephone line, to find that opening the field to private players, a process begun in the mid-1990s, had not only made both landlines and cellular phones easy to buy but also the cheapest in the universe.

Leaked versions of the CAG report had been circulating for weeks, and when it was finally tabled in parliament, every Indian – the telephone subscriber base had already ballooned to more than 800 million that year – felt he had been robbed in some way. Rai himself became a national hero, taking on the halo of a corruption fighter. On the other hand, the documents cited in the CAG report indicated that the prime minister had sat back and done nothing as the minister involved, who was from the DMK party, a key coalition ally, boldly went about his ways. All of India now thought they had evidence of what they had long feared; India was led by a prime minister who had little control over his Cabinet.

Now, on August 9, 2011, just as the Hazare-led agitation was coming to a boil, the CAG unveiled another crushing report. This time, it was a 700-page indictment on the government's handling of the 2010 Commonwealth Games. For the past three years, as Delhiwallahs watched the ham-handed way in which the government prepared for the Games, reports had circulated of massive corruption in construction contracts and equipment purchases. The CAG only confirmed their most dire suspicions. Fanned by an excited media, which did not have to travel far to record the sense of outrage, the crowds had come to Ramlila Grounds.

So there sprawled Hazare, in front of a crowd of 60,000. Across India, in town and country, hundreds of other similar meetings were being held that Sunday. For a time, the great divides of India had melted away. The atmosphere was almost festive. Many sported armbands with the Indian tricolour. There was much embracing. Someone took an electric guitar on stage while another man, long hair tied back in a ponytail, was singing a mellifluous tune in support of The Cause. Everyone agreed the government was rotten, and everyone wanted to do something about it. Camera shutters of a hundred Nikons and Nokias rattled and clicked as the smart set, some clad in Armani jeans and Cavalli eyewear, positioned themselves to make sure the huge stage with its picture of Mahatma Gandhi got into the backdrop of their frames.

Hazare's team had adroitly captured for themselves the magic of the Mahatma, whose principal weapons to overthrow the British Raj were non-violence, non-cooperation and the threat of the death fast. Hazare, who sometimes speaks of "shooting" the corrupt, had come to the fast after visiting the mausoleum of the Mahatma. Visuals of him kneeling there had upstaged the television and photo coverage of the prime minister addressing the nation on Independence Day, August 15.

Hazare himself made for an interesting study. Once a jolly, rum-loving driver in the Indian Army, he had turned his attention to social causes after reading the works of Swami Vivekananda, a mid-19th century monk and reformer from Bengal, who is also much admired by Narendra Modi. All but two of Hazare's 15 fasts until then had been targeted at the state government of his home state, Maharashtra, whose capital is Mumbai. All along, he had almost always succeeded in bending his intended target to his will.

Thus emboldened, he had boasted that April that Manmohan Singh would have been compelled to resign if he had continued to fast another couple of days. "India is Anna and Anna is India," said his cheerleaders, which included Kiran Bedi, the first woman to be admitted to the Indian Police Service.

And it was an incoherent narrative that emerged from his camp. For instance, Hazare and his supporters went around saying they had faith in parliament, but not its MPs. While this sounded contradictory – MPs constitute the House after all – there was a point there, of course. In the Lok Sabha, the powerful lower house of parliament, no fewer than 150 of the 544 MPs had faced criminal cases, according to the non-governmental organisation, National Election Watch. They included MPs sitting on both sides of the House, Treasury and Opposition.

Walking around Ramlila Grounds, I spoke to dozens of people. Nine out of 10 I spoke to had not read the Lokpal Bill, but they all figured Hazare must be right. Why else would a government jail him, only to sheepishly release him in the face of a national outcry?

Eight days after he began his fast, the government buckled and agreed to table the Lokpal Bill. So much for the government's credibility.

This surely was the magic of India's democratic polity, with its established freedoms to dissent and challenge. But it was difficult to avoid a sense of unease as well: Wasn't the festival of democracy descending into farce? Yet you also could not but marvel at the sophistication of the Hazare campaign, India Against Corruption, with key members assigned precise responsibilities from media management to crowd control. Could all this truly be the work of a largely unlettered man? Surely, a clever coterie was pulling many of the levers from behind the curtains.

And this is where attention centred on the personality of Arvind Kejriwal, a former income tax official with the government. Slight of build, dressed casually in shirt and trousers over open sandals, with a mildly nasal voice, Kejriwal had built a reputation as an anti-corruption campaigner, using the Right to Information Act to great effect. The Ramon Magsaysay Award Foundation in Manila, Philippines, had given him an award for his contribution to the fight. At that time, there was no hint that the India

Against Corruption movement would morph into a political party. Indeed, Kejriwal would often say that the movement had no intention to enter politics directly.

Kejriwal insisted that the government bill was a sham and the government must switch the text with the one offered by his group. It did not seem to matter to him that Hazare's health could be badly affected by the fast – "Anna will fast until his demands are fulfilled," he would tell all who came to him. "For the most part, Anna's health is normal."

Kejriwal's inflexible position and his apparent lack of concern for Hazare's health disturbed many who watched him, including his one-time mentor, Aruna Roy. She voiced concern about the scope of the Lokpal Bill, with its all-powerful ombudsman, as well as the truculence, "the props and the choreography" of the campaign. Above all, said Roy, Hazare was wrong to undermine democratic institutions.

On August 28, shortly after 11 am, Hazare broke the fast he had started 288 hours earlier by accepting a glass of coconut water from two children. With Kejriwal, Kiran Bedi and a bunch of others standing next to him, he claimed victory in his fight to bring about the Lokpal Bill. In truth, the victory was hardly complete. The government had agreed only to refer Hazare's demands to a standing committee, but it did not seem to matter. Kejriwal, a diabetic who had not joined the fast, furiously gave the victory sign to every photographer within view.

Kejriwal would go on to co-found the Aam Aadmi Party, which means Common Man's Party, the following year, and eventually emerge as chief minister of Delhi, helping himself liberally to the constituency that once belonged to Congress.

As he moved from social activism to politics, the ruling Congress began to recognise the threat Kejriwal posed and tried every trick to trip him up, including a charge that he had not fulfilled the obligations of his scholarship bond while still a government employee. A senior officer in Delhi Police told me how the government had quietly set its investigation agencies on the man. "They looked through everything – his bank accounts, his every decision as a government employee, anything you could think of – and came up with nothing," this person told me. "Kejriwal's record in the bureaucracy was spotless. Ultimately, they knew they would have to fight him politically."

Anna Hazare is no longer a major player in Indian politics but Kejriwal is in the headlines almost every day. At the formative stages of the AAP, his fire was trained on Congress and its ruling family, as well as Sheila Dikshit, the incumbent chief minister of Delhi. At one public meeting, he waved a thick file in the air, saying he had 700 pages of "evidence" against Dikshit. Nothing came of it and Dikshit has not been prosecuted.

In 2011, he would generally avoid criticism of the BJP or Modi, fearing that this would not be popular with the masses, which had begun looking for a change.

Then, as his ambition widened after his brief stint as Delhi chief minister at the end of 2013, he journeyed to the Hindu holy town of Varanasi in Uttar Pradesh, which Modi had picked as his constituency for the 2014 national election and stood against the BJP's top man. The AAP fought for seats across the nation, and ended with four seats in the 544-member lower house as the BJP swept the poll. While he lost in Varanasi to Modi, he still collected more than 100,000 votes.

But his hold on Delhi is unassailable for the moment. In late 2013, campaigning not just on his anti-corruption platform, but also with promises of free water and electricity to the poorer settlements around the national capital, AAP emerged with 28 seats in the 70-member Delhi Legislative Assembly while the BJP got 31. Taking the support of eight Congress legislators, which gave him the necessary majority, Kejriwal governed Delhi for less than 50 days, before quitting abruptly. He blamed the BJP and Congress for not backing his efforts to bring an Ombudsman Bill.

In early 2015, elections were held again to fill the Delhi state assembly. This time, Kejriwal and his AAP romped home, taking 67 of the 70 seats. It was a huge setback to Modi, now prime minister, and the BJP, which got only three seats in the assembly. Congress, which had ruled the Delhi state assembly for 15 years at a stretch before Kejriwal appeared, drew a blank. It was emblematic of the situation the party of freedom had been reduced to.

Today, Kejriwal's vitriol has been transferred fully to Modi and the BJP, which he assails daily in tweets, interviews and speeches. And much like Modi with the BJP, he has taken control of his party, heaving out anyone who does not toe his line. The future battlelines of Indian politics could well revolve around the ideas of these two men – one intent on swiftly building the cake, the other on distributing it first.

15
The Gandhi Clan and Its Reluctant Candidate

> "Last night, every single one of you congratulated me. Many of you hugged me. But last night, my mother came to my room and sat with me and cried. Why did she cry? She cried because she understands that the power so many people seek is actually a poison. She can see it because of what it does to the people around and the people they love. Most of all, she can see it because she is not attached to it. We should not chase power for the attributes of power, we should only use it to empower the voices."
>
> — Rahul Gandhi, in January 2013, upon being made vice president of the Indian National Congress party.

THE YEAR IS 1980 and Rahul Gandhi and his sister, Priyanka, are in a parked Ambassador car at New Delhi's Palam Airport, not yet named Indira Gandhi International Airport. There is an argument, a little pushing. In the door frame, unnoticed, appears a handsome man in the uniform of an Indian Airlines captain, smiling as he peeks in at the scrapping pair. A word from him and the duo are separated, their dispute forgotten. The car drives off noisily, children now focusing on Rajiv Gandhi, India's future prime minister.

Some weeks later, as New Delhi's Raghubir Singh Junior Modern School on central New Delhi's Humayun Road celebrates Sports Day, Rajiv and his wife, Sonia, turn up in T-shirts and jeans to mingle unobtrusively with children and fellow parents, whose children share Priyanka's class. Gamely,

Rajiv joins a potato-sack race organised for parents. As the contest starts, he tumbles over and so do a few other parents. In a trice, portly sports minister Buta Singh, chief guest at the event, leaps to his side, obsequiously dusting off the younger man's clothes as other parents fend for themselves. What a fool the politician, attempting to ingratiate himself so plainly! Indira's older son waves him away, and he and Sonia exchange winks and nudges.

Dad and Mum, dinner over at the joint family home they share with prime minister Indira Gandhi, drive the short distance to the India Gate monument to the war dead, for the popsicles and ice cream sold by a fat Sikh man whose trolley rolls up every evening and stays until just after 11pm. Which kid would not like Mum's pasta, especially when the recipe is straight from Italy and she is only too happy to enter the kitchen? For the pre-teen Rahul and Priyanka, life would have seemed complete.

Forward to 1988, and Rajiv is prime minister of India, having been elected with a record parliamentary majority that beat the best results delivered for his Congress party by even his famous grandfather, Jawaharlal Nehru, thanks to the flood of national sympathy over the assassination of Indira Gandhi. It is the 100th anniversary celebration of a key government department, and Rajiv, as chief guest, has brought his family along for the dinner. The dessert is a sweetmeat common in northern India called *revdi,* a hard, sugared candy made in flat rounds encrusted with sesame. Food aficionados credit the *revdi* made in Meerut, a busy cantonment town 70 km to New Delhi's northeast, to be the finest in India. Spotting the sweet in the buffet line, Sonia turns to mutter to Rahul in rapid-fire Italian, the boy vigorously nodding in agreement. Her husband, who follows Italian, explains to a curious onlooker: "She is telling Rahul: 'Remember, before Dad became prime minister, we used to drive down to Meerut over the weekend to eat their *revdi*. Don't you miss those days?'"

These and other similar moments must surely play through the minds of the Gandhi widow and her two children a thousand times as they dutifully trudge the dusty hinterland of India, even as the tide of public opinion has swung so sharply against the Congress party they inherited, and lead. The assassinations of father and grandmother aren't the children's only painful memories. Uncle Sanjay, their father's politically active younger brother, was killed when the stunt plane he was flying crashed in June 1980. That was when Grandma, bereft of Sanjay's muscular support, turned to Dad, forcing him to leave his Indian Airlines job to "help Mummy". Sonia wept that day, knowing her calm and carefully ordered life was soon to turn upside down.

And of course it does, starting within the household. Indira Gandhi's turning to Rajiv upsets Maneka, Sanjay's young widow, who had stood by Indira Gandhi during her bad times and now assumes the political legacy will come to her. There are tensions in the joint family, shouting, and then the spunky aunt is bounced out of the house by Grandma. With her goes Priyanka's toddler cousin, Varun Feroze, the boy who carries the name of Indira's husband, and is loved by one and all.

Outside the home, Indira Gandhi is facing Sikh separatism in Punjab, partly fanned by her own home affairs minister, who is in a political battle with the Akali Dal group that governs Punjab. Forced to send in troops to oust the rebels from the Golden Temple, the holiest Sikh shrine, Indira draws outrage from the Sikh community, even those who have no sympathy for militancy. One day, the car carrying Rahul and Priyanka to school is bumped by another vehicle. Indira, fearful it is an attack on her grandchildren, or at the very least a warning, gathers the kids and takes them on a short holiday to Kashmir, seeking peace amid the maples, evergreens and pines of the Valley. Short weeks later, on October 31, 1984, she is cut down by bullets fired by her own Sikh bodyguards, and it is Mum, Sonia, who rushes the mortally wounded prime minister to hospital. In less than seven years, their own father, who succeeds Indira as prime minister, would be killed too, blown up while campaigning in Tamil Nadu by a woman suicide bomber dispatched by the Sri Lankan Tamil Tiger supremo Velupillai Prabhakaran. So massive is the blast that Rajiv is recognised only by his running shoes. The body is accompanied to New Delhi by his school chum, Suman Dubey, who has since remained a father figure to the Gandhi kids and Sonia's most trusted counsellor.

Whatever you may say about the Gandhi clan, their vanity, lack of intellectual depth or propensity to fall for flattery – the obsequious Buta Singh rose to be home affairs minister in Rajiv's Cabinet – it is indisputable that a streak of public service runs in their veins. So, too, a concern for the dispossessed and the people who lead marginal existences. Rahul's self-image, for instance, is clearly of one selflessly and unceasingly defending the interests of the poor and the underprivileged, in the tradition of his grandmother, Indira, and great-grandfather Nehru. It is a role he takes seriously. Ashutosh Varshney, head of the political science department at Brown University in the US, recalls sharing a Virgin Atlantic flight from New Delhi to London. Rahul had dozed off for a while and when he awoke, Varshney, seated near him in Business Class, suggested a chat at the bar. For the next three hours, Rahul stood there sipping orange juice and discussing poverty and other developmental issues with the Ivy League don.

His critics, and there are millions of them now, refer to Rahul as *Pappu* – a Hindi word for dupe. Jokes about his intellect abound within India's swelling middle classes. A Doon School contemporary remembers him as not a particularly bright spark in an institution that emphasised a well-rounded personality and sound instincts over academic excellence. Rahul was removed from school early and abruptly because of fears for his safety – Rajiv, reportedly driving himself and with a security car following at a discreet distance, showed up early one morning and took the lad back into the security of the prime ministerial home. From then on, for the cocooned lad, some of his best pals were his father's security officers, all older than him, and alongside whom he sometimes practised at the Special Protection Group's firing range in Mehrauli, emerging as a crack shot.

Those who know the man better have a different take on his intellect. Like Varshney, senior people in Singapore who know Rahul speak of an earnest person with a keen interest to debate, and learn about, development issues. One Singapore minister who hosted Rahul in his house spoke of spending the entire evening in serious discussion. In New Delhi, former external affairs minister K Natwar Singh, no friend of the Gandhi clan these days, once noticed that a book I was carrying had several passages underlined with a pencil. Rahul, he said, was also a voracious reader and, like me, tended to highlight key passages or thoughts in his books. Despite their falling out, Natwar Singh seemed to have no animus towards Rahul. And he was firmly of the opinion that Congress would not survive if the Gandhis were not around. Both Sonia and Rahul, he pointed out, were unquestioned dynasts – but they were also *elected* dynasts, repeatedly endorsed by people in parliamentary elections. Sonia too, it appears, is a book lover.

Nevertheless, the image of Rahul stuck in people's minds is that of a genial dunce, or *Pappu*. A series of gaffes has contributed to the reputation. In April 2013, a year before he led the Congress party into the national election that got it all but wiped out, Rahul spoke to the country's top businessmen at an event organised by the Confederation of Indian Industry. There he warned about investing too much hope in Modi, saying "We go into this model where you have one guy who will come and fix everything. He is going to come on a horse, the sun is in the background. There are a billion people waiting. He is coming and everything is going to be fine. No, it's not going to work like that."

Rahul was right of course, but the intelligence of his words was obscured by his clumsy articulation on these and other issues that headline writers seized upon. One of them was to liken India to a beehive. "People call us an elephant... We are not an elephant... we are a beehive. It's funny but think about it. Which is more powerful? An elephant or a beehive?" Rahul was speaking about inane comparisons of China as a massive dragon with its insatiable appetite for infrastructure and India as a slow-moving elephant. He meant to speak about Indian society's resilience, like a beehive that survives strong winds by swaying with it. But while the idea makes sense, the words came out all wrong. People in the audience looked at each other, not sure of what they were hearing. Six months later, he told a conference of India's Scheduled Castes – former Hindu outcastes now called Dalits – that India's Dalits needed the escape velocity of Jupiter to escape their plight. To escape Earth's gravitational pull, he explained, you need to travel into space at a speed of 11.2 km per second. In Jupiter, that was 60 kmps. Since Rahul was illustrating the social plight of India's most underprivileged social classes, he was perfectly within reason to use the analogy, but India's media, particularly television and the English print press, is mostly composed of urban, English-educated classes who unconsciously sneer at the lower classes. A fresh round of jokes began to circulate about Rahul. The subtext was that his audience couldn't be trusted to handle a concept like escape velocity. It was as though there was little he could do without attracting ridicule.

At other times, he simply bombed as a politician. In January 2014, Rahul gave his first television interview, with the Times NOW channel landing the coup. Arnab Goswami, the channel's combative anchor, mentioned Modi more than two dozen times during the 80-minute interview. Rahul, trying to focus on issues, avoided saying Modi's name for the most part, and instead talked of issues such as development, women's rights and corruption. At times he rambled, frequently referring to himself in the third person. *The New York Times* later wrote, "Mr Gandhi fumbled, stared with a blank expression and a tilted head and looked wounded at times." There was no question about it. The interview was a failure: it made the self-assured Modi, in contrast, look not only like the more formidable contender but also overwhelmingly more competent as a leader.

Meanwhile, as the polls approached, Congress was a house divided. The old boy herd, whose power was built around a lifetime of influence peddling, gathered around Sonia while Rahul was trying to push his own ideas, including promoting a younger crop of idealistic candidates. The vital southern state of Andhra Pradesh was particularly riven with Congress feuding and some key moneybags refused to open their kitty to the party, even if funds had been gathered in its name. Television channels, sensing the mood was massively for Modi, often offered split-screen live coverage of Modi and Rahul speeches, but while Modi could be heard, Rahul was muted out most of the time.

Nor was it any better after the election, which delivered the Congress party its worst drubbing. With Congress strength in the powerful lower house of parliament cut to 44 seats, a historic low, Sonia and Rahul came out to accept defeat before the national media. After congratulating the new government and wishing it the best, Rahul acknowledged that his party had done very badly.

"As vice president of the Congress, I hold myself responsible," he said. Then, standing to his mother's left as she took the microphone, Rahul seemed a picture of relief and joy, smiling throughout the brief session. India's media, sections of which suggested he had been smirking, quickly speculated on the reasons for Rahul's behaviour. Many surmised it signalled relief that he would not be called upon to pursue an occupation he didn't quite relish, but had been pushed into by a sense of duty, or his mother's ambitions, just as Meryl Streep pushes her son's political career in *The Manchurian Candidate*.

Watching his performance on television, I, too, got the same sense. Rahul was radiating unparalleled relief. Later, checks with people close to the Congress leadership offered up a totally different picture. On that day, when Sonia and Rahul announced at short notice they would face the cameras, beat reporters were mostly out of the office, contacting people in the new government. In many newsrooms, the youngest staffers – many of them women barely into their twenties – were told to hurry down to Congress party headquarters. These young women, eager to take photographs of the handsome Rahul or shoot selfies with him in the background, frequently squealed out to him to smile and look their way. With no sense of the moment, Rahul had obliged. Television cameras, stationed in the back of the press scrum, had caught only Rahul's expression, not the entreaties to which he was responding.

Later, when Sonia, as chair of the United Progressive Alliance, hosted dinner for the departing Manmohan Singh and his Cabinet, Rahul was nowhere to be seen. He was overseas on holiday, after a gruelling election. Many thought poorly of the Gandhi scion for not having the grace to show up at the dinner for the elderly Manmohan. Once again, the Indian media noted, he was the absentee landlord of the dwindling family estate.

It is hard to tell why someone so steeped in his family's political tradition, and with the best recognised family name in Indian politics, should prove so lacklustre as a leader. Rahul's parliamentary interventions are remarked upon only because they are so rare. He has one of the worst attendance records. In early 2015, he missed the entire budget session of parliament, having disappeared from India for nearly two months with no explanation about his whereabouts. And he is invariably remembered for the wrong reasons. In August 2015, a journalist with a telephoto lens captured him walking into parliament with a cheat sheet in hand, the key points of his speech, to be made in Hindi, written out in Roman script. Twitter and other social media lit up with #Pappu talk for days.

Vayalar Ravi, a longtime Congressman and minister, says Sonia once asked him for advice on how Rahul should go about building his political career. "Madam, in youth politics you have to be a little aggressive, burn a few buses and things," Ravi offered. Sonia vigorously shook her head in disagreement and changed the subject.

One explanation offered to me by someone who has known the family since the 1960s is that after four generations in power, the biting urge and burning hunger to hold high office à la Modi are simply not there in Rahul. Instead, there is a sense of fatigue. Another could be fear of one more great tragedy being inflicted upon the family, should it accept power directly. It has now come to light that the reason Sonia declined to be prime minister, when the post was available to her in 2004, was not because of any advice from president APJ Abdul Kalam or her own self-confessed "inner voice". in his book, Natwar Singh described a scene between Sonia and Rahul witnessed by him, Manmohan Singh and Suman Dubey. Sonia apparently was willing to be prime minister but Rahul stepped in and vetoed the idea. As a son, he would not allow her to come in harm's way after his father and grandmother had fallen to assassins, he insisted. Sonia, of course, famously told the world later that an "inner voice" had stopped her from taking the job.

According to Natwar Singh, the Gandhi clan tried its best to stop the story from surfacing. Indeed, he told me, pointing to the chair on which I sat, Sonia had sat in his drawing room with Priyanka, after years of ignoring him, pleading that he not go public with the event. Natwar could not oblige them – the book, he told them, was already with the printers.

The pity is that young Rahul had shown much promise initially. In March 2006, when he made his first major speech in parliament, he had focused on education. In fact, reading that speech, I discovered that he'd spoken of ancient Nalanda University even before the idea of its revival was mooted by president Kalam. His travels around India, he said, had convinced him that education was not about schools and universities but fulfilling aspirations. "A successful education system must do two things: it must allow all young Indians to dream, and it must teach them the skills to turn those dreams into reality," he said, to resounding cheers from every section of the House.

The candour and sincerity in his address touched a chord. Word then was that Rahul might be planning to step into the shoes of human resource development minister Arjun Singh, who was ailing. It made sense: more than a third of Indians were below the age of 15 and many would soon be eligible to vote. A new minister tuned to the latest thinking was probably just what the country needed. After all, his father, Rajiv, was credited with laying the foundations of India's rise as a power in computing and software.

Rahul's reluctance to enter government was a point of frustration for many young MPs in Congress, who felt their own progress was hampered on this account. While many of the younger guard – Sachin Pilot, Jyotiraditya Scindia, Milind Deora and some others – did get junior ministerial berths, some, like Pilot, clearly had potential to go higher. Scindia, too, while no bright spark in school, had flowered in adulthood and won the respect of the bureaucrats who dealt with him. They spoke of his keen grasp of matters and the preparations he made for meetings. But because of his lineage – he is the current head of the Scindia clan that ruled the erstwhile Gwalior state – Jyoti Scindia and others like him had to be particularly careful to not grab too much limelight, lest it touch off some of the famous insecurities endemic to the Gandhi household. So they bit their tongues and bided their time. Many were plainly frustrated but they kept their thoughts mostly private, or confided only in a rare few.

Manmohan Singh repeatedly said he would like to see Rahul in Cabinet but Rahul held firm, insisting he wanted to learn politics "brick by brick". Having successfully managed his mother's 2006 by-election with spectacular results, he withdrew into a shell, just when party colleagues felt he had built up the right momentum to make a spectacular lunge for the national stage. There was also fear of being lured into a trap by his coalition allies. To take charge of Congress and then lead the party into disastrous showings in elections would be the kiss of death to the dynasty. Sadly for him, that would be his fate in 2014, except that Congress, desperately short of ideas and appeal, continues to cling to the dynasty.

"Rahul had everything to offer a young person but his gestation period was too long," noted political anthropologist Shiv Visvanathan told me, as he watched the 2014 election results unfolding on television. "It created a 'Prince Charles effect'. He was seen as a pupa that refuses to fly."

There was, of course, the desire to live a life as near normal as his pedigree and position would allow. Rahul loved to race motorcycles, for instance. A ranking bureaucrat, whose government bungalow was not far from Rahul's, told me of the nuisance that the Gandhi scion and friends often created – getting the Special Protection Group to close off Aurangzeb Road, now renamed APJ Abdul Kalam Road, in central New Delhi so they could race around on high-powered motorbikes in the middle of the night.

A trip to Singapore in 2006, where he had two lengthy sessions with founding father Lee Kuan Yew, may also have influenced his thinking. "Rahul came back with two insights from his various meetings in Singapore," someone who used to speak to him frequently told me. "One is, do not be in a hurry. Second, build a team of able and reliable people that you can count on to implement your vision once you are ready for the job."

Rahul's dual persona was in view in the week he spent on the prosperous island in the heart of Southeast Asia. Keen student of the city-state's development story by day, he was a lounge lizard at night. At least once he was spotted late at the Ministry of Sound nightclub, swilling whisky and enjoying himself. But his instinct for people was present throughout. His tour included a visit to an oil-rig building facility operated by Keppel Corporation, one of Singapore's top conglomerates. Indian workers on site recognised Rahul and stopped to cheer, a witness to the event told me. Pleased, he turned to meet them. One janitor held up his broom and joined his palms to greet him in the traditional Indian way, signalling he didn't want to shake hands lest Rahul feel defiled if their hands touched. Jawaharlal Nehru's great-grandson strode up, yanked the broom away, and vigorously pumped hands with the delighted cleaner. That day, in Singapore, the Gandhi family won one more admirer and perhaps hundreds more in that man's village.

Was Rahul putting on an act? Not at all. His father, who was as completely at ease sipping a roadside vendor's tea as dining with the president of the US, would perhaps have done the same thing.

Rahul's demise as a vote catcher has been sealed with Congress' performance in the Delhi state assembly polls of February 2015. The fledgling Aam Aadmi Party, led by former tax officer Arvind Kejriwal, swept all but three of the 70 seats in Delhi.

"Aam Aadmi" stands for "Common Man", and in fact was a phrase adopted by Congress in 2004, thanks to the astute Jairam Ramesh, a speech writer for Rahul and his mother who was subsequently given a Cabinet berth. Against the BJP's "India Shining" campaign, Ramesh, who did his tertiary education at Massachusetts Institute of Technology and remembered Walter Mondale's "Where's the beef?" punchline from his days in America, thought up the slogan for Congress. The phrase delivered stunning results in 2004 by successfully portraying it as the party of the masses and the BJP as an effete, urban force. It was telling that not only have the poor of India now deserted Congress, but that its key planks have been usurped by all manner of pretenders. Of course, voter fatigue with Congress was a factor as well for its rout in Delhi.

For 15 years from 1998, Delhi had voted in successive Congress state governments, the last of which sank in the stink of corruption scandals associated with preparations for the 2010 Commonwealth Games. Yet Rahul, save for one campaign speech, was nowhere to be seen. It was as though he had either lost the zest for a campaign, or had given up hope and did not want to be associated with a lost cause.

For both Congress and the BJP, which too suffered equally despite rolling out prime minister Narendra Modi as its champion campaigner, the opponent to beat was Kejriwal. In December 2013, the mercurial taxman had stitched up a minority government in Delhi with Congress support, then abruptly quit after 49 days when Congress and the BJP refused to support his anti-corruption legislation for the appointment of an ombudsman. When Delhi voted in the elections to national parliament that followed a few months later, it had given all its seven parliamentary seats to the BJP. Yet, barely eight months after that, here was AAP and Kejriwal returning with a stunning and unprecedented electoral showing in the state elections.

Writing in the *Business Standard* newspaper after the state polls, TN Ninan, perhaps India's most respected editor, summed up Rahul's predicament. "A year ago, Mr Kejriwal was in a bigger mess than Mr Gandhi," wrote Ninan. "He had thrown away a mandate, angered voters, and then eaten humble pie in the Lok Sabha elections. Since then, Mr Gandhi has played hide and seek while Mr Kejriwal has rebuilt his reputation and his party, in the very city where Mr Gandhi lives. While one has delivered resolute reconstruction, the other has been missing in action. There is no further proof required that Mr Gandhi has no taste for the job of rebuilding his party, and no stomach for a political fight. The best thing he can do for the Congress is to get out of the way."

Ninan is right. For all his earnestness, Rahul just doesn't have the pull of the Gandhis. His standing in the party is almost exclusively because no one wants to get on the wrong side of his doting mother, whose grip on Congress is absolute. Aside from the perception deficit that afflicts him,

Rahul's is a limited agenda for one who is projected by his party as a national leader. Unlike his great-grandfather, Nehru, or his grandmother, Indira, he seems to have little interest in foreign policy. Instead, he is so focused on development issues that even the young and upwardly mobile Indians do not connect with him. Perhaps it was because he grew up with the legend of the Nehru-Gandhi family's deep link with the rural masses. In the early 1970s, Indira Gandhi's rallying cry, one that helped her win power and dominate Congress, was "*Garibi Hatao, Desh Bachao*" – Remove Poverty, Save the Nation! Rahul is stuck on that groove.

"My politics is very simple," he once said. "As long as there are poor people in India, I will stand by them. I do not care what his religion, caste or colour is or where he comes from."

Rahul's failing, and Sonia's too, is to stay frozen in old ideologies without realising that both Indira Gandhi and her son, Rajiv, ruled with more pragmatism than is recognised generally. As early as 1982, for instance, Indira had begun to reduce India's reliance on the Soviet Union and build ties with the US.

Thus, when Sonia and Rahul oppose government acquisition of agricultural land for industry, they fail to acknowledge that it was Nehru who put land acquisition outside judicial review, saying national interests would sometimes entail displacements. Indira, too, had amended Indian laws to declare that farmers whose lands were taken by the government were entitled to an "amount" but could not expect full "compensation". Her son, Rajiv, was a practical man when it came to policy, with little fear of private enterprise. This is where Rahul is not easy to understand; surely, with his deep interest in development economics, he must be aware of the importance of industry to growing the employment pool. Factories cannot be built without land.

But Sonia and Rahul soldier blithely on, peddling old mantras, increasingly at odds with even the people they claim to represent while causing immense damage to India's development prospects at a time when a window of opportunity has opened for it. Alongside, of course, is a conviction that they, and they alone, were born to rule party and government, and almost everyone else is an interloper. While Rahul seems a writeoff – many in India refer to him now as the "former future prime minister" – increasingly, there is resistance to him even within Congress. The old boy clique of Congresswallahs insist that Sonia continue to lead them, which is another way of saying they don't want the son.

Against the growing realisation that the little emperor has few votes, one tantalising question that will not go away is whether his sister, Priyanka, will one day step into active politics. There is a ready-made constituency waiting for her. The Gandhi women are made of stern stuff and in Priyanka, people sense determination and flair, just as, in her time, Indira Gandhi was hailed by admirers as an incarnation of the Goddess Durga, embodying power and invincibility. Priyanka does have a resemblance to her grandmother, particularly in the way she wears her hair. In repose, she actually looks more like her father.

The spunk in Priyanka surfaced early. In 1991, barely out of her teens, she campaigned against Arun Nehru, Rajiv's cousin who had fallen out with him and then sought to usurp his parliamentary seat of Amethi after Rajiv was killed. Her entry into the battle proved a success. Arun Nehru was defeated and Rajiv's friend and flying associate, Satish Sharma, won through in Amethi, establishing Priyanka as a political draw. Captain Sharma yielded the Amethi seat to Sonia in 1999, who then vacated it for Rahul in 2004. Since then, Priyanka's focus has been on ensuring that Amethi and nearby Rae Bareli, her mother's current constituency, have been safe for Congress, freeing mother and brother to campaign across the nation. Her best performance came in the 2007 Uttar Pradesh state assembly elections, where Congress won seven of the 10 assembly segments within the parliamentary constituencies of Amethi and Rae Bareli.

And she was one Gandhi who could match Narendra Modi word for word. In the heat of campaigning for the 2009 general election, Modi had come down from Gujarat to carry his fearsome oratory to UP, repeatedly sneering at Congress as a "125-year-old hag who is a burden on the family".

Congress was a bit uncertain how to respond. It was Priyanka who slew that jibe with characteristic elan. "Do Sonia Gandhi, Rahul or I look old to you? If elderly people feel young, it is good for their health."

Yet, that solid performance on the stump can no longer be taken for granted as the party loses its roots one by one. In the 2012 state elections, Congress lost in three of the five assembly segments in Amethi. And in the 2014 parliamentary election, despite her hectic campaigning for Rahul in his Amethi constituency to stem an onslaught by the BJP and Modi, the brother retained his seat with a much thinner margin. Still, there is not a Congressman who would not welcome Priyanka taking a bigger role in the party, if nothing else, because she is such a draw and Congress could use her fresh, feisty personality. Indeed, Natwar Singh speaks of her with admiration: "She is superb, witty and great with one-liners that instantly communicate with her audience."

But Priyanka has steadfastly refused to be drawn in, instead ensuring that the *maidan* (ground) is reserved exclusively for her brother. She is adamant that her principal focus is her children, son Raihan and daughter Miraya. With Raihan now a resident scholar at Doon School, Congresswallahs have not given up hoping she will seize the mantle. Hours after the Delhi state election results were announced in February 2015, signalling a complete rout for Congress at Arvind Kejriwal's hands, a crowd showed up at Sonia's door, demanding Priyanka be drafted into the party.

Priyanka's political Achilles heel is her husband, Robert Vadra, known for his cosy relationships with top realtors around the capital. Vadra's deals had become an election issue but the BJP has held fire since coming to power, partly because it wants to hold the issue in reserve to pressure the Gandhis when it needs to, which would be if Congress showed signs of a reawakening. As TVR Shenoy, one of the most astute observers of Indian politics, told me, "Modi wants the luxury of being able to choose his opposition at the appropriate time and he will keep Congress alive with this in mind."

While Priyanka has defended the business dealings of her husband, it is not certain whether this comes from conviction that he is blameless or from a wifely instinct to defend the family name against attack. In her time, Indira Gandhi's husband, Feroze Gandhi, had also given plenty of trouble to his father-in-law, Nehru. But Feroze, an MP who had changed his original surname, Ghandy, to match that of freedom fighter Mahatma Gandhi, had done so by exposing possible corruption in the Nehru Cabinet.

Vadra, a man who was introduced to Priyanka when she was in her teens, is a different kettle of fish. His life has been troubled too. A brother committed suicide, a sister died in a car crash and his father was found dead in a cheap motel some years ago. His mother, Maureen, is listed as a partner in his business ventures, many of which have shown astounding success after the Congress party regained power in 2004. Vadra is also known to be fast friends with the owners of DLF, one of India's biggest real estate firms, and he occupies a massive apartment in the DLF-built Aralias development in the suburb of Gurgaon. Neighbours say that when he entertains, DLF Golf and Country Club, whose verdant greens his apartment overlooks, obliges by keeping the floodlights on until the party is over.

While he gets along well with Rahul, his relationship with Sonia isn't apparently quite so warm any longer. Vadra showed up with Rahul as he filed his nomination papers from Amethi but kept a low profile during the remainder of the campaign and was not around when Sonia filed her own papers in the adjacent constituency. That he is a political liability for Congress is undeniable. During the 2014 campaign, Modi repeatedly targeted Vadra's business deals and often caricatured Congress as no more than RSVP – standing for Rahul, Sonia, Vadra and Priyanka – a jibe that even the feisty Priyanka found hard to put down, although she did try. Priyanka's counter was to ask Modi to stop trying to be a schoolmaster teaching children the letters of the alphabet such as ABCD and RSVP.

Yet Priyanka's public image is at odds with the woman she is. Most people see her as gregarious, outgoing, a natural politician. In truth, outside the five-year election cycle, she is a private person, often showing up quietly in New Delhi's Santushti Shopping Complex or Khan Market to shop alone for cotton clothes. Sometimes she flies Raihan and Miraya to Singapore, where the family can move around with minimum security. Her big intellectual interest is Buddhism.

Of the two Gandhi siblings, Priyanka, particularly, has had more difficulty exorcising the ghosts that haunt them. In 2008, she travelled to Vellore Central Prison in Tamil Nadu to meet Nalini Sriharan, one of the women who plotted her father's assassination on behalf of Sri Lanka's Tamil Tigers. Sriharan, sentenced to death, had her punishment reduced to life imprisonment on a plea from Sonia.

"Visiting Nalini was my way of coming to terms with the violence and loss that I have suffered," Priyanka explained later. "I do not believe in anger, violence and hatred and I do not let these things overpower my life."

16
Dysfunctional Diarchy: The Manmohan Singh Paradox

> "I firmly believe that the emergence of India as a major powerhouse of the evolving global economy is an idea whose time has come. Blending tradition with modernity and unity with diversity, this nation of ours can show the way forward to the world. Serving this nation has been my privilege. There is nothing more that I could ask for."
>
> — Manmohan Singh's last speech as prime minister, May 17, 2014

IN EARLY MARCH 2014, a few days after the shock resignation of his Navy chief over a string of accidents involving naval assets, prime minister Manmohan Singh invited admiral Devendra Kumar Joshi and his wife, Chitra, to a farewell tea at his residence. The Singhs went out of their way to make the Joshis feel welcome, pressing on them a meal of *dhokla* savoury, cakes and Indian sweetmeats.

Facing India's first armed services chief to quit on an issue of moral responsibility, India's first Sikh prime minister perhaps felt he owed a word of explanation to the gentleman-officer sitting rock steady in his seat, even as the prime minister himself shifted uneasily, repeatedly.

"Admiral, there were many times when I, too, thought of resigning," said Manmohan, who comes from a community with a long martial tradition. "Every time, I thought of the nation and decided to stay on."

The words, in so many ways, underscore the paradox of Manmohan Singh. Born poor in the village of Gah, in a district of Punjab that went to

Pakistan after the Partition of India in 1947, Manmohan as a teenager was witness to the trauma of that event, with its large-scale killings as Muslims migrated west to the new nation created for them, and Hindus and Sikhs like him moved southeast to the safety of Hindu-majority India. His birth date, September 26, is a matter of conjecture for no actual record exists – that was the date a relative entered when filling up his school application. Raised by his paternal grandmother after his own mother died early, Manmohan moved to the Sikh holy town of Amritsar, where his father, Gurmukh Singh Kohli, ran a small business. As commonly happens to children who lose parents early, it is possible that the young Manmohan suffered indignities at the hands of less caring kinfolk. If so, he has not talked about it.

India's Sikhs are generally known more for muscularity than intellect, the reason that so many choose the military and constabulary as a profession. Manmohan was the opposite, fascinated by knowledge and learning. Indeed, he credits his poor eyesight to the early years of reading in inadequate light without electricity. Manmohan's father would have liked him to join his fruit business, but the young man demurred, insisting he wanted to study. Winning a scholarship to study at the Dayanand Anglo-Vedic (DAV) College in Jalandhar, he is remembered by his contemporaries as a man devoted to his books. Manmohan is almost completely bald under his turban now but in his younger days he had wonderfully long hair. On weekends, when his hostel mates were out in the field playing football and hockey – cricket then wasn't quite the rage it is now – they would find Manmohan under a tree, fresh from a bath. There, he would be reading a book while he waited for the sun to dry his hair so he could gather it up to make his *pugree*. The reading habit stayed through his life, until the demands of the prime ministership shrank his time. His girls say that most of the birthday gifts that came from their father were books. Even as prime minister, Manmohan tried to keep his Sundays free, so he could read the papers at leisure, and turn to some book he needed to consume.

Brilliant in college – he stood first in Economics both in his bachelor's and master's courses – Manmohan won a scholarship to Cambridge, finishing his Tripos in 1957 under the tutelage of Joan Robinson and Nicholas Kaldor, two of the biggest names in academia. He returned to Punjab to marry a woman he'd met and wooed – Gursharan Kaur – and to serve out his scholarship bond at Panjab University, starting a family and siring three girls. The presence of a third child suggests that Manmohan may have wished for a boy after two girls but it was also not uncommon in those times to have more than two children.

Three years later, he was back in Britain, doing a doctorate at Nuffield College, University of Oxford. Once that was done, he returned to India, before working at UNCTAD, the UN's trade and development body, for five years. He then did a brief stint as a trade adviser to the Indian government and subsequently joined the DSE in 1969 as a professor of international trade. The DSE, styled on the London School of Economics, was one of the most prestigious academic institutions of the era. It drew notables like Amartya Sen, who would win a Nobel Prize decades later, and other big names such as Jagdish Bhagwati, Sukhamoy Chakravarty and Mrinal Datta Chaudhuri. It was an era when ultra Left movements were sweeping parts of the country and many University of Delhi students too were affected by the radical ideology. Amit Mitra, currently finance minister of West Bengal, who as secretary general of the Federation of Indian Chambers of Commerce and Industry did much to lobby for private enterprise in the country, was a student of Manmohan's at DSE. A right-winger committed to private enterprise, Mitra always carried a knife hidden under his clothes to protect himself from hot-headed radicals influenced by Naxalism, as Maoist ideology was known at the time. One day, Mitra said, Manmohan called him in for a quiet word and advised that he be less strident about his right-wing views, given the climate at DSE and the presence of Maoist elements in the university. Mitra took the advice.

Manmohan left the DSE in 1972 to return to government, quickly gaining a reputation as a clear-headed man who could be relied on for valuable advice. His various appointments, as his career progressed, include the prestigious posts of governor of the RBI, the central bank, and deputy chair of the Planning Commission, a legacy of the socialist era of central planning, but influential because it was chaired by the prime minister, while the deputy had Cabinet rank. (The Modi government scrapped the Commission soon after taking power.) He was also secretary-general of the South Commission – the predecessor of the intergovernmental organisation of developing countries, South Centre – between 1987 and 1990.

Manmohan returned to a new India. Rajiv Gandhi had been booted out after a corruption scandal involving arms purchases from Sweden. Vishwanath Pratap Singh, then prime minister of India, appointed him as an economics adviser but that government soon fell and Manmohan Singh, looking for something to do, turned to an old friend from Punjab, Professor Surinder Goyal, who chaired a think tank that tended to lean left on economic issues. Goyal, who was close to VP Singh's successor, Chandra Shekhar, was happy to oblige an old friend and fellow Punjabi. He put in a word with India's ninth prime minister and Manmohan was soon chairman of the University Grants Commission, a powerful regulatory body that also determines funding for government universities.

Then the wheels of fortune turned again. In 1991, Rajiv Gandhi, campaigning for a comeback, was assassinated at a rally in the southern state of Tamil Nadu. Partly due to the sympathy vote on that account, Congress returned to power and PV Narasimha Rao, a dour polyglot who had served Indira Gandhi loyally, was named prime minister. India was facing a balance of payments crisis at the time, and in return for a bailout, the IMF laid down several conditions, including economic liberalisation. There was no choice; Rao went with what he had promised and hired Manmohan as finance minister to implement the task.

Throughout his career, Manmohan was careful about his image. But even as he rose higher and higher, it seemed he found it difficult to shake off his diffidence and self-image of being more of a civil servant than a true master. While avoiding the temptation of the loaves and fishes of office, he would apply for every privilege legitimately available. When he was appointed governor of the RBI, he had finished 13 and a half years in government service. But becoming RBI governor meant officially severing ties with government, in order to maintain the independence of the office. Since service rules were clear that a minimum of 15 years service was required to be eligible for government pension, Manmohan petitioned Indira Gandhi on the matter, seeking a waiver. The prime minister responded on the file saying no one would grudge Manmohan getting the special treatment, given his outstanding record of service, said Vinod Prakash Sawhney, a retired secretary for banking.

Sawhney called on Manmohan more than once in the Mumbai official residence of the RBI governor. Manmohan knew "Gullu" Sawhney liked his evening drink so the scholarly Sikh would draw the curtains, lock the door and pour the bureaucrat from New Delhi a glass of whisky. "Manmohan was not a teetotaller as many believe," Sawhney told me. "He would permit himself the occasional tipple. But he was not the most generous of hosts."

Just as the Partition in 1947 had seared his consciousness as a young lad, the riots in 1984 that followed the assassination of Indira Gandhi by her Sikh bodyguards in 1984 would affect Manmohan deeply. A mob gathered outside his Ashok Vihar home on the fringes of University of Delhi, and only melted away when his son-in-law, a Hindu, came out to confront the attackers, identifying himself by his faith. In the mob, shockingly, were known faces from the neighbourhood. Across India, more than 2,700 Sikhs were slaughtered but the bulk of the deaths was in the capital, New Delhi.

Rajiv Gandhi had just been installed as prime minister, succeeding his assassinated mother, when the riots started. Credible anecdotal evidence suggests the police did little to stem the violence and some Congress figures were accused of supervising parts of the outrage. In contrast, the number of Muslim deaths in the 2002 Gujarat riots was fewer than a third of that figure and it is not widely recognised that more than 250 Hindus were also murdered in the Gujarat riots. While every life matters, it is noteworthy that a greater stigma has attached to Narendra Modi for his inability to protect minorities in his state. Indeed, Sonia Gandhi, campaigning in Gujarat, once described him as *maut ka saudagar* – a merchant of death.

The writer, Daman Singh, Manmohan's middle daughter, recently said that apologising for the anti-Sikh riots on behalf of the Congress party was one of the most painful moments in Manmohan's life.

"I apologise, not just to the Sikh community, but to the entire nation on behalf of our government. I bow my head in shame about what happened," he told parliament in August 2005. Those who know him closely believe Manmohan's decision to sell the Delhi property and buy one in Chandigarh, the joint capital of Punjab and Haryana states, was influenced by that 1984 attack on Sikhs.

Under the benign smile, some people also see a spot of hubris – when he was finance minister, journalists who went to interview him were often handed a lengthy biographical profile of the man, complete with the smallest award handed to him by a district Rotary Club. Former external affairs minister Natwar Singh, who left his Cabinet after Congress declined to defend him over allegations he had profited from Iraq oil sales, said Manmohan Singh remembers every slight he has endured. Some also spot a mildly vindictive streak, which he keeps hidden for the most part. Goyal, who had helped him get the University Grants Commission job, would turn bitter about his friend after Manmohan became finance minister to Rao and quickly set about to unshackle the socialist era controls.

"He repaid my favour by withdrawing the government grants that my institute used to get," Goyal complained to me once. "And all because I made a few critical noises about his pro-market moves."

Manmohan's irritation with Goyal was probably brought on by impatience that Goyal persisted in taking rigid ideological positions even when he knew the finance minister was fighting a crisis situation, and doing the correct thing. Because with other old friends, particularly from Punjab, Manmohan could go out of his way to help.

This was the background – solid Punjabi roots, the upheavals of Partition, a sterling record in academia and government and a well-grounded family – that Manmohan brought to India when he was given charge of the country in 2004. In addition, he had that quality rare among

India's politicians – high personal integrity. That integrity was sometimes narrowly defined though, and some have suggested that the moral standard is not always so unbending. In a long examination of his life and record in October 2011, *Caravan* magazine wrote about how Manmohan bent his high standards in the 1999 election he fought from south Delhi – the only time he entered a direct race for parliament. Aware that the official quota of funds allowed for a campaign would not suffice, and that he risked losing on account of it, Manmohan would receive fawning industrialists in his home.

"I want only your good wishes," Manmohan would tell the tycoons who came with offers of financial aid, according to *Caravan*'s account of its conversation with Harcharan Singh Josh, Manmohan's election agent. Then the industrialists would go to the next room and, according to *Caravan*, hand a cash pile to Gursharan Kaur. After the election, Manmohan passed the unused funds to the Congress party. Manmohan, who never denied the *Caravan* report, learnt the grubbiness of politics first-hand in that election, which he lost by less than 30,000 votes.

Having lost the only direct election to parliament he contested, Manmohan never chanced his luck again at the hustings, instead entering parliament through its upper house, Rajya Sabha, which gets MPs from an electoral college comprising members of state legislative assemblies. To enter, he merely needed to make sure that his party president put out the word to state legislators to vote for her man. Manmohan, who is from northern Punjab, was elected as a Rajya Sabha MP from the remote eastern state of Assam, a province that Congress has dominated for years. To qualify as a resident of Assam, he rented a house in Guwahati, its state capital, and hung his name plate on the building, visible from the street.

More than almost anyone else in India, Manmohan came into office fully aware of the remedies the nation required to pump up the economy and project it to the front ranks of the world. He was also uniquely inhibited from performing his role. Made prime minister only because Sonia did not take the job, he was completely aware of his handicap while almost every other important figure in Cabinet could claim to have a direct mandate.

The Cabinet list was almost entirely drawn up by 10 Janpath, Sonia's residence and the true seat of power. Manmohan had say over only his own PMO, but even here he was checked from appointing his first choice as principal secretary – Montek Singh Ahluwalia, a top economist and former IMF official – partly because two Sikhs in top positions, working in close proximity, may not be advisable. So, on the advice of his Punjab circle, he had picked TKA Nair. He got his choice of NSA in Mani Dixit, a feisty diplomat widely recognised for his brilliance, but also had to accommodate Gandhi family loyalist MK Narayanan, intelligence chief to four prime ministers, in the role of special adviser for internal security.

In the early months of the Manmohan government, his spin doctors, led by Sanjaya Baru, put out word of how well the diarchy was functioning – he in charge of government, Sonia in charge of party and coalition affairs. The narrative was that the two met regularly and comfortably, dropping into each other's home by turn. Yet, behind the scenes, it was hardly so comfortable. On July 4, bare weeks after he was sworn into office, Manmohan was forced to announce a National Advisory Council headed by Sonia who would have the rank of Cabinet minister. Everyone knew what it meant – a sort of super Cabinet would now keep watch over the government, and the nature of its membership indicated the left-of-centre thinking that would rule the NAC.

Fond as Sonia was of Manmohan Singh, they were poles apart. One was fixed on growing the economy, the other on improving her party's chances of winning the next election, and hopefully, pitchforking her son to power. While good economics is said to translate into good politics, the route is seldom common. Sonia, whose political learning came from watching her late mother-in-law's populism, focused on redistributing the pie that Manmohan had not been given enough leeway to bake.

To complicate matters for the prime minister, long-serving Congress figures were in charge of key ministries such as foreign affairs, home affairs and human resource development. These were powerful men with a history of loyalty to the family and party. Human resource development minister Arjun Singh, for instance, was a man who had stuck to the clan even though

Jawaharlal Nehru had his father jailed for corruption. Defence minister Pranab Mukherjee had been a junior minister when Manmohan Singh was still a bureaucrat.

Two months after he was sworn in as prime minister, said Natwar Singh, who was foreign minister at the time and claims a connection to the Nehru-Gandhi family dating to July 1944, Manmohan Singh had begun to complain the arrangement was not working for him. On a visit to Bangkok in late July, he summoned Natwar Singh to his hotel suite one evening to say that the situation could not be tolerated and he was thinking of calling it a day. Natwar Singh soothed his feelings and told him he had been given a job and he had to do it, and that he had the full support of his team. That is Natwar Singh's version. Earlier that month, the Opposition figure, George Fernandes, who was formerly India's defence minister, had charged at a press conference that Natwar Singh had been ignoring the prime minister, avoiding briefing him or even meeting with him. Mukherjee, who was defence minister in Manmohan's first Cabinet, would do the same, with the prime minister chafing quietly at the insult, yet not bold enough to discipline his colleague.

In March 2005 came an event that would test the tenuous arrangement even further. SS Razi, governor of Jharkhand, a tribal-dominated state carved out of Bihar, was at the centre of a controversy after Jharkhand delivered a hung verdict in state elections. The BJP and its ally turned in 36 seats in the 81-seat state assembly. Congress and the local ally, Jharkhand Mukti Morcha, claimed 26. That swelled to 33 with another party pledging support to Congress. That still left the coalition short of a majority. To everyone's surprise, Razi invited the smaller group to form the government, leading to a national uproar. Manmohan, not privy to the instructions that are believed to have flown from New Delhi, was angry and upset. Eight days later, in a damage control exercise that followed loud complaints from the party that the prime minister was "invisible", the state government was handed back to the BJP. Talk was soon rife about the widening rift between the prime minister and his party chief. *India Today* magazine, well-sourced with Congress, ran a cover story detailing the friction between government and party.

"The rise of the maximum leader, reminiscent of the Soviet era, is directly proportional to the steady thinning of prime ministerial power," it said. "Looks like the odd couple is in danger of becoming a couple at odds."

Still, on the first anniversary of the coalition government, in May 2005, Sonia and Manmohan sang each other's praises in an effort to quell talk of their frayed ties and persistent chatter that she might want to be prime minister herself. Aiming her words as much towards Manmohan as the nation, she said, when asked whether she may reconsider her decision to decline the national leadership: "Why should I want to become PM now? There is a prime minister in place, a man of integrity who is doing an excellent job. He has a five-year term." She added, "I think the government has done a good job, but not perhaps the Congress party itself."

Manmohan gave himself a 6/10 for his first year's performance but the taunts that he was not in charge of the government would not go away. He was accused of being "invisible" and worse, "ineffective". The talk in New Delhi was that he continued to act as though he was not prime minister but still Indira Gandhi's economic adviser. The nation itself, however, seemed to like the man, as subsequent events would prove. As Pratap Bhanu Mehta, the respected political commentator, told me at the time, "The big problem is that the government is a bit reluctant to project its best asset – Manmohan Singh – for fear of alienating the old guard in the Congress."

Two years into his term, it appeared that Manmohan was still trying to assert himself, at least in matters of his economic agenda. After the FTA with Thailand and the Comprehensive Economic Cooperation Agreement with Singapore, some Indian industrialists began to moan that their businesses were being affected by the competition that arrived with the accords. One leading businessman, who had signed with a prominent multinational to manufacture car tyres in Pune city suddenly found the partner pulling out. The global company now found it more profitable exporting to India from Thailand. When the Asean and India FTA was being negotiated, Sonia lent her weight to the go-slow lobby. In April 2006, she wrote to Manmohan, advising him to move with caution on trade deals, particularly where it concerned farm imports. He wrote back a week later, standing his ground. In fact, he went further. At the Asian Development Bank's annual meeting, held that year in the southern city of Hyderabad, he called for a pan-Asia FTA, himself promising a "web of partnerships with countries of the region through free trade and comprehensive economic cooperation agreements".

It was only a matter of time before Manmohan wilted. An Early Harvest Programme that was part of the FTA was shelved, ostensibly with the intention of going directly into the full FTA. Many Asean states were upset. Malaysia's feisty trade minister, Rafidah Aziz, wrote her Indian counterpart, Kamal Nath, a stiff letter of complaint, pointedly using large font. Her irritation was understandable; Malaysia was the coordinator for the Asean-India FTA negotiations.

By the beginning of Manmohan's third year in office, it was evident to some in the know that the twin-pillar edifice that had held so much promise was seriously beginning to totter. A poll by *India Today* magazine showed that of the 39 ministers, 22 failed to score the passing grade of 35 on 100, and a majority were from the Congress party, the coalition leader. Among those with failing grades was human resource development minister Arjun Singh, Manmohan's nemesis and an old-style Congresswallah who had recently embarrassed him by prematurely revealing that the government was considering extending caste quotas in higher education. Barring announcements on the privatisation of Mumbai and Delhi airports, there was little forward movement on economic policy either. And, more importantly for a scholar like Manmohan, the intellectuals who had backed him so much now began to look askance at him. Andre Beteille, Manmohan's former colleague at DSE and the nation's top expert on social stratification, would quit the Knowledge Commission over the government's decision to extend caste-based quotas to as much as 49.5% of the intake in top colleges, including the famed Indian Institutes of Technology and the Indian Institutes of Management.

Castes categorised as Other Backward Classes, or OBC, form 52% of India and no government in a full-fledged democracy could overlook their claims to enforce a merit-only policy. Still, the decision enraged upper caste students. In New Delhi, the top medical school, All India Institute of Medical Sciences, was the focal point of their protests. Partly for that reason, Manmohan, when he needed surgery to relieve carpel tunnel syndrome, avoided going to AIIMS, where the surgery on the other wrist had been done the previous year, and chose the Army Hospital (Research & Referral) for his treatment. Along with Beteille, the Knowledge Commission's convener, Pratap Bhanu Mehta, would also leave. As he departed, Beteille wrote to Manmohan complaining that aspersions cast on the competence of the Commission "have been received in silence by your office".

Manmohan stayed mute. It was clear that he was increasingly unable, or unwilling, to stand up even for his oldest friends.

Still, the prime minister could claim credit for two significant developments – the social safety net for the rural poor called the National Rural Employment Guarantee Act, and markedly improved Hindu-Muslim relations, important in a nation which has had its periodic communal upheavals. Within the majority Hindu fold, caste tensions were down as well. Years later, both claimed successes would prove ephemeral. The jobs guarantee caused massive distortions in the job market. (Punjab farmers, for instance, would have trouble employing migrant labour from Bihar for the cropping season and even cottage industries such as silk sari-weaving would suffer.) And communal tensions, it would emerge, were subdued only because of the opportunities that arose from an expanding economy – and this was no direct contribution of Manmohan's but more from the lag effects of economic policies put in place by the predecessor government led by the BJP's Atal Bihari Vajpayee.

Overseas, though, Manmohan was hugely respected for what he stood for, the way he conducted himself, and of course, as the leader of a nation that once again was catching the attention of the world. Attending a G-20 summit in his first term, his turn to speak came after British prime minister Gordon Brown's address. Brown's speech was scholarly, and was received with polite applause. Then it was Manmohan's turn. In simple words, he sketched out complex ideas, and was heard with rapt attention. When his speech was over, spontaneous applause broke out and leader after leader endorsed his words. Brown himself walked over to congratulate him.

"I say, Prime Minister," Brown told him. "I thought I'd made a great speech, but you overshadowed me completely."

Manmohan's big moment came in 2008 when he stared down the Left parties that gave his coalition parliamentary support without participating in government. Enraged that he would go through with the nuclear deal with the US, the Left withdrew support, bringing the government to the brink of collapse. Only intense backroom negotiations with other parties that stepped in with support saved the day for the UPA government. For Manmohan, this was an unmixed blessing. Not only could he now move swiftly on building ties with the US – his strategic instincts told him this was critical – he could also move on economic policy without feeling the Left's restraining hand on his collar. This also affected his equation with Sonia. It meant that, in his second term that started in May 2009, he could be more his own man because the coalition chairwoman had fewer allies in the left of centre.

Indeed, if Sonia's NAC was behind landmark moves such as the Right to Information Act and the National Rural Employment Guarantee Act in UPA-1, she found herself more circumscribed in UPA-2. Activists such as Aruna Roy had helped push through the RTI, thanks to Left support. But in UPA-2, the leftist yoke was off the government's neck. Among those who joined the NAC in UPA-2, and contributed greatly to its orientation, was the former Indian Administrative Service officer turned NGO figure, Harsh Mander, my contemporary at University of Delhi.

The son of a civil servant himself – his father, Har Mander Singh, was the deputy commissioner of Bomdilla who performed the tricky mission in 1959 of meeting and transporting to safety the young Dalai Lama as he fled Chinese oppression in Tibet – Mander was the brain behind some of the controversial NAC-led initiatives such as the Food Security Bill, the Communal Violence Bill and the Land Acquisition Act. Other initiatives that flowed from him included legislation to improve the lives of street vendors, abolition of child labour and manual scavenging.

Sonia's NAC has been portrayed as a super Cabinet, with vast influence. In reality, things were a bit different. Its members worked pro bono, conducting their own research, and while the NAC's working groups functioned throughout, it met its chairwoman only once a month and usually for no more than half a day. The NAC mandate covered all aspects of social policy, with an emphasis on measures that would benefit the poor and the disadvantaged. Usually, the NAC constituted about a dozen members, whose tenures were renewed annually. Board members often disagreed vociferously, with the issue going to Sonia for the final word. Every time, she could be counted upon to display a strong social democrat instinct.

"She was always on the side of the disadvantaged and she would always look for a strongly secular angle," Mander told me. "Congress party itself was really a coalition of ideologies and she represented the left of centre, secular ideology."

This firmly secular orientation was the area where Sonia and Manmohan really converged. Otherwise, Manmohan's economic ideology was not too different from the BJP's. Several NAC members I knew, including respected former bureaucrat Naresh Saxena, speak of how well prepared Sonia used to be at meetings. She was also recognised for her sense of dignity and grace – the years of watching mother-in-law Indira Gandhi had rubbed off on her – as well as ideological clarity.

And she could be fantastically droll. For a time, the NAC had the interesting presence of Narendra Jadhav, who also served on the Planning Commission as a member with minister of state rank. The Commission, later disbanded by Modi, was led by Montek Singh Ahluwalia, a brilliant right-wing economist who was close to Manmohan and his wife. Once, when Jadhav strenuously argued against an NAC plan targeted to help the marginalised, Sonia looked at the man. "Clearly, your boss has trained you well," she told him, referring to Ahluwalia. The NAC dissolved in laughter.

The general perception is that Manmohan rubber-stamped the proposals from the NAC. In fact, the situation was far more nuanced. Manmohan often firmly disagreed on issues and would use a classic bureaucratic tactic – delay – to slow or halt plans he did not favour. Sanjaya Baru says in *Accidental Prime Minister* that Manmohan "received enthusiastically" the proposal for the National Rural Employment Guarantee Act when it travelled from the NAC to the PMO. But Mander insists that, if anything, Manmohan was deeply uncomfortable about it. Indeed, Mander said, in his direct discussions with Manmohan, the prime minister voiced his opposition to the bill, and even after it was enacted, did not give it full support.

Likewise, Mander said Manmohan stalled for time and resisted the Food Safety Act until six months before the government's tenure ended. As an economist, Manmohan recognised the terrible distortions food guarantees could cause and he resisted it stoutly. And when Sonia, enthused by Congress chief minister Ashok Gehlot's experiment to distribute free medicines in hospitals run by Rajasthan state, pushed for a nationwide scheme, Manmohan stood his ground and ruled out the idea. Had the food bill been enacted earlier, giving the government time to implement it, the history of the 2014 elections may have been a little different.

"What Singh did was to stand firm on big ticket items and concede the smaller stuff such as legislation on street vending, manual scavenging, etc," said Mander. "Congress was almost at war with itself and didn't have a clear story to tell, or sell. It ended up doing neither pro-poor or pro-business policies with any conviction." Mander is not wrong. Neither were the pro-business policies done with enough thought, as is obvious from the several scams that were exposed subsequently.

The NAC ended with the Congress government. One of Sonia's last acts was to gather the lower staff of the Commission for a group photograph with her. Everyone knew her government was dying, so there was a special poignancy to the moment. Sonia did not need the picture with the lower staff but she knew it was important for them. Hence that little deft touch that begets the loyalty that money cannot buy.

It is clear that on many other matters of critical national importance,

Manmohan could not stand up to Sonia at all. Saxena said he once expressed to Manmohan his worries over the growing culture of corruption in New Delhi, particularly in ministries led by coalition allies. Manmohan's response baffled him: that is not my problem to solve! Too often, the prime minister buckled, using the excuse of "coalition dharma" – that you had to compromise to steady the ship. Ultimately, it would prove disastrous for India, stilting its growth, weakening institutions, reducing faith in government.

When Manmohan hosted admiral Joshi that March weekend in 2014 as he prepared to yield power, he may also have been musing on how history would judge him. Even a child in India knew that had their prime minister had his way, and not agreed to be so subservient to the Gandhi family "high command", things would have been so different. Indeed, so weak was Manmohan that India, under him, failed to mark the 20th anniversary of economic reforms that had changed the face of the country – reforms that Manmohan had implemented under the instructions and political tutelage of Narasimha Rao. Rao, as prime minister, had begun to ignore Sonia, leading to a falling out so severe that while she personally visited the homes of all Cabinet ministers to invite them to her daugher Priyanka's wedding, she merely mailed the invitation to the prime minister. Fearful of upsetting the Gandhis, no government department celebrated the anniversary either, which passed in 2011.

If Manmohan's well-wishers, including former media adviser Baru, are to be believed, one of his three daughters would have liked him to quit mid-term, particularly in 2013 when he was insulted by his fellow party man and putative successor – the two-time MP Rahul Gandhi. Rahul had unexpectedly shown up at a junior party colleague's press conference to attack legislation just passed by Manmohan's Cabinet that would have effectively voided a Supreme Court order banning from parliament those who had received criminal convictions.

Sonia had forced the Manmohan Cabinet, to the prime minister's deep discomfiture, to process the legislation in order to save the Bihar strongman Lalu Prasad Yadav, a coalition ally. He had been convicted in court on several counts of corruption during his term as chief minister of the sprawling province. As can only happen in India, when forced to leave office, he had installed his homemaker wife as chief minister.

Now, Sonia, as the coalition head, was trying to save him, only to find the son stepping in unexpectedly. Calling the intended legislation a piece of "nonsense", Rahul proceeded to dramatically tear up a copy of the ordinance in full view of the gathering in the Press Club of India.

Manmohan was abroad at the time for a meeting with US president Barack Obama, and the press feasted on the news of the clash within Congress. Many, including Baru, wanted Manmohan to quit immediately to save himself and his office from being demeaned by the upstart Congress vice-president whose intention, farcical or otherwise, clearly was to distance himself in the public eye from the government so influenced by his mother.

Manmohan's uncomplaining acceptance of Rahul's slight in his second term contrasts with the way he handled the stripling during his first term. Campaigning for Congress in the heartland state of Uttar Pradesh, where Muslims make up a fifth of the population, Rahul suggested in a speech that had someone from his family been in active politics in 1992, Hindu zealots would have been prevented from destroying a 16th century mosque in Ayodhya, seen as a watershed event in the communal history of the country. A Congress government led by Rao was in charge of India at the time. Manmohan bristled at the insult to his predecessor and political mentor. A rare snub followed for Rahul.

"He was truly a *sanyasi* in politics," Manmohan said a few days later, using the Hindi word for 'renunciate' to describe Rao. "He was a moderniser who was steeped in our tradition and ethos. He was a rare scholar and statesman who gave a new sense of direction not only to our economic policies but also foreign policies."

But now, as on countless occasions before when his writ did not run past the powerful Gandhi clan, Manmohan stayed on, swallowing the phlegm.

Why did he take the insult? Some critics say he did so because he, or people in his immediate family, had come to enjoy the trappings of office and were reluctant to let it all go. A senior PMO official told me he was once confronted by Gursharan Kaur and one of her daughters, while on an overseas tour. They wanted to know if the prime minister intended to quit. Amused that they should come to him seeking answers to a question that should have been put across the family dining table, he asked them to talk directly to Manmohan.

Perhaps Manmohan was only too aware that he served at the pleasure of the Gandhi mother and son. Throughout his first term he was seen as a mere seat warmer, and the press, without any subtlety, would often beard him with the poser – how long do you expect to be around? Manmohan would show no irritation and always came up with a stock response – to lead this great nation was an honour no one could refuse. By showing no apparent ambition to consolidate his power, and always expressing a willingness to step aside for the Gandhi scion if asked to, Manmohan successfully deflected any insecurities the Gandhis may have had on his account. Baru often said Manmohan is overestimated as an economist and underappreciated as a politician. And he is right.

"Even at the height of the political crisis over the civil nuclear deal with the US, there really was no threat of Singh quitting. He loved the job too much," a PMO person, who met him several times a week, told me. "If he came close to quitting, it was only towards the end of his second term when his image came apart, thanks to the scam after scam that erupted in his government. Even then, I am not sure that even if he wanted to leave, Gursharan would have allowed him to."

But the source close to Manmohan gave me another reason why he would not go – fear that if he quit, embarrassing Congress and the Gandhis, they would round on him and frame him in some way. "For a middle-class Indian, there is no bigger embarrassment than seeing a policeman at your door. The lasting television images of Narasimha Rao are of him emerging from one lower court building after another, in some corruption case," said this person. "Rao was Singh's political mentor. His worst fears are that the Gandhis will embroil him in some corruption case once he steps down. The

Gandhis are capable of doing that, never mind how loyal he has been to them."

Others who remember the lengthy biodata of Manmohan that his office put out, think he was chasing a record of being the only prime minister since Jawaharlal Nehru to serve out two consecutive full terms. The most charitable, and noble, explanation – and his words to admiral Joshi bear this out – was Manmohan may have been reluctant to make way for a possibly corrupt successor gaining office merely on the basis of his personal loyalty to the Gandhi mother and son. Certainly, there were many who fancied their chances. Pranab Mukherjee, Manmohan's former boss in the commerce ministry, and the most powerful minister in Cabinet until he was elevated to the largely ceremonial role of president of India, was one. Another was Sushil Shinde, who thought he could parlay his under-caste status to make a claim for the job. The list included two others who concealed their ambitions better – AK Antony, the defence minister who had cultivated a scrupulously clean image, and the haughty and brilliant P Chidambaram who had excelled in every portfolio given him, including, latterly, finance and home affairs. But Antony knew no Hindi and his English sometimes could not be understood while it was not clear if Chidambaram would be as malleable if he got the big job. There was also lower house Speaker Meira Kumar, an English-speaking woman candidate from a caste so low in the social order that they were regarded Untouchable by Hindus a half century ago. The former outcastes, now called Dalits, form a significant vote bank. They had voted Congress for decades until groups such as Mayawati's Bahujan Samaj Party emerged to aggregate their vote, weakening Congress.

Whatever his reason for not quitting, history will record that Manmohan was unable, or unwilling, to intervene as he presided over what is generally regarded as India's most corrupt period since the nation's independence from British rule in 1947. Indeed, his silence was so resounding that it had become the subject of jokes around the nation, spreading to the diaspora. At a concert by top Indian and Pakistani musicians at Singapore's Star theatre in 2013, the Indian master of ceremonies began by requesting that the audience "switch your cellphones to Manmohan Singh mode".

Perhaps he was also driven by a deep sense of duty. "Things are not entirely the way I would like them to be," he told a select bunch of television editors in early 2011, when they peppered their tough questions on government with references to his own clean image. "Quite frankly, I never felt like resigning because I have a job to do. I will stay the course. I did not think of giving up halfway."

His helplessness cemented a conviction about India's abysmal state of governance. Behind his back, some key figures in Congress had started referring to him as MKK – *mein ki karaan*, a Punjabi phrase that translates as the lament, "what am I to do?" The public sensed a paralysis in their prime minister that was almost physical. His movements, caught on television, seemed to be spasmodic and he looked wooden at the best of times.

Unknown to most, there was a reason: Manmohan had, according to a credible medical source in Bangalore, started showing signs of early stage Parkinson's disease. It was a closely guarded secret, unknown even to many senior officers in the PMO. Manmohan's medical team had reached out and consulted Dr Satish Chandra, the director of National Institute of Mental Health & Neuro Sciences, based in Bangalore. The disease was in check, my sources told me. So, as the nation chuckled at Manmohan's "Energiser Bunny" gestures and mannerisms, only a small band of people knew why this was so.

Sonia too was in poor health. The Gandhi dowager had always had a history of asthma but a new complication turned up. Some say this was diverticulitis, or inflammation of the diverticulum, especially in the colon. For this, she had been admitted to Sir Ganga Ram Hospital, not far from her home. In late July 2011, she unexpectedly left the country for medical treatment abroad. No explanation was given. Rajdeep Sardesai, the television personality behind CNN-IBN news channel, said he was threatened with a lawsuit by Ahmed Patel, Sonia's political secretary, after his channel said she was being treated at Memorial Sloan Kettering Cancer Centre in New York City. It is generally accepted – and never confirmed – that she was being treated for cancer.

The Bangalore daily, *Deccan Herald*, had the clearest version of that treatment. On August 5, it revealed that the surgery was for cervical cancer and had been performed under the supervision of Dr Dattatreyudu Nori, a leading Indian-American doctor. Cystography reports were awaited, the paper claimed, and further treatment to be determined subsequently.

The report was never confirmed and her illness remains a mystery. The Congress party, typically taciturn on matters involving the first family, merely said in a statement: "Mrs Gandhi was recently diagnosed with a medical condition and upon the advice of her doctors, has travelled abroad for surgery." Upon her return, Narendra Modi, ever the gentleman, sent her flowers and a get-well card.

Today, the decade of Manmohan is widely remembered for the multitude of scandals. Yet, to judge Manmohan on the basis of those alone or the government he ran for 10 years, however timorously at times, is not to get the full picture. For the record is mixed. Among his top achievements, no doubt, is the reset of ties with the US and Japan. At home, India enjoyed a period of social harmony, a significant achievement for a nation whose religious communities – and castes – have often clashed. Now, as India's minority groups grow worried under Modi, Manmohan's time, at least on that account, seems like a gilded age.

While his own background as a minority Sikh played a small part, recent research also indicates that the strong growth registered in his first term starting in 2004 – thanks to the sound economy he inherited from the BJP-led government and, reaching further back, the unshackling of the economy he performed under prime minister Rao's directions – also contributed to social peace as people focused on improving their lives. But it is also undeniable that growth slowed significantly in his second term on the back of his government's policy paralysis and persistently high inflation. His last two years saw average economic expansion of less than 5%, bringing to the surface once again the acid label of "Hindu rate of growth". Worse, he failed to overrule a dirigiste finance minister who slapped a retrospective tax on key multinationals such as telecoms giant Nokia, scaring away investors.

"His credentials as the architect of the 1991 reforms were an important factor in his being chosen prime minister, yet the promise that his elevation held remains only partially fulfilled," the respected newspaper, *The Hindu*, said in an editorial in May 2014.

Sadly for Manmohan, the foreign policy breakthroughs he sought failed to materialise. Under pressure from allies in West Bengal state, which shares a border with Bangladesh, he had to renege on a deal to give that country a larger share of common waters, severely angering the friendly Sheikh Hasina government in Dhaka. Tamil Nadu's politics prevented him from building a closer relationship with the strategically perched nation across the water, Sri Lanka, where China subsequently made rapid inroads. And his dream of visiting Pakistan, the land of his birth, remained unfulfilled. Meanwhile, China had been making several border probes along their undemarcated frontier and finding the Indian response weak.

Much has been made about Manmohan's burning desire to visit Pakistan as prime minister. His decision to oust MK Narayanan, a noted Pakistan sceptic, and replace him with the more pliable Shivshankar Menon as NSA, is cited as born out of a desire to get to that outcome. And it is true that Manmohan would frequently inquire with the Pakistan desk of the Ministry of External Affairs when he could go to Pakistan. Yet, a senior official who worked closely with Manmohan told me that while it was true Manmohan had a "rose-tinted view" of Pakistan, he "always listened to reason; there was never any question of him pushing the envelope".

The sentimentality may be overstressed. Manmohan's view of his land of birth is probably not much different from that of others of his generation, who had suffered in the violence and upheavals of the Great Partition of India. I once asked my wife's grandmother, who died just short of her 102nd birthday in 2015, whether she would like me to arrange for her to visit Bhera in Pakistan's Sargodha District, scene of her childhood. Indians have great difficulty getting a Pakistani tourist visa, so I thought she would leap at the offer. Instead, her response was philosophical: "Why rake up memories? All that is behind me now." Some years later, after a trip to Pakistan, I described the road journey from Lahore, capital of Punjab, to Islamabad, the national capital, and the orchards full of the kinnow variety of mandarin oranges that came into view as I drove through Sargodha. She looked away and did not pursue the subject.

For that reason, I am inclined to think that Manmohan, who lost kinfolk in the Partition riots, was probably driven not so much by sentiment as a desire to find a diplomatic breakthrough that could help cement his legacy as a peacemaker with India's most important, yet nettlesome neighbour. As a collector of awards, perhaps he had eyed a potential Nobel Peace Prize as well. Who knows?

Domestically, the Congress-led government under him ran aground and made several political bungles, notably in its stronghold of Andhra Pradesh, where it had won 34 of the 42 parliamentary seats in 2009. Today, after the 2014 polls, Congress stands decimated there, even after agreeing to split it to cater to local sentiments in a key region, Telangana.

Manmohan's notable foreign policy success was the nuclear deal with the US, which helped lift global sanctions on India's nuclear programme and enhanced its strategic elbow room in Asia. But even the US account had gone "off the rails a bit", as a senior Indian diplomat told me, towards the end of the government's tenure. American companies such as Westinghouse Electric were shying away from building nuclear plants in India, thanks to onerous legislation and responsibility clauses. The US also bungled the treatment of an Indian diplomat arrested for making false declarations on the money she paid her domestic help in New York, leading to the withdrawal of special privileges accorded to American diplomats in India and part of their security. It was not until Modi, a man who had been denied a US visa for 10 years, arrived in New Delhi that the relationship once again picked up pace.

Could Manmohan have done better? Certainly. His government was returned to power with a larger majority because people saw in him an honest and competent administrator, the very qualities for which they later turned to BJP's Modi. But rather than using the 2009 victory to assert himself, and put his own stamp on government, Manmohan too meekly yielded to his coalition allies and the Gandhi household. A *Time* magazine cover story on Manmohan, published in July 2012, was appropriately titled "The Underachiever". Baru, his former media adviser, revealed that Manmohan told Baru he was reconciled to the fact that "there cannot be two centres of power". The consequences have been lethal for not just his reputation, but India's future too.

Perhaps it is fitting then that the last word on Manmohan should come from a senior politician of the rival BJP. "The prime minister goes out with dignity and grace," Arun Jaitley, leader of the Opposition in the upper house and later finance and defence minister to Modi, said in a blog post shortly after the 2014 election results were announced. "He will remain an elder statesman and a man of credibility to guide the nation. Only if he had stood up at the right time and disagreed, he would have been regarded with still greater honour."

PART V

INDIA RISING

17
A Murder in Mumbai: The Rise of Narendra Damodardas Modi

"I have come with one medicinal herb that I am offering as a remedy to India's problems. And that herb is 'development'."

— Narendra Modi

TWELVE YEARS AGO if you had asked who in the BJP's younger guard had the best chances of rising to national leadership, the line would have started with Pramod Mahajan, a dynamic figure known for his fundraising abilities, deep knowledge of the political lie of the land, terrific networks and strong organisational capabilities. He was also affable and accessible, which made him a draw to journalists, many of whom chose to overlook the less savoury sides of his personality, of which there were several. During the early 1990s, as a correspondent for the Hongkong magazine *Asiaweek*, I was an occasional visitor to his flat near Gurudwara Bangla Sahib, always received with great hospitality and sent away with fabulous insights, and, when required, perfect quotes for a story.

Mahajan had come to national notice in 1990 when he organised the *rath yatra* – chariot ride – that propelled Lal Krishna Advani as the champion vote-getter of the party. Advani, who coined the phrase "pseudo secularism" for the minority vote-bank politics of Congress, used the *yatra* – which loosely translates as journey or pilgrimage – to garner support among the majority Hindus of India for the building of a temple to Rama on the site of a mosque built by the Muslim invader, Babur.

Varnas are the main orders of Hinduism – including Brahmins, Kshatriyas, Vaishyas and Sudras – and each *varna* includes hundreds of castes and subcastes. Beyond are the outcaste Dalits, so low in the order that they aren't even considered a part of the caste system. The *yatra* was a huge success because, for a brief period, it managed to aggregate large sections of Hindus, a community generally riven along caste and *varna* lines. When Mahajan was romping around as the champion organiser, Narendra Modi's role was limited to making arrangements for the *yatra* in his home state of Gujarat.

On the morning of April 22, 2006, Pramod Mahajan was in Mumbai visiting his family when his younger brother, Pravin, entered the room holding a .32 calibre Browning pistol. Old resentments in the younger man had come to a boil. There were hot words, four shots were fired. One missed; the other three lodged themselves in Mahajan's liver and pancreas. Bleeding and barely conscious, he was taken to PD Hinduja Hospital & Medical Research Centre. Thirteen days later, he was dead after suffering a heart attack in hospital.

Barely a month after his death, his only son, Rahul, was battling for life after a late night binge went wrong. The family secretary, Vivek Maitra, was dead, possibly from a cocaine overdose. They were supposed to have been in mourning and indeed, were to leave soon for a holy spot as part of the ritual for the dead. But, just after 10.30 pm, they were said to have ordered food as they swilled champagne. Three of their drinking companions, whom the domestic help did not appear to recognise, left, but returned later. By 2 am, Rahul Mahajan was on the floor unconscious and Maitra on a sofa, most probably dead. A sachet of white powder apparently found in Maitra's pocket matched traces in the champagne glasses, police said.

Maitra, the elder Mahajan's close aide for 15 years, was one of those louche personalities of whom there is no shortage in the BJP and its periphery. On a visit to Singapore, accompanying Pramod Mahajan, then India's minister for information technology, Maitra had told me his story. A man who rose through student politics in Maharashtra, Mahajan's home state, he had been assigned to "assist" Mahajan by the Rashtriya Swayamsevak Sangh (RSS), the umbrella Hindu organisation that is the ideological fountainhead of the BJP. From then on, he had become Mahajan's shadow and claimed to have performed many "special assignments" for the politician. Unlike the smooth Mahajan, his special assistant was a coarse hood. Archetypal RSS figures tend to have a modicum of restraint and discipline, but this fellow was a hard-drinking man who suffered from hypertension and other ailments.

At a dinner for the visiting minister, held at the Harilela-owned Holiday Inn Hotel's Tandoor restaurant, Maitra made a complete fool of himself, ordering drink after drink and hitting on the petite Malaysian-Chinese waitresses from Ipoh. If Mahajan noticed, and it was difficult for anyone to have missed Maitra's behaviour, he ignored it. Indeed, he seemed most indulgent towards his man, smiling benignly at him all the time. It made me wonder what grip this lout had on Mahajan that he could be excused so many trespasses.

The drinks and drugs binge would not only end Maitra's life but also the political career of his late master's son, then only 31 years old and already labelled by a non-sceptical media as "BJP's Rahul". For Rahul Mahajan, a former civilian pilot, had been pitched as a putative vice president of the BJP's youth wing, pushed, partly against his instincts, by the ambitious Maitra himself. Newspapers were going to town with the story of Rahul Mahajan sitting in his jacuzzi snorting heroin with 500 rupee notes while Maitra watched. Interestingly, while the BJP spokesmen quickly tried to distance the party from the scandal, calling it a "family matter", no less than former prime minister Atal Bihari Vajpayee defended the younger Mahajan, describing his follies as the peccadilloes of youth.

"Rahul had nurtured friendships with people of questionable integrity," Vajpayee said. "We will see how the boy can be brought back on the right track from where he has strayed."

Interestingly, the Congress government also let the matter drop, perhaps returning the favour that Vajpayee had shown the party when one of their significant young got into trouble at a US airport some years earlier. At the time, the lad had reached out to Indian ambassador Naresh Chandra, who in turn had called Vajpayee. The wise old Vajpayee had issued instructions to do everything in the ambassador's power to spring the youngster, setting up a connect across the political divide that would hold for years. (Until Modi, beholden to none, frequently attacked Priyanka Gandhi's husband Robert Vadra's land dealings during his 2014 election campaign, sneering at *daamad-ji* – Mr Son-in-law!)

With Pramod Mahajan out of the way, the BJP's list of Next Gen leaders narrowed considerably. There were highly articulate figures in the younger crowd, including the legally trained Sushma Swaraj and her bête noire, Arun Jaitley, urban and urbane faces of the party. Modi was the one born on the wrong side of the tracks, as it were. But he was swiftly building up a favourable track record. And certainly, unlike Pramod Mahajan, who was older than he by a year, he left no trace of personal misdemeanour in his wake.

Born into a backward Hindu caste of Ghanchis, or oil millers, in Vadnagar, 110 km north of the Gujarat capital city of Gandhinagar, the young Modi knew poverty – but not deprivation – in his early years. By all accounts his youth, like that of millions of other Indians, was unremarkable. He helped out at his father's tea stall, loved drama in school, and was a strong swimmer. Like many of his time, at age three, he was engaged to a woman chosen by his parents, an alliance from which he walked away in his late teens, before they lived as man and wife; so no great ill-will touches him on account of that action. There is another nugget from his past, though, that is important: there were Muslim Ghanchis as well, and Modi, the man who refuses to accept headgear gifted by Muslim ulemas in public, saying he had no time for tokenism in the name of appearing to be secular, had many friends from the minority community in his early days.

At the age of eight, he began attending the local unit of RSS and from that point on, in so many ways, the Sangh Parivar – Sangh Family – would be his family, nurturing him in youth, building his consciousness around a

Hindu identity, its emphasis on physical strength and martial preparedness all built around a core credo of "renunciation, dedication and hard work". Four years after his induction into RSS, China would attack India, leaving a national scar on the Indian psyche, including the 12-year-old Modi's. Then in 1965 came another war. Pakistan attacked India and the tea boy at the railway station would watch wounded soldiers being ferried home from the front, seminal influences that would be reinforced in later years as he dealt with China and Pakistan.

Two years later, then 17, Modi left home to travel around India, the nomadic existence combined with spartan living and celibacy perhaps evoking a mental connection in him with the sadhus and renunciates of old, particularly the Bengali monk, Swami Vivekananda, whose work and speeches would influence him greatly. He would return home to Ahmedabad briefly after two years on the road, to a city that was just recovering from communal riots. The war with Pakistan over Bangladesh would follow in 1971, and the victorious Indira Gandhi, now hailed as the incarnation of the Goddess of Power, would take India into Emergency Rule in 1975. Modi was jailed in 1971 after participating in an RSS rally demanding that RSS workers be allowed entry into the Indian Army, one of the country's most secular institutions, from which the RSS had been banned. Modi became increasingly active as a covert operative for the RSS during the Emergency, even learning the art of disguise.

If Modi today sleeps less than five hours daily, and spends up to 16 hours on meetings and files, and an hour on exercise, he is harking back to that early training and the influences he absorbed before entering his teens. And when he denies ever feeling lonely, or the need for a life partner – "I am not lonely because I am always among the people" – it does not sound insincere. That was how he lived for the past 40 years.

By the time he entered his 40s, he had become a force to be reckoned with in the Gujarat BJP. But Modi came to national notice as a capable organiser only after the March 1995 state elections in Gujarat, where the BJP, for the first time, got a clear majority to run the state, winning two-thirds of the 182 seats and toppling the Congress party. He had been named Gujarat state secretary of the BJP the previous year by Advani, who had once again become the BJP's national president. Keshubhai Patel was named chief minister and with him came other names, including Shankersinh Vaghela, Modi's old friend and soon-to-be enemy. (Vaghela is now the Opposition leader in the Gujarat assembly after he cut away from the BJP to set up his own party, then ended up with Sonia's Congress.)

But Modi, already powerful and rising, was accused of unsettling Patel's regime, which ended with the BJP swapping Modi for Vaghela six months later. Seen as deeply divisive, Modi was packed off to New Delhi as a national secretary of the party, the watchful Advani again intervening on his behalf to secure him a soft landing. There his bonds with Advani, his great backer for a decade, would tighten. He would also build other networks in the party and in the wider world. There was one more thing: he would also taste and master the ability to use national media, including a perfect understanding of the power and peculiarities of television and the vulnerabilities of the key figures in each channel. Later, after a series of bad experiences with media, including partial use of his comments and deliberate distortions of truth, would come a certain wariness. Hence, all too often, a difficult question is met with a cold look that often reduces the questioner to a stuttering jelly: *Aap ka agenda kya hai?* What is your agenda?

But he was still only a sideshow, the quiet organiser. Others more flamboyant, including city-bred lawyers like Arun Jaitley and Sushma Swaraj (now finance and foreign ministers in Modi's Cabinet) were the rising stars in the BJP's forefront while backstage, the brilliant K Govindacharya, a polyglot who continues to have a fan following in RSS ranks, held court in the BJP's national office. But Modi was attracting attention too, including that of the popular and respected prime minister, Atal Bihari Vajpayee, who sent him on several overseas trips, including to the US.

For all that, according to accepted wisdom, Modi's mind at the time was never far from Gujarat, where Patel had returned to power. In his autobiography, *Lucknow Boy*, the late Vinod Mehta, who gave the breath of life to the sassy weekly, *Outlook*, recounted Modi showing up at his door and attempting to plant negative stories about Patel. Perhaps Modi was being vile but he had good reason to want a government change in Gujarat. The state government had badly mismanaged the handling of the devastating earthquake that struck its Kutch region in January 2001, and came after a severe drought in many regions the previous year. Popular support for the government was severely eroded. The state, with its deep vein of entrepreneurship, was flagging under years of misrule by first Congress and latterly, the BJP. In the year before Modi took full charge of Gujarat, its economy had shrunk by 5%.

In October 2001, five years after he had been bounced out of Gujarat, Modi was back in the state, with Patel forced into exile. This time, Modi was the chief minister. In a state until then dominated by a long list of Patels starting with the Independence figure, Sardar Vallabhai Patel, the nation's first home affairs minister, here was a backward caste boy catapulted to power. In his highly sympathetic *Narendra Modi – A Political Biography*, Andy Marino, who seems to have had unprecedented access to the man, said Modi had not expected to be made chief minister. Indeed, when Vajpayee gave him his orders to take charge of Gujarat, Modi had demurred and offered to spend 10 days in a month in the state. It took two days of persuasion, according to Modi's version as relayed by Marino, to persuade him to accept the task.

Having been appointed chief minister, Modi needed to get elected to the state assembly soon. India's rules prescribe that a person can hold ministerial office as long as he is elected to the state or national legislature within six months. Modi would do that through a by-election in February 2002. Still not certain of his public allure despite his formidable grip on the party machinery, he decided to contest from Rajkot-II Assembly constituency, a "safe" BJP seat the party had comfortably won since 1985.

Modi took the seat with 57% of the votes but his victory margin of 14,000-plus votes was half the previous BJP candidate's margin in the 1998 state assembly poll for the seat.

Crucially, Keshubhai Patel, target of Modi's manoeuvres, did not campaign for Modi, pleading ill health. Perhaps it was a blessing; Gujaratis had tired of Patel, tainted by his poor track record in office. In two constituencies that also went for by-elections at the same time and where Patel did campaign, the BJP lost both seats. Modi also got little help from Viswa Hindu Parishad and the Bajrang Dal, both hardline Hindu outfits. But the RSS turned out in strength to lend a hand to its loyal underling, helping him win and setting up a political connection that Modi finds useful still and difficult to shed.

There was another result from that by-election and *The Times of India* headline of February 26 said it all: "Modi wins, but party loses in Gujarat". The personality-before-party cult that so marked his later years of dominance was just about to begin.

Two days after he legitimised his rule with his election victory came the shock that would shape the way the world would look at Modi since.

On the morning of February 27, the Sabarmati Express pulled into the station of Godhra with more than 2,000 passengers. The train was five hours late as it headed for its final destination, Ahmedabad. Most people on board were Gujaratis coming home after visiting the town of Ayodhya in Uttar Pradesh, where a decade ago a Hindu mob, watched by Advani, had destroyed the 16th century Babri Mosque because it stood on what is purported to be the birthplace of their God, Rama.

Godhra is a town just inside Gujarat. Had the incident that was to follow taken place a hundred miles earlier in the journey, Indian political history may well have been different. As it happened, as the late-running train with its Rama devotees pulled out of Godhra Station, it was pelted with rocks. Someone pulled the emergency chain and the train came to a stop less than a kilometre from the station. A crowd of Muslims, as many as the passengers in the train, had gathered hurling stones and abuse, calling for blood. Some of the calls for violence apparently emanated from the local mosque's loudspeakers. Before long, Coach S-6 of the train was aflame, set alight by Molotov cocktails. Those who jumped out of the burning carriage were assaulted with iron rods and other weapons. The two fire tenders of the local fire brigade were rendered useless by suspected sabotage. When the firefighters finally set off for the station, a crowd led by a Congress politician – now in jail – blocked their progress. Within the hour, 59 people lay dead, more than half of them women and children.

Modi rushed down to Godhra and a quick check of the crime scene and conversations with local officials suggested this was no accident, but a staged attack with a larger goal, just as the terrorist attack on the Indian parliament a few months before had been. "This inhuman terrorist crime of collective and mass violence is not an incident of communal violence," he said in his first reaction to the outrage.

The news would spread like wildfire in a state that was always a communal tinderbox. Next day, the Viswa Hindu Parishad, the extremist Hindu outfit behind the Ayodhya outrage, called for a statewide shutdown. It was a matter of time before the retaliation began, and it did, fetching counter violence as well, as the state burned for three days. On February 28, as the first reports of violence came in, Modi went on Doordarshan, the state-run broadcaster, to appeal for calm. He noted that 58 people had perished in a single compartment, a tragedy that would bring tears to the eyes of the strongest men. Vowing to punish the guilty, he said "an example would be set that in future no one will ever dream of committing such an inhuman act". At the same time, he went on to say, "creating disturbances, indiscipline and venting anger publicly is not the solution". "I pray to you that the need of the hour is to maintain peace and self-discipline." He ended his speech by noting that while the 18,000 villages of Gujarat had been largely peaceful, the violence that had started in cities was disturbing. "It is my request that tit for tat is not a solution."

The incensed mobs were in no mood to listen. By the end of the fourth day, the time it took to quell the violence, more than a thousand people would be dead. The majority – 790 – would be Muslim but 254 Hindus would also die. The violence would shame India. The scars caused by the Congress party's inept handling of the Ayodhya crisis in 1992 had been barely healing when Muslims would feel a second blow, this time from Gujarat, 1,200 km west of Ayodhya. Few remember the trigger for the violence, which was the arson attack on the train. Thirteen years later, whenever Indian intelligence agencies interrogate suspected Muslim terrorists, Gujarat comes up again and again.

Visiting Singapore a few weeks later, Vajpayee was so embarrassed by the events in Gujarat that he failed to appear before the local media. Instead, he fielded Arun Shourie, his minister for disinvestment, to talk to journalists. It is widely known that Vajpayee had wanted Modi fired, but Advani stepped in to shield him once again, and Modi stayed.

In later years, a more nuanced perspective of his handling of the riots would emerge that would suggest Modi was not so callously immobile as was widely alleged for years. At the annual India Today Conclave of 2008, after being provoked by Digvijaya Singh, a feudal figure who rose to be chief minister of Madhya Pradesh, and later a key adviser to Rahul Gandhi, he seemed to lose his patience over being repeatedly accused of not doing enough to quell the violence.

When the riots took place, Modi said, his administration had sent urgent requests to all of his neighbouring states for police forces. "Diggy Raja", too, he said, using Digvijaya's nickname, had been approached. All three states ruled by Congress, including Digvijaya's Madhya Pradesh, as well as Maharashtra and Rajasthan, declined to send reinforcements.

It was true, as investigations ordered by the Supreme Court would reveal. Modi was speaking the truth. Digvijaya sputtered but had little defence.

That said, even many of his well-wishers are baffled that Modi has shown little public remorse for the killings early in his watch. His steadfast response is "If I am guilty, hang me." Beyond that, he says nothing. Perhaps it suits him politically with the Hindu hardliners who see him as a man who can stand up to terrorism or the demands of the principal minority community for unique treatment. Indeed, he can seem to be callously cold to Muslims. In July 2013, in an interview with Reuters, he said he had done "absolutely the right thing" during the 2002 riots. He went on to say in the interview, "If we are driving a car, we are drivers, and someone else is driving a car and we're sitting behind, even then if a puppy comes under the wheel, will [it] be painful or not? Of course it is. [Whether] I am a chief minister or not, I am a human being. If something bad happens anywhere, it is natural to be sad."

In December 2002, with communal tension still high and hundreds of thousands of Muslims still displaced, Gujarat went to the polls. Narendra Modi delivered the BJP's biggest ever victory in Gujarat with 127 seats, winning 50% of votes. This was an improvement over the BJP's win of 117 seats in 1998, itself an impressive performance. The BJP's vote share had improved by more than 5 percentage points.

There was no looking back. Modi felt confident enough to raze illegally constructed Hindu temples that were blocking roads in his state, surprising Muslims and the national intelligentsia, whose interest perked up in the man. Slowly, some Muslims in his state would begin to change their minds about Modi. In contrast to the suspicion with which Muslims in the populous Hindi-speaking heartland regard Modi, the sharp edges have rubbed off in Gujarat's Muslims' perception, which is more favourable of the man, and one in four of them is estimated to have voted for his government in the 2012 state elections. Certainly, it is easily proven that unlike the Gujarat of the past, even including the periods under Congress governments, the state has had no major communal conflagration under Modi since that awful first quarter of 2002.

By the time the next state election came around, in 2007, Modi's single-minded focus on development had begun to attract national and global attention. Singapore, always keen to see India do well, was intrigued by Modi very early in the day. In March 2006, I travelled to Ahmedabad and Gandhinagar with the Singapore elder statesman Goh Chok Tong and a couple of other Singapore MPs. Modi, from all accounts, listened carefully to what Goh had to say, including a view on how the Sabarmati riverfront could be developed to the benefit of the state. Later that year, Modi would be invited to Singapore, spending several days on the island before embarking on a tour of China to study its Special Economic Zones.

Modi is said to count Goh as one of his economic mentors. Certainly, they have a very comfortable relationship. It is possible that the island state's non-ideological approach to policy – whether economic or foreign – appeals to him. But he also could not have missed the absolute emphasis Singapore places on religious harmony and the benefits the island has gained from a Muslim minority that trusts its government and feels secure in their land, feeling no particular allure for the neighbouring nations of Indonesia and Malaysia that are predominantly Muslim.

By 2007, with Pramod Mahajan out of the way, it was clear that Modi was the man to watch in the Opposition. Within the BJP, the knives were being sharpened against the star rising in the west of the country. As Gujarat, his dominion, went to the polls that December, BJP's leadership moved swiftly to block his claim to be the candidate for the prime minister's job in the national polls due in less than two years. They abruptly announced in New Delhi that Advani would lead the campaign in the parliamentary elections, thus pitching him as the putative prime minister should Congress be toppled.

Advani had been Modi's mentor and shield for more than a decade. But times had changed. Now Advani was wary of his understudy, and with good reason. When Advani went on the stump in Gujarat, few turned out to hear him. The local BJP members appeared to be listless backers. When the crowds showed up, they hollered for "Narendra-bhai". This was insulting, and Advani did not miss the message. Modi had accepted his party's decision that Advani would lead the campaign in the national election, but he could not resist playing with him.

It wasn't just Advani who had come to resent Modi. His abrasive style was earning him plenty of enemies. There were many in the state bureaucracy, for instance, who were Modi cheerleaders. But a good number also detested his style and methods. So many portfolios were concentrated in his hands. In the 2007 state elections, several dozen of the 182 constituencies had BJP rebels contesting against the official candidates picked by Modi. Many BJP MPs flew down from New Delhi to queer the chief minister's pitch. They would not succeed. Modi had Gujarat in his thrall.

There are seminal moments in every politician's life that define his future. In India, the 1965 war with Pakistan was one for the diminutive Lal Bahadur Shastri, who displayed quiet determination. In 1977, Indira Gandhi, in Opposition, mounted an elephant to cross treacherous floodwaters in Bihar to reach the village of Belchhi, scene of a caste massacre, igniting her in the national consciousness as a champion of the underdog, just as much as her decisive splintering of Pakistan in 1971 had helped her gain an image of all-consuming power. For the handsome Rajiv Gandhi, it was the image of composure he presented in grief as he stood, with young son Rahul, at his assassinated mother's cremation in November 1984.

For Modi, his second big moment came on October 7, 2008.

Ratan Tata, India's best-regarded industry figure, presided over an empire that encompassed salt to software. The group, which began in steel, owned hotels, chemical plants, construction and power generation companies. Tata Consultancy Services, its outsourcing arm, was the group's principal money-spinner and India's top IT services company. Ratan Tata's passion, though, was automobiles, and against the misgivings of many Tata directors, he had pushed through Tata Motors' purchase of the British marque Jaguar Land Rover, perhaps the group's best overseas acquisition to date. Now Tata wanted a vehicle for India's scooter- and motorcycle-owning lower middle class to travel in safety and comfort without being exposed to the harsh elements. He dreamed up a car that would sell for less than 100,000 rupees (hence the one-lakh car, as it came to be known at its launch) and put together a team of engineers to execute the project.

The site chosen for the Nano plant was in West Bengal and Tata went there for two reasons. First, the Marxist government of the state, after decades of dirigiste policies, was awakening to the need to create industrial employment for the masses displaced from the land and was welcoming of investment. Second, rural purchasing power was strong in West Bengal, partly because the reds had neglected urban Bengal in favour of the rural. Unfortunately, the site picked for the plant was on one of the most fertile patches of land in the Hooghly River delta, provoking farmer unrest, labour agitation and shutdowns. Mamata Banerjee, then in Opposition as the head of All India Trinamool Congress, used the unrest to emerge as a champion of the Bengal *kulaks*. Work on the factory ground to a standstill. Angered and dismayed, the Tatas decided to look for an alternate location and walked into the waiting hands of Modi, who moved with unprecedented speed to line up land and other incentives for Nano to move to the area of Sanand in his state. On October 7, Ratan Tata appeared at a press conference with Modi to announce that Nano "had found a new home". More importantly, and rare for his upper crust, genteel persona, he went on to say: "There is a good M and a bad M."

There was no mistaking his meaning. The good M was Modi, the bad was Mamata, and the endorsement had come from no less than India's most respected industry captain.

True to his personality, even as he savoured his success, Modi could not help poking his opponents in the eye. He wrote to both Mamata and West Bengal chief minister Buddhadeb Bhattacharjee, offering them advice on good governance and the proper attitude to industry. To rub it in, he shared the letter with *Anandabazar Patrika*, the state's largest circulated Bengali language daily.

"The fact of the matter is," he crowed to Bhattacharjee, "Bengal does not yet have the work culture to produce a Nano."

Sanand has done well since and a vast production hub is gathering around the town. In March 2015, Ford Motor Company said it would spend more than a billion dollars to set up its second plant in India there, a facility that would initially deliver 240,000 cars a year and 270,000 car engines. Ford CEO Mark Fields said he was drawn to Sanand because of Gujarat's infrastructure and access to ports.

It used to be commonly said that border states like Gujarat and Punjab could host no major industry because of the perennial threat of a war with

Pakistan and the likelihood of attack on economic targets. Incredibly, Modi has defied that wisdom.

The Nano itself is not a success. Tata knows it misread the Indian consumer by portraying it as the world's cheapest car and is now scrambling to rebuild the car's image. But regardless of Tata's fortunes with the vehicle, Modi's sped along. Until then, he was tainted by the shame of the riots. Despite the thin evidence that could link him to wilfully allowing Gujarat's Muslims to be "punished" for Godhra, the known-unknown, as political scientists would say, was that he was somehow culpable. The Nano's move to Gujarat would grab global attention for Modi. From that point on, he would be seen as a doer and a nationalist. Just the kind of leader India had sorely missed for so long.

Around the time, keen observers of India's polity began to sense that the country was poised for a rightward lurch. Sonia Gandhi, campaigning for Congress in the Gujarat state polls, labelled Modi a *maut ka saudagar*, or "messenger of death", in one speech, then quickly dropped the epithet, possibly fearing a backlash from the Hindu community. Gujarat, certainly, wasn't seeing their leader as *maut ka saudagar*. Instead, they saw a man who had electrified its villages, improved roads and talked not of a vague secularism or strident *Hindutva*, but of sending girls to school and development and more development. Modi retained power comfortably in the 2007 polls.

Still, no politician aiming to lead India can afford to achieve success by playing to a single gallery, however well-stacked the stalls. Advani, readying his bid to national power, had tried to soften his hardline Hindu image by visiting Pakistan and hailing its founder, Mohammed Ali Jinnah, as a secular politician committed to Muslim-Hindu unity. This had discomfited hardline Hindu elements, including the RSS, whose core philosophy, influenced greatly by the emigres who migrated to India during the Partition, was built around a core of hatred for Pakistan and suspicion of Muslims.

Advani was on the right track but the gambit would not work for him. Poor losers in 2004, the BJP had turned on the Congress government in fury. Advani repeatedly trashed Manmohan Singh as India's "weakest ever prime minister" in parliament and outside, sounding mean, petty and vindictive against the dignified silence of the scholarly Sikh, then regarded as incorruptible. Indeed, the BJP had behaved most cussedly, attempting to block the nationally popular nuclear deal with the US and the introduction of a goods and services tax, both of which it had initiated in its years in power. Its acts would come back to haunt the BJP when the electorate handed Congress a bigger victory in 2009. Advani's dreams of leading India, it was clear, would not materialise in his lifetime.

It was only a matter of time before the BJP would turn to Modi, and he knew it. Had it not, Modi would have cut away from its folds a long time ago. Jairam Ramesh, the Congress ideologue and occasional speech-writer for the Gandhis, said he bumped into Modi one day in 2011 and the Gujarat leader told him candidly that if the party did not make him its candidate for prime minister in the 2014 elections, he would leave to form his own group.

It was a threat not to be taken lightly. Indian industry, vexed by the slowfootedness of Manmohan Singh's last years, were turning to Modi as a messiah. So funds would never be the problem. India's youth – two-thirds of the country are below 35 – had turned to him, seeking the qualities they so missed in a leader: decisiveness, self-confidence, free of graft and a man asking for votes on the plank of development for all.

Modi was now ready to take his message to all of India. The test bed would be New Delhi and the carefully chosen venue would be the Shri Ram College of Commerce (SRCC), one of the most sought-after institutions in University of Delhi. When he arrived that morning of February 2013 to speak to the students, Modi was aware he was speaking to an audience of the educated urban young. Nearly 1,800 of them crammed into the sports complex. To his delight, the invitation from the SRCC had come after an internal poll in the college indicated that he was the national figure the students most wanted to hear. He did not disappoint them. When it came to numbers, Modi had them at his fingertips. Cotton production had been 23,000 lakh (10 lakhs equals a million) bales when he took office, today it was 123,000 lakh bales; the milk sold in New Delhi and Singapore, he boasted, came from Gujarat. Most importantly, something that resonated with the growing consciousness of youth in the environment – Gujarat, he claimed, was the only state in the union where the water table was rising.

And displaying the confident ease that came to be his trademark on the stump, riveting crowds and television audiences, Modi would tease his listeners that day. Half an hour into his speech he looked at his watch and said he was aware that college lectures lasted 45 minutes and he was afraid of going over time. The students shouted back to him to continue as long as he liked. Pleased, Modi went on to speak for a full hour, peppering his address with catchphrases such as India's success in IT having moved the nation from "snake charmers to mouse charmers". Along the way, he would also offer the audacity of hope. Picking up a water glass he remarked that some would see it as half full and others, half-empty. "I have a third point of view. For me the glass is always full; half with water and half with air. We can turn over the situation." The SRCC students went into raptures. They had never heard a mass leader like this before. If those students were a focus group, there could be little doubt now who the teeming youth of India wanted as national leader. Not Rahul Gandhi, who had just entered his 40s but a man two decades older who'd captured their young minds with his energy, vision and optimism. Narendra Damodardas Modi.

Every week that passed, it was clear that Modi was the Opposition front runner. That September, the BJP officially named him its candidate for prime minister. The frenzied media following Modi was piling up, made it clear that there could be no other figure to lead the Opposition into battle in the parliamentary election due by May 2014. Modi's speeches were often telecast live, without a break for commercials. He was gathering steam on social media as well. His Twitter following expanded by the hundreds every hour, and he would often use the medium to share his thoughts and sometimes, break news, frustrating newspaper and television platforms that were used to intermediating the news exchange.

In December, state assembly elections were held in several states of the Hindi-speaking heartland and the debacle suffered by Congress in Rajasthan, which it controlled, and in Madhya Pradesh, where the BJP was the incumbent, gave an indication of the mood of the voters. The campaign, increasingly, began to take on the air of a presidential election. *Ab ki baar, Modi sarkar* – After this, a Modi government – was the catchphrase. Even in the remote corners of India, including its northeast, Modi was a draw. In southern India, where Modi's Hindi is not understood, the BJP sold tickets for his rallies to show its man's allure to the masses.

Then, as 2014 came around, Congress tried to revive itself. But there seemed nothing it could get right. For good measure, it led with its chin many a time. One classic case was a flippant remark by Mani Shankar Aiyar, Rajiv Gandhi's senior in school who had followed Rajiv into politics and held the portfolios of petroleum, then sports, in Manmohan Singh's first Cabinet. The All India Congress Committee held a taking-stock session in mid-January, as it geared up for the polls. After a morning of dull speeches, Rahul Gandhi stepped up to the mike mid-afternoon and delivered one of the most rousing speeches of his political career, combative and folksy. On the same day, however, Aiyar, a champion school debater who had delivered an impassioned speech in May 2004 begging Sonia to accept the prime minister's post, stepped forward again with his own jibe at Modi.

"If he wants to distribute tea here, we will find a place for him," said Aiyar. "I give you my word: in the 21st century, Narendra Modi will never become prime minister of the country."

It was just the sort of supercilious, elitist remark that the BJP needed to galvanise its campaign. Overnight, Modi became a celebrity among tea sellers across India, where people held special sessions in his honour. For the BJP, it was another handle to attack the privileged prince – *shehzada* – and compare him with the hard-grinding Modi. "The strength of India's democracy will be proved when a former tea vendor defeats a dynasty's representative," said the BJP's Arun Jaitley.

Congress quickly distanced itself from the remark, but the damage was done. It was a spectacular own goal for his party from the Aiyar loudmouth.

In the weeks to follow, Congress would be left speechless again by the agility of its principal opponent. When Rahul's sister, Priyanka, attacked Modi over his "low politics", Modi artfully turned it to his advantage, saying the Gandhis were attacking him over his low-caste status.

India's elections are called a festival of democracy with good reason. But this was classic theatre as well. Around the nation, theatres sold fewer seats in the popular evening shows because people were glued to prime-time television, which usually focused overwhelmingly on the ebullient, chest-thumping Modi.

The BJP, once bitten by its disastrous "India Shining" campaign of 2004, dropped its fears about a second failure. Its campaign slogan now was a confident *Acche din Aane Waale Hain* – The Good Times are Coming.

And this time there was no comeback from Congress. Jairam Ramesh, the Congress bright spark who had coined that superb rejoinder, *Aam aadmi ko kya mila?* – What's there for the common man? – was tongue-tied, aware that the wages of 10 years of incumbency and the weight of scandal after scandal had to be paid. Ramesh's daily habit of crossing the road from his government bungalow to New Delhi's historic Lodi Gardens and ruminating as he enjoyed his constitutional would yield no fresh ideas. Like an aging heavyweight boxer mauled by a nimbler, more muscular opponent, Congress was on the ropes and gasping for relief. The knockout had to come from the opponent directly. And so it did.

The staggered election process began on April 7, 2014. Eligible to cast their ballots were 814 million people, the largest number ever to participate in a free election since the birth of democracy. The turnout on the first day of voting suggested unprecedented interest in the election. Clearly, a wave was building and it was obvious in which direction. Not content in the knowledge that the election was going his way in a substantial manner, Modi went for the jugular, displaying that he had in full measure the key ingredient of success in climbing the greasy pole: a killer instinct.

It is an unspoken understanding in Indian politics that the personal lives of key leaders and their close relatives are generally not targeted. Another is a live-and-let-live attitude, whereby leading political rivals generally do not campaign in each other's constituencies. It is a useful arrangement; today's Opposition can well be tomorrow's government and vice versa. In late April, a friend who was close to both Advani and Modi and was well-regarded by both as a political strategist, told me that the challenger was considering holding a rally in Amethi, constituency of two-time MP Rahul Gandhi. The BJP candidate there was the television star Smriti Irani, who, while new to the Gandhi bailiwick, was drawing sizable interest. Taking the fight to Amethi would also keep the Congress campaign chief on the defensive. "The BJP thinks that while Rahul will still win in Amethi," this person told me, "it believes it can significantly narrow the margin of his victory and thus prove to the Congress party that its dynastic leaders have outlived their usefulness as vote getters." I promptly reported this in *The Straits Times* of April 28.

My source proved accurate. Exactly a week later, on May 5, two hours before the campaign closed, Modi arrived on a dusty fairground in Amethi by helicopter. For 53 minutes he spoke, despite a sore throat that made his voice rasp, wrapping up the address five minutes before the 5 pm close of campaigning in the constituency with a glance at the Movado timepiece on his wrist. Point by point, he took down the Gandhi family and its record in office. Then he came into his element as he focused on the Congress charge that his was the politics of hatred. If anything, he said, it was the Gandhi family that played the politics of hatred. Rajiv Gandhi in his time had insulted a hapless chief minister of Andhra Pradesh for bringing him flowers, reducing the man to tears and stamping on the pride of the Andhras. Sonia had bounced out a low-caste man who occupied the office of Congress president. When former prime minister Narasimha Rao died, she would not let his body be brought into the Congress office or even cremated in New Delhi. Because of this, Rao had to be cremated in Hyderabad. And what of Rahul? The Gandhi scion had insulted his own prime minister, Manmohan Singh, by tearing up an ordinance passed by his Cabinet and calling it "nonsense". He also had a dig at Priyanka, who had labelled him as a man who played low politics. Congress, he said, resented his low-caste status. Tell me, he asked his audience, who plays the politics of anger?

It was vintage Modi: acerbic, interesting, captivating. Also, masterfully strategic because he was aware that Andhra Pradesh was going to the polls in two days and his words about the poor treatment handed out to two of the state's most famous sons would resonate there. While talking to Amethi, he was also talking past the crowd and taking aim at his audiences more than 1,200 km to the south.

"Now, no one can save this mother-son government," he stormed.

And of course, he was proven right. When the results came in, the BJP had a clear majority in the powerful lower house of parliament, the Lok Sabha. Together with allies, it had a comfortable 336 seats in the 543-seat house. Not since 1984, when Rajiv Gandhi had ridden the sympathy wave over his mother's assassination to deliver a landslide for Congress, had a single party got enough seats to rule by itself. In the heartland state of Uttar Pradesh, which includes Amethi, the BJP took no less than 73 of the 80 parliamentary seats from the state. It was estimated that one in four who voted for the BJP did so because they saw themselves as voting Modi. For that reason, anywhere between 60 and 100 BJP seats, political scientist Ashutosh Varshney told me, could be credited to Modi's charisma. Congress had been cut to 44 seats, a number so tiny that Congress did not even qualify to be Leader of the Opposition. Rahul would prevail in Amethi, but his victory margin would be a quarter of his 400,000-vote margin in the 2009 polls. Never in the history of that grand institution had Congress suffered so much humiliation before. Modi's victory was unparalleled, and complete. India was his to run for at least the next five years.

18
Mass Culture and Nationhood: The Masala Dosa-isation of India

> "The chief characteristic of our civilisation has been unity in diversity. We have never attempted to impose uniformity or dilute diversity. We have believed in a composite culture where, while individual identities are retained, traits are shared."
>
> — Manmohan Singh, 2009

IN LATE 2009, *Outlook*, a feisty weekly magazine that was propelled to great popularity by its founding editor, the late Vinod Mehta, published its annual food survey. The 13-city poll established the South Indian *thosai* – or *dosa* – as India's national dish, beating to second place *tandoori* chicken, the staple of every menu in most "Indian" restaurants overseas and, of course, popular thinking about Indian food.

While the *thosai* predictably scored heavily in the southern states, it ran up impressive numbers as the food item of choice across the country. In Bhopal, capital of Madhya Pradesh, India's largest state by area, 46% of people voted for the fried pancake that can be eaten with or without a filling of the traditional boiled potatoes and fried onions – or, these days, as people experiment with it, cottage cheese and even spicy minced lamb. Only among the culturally chauvinistic Bengalis, and the Punjabis, who pride themselves on their machismo and swagger, did it fare poorly. The *thosai* scored a 5% popularity rating in West Bengal and 6.8% in Punjab.

The rise of the *thosai* in some ways underscored not just the rapid strides southern India has taken in the Indian national consciousness but also the steady and swift progression towards a truly composite all-India culture. That is an amazing achievement for a nation that has 24 official languages, hundreds of dialects and all the major ethnic groups and religions of the world along with their various food habits and quirks.

As John Dayal, a member of the National Integration Council (NIC), told me: "There is a super identity of the Indian as a multicultural being that is emerging for the first time in four millennia. You see it in the popular culture and the *thosai* is one manifestation. On the other hand, the hardcore Punjabi who once feared he would get pneumonia by eating rice, now doesn't mind the rice-based *thosai* for breakfast."

Yet not too long ago, the differences were stark. And so, too, the prejudices. Indeed, Dayal's NIC had been set up by Jawaharlal Nehru to promote harmony in light of India's massive diversity.

People across the populous North tended to club people from the five South Indian states as "Madrasis", a throwback to the days of the British Raj when the Madras Presidency encompassed most of southern India, comprising the states of Andhra Pradesh, Tamil Nadu, Karnataka and Kerala, and tiny Pondicherry, a federally administered territory. Madrasis in turn seemed to lump all North Indians as "Punjabis", although Punjab is but one of the northern states.

While being a Madrasi had its advantages – landlords in the North tended to prefer them because of their reputation for being good tenants diligent about paying rent on time and not prone to overstaying the lease – knowledge about the South was thin. Chaudhary Charan Singh, who briefly held the office of prime minister after succeeding Morarji Desai, made his first trip to southern India only after he became home affairs minister following the 1977 national polls, by which time he was already into his 70s.

People also poked fun at the Madrasi's frugality and parsimonious ways. Their exaggerated body language and spoken tongues were the stuff of caricature, as too the wraparound white sarongs they wore. *Sambaar*, a mildly spicy, runny broth that is a weaker cousin to the *mulligatawny*, and is served across the South, was an object of mirth. Better off people ate real vegetables, not spicy water with the odd piece of carrot or potato in it – so went the northern mind. And now here was the humble *thosai* crisply standing up to be counted as the national dish. Where was India heading?

Several developments contributed to the blurring of the divide. India's military, drawn from around the country, was no doubt a great factor. So, too, the All India Civil Services. Indeed, the elite Indian Administrative Service, which dominates the bureaucracy, is distributed such that only half of its officers stationed in each state were born there. The other half are out-of-state officers. And all of them rotate frequently between stints in the states and the central government in New Delhi.

Other factors, not always intended, also contributed to the national cement. First was rationing, introduced during the food shortages of the 1960s. Public distribution shops offered wheat flour as part of the rations, and for many Southerners this was their first introduction to the cereal from which is made *chapati* bread. Of course, some of them soon found merit in *thosai* made with *atta*, as wheat flour is called. Then, in the early 1970s, Indira Gandhi offered all federal government employees a facility known as Leave Travel Concession. While they could use this to travel to their native areas every year, once in four years government staff were allowed to take their family anywhere in the country. (The Modi government is now thinking of extending the facility to cover SAARC states, a move that has immense potential to do good, albeit with some attendant risks if, for instance, too many Indians turn up in tiny Bhutan or the Maldives.)

Naturally, most beneficiaries tended to make maximum use of the facility. The Madrasi began to travel as far north as Kashmir. When he descended from the snowy hills of Kashmir's Gulmarg resort, he was received by enterprising restaurateurs offering him crisp *masala thosai* and hot, brewed coffee, southern style. In turn, when the Northerner arrived in Kanyakumari, Thiruvananthapuram and other places in the southern tip of India and as far east as Port Blair in the Andaman & Nicobar chain of islands, lentils, leavened breads, butter chicken and kebabs followed him.

Anup Jain, who used to be marketing director for Pizza Hut in India before moving to his current job as chief operating officer of the shoe giant Bata India, noted how food habits were blending across India. "I was in one of the most traditional South Indian restaurants in Chennai some time ago and upstairs they were showing Shah Rukh Khan movies and offering Punjabi and Indian-Chinese dishes. That's how good the blending is these days," he mused, as he pondered ways for Pizza Hut to tap into the trend.

The acceptance of alien food and dress in the unlikeliest places came home to me starkly in 2009 while I was travelling in Tamil Nadu state from Coimbatore to the textile town of Tiruppur. Tamil is one of the great languages of India and Tamil Nadu politicians have played on language chauvinism to grab power from Congress, the party of freedom. In the 1960s and 1970s, which saw anti-Hindi movements in Tamil Nadu, Hindi disappeared even from signs on railway station platforms, which in other states are written in English, Hindi and the local language. Throughout Tamil Nadu, women, particularly the younger generation, were clad in the *salwar kameez* – tunic and pyjamas – of the North. The route was punctuated by roadside kitchens offering food baked in the *tandoor* clay ovens of the North, clearly aimed at the truck drivers who brought cotton from Gujarat and elsewhere to be milled and stitched in the factories of Tiruppur.

Politically, the balance began to even out as the North's traditional dominance, centred in Uttar Pradesh, began to wobble. India got its first prime minister from the South when Narasimha Rao, who was from Andhra Pradesh, took charge of India in 1991 shortly after the murder of Rajiv Gandhi. HD Deve Gowda, another Southerner, from adjoining Karnataka, followed in Rao's shoes. At the time the *Outlook* survey was published, three of the four most powerful men in the Cabinet after Manmohan Singh were Southerners – home affairs minister P Chidambaram, defence minister AK Antony and external affairs minister SM Krishna. And the fourth, finance minister Pranab Mukherjee, was a Bengali, while the prime minister himself was from Punjab. While Krishna, a Fulbright scholar, preferred to be seen in close-neck tunic and trousers, Antony and the Harvard-educated Chidambaram confidently asserted their southern identities by wearing shirt and sarong outfits to receive even the biggest foreign dignitaries.

But it was the IT revolution of the 1990s, as the world braced for the Year 2000 problem and sought help from Indian code writers to protect their data, that placed South India firmly on the map. Indeed, it even shifted India's growth momentum southward. The big software firms – Tata Consultancy Services, Infosys, Wipro, and now Cognizant – are all South-based even as they draw talent from across the nation. Manufacturing is moving too. The ubiquitous Maruti Suzuki sedan, manufactured outside New Delhi, now shares space with Hyundai, Ford and Toyota models made in southern India.

Inevitably, global consciousness too began to focus on southern India. While New Delhi, Bombay (Mumbai) and Agra – city of the Taj Mahal – were well known to the world, suddenly Bangalore, capital of the southern state of Karnataka and the country's principal software hub, began to gain recognition around the world. Indeed, back office workers in the West began to complain they had been "Bangalored" as many white collar jobs moved to the southern metropolis.

More and more, India is beginning to look like a lesser version of the United States, with multiple centres of excellence, fluidity of talent across state borders, and several gateways to the world. And the newer ones are all in the south of the country.

This is not to say that the stereotypes have vanished entirely. Indeed, four months before the *Outlook* survey, a Bollywood release, *Quick Gun Murugun*, had sought to further the stereotype of the South Indian. A Madrasi cowboy who was evangelical about his vegetarianism, Murugun settled down at restaurant bars with his favourite order: "*Oru* whisky, *oru masala thosai*" – a whisky and a *masala thosai.*

"The North-South divide has broken partly because cities like Bangalore and Hyderabad in the south and Gurgaon in the north are stamped on the national consciousness," said social anthropologist Shiv Visvanathan, referring to the country's hubs for the outsourcing industry. "But Indians do not yet have the kind of diversity and cosmopolitanism that you see in, say, San Francisco. Scratch a man in Gurgaon and you see his true identity."

Professor Visvanathan, a foodie, complained to me that the standardisation of the *thosai* has come at the expense of quality established by the master chefs of southern India's Udipi region who invented the dish so long ago. As he said in jest: "Call me a Brahmin purist if you like, but then I am a purist for butter chicken too."

To the uninitiated, India looks frighteningly splintered into regions, states, languages, religions, and of course, caste. Even Lee Kuan Yew, Singapore's founding father and universally acknowledged as one of Asia's greatest minds of his time, failed to fully grasp the unity and mass culture that has emerged under the surface.

"Despite the best efforts of the British and the Indian nationalists, India as a nation is still more of an aspiration than a reality," Lee said in his book, *One Man's View of the World*. "To ask if India can achieve what China can is to ask if you can make an apple into an orange. The results of these fundamental differences between India and China are quite apparent. One country gets things done. The other talks incessantly but seldom finds the will or ability to get up and go."

Lee saw India as "trapped by the almost unchangeable realities of its internal composition and the persistent grip of the caste system". Still, he also recognised that India would not have held together under a unitary system like China's because of its disparateness. "The great strength that they have is also their weakness," said Lee. "They are so diverse and different. Every earthquake that they have, the stones somehow move with each other and do not fall apart. They are still in place. I am not saying that the Chinese stones will fall apart. But in the case of India, there are different state governments and chief ministers, they keep on shifting but it coheres together somehow."

Without question, Indian identities are blending significantly even as television, mass media and communication help people retain and reach into their roots with a multitude of regional news channels, entertainment programming and the cheapest mobile telephony available in the world. Procter & Gamble, Unilever and myriad other companies manage to reach all of India with a single advertisement spot, especially if they feature a cricket star or a Bollywood actor, rather than tailor advertisements to regional tastes.

Indeed, caste, for which India always gained a bad odour, is increasingly more of an economic and, to an extent, political, rather than a social phenomenon. Caste's social characteristics – rules on touch and inter-dining – have long faded in urban India and are rapidly disappearing in the hinterland as well. Take the backward class movement, which has propelled new political configurations across India, particularly in Tamil Nadu, Bihar and Uttar Pradesh, which are all ruled by once-marginalised castes that have found new voice through political aggregation. India's Constitution prescribes, under Article 340, the appointment of a commission to investigate the condition of socially and educationally backward classes in addition to the castes and tribes scheduled under Articles 330 and 332 (hence called Scheduled Castes and Scheduled Tribes, or more popularly, SC/ST). The first backward classes commission, which reported in 1955, listed 2,399 Other Backward Classes (OBCs). In 1980, when a new commission headed by BP Mandal submitted its report, the number of so-called OBCs had risen to 3,743 as more castes laid claim to be included in the list. Far from attempting to rise in the social hieraracby, "backwardness" had become a useful badge of privilege in gaining access to education and employment!

Likewise, in the summer of 2007, the desert state of Rajasthan and parts of northern India were rocked by a spreading revolt of farmers demanding to be pushed down the Hindu social order in the official record. The pastoral Gujjars, who were classified as OBCs, were demanding to be listed as Notified Tribes. This collided with the interest of the Meenas, who resent any new entrants into the tribal category. Classified in 1954 as tribals, they had, for 50 years, enjoyed access to special privileges that had given them sizeable clout in the powerful civil service because many Meenas entered through the quota route.

Gujjars are classified as tribals in some states like Jammu & Kashmir, but in Rajasthan, they are OBCs because they live a more settled life and are generally well-off. Were the Gujjars, whose community leaders include former corporate affairs minister Sachin Pilot, who has a Wharton MBA, justified in their protests? It depends on which way you saw it; in 2003, as the BJP campaigned for state elections, which it eventually won in Rajasthan, it had promised Gujjars that they would be classified as tribals. The Gujjars delivered their votes and were demanding the BJP keep its word.

Periodically, some politician eyes extending these quotas to private sector employment, hoping to tap into a lucrative vote bank. Fortunately for India, no government has been so desperate as to draw this weapon, for doing so might deal a killer blow to private enterprise. But even without legislation, it is heartening that the normal hiring process itself is bringing the lower castes into employment in a natural way. At Hindustan Unilever, Unilever's Indian subsidiary that is the country's top consumer goods company, the lowest castes, tribes and OBCs have made up more than half the rolls for more than a decade.

Indeed, some political scientists say even if caste-based quotas were to be introduced in the private sector some day, it may not be so much of a disaster at all, judging from the experience of southern India, where the teeming lower castes got political power way early compared with the North, where the OBCs came to dominate power only in the 1990s. Some serious India scholars like Ashutosh Varshney believe this was why southern India's growth rates have soared since the 1980s, and even more since the economic liberalisation measures introduced by Manmohan Singh in 1991 when he was finance minister to prime minister Narasimha Rao. For the quarter century since 1980, incomes of South Indians rose at twice the pace of those living in the North.

"The southern Indian states are some of the biggest growth engines of the economy," said Varshney, who heads the political science department at Brown University, United States. "Yet, these states have had the highest percentage of affirmative action reservations. Clearly, the disturbance caused to the established social order has released vast entrepreneurial energy in South India. And that is partly because the relationship between caste on one hand and business and occupations on the other, has broken down."

Such insights are increasingly shared by industry as well. Sanjeev Bikhchandani, who runs naukri.com, India's No. 1 jobs portal, said statistics from the Indian Institutes of Management, the nation's most sought-after business schools, indicate that successful OBC students score only marginally less than merit category candidates in entrance exams. At that level, the quotas do not harm talent because the quota candidates score only about 2 percentage points below the merit candidates. Of course, Bikhchandani conceded, this statistic for OBCs includes the "creamy layer" that the Supreme Court has ordered should not gain from quotas. Without this layer, the OBC performance may drop.

Without question, democracy, now fully entrenched and with elections the only route to power, has been a major factor in the coalescing of India. As the national elections of 2014 showed, and the February 2015 polls to the Delhi state assembly endorsed, India is in the middle of a democratic upsurge of a kind that could become a model in the history of democracy. The participatory upsurge from the bottom up has helped the birth of new political parties and is swiftly changing the social profile of the political class. Many of the voters are former Untouchables, tribals and other classes that suffered centuries of oppression but now rejoice in their democratic freedoms. Election studies show that Dalits, among the most oppressed socially, are among the most enthusiastic voters. Even the widening middle class, which traditionally tended to sneer at the politician, is taking a big interest in the political life of the nation.

"The most important thing about India is that democracy now has the passion of a religion, the thrill of a mystery," noted political thinker Pratap Bhanu Mehta wrote in an essay for *The Indian Express* newspaper. "Anyone who doubts, it, or shows contempt for it, through hubris or condescension, will come to grief."

From all these has emerged a true sense of nationhood. In *Battles Half Won*, a superb book on Indian democracy, Varshney cited surveys conducted by the University of Michigan at Ann Arbor and New Delhi's Centre for the Study of Developing Societies, on whether Indians are proud of their nation. The proportion that was "very proud" or "proud" added up to more than 85% in each survey. Likewise, in studies on subjective national identity conducted between 1998 and 2005, roughly two-thirds said their identity is only Indian, more Indian than state-based, and equally Indian and state-based.

In other words, India's diversities have not affected the rise of a national consciousness. Indeed, the nation is rapidly becoming a melting pot even as it retains the characteristics of a mosaic.

19
Thy Partner's Wife: Changing Social Mores Amid Repressed Sexuality

> "Housework and housekeeping are for girls, not roaming in discos and bars at night doing wrong things, wearing wrong clothes. About 20% of girls are good."
>
> — Bus driver Mukesh Singh, sentenced to death in the 2012 Delhi rape case, to Leslee Udwin, maker of the BBC documentary, *India's Daughter*

PRAKASH KOTHARI, INDIA'S best-known sex therapist, recalls the time he fixed an appointment for a businessman from Surat, a city in Gujarat known for its gem-cutters and conservative ways. At the appointed hour, Dr Kothari was taken aback to see four couples pushing into the cramped consulting room of his clinic in Mumbai's KEM Hospital.

"I told them, 'Hello, I occasionally let a relative sit in, but not such a big crowd'," the famed therapist told me. "At that point a man stepped forward and said gently, 'Doctor, allow me to explain'."

The story that unfolded took even Kothari by surprise. The couples, all of whom had been married for more than a decade, were friends who occasionally swapped spouses. They wanted Kothari's help to learn new erotic games they could try as a group. "We are honest with each other," a male member of the group explained. "We support each other in business and in our personal lives. We work on our problems together."

Although India is famous for its 4th century sex treatise, the *Kama Sutra*, its people used to carry a reputation of being notoriously straitlaced in bedroom matters. People avoid touching in public, much less holding hands. Prudery is common; politicians are apt to attack the presence of cheerleaders in revealing clothes at Indian Premier League cricket matches.

Under the surface, though, things are stirring. The case of the Surat wife-swappers underscore just how rapidly tradition-bound India's social mores are changing. Amid rising incomes and exploding consumerism, personal gratification of every sort is increasingly seen as a legitimate aspiration for everyone, and particularly the upwardly mobile classes.

The urban young, especially, are going through an era of immense sexual liberation. A senior Delhi Police official once told me of a case where his men had picked up a young woman suspected to be a sex trafficker. It turned out that she was comfortably middle-class, the daughter of an army colonel.

"When we asked her why this, her answer stunned us," the official said. "She said, 'I just do it for the fun'."

Likewise, a college friend of mine, now living a bachelor existence in New Delhi after separating from his wife, told the story of a young woman he knew intimately for several months. Samir (not his real name) hangs out twice a week at Rick's Bar in The Taj Mahal Hotel, a watering hole popular with yuppies.

Late one evening, he was standing at the bar when he fell into conversation with a young woman standing next to him, waiting for her boyfriend, a banker, to arrive. An hour or so later, it was evident that the banker was going to show up very late, if at all. Samir, who lives in the tony Friends Colony area, offered to drop the young woman off at her home in nearby Maharani Bagh, an equally upscale estate.

The woman, it turned out, came from a rich, tradition-bound Hindu family with roots in Rajasthan, a state whose womenfolk regularly observed *karva chauth,* the annual fast for the husband's longevity. Rajasthan was the last of the provinces to eradicate the awful ancient practice of *sati,* where a widow immolates herself on the husband's funeral pyre.

As she stepped out of his Mercedes, Samir gave her his card, suggesting they should catch up over coffee sometime. The response surprised him.

"You live alone, don't you? Why do you need a restaurant; don't you have coffee in your house?"

"She drove up to my flat next day, parked and came upstairs," said Samir. "For the next three months, she slept with me once or twice a week, often seeing me just before she went for a date with her boyfriend, or just after seeing him. Then, one day, she ended all contact without explaining why."

Some months later, he saw her again at Rick's. She was with a man whom he guessed was the banker. They nodded to each other and that was all.

Samir, who is about twice the woman's age and well-travelled, said he made no further attempt to make contact with her. Neither did she reach out to him again. But the casualness of the young woman's approach left him more than a little stunned, he said.

A survey of urban India published in 2011 by *Outlook* magazine, in collaboration with market research company MDRA for the Moods condom line, indicated that Mumbai remained the top city for casual sex, followed by New Delhi and the western coastal city of Goa. While parties were where most of the casual encounters started, social networking sites are increasingly another starting point for liaisons. Sachin Bhatia, co-founder of TrulyMadly, a dating app launched in 2014 which now has more than 500,000 active users, told my colleague, Nirmala Ganapathy, he decided to remove an option for users to reveal their religion within a month of the app's launch. Women users said the option was irrelevant. A third of respondents in the cities cited by MDRA confessed to having had casual sex at least once. Most interestingly, three-fourths of respondents in Guwahati, a major city of the eastern Indian state of Assam, reported that casual sex encounters were initiated by women. And in Hyderabad, fully a quarter said their preferred sexual indulgence was partner-swapping.

Still, some prejudices remain; more than nine out of 10 in tradition-bound Chennai, capital of the southern state of Tamil Nadu, said they would not have sex with a partner from a different religion or ethnicity.

If the young are increasingly finding free release for their libido, the older ones too are finding sexual liberation, and in the unlikeliest corners of the country. Anecdotal evidence suggests that wife-swapping, for instance, exists not just in the big metros but also in smaller cities such as Chandigarh in the north, Kochi in the south and Ahmedabad, Gujarat's textile centre and administrative headquarters. Indeed, some say that Ahmedabad, a city whose *memsahibs* travel in limousines with their heads covered, has several of these cosy circles.

A person who was invited to attend one such group encounter in the city described the event, which took place in a farmhouse on the edge of town. Among those present were a hairdresser couple, a mid-level banker and his wife, a top tycoon and his spouse, and a husband-wife pair of senior bureaucrats. The rules were clear: no paid women to participate, only spouses. All present had their HIV tests done regularly and could produce the certificates on demand. Car keys were dropped into a bowl and women picked one set each, spending the night with the man who owned the vehicle. Or the women took off some item of clothing and dropped that into a bin to join the handkerchiefs of men. The clothes would then be taken out in pairs. Occasionally, the women at the party gave themselves names of movie stars while the men were tagged after famous politicians.

The man most women batted for was the hairstylist, who was the youngest of the lot.

"This group has stayed loyal to each other for years," said the person, who has not accepted a second invitation with them. "There is a sense of equality in their behaviour although their income strata is so different. Between themselves they jokingly call this 'women's empowerment'."

Businessman Ajay Anjaria, who moved to Bangalore from Ahmedabad some years ago, said he routinely heard wife-swapping stories during the years he spent in the city.

"Perhaps it harks back to a time when the textile tycoons of the area sent one of the males in the family to represent them in Mumbai," said Anjaria, who has no direct knowledge of the matter. "They were envious of the fun such people had in the big city's bars and other nightspots and wanted to prove that life wasn't too dull in Ahmedabad either."

Deepal Trivedi, an Ahmedabad-based writer and socialite introduced to me by Mumbai journalist Sangeeta John, told me that the phenomenon involves no pressure or coercion. "For the couples involved it probably is a relief from the hypocrisy that surrounds them," she said. "Certainly, it is not a matter of money."

Still, complications can arise even in the most broad-minded groups. Some years ago, two women were murdered in Ahmedabad for refusing to oblige their husbands, who suggested swaps. And a former banker in Mumbai spoke of a school chum who separated from his wife after 15 years of marriage and three children.

"They are rich plantation owners from Kerala with conservative backgrounds and lived in a southern metro," he said. "The woman had apparently got too fixated on a member of their group and didn't want to share him. That led to the end of her marriage."

Wider Indian society is slowly becoming aware about these circles even as the practice is limited to very tight, elite groups. In 2006, Bollywood produced a movie on the theme, *Mixed Doubles*, starring the dusky Konkona Sen Sharma as an innocent housewife introduced to the practice against her will. The movie had an average run at the box office and caused no great stir. But the track song of *Omkara*, a movie about a hitman who works for political masters, did cause a stir. *Beedi jalaile* (light my cheroot) became a massive hit on the airwaves. Risque throughout, the song suggests that a good place to light up the *beedi* would be the clay oven of the neighbour's kitchen. And it went on to advise: "Light your fire, dearest, from my bosom. There's a lot of heat in here but don't let the smoke out of your mouth, for people will know ... the world is a cheat."

What was most surprising was that the lyricist was the famed and hugely respected Sampooran Singh Kalra, better known as Gulzar, a man who has won every big Indian award in cinema. What's more, he wrote the song at age 70.

Likewise, two movies a generation apart, *Bobby* starring Rishi Kapoor in 1973 and *Bachna Ae Haseeno* (Watch Out, Beauties) starring his son, Ranbir, in 2008, capture the changing mores in urban India. Ranbir played Raj Sharma, who designs games for Microsoft's Xbox, lives life in the fast lane, downing tequila shots at fancy bars and sporting designer labels. After dumping two women, he meets and falls for doe-eyed Gayatri. But he has to do some penance before winning the love of his life. His father, in *Bobby*, was a rich teenager out of boarding school named Raja. In love with the 16-year-old granddaughter of his old governess, Raja has to confront parental displeasure. The two young lovers elope on a motorcycle, and later, the parents yield.

Bobby was a watershed moment in its time for two reasons. First, it was among the first movies to portray teenage rebellion. Second, it was the first recognised instance of product placement in an Indian movie – the 175cc Rajdoot GTS motorcycle made its first appearance in the movie and became a sensational marketing hit thereafter. Raja in *Bobby* was smitten with a love that was pure and simple. The Raj Sharmas of today's India do not pledge their troth too rapidly and even as they consummate one attraction, they are fully aware there will be more to come. What's more, in *Bobby*, the director, looking to put short skirts and tight blouses on a busty body, characterised the heroine as a Christian girl of Anglo-Indian descent who lived in Mumbai, then the country's most forward city. In *Bachna Ae Haseeno*, Radhika, Raj's second conquest, is a dusky, iron-pumping siren born into a Hindu family from Jharkhand, a tribal state deep in India's Hindi-speaking heartland. Modern India, clearly, is more at ease with itself. There is another message: for a culture transfixed with the idea of the transmigration of the soul, a fit body is increasingly seen as a virtue.

Slowly, the political class, which surely deserve to be called India's worst humbugs, are also shedding some of their pretensions. India's media looked the other way on Jawaharlal Nehru's love affair with Edwina Mountbatten, wife of the last viceroy, and several other rumoured liaisons. Chandra Shekhar's rugged handsomeness was a huge draw to women, especially those with political ambitions. Even the staid and sober Narasimha Rao left hints that he had romantic interests. Rao's successor, Atal Bihari Vajpayee, was a bachelor who lived with a woman who was not his wife.

But that was all very private. Today's India is fast losing its prudery. Shashi Tharoor's third wife, Sunanda Pushkar, was a trophy he flaunted with impunity, until her sudden death in January 2014 stunned the nation. The circumstances of that death did not seem to affect his electoral chances – he retained his seat in Kerala, even as his party was swept aside in an anti-incumbency wave. Tharoor's senior in the Congress party, Digvijaya Singh, a former chief minister of Madhya Pradesh, announced his relationship with a married television anchor in the midst of the May 2014 elections. At 67, Digvijaya, who has prime ministerial ambitions and was widowed just a year earlier, had daughters older than the woman he said he wanted to marry. Weeks earlier, at 89, Narain Dutt Tiwari, another Congress stalwart who was chief minister of Uttar Pradesh and Uttarakhand, finally accepted a 34-year-old man as his son after the younger man took him to court, which then ordered DNA testing to establish paternity.

Still, for all the experimentation and adventurism that is said to go on, most Indian couples remain steeped in their conservative ways. Certainly, not everyone in India is saying: *When skin meets skin, where's the sin?* What's more, Indian men still retain their deep-seated insecurities.

"They are more aware no doubt, and inclined to adventure," said Dr Kothari. "But when it comes to marriage, they are obsessive about wanting their brides to be virgins."

This obsession with virginity, combined with the fixation on the male child, is one of the reasons there is so much sexual repression, especially at the lower end of society. Women are forced to marry early, even if they would prefer to wait until their mid-20s. Village elders round on young couples going on dates or even texting each other, a phenomenon difficult to control in a nation with more than 900 million cellphone connections. Lovers who elope are hunted down and sometimes murdered, often by their own kin. These are described as "honour killings" in Indian media.

In February 2005, shortly after I returned to India, a curious event outside University of Delhi's Hansraj College highlighted the contradictory pulls tugging at Indian society. A group of 50 gathered, shouting slogans against Western values and demanding a ban on Valentine's Day celebrations. They were from militant Hindu group Bajrang Dal and another Hindu-oriented outfit, Shiv Sena, whose base is Mumbai. Police held them for a bit, and less than an hour after they had assembled, they melted away. It is not clear what they had gained with their protest; around the tree-lined campus, many young couples embraced or held hands. In the shops of nearby Model Town, Valentine's Day sales moved as briskly as ever.

To the outside eye, it would have seemed odd that a festival which began with the legend of a third century Roman priest should find increasing acceptance in a land that gave the world the Taj Mahal, the greatest monument to love, as well as the *Kama Sutra*, the book that details the practice of love's fulfilment. But the protests, as well as the disdain with which campus students reacted to the protesters' call, underscored to me both the rising Westernisation of urban India and the resentment at the fringe about the phenomenon. It also spoke for India's ability to accommodate both sentiments and move on, which was, of course, the correct way to deal with it. Because, truth to tell, the Valentine's Day celebration was really a manifestation of Indian entrepreneurship.

Back in the late 1980s, when cable television had just begun to spring up around India, Anil Moolchandani, a former sari trader, sensed the consumerist instincts of Indian society and launched Archies greeting cards. Initial attempts to diversify from birthday, Deepavali and Christmas cards saw Archies selling "Miss You" and "Get Well Soon" cards, greetings that were still alien to large parts of Indian society. But it was not until late 1988 that Moolchandani launched the first Valentine's Day cards, along with Mother's Day and Father's Day cards. Until then, February 14 had been associated in the Indian public mind with the massacre of upper-caste Hindus by a teenage woman outlaw by the name of Phoolan Devi, later immortalised in the movie, *Bandit Queen*. On that day in 1981, Phoolan

Devi and her gang entered a village in Behmai, northern India, lined up 30 youths of the Thakur caste who had refused to surrender a village elder who had killed Devi's lover and proceeded to gang-rape her. Then she shot and killed 22 of them.

Indians used to place a massive premium on gaining a virgin bride, and it is true that many still do. But increasingly, infidelity is being forgiven. A survey conducted on 75,000 respondents living across 10 cities by the global dating website Ashley Madison and reported in *The Times of India* suggested that 76% of Indian women and 61% of men do not regard infidelity as sinful or immoral. What's more, 81% of men and 68% women thought their extramarital affairs had a positive effect on their marriage.

Of course, a good number – eight out of 10 males and nine out of 10 women – said they had never been caught. Even for most of those who did get found out, the discovery did not lead to divorce.

Bollywood, not an unreliable bellwether for Indian society, has been aware of this for a while. Some years ago, *Kabhi Alvida Na Kehna* (Don't Ever Say Goodbye), a tale of fractured and unworkable marital relationships, set in New York, captured this. In the movie, which many people quickly shortened to its initials, *KANK*, widowed lothario Samarjit "Sam" Talwar, played by Indian cinema's biggest name, Amitabh Bachchan, condoles the infidelity of his daughter-in-law as he lies dying. Sam dotes on his son. Yet he advises his daughter-in-law to leave her husband – played by his real-life son, Abhishek – and pursue her true love, Dev – played by Shah Rukh Khan – an embittered man with a career-oriented wife, played by Preity Zinta.

The same week that *KANK* was released, actor-producer Amol Palekar released *Quest*, a movie made in English and Marathi, the language of Maharashtra. *Quest*'s storyline involves infidelity, bisexuality and a family's reaction to the father's confession of having had a gay partner.

Yet, it was not too far back when Bollywood was portraying the reverse theme. In the high-grossing *Astitva* (Existence), a housewife's dull family life disintegrates when an unexpected inheritance from her music teacher arouses her husband's suspicions. When she confesses that her 25-year-old son was sired by the teacher, even the young man does not stand by his mother.

Without question, people watching the movies have changed. On any night, outside the south New Delhi multiplex cinema called PVR Anupam (PVR is an abbreviation for Priya Village Roadshow) in Saket, the street is jammed with Toyotas, Fords and the rare Mercedes sedan. The people streaming in wear designer jeans shredded at the knee or higher. Some carry cartons of tortilla chips, which they would wash down with sugared soda. Holding hands is no longer taboo. Several of the young walking around would have perhaps had more than one relationship. Just as in *KANK* the movie, the language they speak is a mix of English and local tongues. Many in the crowd work nights and sleep in the day, thanks to the dozens of back-office firms and outsourcing companies that cater to foreign, chiefly Western, time zones. The air is filled with the smell of opportunity, aspiration, avarice and transient affections.

It was in this cohort, and from this cinema, that one of India's most horrible stories of violent rape and murder began in the late evening of December 16, 2012.

Leaving PVR Anupam after watching the movie, *Life of Pi*, 23-year-old Jyoti Singh Pandey – it makes no sense not to give her actual name although she is widely referred to as Nirbhaya or Fearless – and a male companion looked for public transport to take them to Munirka, 5 km away. A bus with shaded glass windows stopped and a young man called out to the couple. In a massive city like New Delhi, where public transport is thin and trains and buses overcrowded, it is a relief to see a near-empty vehicle where a sly hand may not squeeze your buttocks or an elbow deliberately brush against a covered breast.

Jyoti and her boyfriend scrambled aboard. The tragedy of that decision would be felt not just in India but around the world.

For the attractive Jyoti, the daughter of a baggage loader at Delhi's Indira Gandhi International Airport, the nightmare began immediately. Including the driver, there were half a dozen men in the vehicle, used mainly to ferry schoolkids and office goers to fixed destinations. That night, the six had taken the bus for a joyride. They had been looking for trouble. Now, with the attractive young woman on board, their libidos were aroused. She looked the perfect victim: beautiful, frail and, regardless of the male escorting her, very vulnerable.

The bus deviated from the route it should have ordinarily taken, instantly drawing the suspicions of the two passengers. It was too late. When the boyfriend began to object, he was taunted: "What were you two doing out so late in the evening?"

Then the horror started. The six, one still in his teens, raped the woman by turn as the driver kept the bus in motion. The rape came with unspeakable bestiality. A rusted metal object – believed to be the L-shaped rod that is used to turn a stalled engine – was thrust into her, tearing into her intestines and genitals. The boyfriend was beaten to an inch of his life, and knocked unconscious with an iron rod when he tried to come to the woman's rescue. The woman bravely continued to fight her assailants until she was too weak to move.

Then the six drove to a secluded spot, flung the couple off the bus and attempted to run them over. The boyfriend somehow managed to pull her away and the vehicle sped off. The partially clothed pair were found by a passerby about 90 minutes later, and the police informed. Next day, when police identified the bus and impounded it, they spotted visible attempts to wash away all signs of the crime.

Statistically, given India's 1.2 billion population, the incidence of rape is no more serious than in many other societies. But the Indian rape situation is characterised by two things: the numbers are almost certainly understated, and many of the cases that come to public notice are horribly violent, such as this one involving Jyoti Pandey. The outrage turned into an international cause célèbre and gave India an awful reputation from which it hasn't yet recovered. Manmohan Singh's government, shaky as it was, had a national disaster on its hands.

As she battled for life at Delhi's Safdarjung Hospital, candlelight vigils were reported across India as young and old gathered in schools and street corners to pray for her well-being. Jyoti's father had moved the family to the city, selling land in his village to give his children a modern education so they could escape the misery that he had known as a poor child. In his worst nightmares, he could not have imagined the bestiality his daughter was to encounter. After multiple operations, her condition showed no improvement and she began to weaken. Ten days after the rape and brutalisation, it was clear Jyoti would not live.

Now, the Manmohan Singh government began to worry about the political fallout from her death, which seemed inevitable. Delhi chief minister Sheila Dikshit, her popularity eroded by the corruption scandals surrounding the Commonwealth Games hosted by the city two years earlier, pressed the federal government to fly Jyoti out of the capital, fearing an outbreak of public violence. It was left to Singapore to step in to bail out the Indian government. On December 26, the Cabinet met to take stock of the situation and a decision was taken to fly Jyoti to Singapore's Mount Elizabeth Hospital by air ambulance.

Ostensibly, the hospital was chosen because it had the expertise to do multi-organ transplants. Six years earlier, a Tamil Tiger suicide bomber had made her way into Sri Lankan Army headquarters and detonated herself, killing 11 and critically wounding then-Army chief Sarath Fonseka. General Fonseka was evacuated to Singapore where surgeons succeeded in patching him together and sending him home in a few months. Other desperate cases, from Myanmar generals to Bangladeshi leaders, had been flown there for treatment. Still, despite its impressive track record, there was only so much Singapore's doctors could accomplish. Everyone knew that the Manmohan Singh government was simply trying to avoid having Jyoti die in India.

The poignancy of her death there was that Mount E – as Singaporeans like to abbreviate the hospital's name – draws its paramedical staff from all parts of Asia. Who knows, in life, Jyoti Pandey might well have one day travelled to Singapore on the credentials she had been gathering – a diploma in physiotherapy. Sedated to prevent the pain from being felt by her damaged brain and tortured body, a ventilator machine performing the work for her lungs, and surrounded by her parents, two brothers and senior staff of the Indian High Commission, the 23-year-old died at 4.45 am Singapore time on December 29. In the three days she was alive, not once had she opened her eyes on the island described by former Indian prime minister Atal Bihari Vajpayee as "nothing short of a miracle".

The circumstances of her arrival in Singapore and the shock of her death affected not just Indians on the island, but also Singaporeans. A few hours after she died, when I went to the Indian High Commission on Grange Road, walking distance to the hospital, lines of people had begun to form as the news spread, some just to huddle amongst friends for silent comfort, others to sign a condolence book that had not yet been opened. The mood was one of despondency, as when a nation gets defeated in war.

That afternoon, the dead woman flew home in the comfort that her father could never have afforded – a chartered flight that arrived from India to fetch her back. As happens all too often in India, the official machinery that proved so woefully inadequate to protect her life was in abundance after her trauma and death. Thanks to the power of India's media, the passing had become a cathartic event, a bigger news event than the death the previous month in Mumbai of the firebrand Hindu nationalist Bal Thackeray.

The rapists, for once, did not get away. With unusual speed, the six were brought to justice. One, a man called Ram Singh, was found hanging in his cell in the maximum security Tihar Jail three months after his arrest. His death was labelled a suicide but his family said Ram Singh had been murdered, possibly by fellow prisoners. The prosecution finished its arguments by mid-July and the sentences were out in September. The juvenile was sentenced to the maximum three years in a remand home. The other four got death sentences. The appeal against the death sentence was dismissed by the Delhi High Court in March 2014.

A year after the gang rape and murder, a judicial commission was set up to suggest quicker ways to speed up justice in rape cases. In 2013, several laws were amended and fast-track courts set up to tackle the menace. The death sentences are yet to be carried out but the driver of the bus, Mukesh Singh, remained unrepentant two years after the event. In *India's Daughter*, a documentary on the case filmed for BBC, Mukesh said in an interview conducted from prison that a woman who went out late at night had only herself to blame for attracting the attention of male molesters. "A decent girl would not be roaming around at 9 pm," he said in the documentary. Besides, he said, Jyoti Singh Pandey should not have fought back. "Then we'd have dropped her off after 'doing her' and only hit the boy."

The Indian government, now under Narendra Modi, announced a ban on the airing of the documentary, *India's Daughter*. Home affairs minister Rajnath Singh said in parliament that it "was an attempt to defame India."

The Jyoti Singh Pandey case was an exception for the swiftness with which justice was brought to bear on it. Thousands of other rape and molest cases languish in courts or get nowhere. One reason most rapists and molesters escape appropriate punishment is that society is tilted heavily against the victim.

One of the most egregious cases of molest involved no less than the police chief of Haryana state, bordering New Delhi, a province with so poor a sex ratio that many Haryanvis have to look for wives from other states. This case, which dates to 1990, grabbed national headlines in late 2009 when SPS Rathore, the retired director-general of Haryana Police, aged 67 at the time, emerged smiling from a courthouse after being awarded a six-month jail term. According to the complaint, in August 1990, as founding president of the Haryana Lawn Tennis Association, Rathore had invited 14-year-old Ruchika Girhotra, his daugher's schoolmate at Sacred Heart Convent, into his home on the pretext of discussing her tennis career. When she arrived with a friend, he ordered the other girl to leave and then allegedly made his move on Ruchika.

Most Indian girls routinely swallow such indignities, fearful of social stigma. Ruchika proved stronger. She complained. That triggered a series of shocking developments. Plainclothes policemen were allegedly sent to taunt her family outside their home. Her brother was picked up on charges of auto theft and paraded as a common criminal on the street where the Girhotras lived. Sacred Heart Convent School expelled her. The harassment finally got to the girl. In December 1993, she committed suicide.

The case against Rathore moved only after a judge, responding to public outrage, ordered the Central Bureau of Investigation to probe the case. And justice came only 19 years later, by which time Rathore had advanced steadily and been made head of the state police force. Even so, the trial judge, delivering the relatively mild jail term, had suggested the policeman had suffered enough. Rathore, in the end, served a longer term, but only after India's media picked up on the case and kept it in the spotlight. He continues to receive his pension.

On the positive side, thanks to the Jyoti Singh Pandey case, things are changing, finally. India has moved to set up special courts to try sex offences within six months of a complaint. Schools are being given new guidelines to treat cases of molest with more sensitivity. India finally has enacted a law meant to prevent sexual harassment against female employees in the workplace. The Sexual Harassment of Women at Workplace (Prevention, Prohibition and Redressal) Act of 2013 was enacted almost 16 years after the Indian Supreme Court laid down guidelines making it mandatory for every employer to provide a mechanism to redress complaints related to workplace harassment and enforce the right to gender equality.

The new awareness claimed a high profile personality in February 2015. RK Pachauri, head of the UN's Nobel Prize-winning Intergovernmental Panel on Climate Change, was forced to quit the climate change panel and other posts he held in India after a 29-year-old research assistant in The Energy and Resources Institute, which he heads, accused the 74-year-old Pachauri of stalking and complained of his unwelcome sexual advances. It helps that in Narendra Modi, India has a leader who is unequivocally committed to the dignity of women.

20
India in a Strategic Sweet Spot

> "India has been a model international citizen. It threatens no one."
>
> — Tony Abbott, prime minister of Australia, 2013–15

BETWEEN AD 1024 and AD 1665, the ancient Hindu temple of Somnath in Gujarat, Narendra Modi's home state, was attacked and looted no less than five times by marauding chieftains, starting with Mahmud of Ghazni and finally by the Mughal emperor Aurangzeb. After every attack, it was rebuilt and restocked with ornaments and precious metal. Yet little was done to ensure its protection from the next raid, such was the faith of Indians in the gods that protected them, not to speak of the barrenness of their strategic thinking.

In some ways, that trust in destiny is emblematic of the Indian attitude to the world, built, it appears sometimes, around the Hindu concept of impermanence of the body and reincarnation of the soul. The sense of fatalism and complacency continued into the late 1950s when, after a period of euphoria, ties with China began to sour, leading to a crushing military defeat in 1962. The Chinese would deliver their blow and withdraw, but India would be left with a sense of betrayal.

Thanks to that rude shock, India would embark on a military modernisation programme that would see it acquire modern weaponry, bolster its forces on the eastern and western fronts and take the first steps to build its own war industry, including a credible nuclear capability. The fruits of that endeavour would be revealed decisively not when Pakistan initiated a war with India in 1965, but in the next conflict with Pakistan, in 1971, over what was to become the new nation of Bangladesh. Indira Gandhi, who had stepped into her late father's shoes after the premature death of Nehru's successor, Lal Bahadur Shastri, would midwife the birth of Bangladesh after cleaving Pakistan in two, with the eastern half breaking away to form the new state.

It was India's finest hour in strategic terms. Its intelligence agencies and its military had worked hand in hand to capitalise on smouldering resentments in East Pakistan, brought on by West Pakistan's inability to accommodate the Bengali leader, Sheikh Mujibur Rahman. Then, when the Pakistan Army intervened with jackboots to quell the unrest, India sent its troops to fight on behalf of the Bengalis of East Pakistan, first as irregulars, later in uniform. Thus was Bangladesh born on December 16, 1971. Henceforth, India's dominance over the subcontinent would be uncontested.

Even so, India was content to remain a reactive power, keener to be loved than feared. Examples of a proactive Indian policy have been rare; in 1948, Jawaharlal Nehru sent a planeload of arms to Burma, now Myanmar, to save U Nu's government from Karen rebels who had encircled Rangoon airport. Decades later, in 1987, his grandson, Rajiv Gandhi, would send troops into Sri Lanka to enforce a peace accord between Tamil separatists and the government in Colombo, a costly blunder because of the casualties India bore. A year later, Rajiv would send paratroopers and the Indian Navy to chase down the men who had plotted a coup against the Maldivian ruler, Maumoon Abdul Gayoom.

Beyond these episodic moves, active security policy was never really the norm. As recently as a decade ago, when a devastating tsunami wrecked many installations in its Andaman & Nicobar islands, the government, ignoring suggestions from its military, avoided using the rebuilding opportunity to beef up defence installations along the strategic island chain. It figured at the time that doing so would raise unease in Southeast Asia and spark a response from China, nervous about the Straits of Malacca being a choke point.

Things are changing, though, under Modi, who has set India on a more confident and outward-bound foreign policy path. It has helped that a confluence of circumstances has placed India in a strategic sweet spot – at ease with and courted simultaneously by a host of powers, including the US, Japan, Australia, Israel, France and Russia. Increasingly, the term being used by military men and strategists is of "an Indo-Asia-Pacific region" which, more and more, is shortened to "Indo-Pacific".

Quite a bit of this is happening by default, owing to the rise in nervousness about China after a series of strategic blunders on the part of the Beijing leadership. These are worth recounting.

One abiding narrative about China, and a reason why the mainland has been held in so much awe, was its supposed ability to take the long view. (Some of this perception, particularly in the West, stems from a statement attributed to Zhou Enlai, prime minister in Mao Zedong's China, during Richard Nixon's path-breaking trip to Beijing in 1972. The popular version of the story goes that, when asked what he thought about the French Revolution, Zhou responded "it is too early to say". In truth, as diplomats present at the meeting would confirm years later, Zhou had been referring to the student revolt in Paris that had taken place in May 1968, not the events of two centuries earlier.)

If the Chinese do tend to take the long view, they have been rather remiss lately. Too sure of its power and too eager to assert itself, Beijing has put itself at odds with countries in its East Asian backyard, not to speak of many nations beyond. In 1995, three years after the United States vacated its naval base in Subic Bay and Clark Air Base in the Philippines, China moved into Mischief Reef in the Spratlys, taking the Filipinos, who have always seen the territory as their own, by surprise. Several years before, when Vietnam was not yet an Asean member, China had grabbed the Paracels from Hanoi. At the time, the rest of the world paid little heed, seeing these as one-off events. The narrative of China as a benign, rising power was largely undamaged.

In May 2009, though, China submitted a map to the United Nations with its now infamous nine-dash line markings that laid claim to most of the South China Sea. This angered the Philippines and Vietnam, which immediately lodged protests. Subsequently, Brunei, Malaysia and Indonesia have all spoken out against the Chinese claim and even Singapore, though not a claimant state, has demanded that China clarify exactly what it thinks belongs to it. This has put Beijing in a jam, because it cannot be too sure that its claims, which are based on history, will stand legal scrutiny.

There were good reasons to think that different arms of the Chinese government had not been acting in concert when the claims were published. The Foreign Ministry, it was widely believed, was not in on the policymaking for this move and had to scramble to control the international damage aroused by the claims, believed to have been made under pressure from the People's Liberation Army.

Surprisingly, it was the Philippines, one of the weakest of Southeast Asian nations, that took on China first, dragging it to international arbitration over its maritime claims. Then, as the Chinese refused to participate in the arbitration, Manila gained the moral higher ground, making Beijing look like an unreasonable bully. Analysts pointed out that China had learnt to use international law to its advantage in the World Trade Organisation, particularly the trade body's dispute settlement mechanism. But on the maritime claims, its refusal to agree to arbitration made it look like an outlaw. This is a pity. Many experts on international law believe that China may indeed have rightful claims to at least some of those islands.

China risks losing the plot elsewhere in the region too. Malaysia, for instance, was the first Asean state to recognise the People's Republic – in 1974. Unlike Vietnam and the Philippines, it always tended to deal softly with China on the maritime issue. Yet, in 2015, Kuala Lumpur felt compelled to hedge its bets, raising its strategic ties with Japan from an "enhanced partnership" relationship to a "strategic partnership". And Vietnam, which is culturally and politically close to China, is moving steadily towards the US, once its arch enemy. In addition, it is also growing its military ties with

India, which is helping it with equipment and submarine training. Indian officers are also assisting Vietnam to update its war doctrine.

Beyond the nine-dash line map, there have been other instances of Chinese short-sightedness. China's ties with Japan, for instance, are in a mess. In 2012, China allowed street protests against Japan's decision to nationalise the Senkaku Islands, which China calls Diaoyu. Japan had, of course, stirred the pot by making the first move. Tokyo claimed it nationalised the islands to head off ultranationalists at home. But the move made China react furiously. Violent protests erupted in many towns against Japanese businesses. In the city of Shandong, one Japanese establishment to face attack was the Panasonic factory. If anything, that was the one Japanese facility that ought not to have been touched. Thirty-five years earlier, Panasonic's parent company, Matsushita, had been the first foreign-funded enterprise to enter China. The Japanese company's decision had been the result of a meeting between Deng Xiaoping and Konosuke Matsushita, the company's founder. The company continued to invest in China even after the Tiananmen Square incident, which had put Beijing in the global doghouse. All this had been forgotten by the Chinese, blinded by rage. Panasonic, hurt by the outrage, and also unable to cope with intense competition, ended all television production in China in January 2015.

In November 2013, another big diplomatic miss emerged from Beijing. Typhoon Haiyan struck the Philippines with unprecedented fury, taking thousands of lives. The world turned to help the Southeast Asian nation with money and humanitarian assistance. China, still fuming at Manila for the cultural affront it had suffered on account of the arbitration move, offered $100,000 each from the government and the Red Cross Society of China, initially. The niggardly initial response was noted around the world, and drew adverse comment. The British newspaper, *The Guardian*, reported that China was giving less money than the Swedish furniture company, Ikea.

In contrast, Japan offered $10 million initially, and the US, $20 million. The US military also swung into action with a massive humanitarian mission. China did make amends after a while, sending the hospital ship,

Peace Ark, which delivered invaluable medical help to the stricken region. But few remembered that fine gesture. Too bad for the Chinese, it was their initial pettiness that stuck in public minds.

India's rise, on the other hand, is seen with less alarm across most of Asia, with the exception of Pakistan. Despite its 1987–90 misadventure in Sri Lanka under Rajiv Gandhi, its image as a benign power has largely held. The settling of the Land Boundary Agreement with Bangladesh in July 2015 and Modi's quick acceptance, in August 2014, of an arbitration ruling over a maritime dispute with Bangladesh that did not go in India's favour, have contributed to the image of a well-behaved global citizen. Even with Pakistan, it has acted responsibly, accepting another unfavourable arbitration ruling, in 2013, on sharing waters of the Indus River system.

Such actions, rather than weakening India, have added to its soft power although the country has had its own share of goof-ups. In mid-2015, for instance, its paratroopers entered Myanmar territory to strike at the camps of insurgents who had targeted India, then fled across the border. Unwisely, it trumpeted the action as a sign of its resolve to go in hot pursuit. The jingoism was meant as a signal to Pakistan but it was received poorly in Naypyidaw, which had quietly given India permission for the raid in its territory. Ajit Doval, Modi's national security adviser, had to fly to Myanmar to repair the damage.

India, thus, has an opportunity to move into the centre of the Asian geostrategic sphere. This it could do through two avenues.

The first is its natural weight in the world, brought on by the prospects of its $2.3 trillion economy outpacing China and emerging as a key global growth engine for the region, even as the Chinese mainland slows from its frenetic pace of a quarter century. Many think the Chinese economy is already showing the pain of a hard landing and worry about the consequences. The stock market upheavals in China in mid-2015 and the panic emanating from Chinese economic policymakers, including a surprise devaluation and repeated rate cuts, suggest a swiftly slowing economy. The world now knows that while China's rise is inevitable, its advance cannot be plotted in a straight line. For India, the China events ought not to be more than a sideshow. It has to rise on its own legs.

For now, the prospects for that do not look too bad. The Indian economy is steaming along, although some do worry about the quality of its growth data. Research company Crisil, a unit of Standard & Poor's, reckons that economic growth will accelerate to 7.9% in the year to March 2017. By then, India will pass Brazil and Italy in the size of its GDP. By the end of this decade, it has a good chance of overtaking France and Britain to become the fifth largest economy. But the economies of Japan and China are much more distant targets. Indeed, unless there is a severe implosion of the Chinese economy, which is unlikely, India's GDP will probably not pass China's within our lifetime.

Second, India could emerge as a strong and reliable security guarantor for Asia. Its Navy, whose tonnage is poised to expand by more than a third in a short time, regularly patrols the South China Sea these days, having started mapping the waters since the turn of the century. And, as the post-tsunami relief effort showed, it has the airlift and other capacities to project power beyond its neighbourhood. Its space technology is creditable; in December 2015, India launched six Singapore satellites in a flawless launch aboard its Polar Satellite Launch Vehicle, which some say could double as an intercontinental ballistic missile. Increasingly, it is heading towards a situation in which it can simultaneously draw upon high technology from the US, Israel, Russia and Japan. No other military today enjoys such a sweet spot.

To be taken seriously though, it needs to present a coherent, convincing face to the world. And for that it will need to work on not only its external sinews, including its diplomacy and intelligence services, but also settle into a more cooperative brand of domestic politics. The last may well be the bigger challenge. By the circumstances of its birth as a free nation independent of British colonial rule, India's political development began long before its economic development. The consequences have been evident for all to see – confusion, disorder and a lack of strategic focus. The country has rivals, sure, but it cannot be said to have too many enemies outside its borders; its real foes are within.

Power, they say, abhors a vacuum, and a vacuum is what was manifest within India in the last years of Manmohan Singh's term. The ripples were felt across its neighbourhood, and beyond. It was disheartening to see India lose its way, unable to keep its promises, or fulfil even half its potential. The regard that India was accorded at the start of the UPA government receded into despair, and in East Asia, open contempt.

In many ways, India also failed its immediate neighbourhood. One of the most telling failures of this unfortunate phase was the U-turn that India made in March 2012 on an important US-sponsored resolution concerning Sri Lanka before the UN Human Rights Council in Geneva. After assuring Sri Lanka's defence secretary, Gotabhaya Rajapaksa, of New Delhi's support, the country voted against Sri Lanka. Chidambaram had taken the matter to Sonia Gandhi and, fearful of upsetting Tamil voters in southern India, she had ordered the about-turn.

Two years later, Chinese submarines docked in Colombo Port for the first time, triggering alarm in New Delhi, which had adjudged Mahinda Rajapaksa (the Sri Lankan president, and brother of Gotabhaya) to be an unreliable neighbour. This happened after he turned to China for funds to develop Hambantota, his power base in Sri Lanka's southern tip. In truth, he had first approached India for help but New Delhi had turned him down. Now New Delhi was objecting to his Plan B.

In early 2015, he was ousted after Maithripala Sirisena, one of his closest Cabinet aides, turned on him and contested against the president in the snap election he had called to extend his rule. India's spy agency, RAW, was accused of masterminding the revolt. While Sri Lanka has its fair share of conspiracy theories, this one was not outside the realm of possibility; New Delhi, it came to light subsequently, had withdrawn the RAW station chief just ahead of the election, on a request from Mahinda. The successful ejection of Mahinda – he tried to come back as prime minister a few months later and was defeated again – is perhaps one of the rare external intelligence successes India has scored in recent years. In Maldives, on the other hand, RAW has been a failure; the neutral Mohamed Nasheed was ousted as president and jailed. The new regime has cancelled Indian contracts and sought to give China a bigger foothold in the country.

While the domestic-focused Intelligence Bureau has significantly upgraded its capabilities, RAW is not the agency it was in the 1970s. Its agents within Indian embassies often adopt an ostentatious lifestyle, showing they have access to more funds than the average diplomat. Much of the information it gathers is from newspapers. Former agents say there are fewer agents left in the field with a reputation for boldness, and RAW personnel tend to spend too much time keeping an eye on its own, including MEA staff. While it does all right on Pakistan, for intelligence on China, it is said to depend substantially on friends like the US, Britain and Japan.

Given the influential Indian community in the US, and the presence of Indians in all branches of hi-tech research, many at high levels, one would have expected India's covert agencies to have a first-rate technology gathering programme. But New Delhi has been too timid here, too. Almost all of its work in information technology – one of the four areas that Manmohan Singh had told Menon to make his priority as NSA – is defensive. To be a significant power, India will need to develop a world-class intelligence agency combining feet on the ground, technical capabilities and first-rate analysis. The inputs derived have to be not just for national security, but for commercial use as well. It does not have that strength now.

But intelligence is only a tool. India's security is best guaranteed by a rapid buildup of its economic power. At the moment, it is between 12 and 15 years behind China in its development and the gap is not easily bridged, particularly since Beijing is steering its own economy towards a more efficient model while India continues to flounder with old ways of doing things. Modi is aware of this weakness but his go-it-alone personality shuts out the outreach to rival parties and interest groups necessary to build the consensus on which the pillars of a new economic regime have to rest. Even if India, rising from a lower base, outpaces China's economic growth by 2 percentage points every year for the next two decades, it will still not have the larger economy. Such is the gap between the two.

On the other hand, advances in science can lead to fortune for India. Already, it has leapfrogged what used to be its abysmal communications infrastructure by having the fastest growing market for telephony. The amazing burst of smart phone sales, for instance, is showing up in areas like online shopping. India Post, the 160-year-old postal giant, had been pondering closing many of its 155,000 post offices. Today, after linking up with some 400 e-commerce companies, it is enjoying a revival with cash-on-delivery parcels handled by the department clocking annual growth of 300%. Morgan Stanley and Goldman Sachs forecast that online retail buying in India will leap from $3 billion in 2014 to $100 billion by 2020. Currently, less than half of Indians are connected to the Internet. Small wonder that Amazon is investing $2 billion in India.

Likewise, it has the opportunity to build a clean future. Solar technology, for instance, is getting increasingly cheaper just as sun-soaked India's energy demand is poised to double. For the first time, the cost of producing solar energy has become so cost-effective that it has achieved what is called "grid parity" with coal, thus far the cheapest fuel. China is retooling its economy to repair the awful impact its growth has had on its environment. India has the opportunity to avoid the pain substantially.

Rapid economic growth is important for India's defence posture as well. The military budget has to grow in tandem with the economic pie, or the distortions caused will pull away funds from vitally needed sectors such as health and education. (Already, smaller countries in its neighbourhood like Bangladesh and Sri Lanka have progressed faster on the UN Millennium Development Goals.) India cannot afford to drop its outlays on building skills and improving public health.

If the near-term strategic target is some sort of parity with China, the goal is nowhere close to being reached. India is significantly weaker. Indeed, given India's poor defence preparedness and the character of the nervously fearful AK Antony, China could have walked into Arunachal Pradesh at any time; or at least taken strategically vital Tawang. That it did not do so should be credited more to Beijing's restraint rather than respect for or recognition of India's strength. Perhaps fear of pushing India too close to the US camp was a factor as well in the Chinese calculus. But the Chinese attitude may not stay fixed for all time; already there are signs of a recalibration by Beijing at many levels on its approach to India.

Modi knows that the Asian Century cannot be realised unless China and India settle their outstanding issues and allow their economic relationship to flower. The Indian leader has been pushing China to take a strategic view of the relationship and strive for an early border settlement, but it is difficult to envisage that happening too quickly. Both sides have their limitations. Any honourable settlement will involve tradeoffs but the Indian leader is well aware of the taunts that would await him in parliament, particularly if Congress, emaciated but still the biggest Opposition group in the House, takes a partisan role. A half-century ago, when Jawaharlal Nehru sought to play down Chinese incursions into Kashmir's Aksai Chin area by saying not a blade of grass grew there, Mahavir Tyagi, a prominent advocate for Independence and later, an MP from the Congress party, had assailed Nehru: "There is not a strand of hair on the PM's head; does that mean his head is not important?"

India has to approach China as one united nation, not as a collection of parties bitterly opposed to each other. This is unlikely to happen. And yet talk of a fair boundary settlement that could lead to an acceleration of ties may be putting the cart before the horse. China, which has settled 12 of its 14 boundary disputes on generous terms, is showing little appetite for such an approach with India. Indeed, more and more, the Chinese strongman Xi Jinping is mixing territorial disputes with nationalistic fervour, a potent brew that only limits his negotiating options.

Beijing's turn to the oceans beyond its first island chain and clear signalling that it wants a major presence in the Indian and Pacific Oceans, is another complicating factor. Some analysts also think they are seeing increased activity within pro-China insurgents in India's troubled northeastern states. China had ended all support to such groups in 1988. Even so, the two are not fated to live as tense neighbours.

Worry over what sort of China will emerge in the coming decades is why the Japan relationship is poised to gain salience in India's engagement with the world. Japan is the only other Asian nation with the capacity, and will, to stand up to China. It has tweaked its strategic doctrine and altered laws so its military can now go to the aid of allies. It is building up its military-industrial complex and is ready to export arms, reversing the policies of decades. Japan's rapid advances in robotics, its well-hidden nuclear technology, combined with Indian engineering and software skills, hold great promise for their strategic partnership. There is a strong possibility of India going for Japanese conventional submarines next, after buying the US-2 amphibious planes. The case is helped by Tokyo's willingness to go along with India's "Make In India" ambitions. With the two nations bookending the Indo-Pacific theatre, and the US both in the centre and at the fringes, the relationship with Tokyo is poised for take-off. Modi's hesitation to move faster with Japan is borne of advice cautioning him on China's reaction to such a development. It is not Japan that is hesitating.

Likewise, India's elevation of its ties with South Korea into a "special strategic partnership" – matching its nomenclature for Japan – also bodes well for the country, particularly in the area of high technology.

Technology linkages will play an increasingly larger role in future strategic patterns. A visit to the Samsung Group's technology headquarters in Suwon, South Korea – they call it Republic of Samsung – suggested exactly how this could be so. I was told that 1,400 of the 35,000 working in Samsung R&D were foreigners. Fully half of them were Indians. If Indians like Satya Nadella and Sundar Pichai get to run Microsoft and Google Inc., it is not on account of their talent alone, immense as it is. There is also a comfort level with having them around that plays a role in boardroom decisions.

Seoul is mindful of its relationship with China but Beijing's support for the North Korean regime is pushing it ever more firmly back into the lap of its traditional ally, the US. This works in India's favour. Besides, South Korea needs access to the vast Indian market, especially at a time when China is lengthening its domestic supply chain, crimping opportunities for Korean exports. For its part, India needs South Korea's technology, where it excels in everything from shipbuilding to high-speed railways, even submarines. It is interesting to note that South Korea nudged ahead of Japan and Germany to take first place in the 2015 Bloomberg Innovation Index. Israel, the US, Singapore and Britain are some of the other nations that figure in the Top 10 of that list, all of whom have close ties with India. These things presage well for India's future.

India is also moving swiftly on its strategic relationship with Vietnam, which, at the same time, is elevating its relationship with the US. Their navies collaborate closely and their air forces have a nascent relationship that is poised to grow. Vietnam may well be the first nation to receive the BrahMos hypersonic cruise missile as India tentatively steps into the area of arms exports. Indeed, the Russians, who co-developed the missile, are said to endorse the plan. New Delhi may make its first shipments after it gains entry into the Missile Technology Control Regime. Aside from their shared interests in freedom of navigation in the South China Sea, India sees the relationship as valuable in applying pressure on China's close ties with Pakistan.

There are other opportunities waiting to be seized. Southeast Asia used to be the automatic choice for Japanese investors looking to reduce boardroom risk by finding alternative manufacturing locations to China, where wage costs are rising, the population is ageing and civic unrest is mounting. The Asean Economic Community, with its promise of a unified market rivalling India, was an added draw. But rising country and region risk in Southeast Asia, increasingly a hotbed of Islamic militancy, could lead investors to no longer see Asean as an automatic alternative to China. Vietnam's tense standoff with China makes it less attractive to global investors. Thailand was the Southeast Asian centre for auto manufacturing but the political paralysis there, and now army rule, is affecting the economy and its investment profile. Indonesia's allure as an investment destination was fading, although recent steps by president Joko Widodo to open up the economy somewhat has alleviated some of the gloom. Malaysia's creeping Islamisation is spreading worry and its politics is getting messier.

A stable India, with improved infrastructure and the promise of a billion-plus consumers, is an attractive proposition for everyone, including China. This is already being reflected in the foreign direct investment numbers, which have shot up substantially in Modi's first year and will surely rise more, and faster, during his tenure. Like they do in Europe, investors will pick their spots in India, gravitating to states that hold the promise of being better hosts, and those that have friendlier labour laws.

The rise of India as a manufacturing destination is welcome news for its youthful population, even as it collides with another mega trend – the rapid advance of automation and robotisation of manufacturing. Take the number of employees at Maruti Suzuki, India's No. 1 carmaker. At its original plant in Gurgaon and Manesar, just outside New Delhi, it employs a total of more than 8,000. In 2012, Modi, then chief minister of Gujarat, wooed the company to set up a third factory in his state. Chairman Osamu Suzuki agreed to the plant only after he got Gujarat to agree that he could install 800 robots on the pressing and welding floors, meaning 95% of the work would be automated. At the Tamil Nadu factory of the iconic motorcycle maker Royal Enfield, the paint job is done by mechanical robots with 2.1 metre mechanical arms that cut wastage by half and work four times faster than humans. Robot installations are growing at annual rates of 25% in the country, not unlike in Indonesia, and for the same reasons: robots don't claim minimum wage, are not unionised or go on strike.

With every passing week, it takes thousands of dollars in extra investment to create a single new job. India also has to recognise that 3D printing and advanced robotics in manufacture are contributing to the reshoring phenomenon whereby the big advanced markets of the West may well be producing more locally for consumption. This could curtail India's export hopes.

Also, India cannot assume that all it has to do is hold out the lure of its big market and investors will bang on its doors. It needs an ecosystem – from skill building to infrastructure and a stable political environment – that makes it attractive for long-term investments. Should India not succeed in winning sufficient investment from overseas, and convince its own entrepreneurs to invest at home, it could see its demographic dividend – it has one of the youngest populations – turn into a demographic disaster.

In other words, New Delhi simply has to treat employment as a national security issue on par with its military preparedness, and give it the same attention.

That said, Indians are probably better placed than many others to deal with the disruptive technologies that are emerging. The country now leads the world in smartphone growth, with 160 million operating in 2015. Web users in the period climbed by more than a third to hit 232 million. A report by the respected technology analyst, Mary Meeker, said smartphones accounted for 41% of India's e-commerce. Just as Indians leapfrogged from their British era phone systems to the cell phone age (the country has the lowest call rates in the world), it is now taking to smartphones with the same gusto. This has profound implications for its services economy in the first half of the 21st century.

If its tourism industry can also get off the ground, that alone could guarantee millions of good jobs. Given India's ancient culture, monuments and improving aviation facilities, it is not inconceivable for it to be able to receive multiples of the 7.4 million visitors it got in 2014. As a share of GDP, travel and tourism contributed just 2.2% that year, even less than Pakistan's 2.9% and Cambodia's 13.5%. That's a measure of the potential that exists for India to grow the sector. For instance, it got little of the 117 million Chinese who travelled overseas in 2014 – fewer than 200,000 in fact. Interestingly, more than twice as many travel out of India as visit the country, filling cruise liners in the South China Sea and mountain resorts in Switzerland.

For India to rise swiftly, a peaceful neighbourhood is essential. With Pakistan, a stalemate seems inevitable. The historical baggage was heavy enough, but is now complicated by Great Power intervention as India tilts towards the US, while China, Islamabad's "all-weather friend", embraces Pakistan even more closely. Besides, the entrenched interests of the Pakistani establishment, dominated by the Army, preclude the possibility of any meaningful cross-border relationship. Pakistan will always be used as a proxy by China to mire India in its neighbourhood, even as Beijing remains wary of Pakistan's darker side as a nursery of sectarianism and Muslim militancy, some of it clearly spilling over into Xinjiang. Sri Lanka, Nepal and Bangladesh pose less difficult challenges.

Mountainous Nepal may be the most important of all, and also the easiest to win over, particularly for a ruling Indian party built on Hindu nationalism. Aside from the open borders and free flow of Nepali workers into India, and the several regiments of Gurkha soldiers in the Indian Army, there is sound economic logic to the relationship – for India to build up its manufacturing, cheap power is essential. Nepal, whose main rivers all flow into India, has an estimated 83,000 MW of untapped hydropower, of which half is considered commercially viable. Currently it exploits less than 10% of its potential. Sound, mutually beneficial treaties could ensure cheap and assured power from Nepal across the heartland states of northern India.

Unfortunately, the Nepalese elite are slow learners: Bhutan today has among the highest per capita GDP in the subcontinent because it profits immensely from its power sales to the eastern Indian states. The Nepalese, on the other hand, have been far less willing to share their hydel wealth.

A strong and self-confident India will also reduce temptation in its neighbours to play off the twin giants. At the same time, New Delhi must understand that it cannot react like a spinster in a male locker room every time it sees China showing up in its neighbourhood. China's size and heft will inevitably push it into every corner of the world, and particularly across the vast Indian Ocean. India's strategy should be not to complain, but confidently assert its own presence, if necessary, in China's own backyard. In a small way, it has begun doing that in Vietnam and the Philippines. At the end of the day, nothing is as important as self-belief.

21
Right Man, Wrong Party? The Importance of Being Modi

> "All of us, to whatever religion we may belong, are equally the children of India with equal rights, privileges and obligations. We cannot encourage communalism or narrow-mindedness, for no nation can be great whose people are narrow in thought or in action."
>
> — Jawaharlal Nehru, on the eve of Indian Independence

LEENA SARMA, A senior officer in Indian Railways, recounted an overnight train ride with two politicians from Gujarat in the summer of 1990. The previous day's journey from Lucknow, capital of Uttar Pradesh, to New Delhi, had been a harrowing one for the young woman and a fellow probationary officer. Forced to vacate their reserved seats by thuggish elements accompanying some politicians, the two women had spent the night fearing for their honour and security.

Now, as they travelled on the next leg from New Delhi to Ahmedabad in Gujarat, the worry was greater. They did not have confirmed seats and the Travelling Ticket Examiner temporarily put them into a compartment with a pair of men, also dressed like politicians, mentioning they were regulars on the route. To the women's surprise, and in complete contrast to the behaviour they had witnessed the previous night, this pair squeezed themselves into a corner to make room for them, paid for the meals and, at night, opted to sleep on the floor so the young women could use the padded berths above.

As she detrained, a grateful Sarma asked them to scrawl their names in a diary she was carrying. The younger of the two, a bearded man with a brooding presence, wrote "Narendra Modi". The older man wrote "Shankarsinh Vaghela".

Vaghela would become Gujarat's chief minister in 1996. Modi would take his job in late 2001.

"Every time I see him on TV I remember that warm meal, that gentle courtesy, caring and sense of security we got that night far from home," Sarma wrote in *The Hindu* newspaper in 2014, repeating an anecdote first told nearly two decades earlier to newspapers in her home state, Assam.

It has been a while since Indians felt secure in the knowledge that they had a strong leader at the helm, thanks to the dysfunctional diarchy that prevailed in New Delhi for a decade as the Sonia Gandhi-Manmohan Singh duo lurched around, one protecting her political estate as she waited for her son and firstborn to mature, the other merely warming his seat as the designated estate manager.

In Narendra Damodardas Modi, the first prime minister born in the post-Independence era, however, there can be no doubt about who is in charge. The man is everywhere, travelling around the world, around his vast nation, spending time with space scientists as they successfully eject a spacecraft into Mars' orbit, even occupying cyberspace where his tweets are followed by no less than 18 million people, the prime minister himself often providing the first source of information on government decisions – most recently, a surprise trip to Pakistan. Not since the early days of Jawaharlal Nehru, India's founding prime minister, has the nation seen a man of his vigour and stamina. Indeed, it is remarkable that India, a nation where two-thirds are below the age of 35, chose to vest its fortunes with this politician well into his 60s rather than the Congress party, fronted in the polls by Rahul Gandhi, a man two decades his junior.

Already, thanks to his vigour and charisma, Modi has succeeded in projecting his BJP to power in two key provinces – Maharashtra and Haryana – states that had never had a full BJP government before. Today, even as the party had spectacular failures in elections to assemblies in Delhi and Bihar, the BJP controls states that contribute fully half of India's GDP, seen as positive for economic reform and a key factor that cheers investors who have turned open the tap on foreign direct investments, critical for Modi's "Make In India" programme to boost manufacture. In the first six months of 2015, India topped the global foreign direct investments rankings with $31 billion received, ahead of China and the US, according to figures cited by the *Financial Times*. The previous year it had ranked fifth, behind China, the US, Britain and Mexico. Place by place, India has begun the march up the rankings as an attractive spot to do business.

Lost in the excitement over rising foreign direct investments is a key, but little noticed fact: fewer Indian businessmen are taking capital out of the country to invest overseas. From the $9.2 billion that Indians invested overseas in 2013–14, the last year of Manmohan Singh's gloom-filled administration of India, the outflow plunged to $1.8 billion in the first year of Modi's term. Between 2011 and 2012, at the height of the despondency over the Congress party's administration of India, some $17 billion flowed out as scam after scam rocked the nation. The Indian media's most used description of the prevailing situation in New Delhi then was "policy paralysis".

These days, analysts believe India is the only one of the Bric nations – that also include Brazil, Russia and China – likely to show significant economic acceleration in the 2015–18 period. Russia's oil and gas-export-dependent economy is on the ropes, China is beset with deflation, capital flight and structural adjustment issues that have halved its growth rate, while Brazil's economy is not just slowing, but sliding. In several speeches through 2015, IMF managing director Christine Lagarde described India as a rare bright spot in the global economy.

The Modi effect is palpable overseas too, where Indians are regaining their swagger after having had to cast eyes downward for years, thanks to the perpetual bad news that used to emerge from their home nation. In September 2014, more people showed up in New York's Madison Square

Garden to hear Modi speak than at rock singer Billy Joel's concert at the same venue earlier that month. In Dubai, United Arab Emirates (UAE), a year later, he filled a cricket stadium. There, Modi would not have failed to notice that thousands of Muslim emigres from India were in the audience to wave to him enthusiastically, proving that Modi does have support in the minority community and, perhaps more importantly, exposing the lie that the Muslims of India are somehow less patriotic than their Hindu brethren. On the same trip, in Abu Dhabi, he visited the Grand Mosque, an important gesture that many in India interpreted as a message to Muslims in his own nation, anxious about his conservative Hindu leanings. In turn, the Abu Dhabi ruler announced that Indian Hindus working in the emirate would be allotted land to build their first temple there. Next door, Dubai has two Hindu temples, but for more conservative Abu Dhabi, this was a first. Clearly, a quid pro quo was involved and it is interesting that Modi was prepared to make that concession for a larger cause.

What is that cause? First, with the US slowly losing interest in the Middle East as its oil dependence eases and as its attention focuses on China, the region is in play, so to speak. Modi was only getting there early in the game. Second, more than 7 million Indians work in Gulf states and are a huge source of remittances, particularly for states such as Kerala in the south, which is dependent on the money its emigres send home. But there was a third reason; the UAE, along with China and the US, is among Pakistan's biggest backers. Moving the UAE to the centre weighs on Pakistan to an extent, especially against the backdrop of the tightening US-India strategic embrace. Modi's foreign policy is a quickstepping one.

One abiding worry about Modi is his attitude towards minority communities. At more than 170 million and nearly 15% of the population, India has the world's second-largest number of Muslims in its fold. Christians, at 24 million, are about 2.3% of the population. Both Christians and Muslims have lived in India for centuries – Christianity arrived in AD 52 with St Thomas, the Apostle, while Islam arrived in India around the seventh century, both first in Kerala. In southern Indian states, therefore, the minorities are reasonably well integrated. In school I had a classmate named Sunil Mohamed while my closest friend in New Delhi, Mohan Joseph, is a Syrian Catholic who shared a desk with me in my undergraduate days in Bangalore. Now a high official in the finance ministry, he is married to Shanti and has daughters named Nivedita and Namrata. Thus all the members of the family, church goers all, have names typically heard in Hindu households. This did not happen because it was forced on them but in a natural way, because successive generations felt secure enough in their identities to adopt what they considered the sweetest names available.

Elsewhere though, particularly in North India, minorities, particularly Muslims, have sometimes lived an uneasy existence because of the Muslim invasions down the Khyber Pass and the tortured history of the Independence movement, with its massive bloodletting and the creation of Pakistan as a nation for the subcontinent's Muslims. Their discomfort with every little unhelpful signal from the majority community is therefore understandable. But, in Modi's India, even many Christians have been feeling insecure and vulnerable. Some of this is because of movements like *ghar wapsi* (which loosely translates as "coming home") by Hindu fringe groups under the RSS umbrella, looking to convert poor Indians to Hinduism. Christmas Day 2014, which came six months after Modi took charge of India, was officially also marked as Good Governance Day, upsetting the Christian community. Other moves, such as the ban on beef from cows in the state of Maharashtra and the absence of Muslim MPs on the BJP ticket (the actress, Hema Malini, who converted to Islam to be able to wed a married man, is the nominal exception), despite its huge mandate, also give the minorities a sense of marginalisation.

Indeed, Julio Ribeiro, one of India's most celebrated policemen and one of the key figures behind putting down the Sikh insurgency in Punjab in the 1980s, bemoaned in an editorial page article in *The Indian Express* that "Today, in my 86th year, I feel threatened, not wanted, reduced to a stranger in my own country."

The piece caused an uproar, and even BJP stalwarts like Arun Shourie

– a star of the Vajpayee years but denied a government seat by Modi – rose to complain. Later, Ribeiro said he had exaggerated a bit because that was the only way to get attention in India.

Modi himself has done little to promote such insecurity, but neither has he acted decisively to stem it, perhaps because he feels it is better to let the lunatic fringe vent itself than to stamp on them and create a backlash. Either way, it is a strain on the national fabric. This worries his well-wishers. In January 2015, US president Barack Obama ended his second visit to New Delhi by saying in a public speech that while no society is immune to the darkest impulses of men, "India will succeed so long as it is not splintered along the lines of religious faith." In November the same year, at an official lunch for Modi, who was on a bilateral visit to Singapore, prime minister Lee Hsien Loong pointedly drew attention to the contributions of minority groups, including Muslim emigres from Modi's Gujarat, to the island's success story. The previous day, deputy prime minister Tharman Shanmugaratnam, presenting Modi a ceramic vase after his Singapore Lecture, let drop that the pottery was crafted by "our most eminent Muslim artist".

In a land of exaggerations – from the sights, the sounds, the politics and everything in between, India tends to be an assault on the senses – Ribeiro's was just one more voice, though a big one. But it was also an important signal that India can be ruled only from the centre, not the extremes, whether in faith, economic policy or foreign policy. Such is its size and complexity. As his visit to Abu Dhabi's Grand Mosque showed, the more time Modi spends in office, the more he, perforce, has to drift towards the middle, and that is a good thing for himself and his nation.

Modi had a good record in Gujarat of keeping his party's extreme right wing in check. At his boldest, he had not hesitated to clear unauthorised roadside Hindu temples to open up easier passage for traffic and pedestrians. As prime minister though, his significant failing has been to crack down on the *Hindutva* crowd that have grown increasingly bold since his rise to power. In one of the most tragic instances of *Hindutva* rabidness, Mohamed Akhlaq, a Muslim man in Dadri, a rural settlement less than 50 km from

New Delhi, was lynched in September 2015 on suspicion that he had stored beef in his refrigerator. His young son was beaten to an inch of his life. Akhlaq's other son, who is with the Indian Air Force, was away at the time.

The instigation for the killing had apparently come from a priest in the village temple. Police later said forensic examination had shown the meat in the fridge to be mutton. If it indeed is true that calls from the temple priest had led to the outrage, it would indicate that India's Hindus are taking a cue from their Muslim brethren, who are often accused of allowing their preachers to have an excessive say in their lives.

More interesting was Modi's reaction, or lack of it. For more than two weeks, while India's urban and middle classes worked themselves into a frenzy of indignation, the prime minister, usually quick to respond to events, stayed silent. When he spoke, it was through an interview to a Kolkata daily, where he called the incident "unfortunate" and "unwarranted" while pointing out that Uttar Pradesh, the state where the murder took place, was not ruled by the BJP but by Samajwadi Party, a regional outfit. Not only did the words seem uttered without his usual force, he appeared to have forgotten for the moment that as prime minister, he was responsible for all 1.2 billion Indians.

Many linked Modi's reticence with the ongoing campaign for the state elections in populous Bihar, a province he swept in the parliamentary poll the previous year. Control of the state assembly was important for the larger purpose of governing India, because not only would it add one more state he could directly influence, but also, members of the upper house of parliament are picked by an electoral college that includes state assemblies. Gaining Bihar would help him there. Many of his parliamentary initiatives have been stalled because, unlike the lower house that he dominates, the BJP does not control Rajya Sabha, the upper house. Among the dominant castes of Bihar are the Yadavs, traditional cowherds, and the beef issue, he was aware, could resonate with them. Hence the silence, perhaps. If such thinking is accurate, that would show up Modi to be more of an opportunist than a true statesman. And certainly he can be no Nehru then, or even a Vajpayee.

In any case, the ploy did not work. The BJP fared poorly in the Bihar state election, chipping away at Modi's air of invincibility.

To his credit, Modi has unwaveringly maintained that he is the *vikas purush*, the development man. Yet, he has allowed that agenda to be sometimes circumscribed, or at least in the public imagination, overtaken by the *Hindutva* brigade to which he seems beholden. Indeed, at times he seems oblivious to the risk that he and India face from unsettling its minorities, who number close to 200 million. If the Maoist insurgency was the top national security concern in Manmohan Singh's government, minority unrest could well turn out to be Modi's Achilles heel.

Oddly, no prime minister, not even Nehru, has dominated his Cabinet in the manner that Modi seems to. Even so, in September 2015, several Cabinet ministers appeared before the RSS leadership, which was meeting over three days in New Delhi, to report back to the parent body on the work within their ministries. In the Manmohan Singh administration, Congress Cabinet ministers were known to keep Sonia Gandhi briefed on their work. But she and her son Rahul were at least elected MPs. The RSS leadership is not accountable to the people.

The earlier, therefore, that he cuts loose from the *Hindutva* crowd, the higher the chances for Modi to be the political emperor of all Indians, and for a longer period of time than his current five-year term. Not only will he have to cut loose from the RSS, he may need to cut away from the BJP too. Certainly, he has the national standing to cast a political grouping in his name. Indeed, as he savoured a run for national office, and met stiff resistance from the old warlords within the BJP, he had, for a time, considered setting out on his own.

Besides, the BJP was a mediocre political institution and, until Modi came along, essentially an urban phenomenon. Unlike the hoary Congress, it has no great traditions to lay claim to. Until 2006, when it took power in the southern state of Karnataka, the BJP did not have what could be called a national presence. In the late 1980s and early 1990s, it placed excessive emphasis on the God Rama, whereas the Hindu pantheon is vast; Rama is but one of the incarnations of Vishnu, the Preserver. If anything, the two major events linked to the BJP – the December 1992 razing of the Babri Mosque that unleashed large-scale communal violence in northern India, and to an extent, PM Vajpayee's decision to conduct a series of nuclear tests in 1998 that brought a host of sanctions down on India – are of dubious virtue. And the first event was decidedly a blot to India's reputation for tolerance.

On the other hand, a stress on *Indutva*, or Indianness, would perhaps offer a more lasting glue. That would require Modi to moderate his primal instincts and adopt a line more in tune with his nation's syncretic culture. Two years into his term, his personal popularity remains undiminished. Given his charisma, his focus on development and his unique ability to articulate his vision, India's masses will likely swarm to such a persona because they sense the inherent contradiction between *Hindutva* and development.

That aside, it must also be added that in India even the majority Hindus have their insecurities. For long years, Indians watched with growing unease as neighbouring Pakistan, Sri Lanka and even tiny Bhutan shed their secular moorings and moved to appease their majority communities, Pakistan with a lurch towards Islam and Sri Lanka, towards its Buddhist Sinhalas. Within India, successive Congress governments played the communal card for political ends, heightening consciousness of religion in politics. In 1983, campaigning for state elections in Jammu & Kashmir, Indira Gandhi visited prominent temples in the majority-Hindu Jammu region as she tried to prise the state from the grip of the National Conference Party, whose founder Sheikh Abdullah had died the previous year. Her son and successor, Rajiv Gandhi, trying to appease fundamentalist Muslims, got parliament to pass legislation in 1986 that overturned the previous year's judgment by the Supreme Court that granted Muslim divorcees the right to alimony from their former husbands. This fuelled anger in the majority Hindus, and lent credence to the BJP's charges that Congress pursued "pseudo-secularism".

Now, the aggressive face of Islam coming into view abroad, and even in parts of India, is beginning to be a worry. The spiritual guru Sri Sri Ravi

Shankar, my senior at Bangalore's St Joseph's College, once voiced to me his bitterness about how, in the Muslim majority Malappuram district of Kerala, non-Muslim students who brought lunch to school during the fasting period of Ramadan were told to eat in the toilets.

The BJP has yet to win a single parliamentary seat in Kerala, India's most literate state, but it is only a matter of time before it will. A recent report in *The Hindu*, a respected newspaper known for its robust secular positions, spoke of how even Christian youth were leaving the entrenched Congress and socialist parties to join the BJP.

Modi has also shaken up India's moribund, self-serving bureaucracy. Caddies at Delhi Golf Club complain of a lack of custom as many bureaucrats skip their morning nine-holes to make sure they are in office well in time. At times, Modi has gone about this in school-masterly fashion by doing spot checks. A story doing the rounds in New Delhi has it that he once arrived in the office of a top bureaucrat with the rank of secretary to find the officer not in his seat even though his air-conditioners had been switched on long before his usual arrival time. Modi hung around a bit, then left. The officer, alerted to the presence of the prime minister in his office, scrambled to reach the building, but he was too late. Modi was gone by the time he arrived. At a meeting, soon after, of top government officials Modi fixed his cold eyes on the man and said pointedly: "I keep saying we have to save energy. Yet when I visited a certain officer recently, he not only was not in his seat in time but his room had been cooled a long time before his arrival."

The bureaucracy got the message and the man concerned sulked despondently until his retirement a few months later, his career having effectively ended that day, when once he had been tipped to head the civil service. Modi also has a network of RSS-linked people in every key ministry who pass up useful intelligence, which keeps not only bureaucrats but also ministers on their toes.

But the Modi thrill lies not just in the promise of economic performance and the long due shaking up of the bureaucracy. In him, Indians sense a refreshing absence of humbug. While the classic Indian politician affects frugality while hiding vast corruption, Modi, by contrast, is unapologetically fashionable. The lenses of his eyeglasses rest in Bulgari frames. A Movado, or some Swiss timepiece, appears on his wrist. His wardrobe is vast.

Sometimes, of course, this has backfired on the man. Modi was shown up as a hopeless arriviste when he wore a pinstriped blue suit for a meeting with Obama, and telephoto lenses later revealed that the gold stripes of his suit spelt out his name in tiny gold lettering. Taking aim at both the suit and his penchant for selfies, the Indian media promptly called it the "selfie suit". Modi got rid of the garment in a hurry (the suit was auctioned for the equivalent of $695,000) but it contributed to a drubbing the BJP received at the hands of the Aam Aadmi Party in the Delhi elections that were held soon after the Obama visit in January 2015. It also gave Congress leader-in-waiting Rahul Gandhi a rare stick to beat Modi with. In speech after speech thereafter, the younger Gandhi, mostly dressed in homespun cotton whites, referred to Modi's "suit-boot" government.

There are other things about Modi that set him apart from the rest of India's politicians. Unlike the days of Congress, or even Vajpayee's PMO, top businessmen find themselves shut out of South Block by him. Many of the nation's leading businessmen are infuriated by the lack of special access.

Then there are the issues he focuses on. In his address to the nation on his inaugural Independence Day, August 15, Modi spoke of a "Digital India" and a "Make In India" campaign to woo manufacturing. But what surprised one and all was his call for the need to build toilets and to curb the predatory sexual instincts of male children. No other leader has surfaced such issues from such an important forum. Indeed, even as Modi has shunned his wife for decades, many feminists have begun to claim this macho politician as one of their own.

Modi is fortunate that he has taken office when his nation is staring at two sweet spots – demographic and strategic. With a median age of 25, India has one of the youngest population profiles at a time when China has started aging and Japan is already way over the hill. Also, a mere 33% of Indian women are officially classified as employed, their participation in the labour market having actually declined since 2005 – "a huge missed opportunity" in the words of the IMF's Lagarde. According to an IMF study, the Indian number compares badly with 50% worldwide and 63% in East Asia.

Growth windows such as these will stay open for about two decades more. For that reason, India's chance for the big-ticket reforms essential to find jobs for its teeming youth and propel it into the ranks of middle-income advanced nations is now. Conversely, if it fumbles this opportunity, India could be looking at widespread social unrest because, by 2030, it will have the world's largest workforce.

To be sure, strong as he is politically, his challenges are daunting. First, Modi needs to shake India from the stupor left behind by Manmohan Singh, with growth averaging below 5% in the last two years of Manmohan's rule, the weakest in a decade. To an extent, Modi has done so already. However, since there is often a three- to four-year lag between policy and results, he has to scramble to put India on a higher growth path as he prepares to ask his people to vote him in a second time. The political opposition stands stiffly against his move to reform land and labour laws to promote industry, partly out of cussedness but also because of Modi's inability to reach out to them. The uniform Goods & Services Tax, which the BJP opposed while in Opposition, is moving all too slowly because Congress and other parties are paying him back for opposing these reforms earlier. GST, which has the potential to turn India into a true common market, could help growth tick up between 0.5% and 1%, according to some calculations.

Another criticism of the man is that he is a control freak, and so much in a hurry that he tends sometimes to paper over issues that need deeper consideration. His bench strength in Cabinet is thin. Finance minister Arun Jaitley is an experienced and capable man, and has the prime minister's ear but has not always lived up to his initial promise. Defence minister Manohar Parikkar is well regarded, and so is Suresh Prabhu, the minister in charge of railways. The minister for external affairs, Sushma Swaraj, is a capable politician and administrator but not a Modi camp-mate, having once fancied her own chances for the top job. Critics say, beyond them, the talent in his Cabinet can be squeezed into the back seat of a Maruti Suzuki subcompact. Some, like the telegenic Smriti Irani, in charge of the critical human resource development portfolio, are downright disappointments in their jobs and clearly out of their depth. Commerce minister Nirmala Sitharaman's rigid positions on opening up trade are taking a toll on India's US relationship.

India's media, cowed by his personality initially, and resentful of the lack of leaks from his government, have also begun to pounce. Modi got a taste of it with his "selfie suit". Now, the rising influence of the *Hindutva* gangs has provided the media the excuse to find their strident voice. Slowly, they are losing their fear of him. It is a safe bet that many Opposition figures in India, and some even in his own party perhaps, would like to see him out of the way. Because of all these factors, there is, in Modi, what corporate boardrooms know as "key-man risk". In a perverse way, in Modi's strengths also lie India's fragility.

AFTERWORD AND ACKNOWLEDGEMENTS

I lay full claim to being the author of this book but it was conceived by two other people, Sharmila Kapur and Warren Fernandez.

In the years she spent in Singapore, Sharmila, who now lives in Washington DC, repeatedly urged me to write a book on India after following my reportage of the country for *The Straits Times*. She and my wife, Geetika, were teenage friends and her husband, Sanjiv, a partner with Wolfensohn & Co., my frequent golf buddy during our trench-digging days at Singapore's Transview Golf & Country Club, a picturesque facility along Dover Road that has now made way for the country's expanding education sector.

To Warren I owe too much; one of his first big moves after being appointed editor of *The Straits Times* in February 2012, was to pull me out of India, where I was happily ensconced, to give me the role of foreign editor, a position he'd himself held earlier. A little over two years into my term, he encouraged me to write this book and gave me time off for the effort. Peh Shing Huei, our Beijing bureau chief, had just turned in a splendid book on China and Warren urged me to match that with one on India. If coverage of India in *The Straits Times* has risen significantly in the past decade, Warren deserves most of the initial credit for providing the space and the resources to do so. His successors as foreign editor – Zuraidah Ibrahim and Carl Skadian – who were also my predecessors, maintained the tempo. Always encouraging, the opportunities they placed in my way to travel around the Indian subcontinent freely contributed many anecdotes to this book.

It is a matter of immense sadness to me that photojournalist Rakesh Sahai, a dear friend who shared many exciting moments with me during those travels, passed away on New Year's Day 2016 after a massive heart attack. He was a patient, keen-eyed, considerate travelling companion and his only vice was the one I introduced him to, a fondness for coffee.

Several people read this manuscript. Geetika, and my younger brother, Hari, who traded in a successful banking career for a more relaxed life, helped correct several errors of fact and interpretation. My colleague, Nilanjana Sengupta, read through several early chapters and offered valuable suggestions in her quiet, firm way. Srikant Kondapalli of Jawaharlal Nehru University in New Delhi helped with my chapter on China. The inputs I received from them have been largely incorporated.

I am also grateful to the multiple sources who spoke with me during my years in New Delhi covering South Asia, and subsequently, for this book. They are too numerous to name individually. I remain grateful to them for their candour and openness.

When I started writing this book, I dealt mostly with Shirley Hew, executive director of Singapore Press Holdings' book division. Unfortunately, she died of cancer in December 2014. Thereafter, the task of midwifing it fell into the able hands of Susan Long, who heads the division now, and Shova Loh, a patient editor with a keen eye for detail. Shova's excitement over the project helped me overcome any doubts I had that anyone would want to read this book.

I am also grateful to Lock Hong Liang and Katherine Lumberio for painstakingly working with me on the design of this book and to *The Straits Times* picture editor Stephanie Yeow for her tireless effort to source photos.

India Rising does not purport to be an academic work of history. It is really the perspective of a person who had a ringside view of the Indian pageant, leavened by the good fortune of enduring friendships and connections with some of the principal actors in government, diplomacy and the military. Reporting for *Asiaweek* and *Time* in my younger days taught me the power of the anecdote and this I took to *The Straits Times*, where I attempted to turn reporting even on the most serious issues into "stories" that can be accessed by all. This I have tried to replicate here as well. I hasten to add that all the stories told in this book are accurate to the best of my knowledge.

As foreign editor of *The Straits Times*, which has the most extensive global coverage for any Asian newspaper outside Japan, I had a thumb rule for my staff – that while we would always be sceptical and *critical* about events, personalities and countries, we would never be *cynical* in our approach. I have always held that developing countries have unique problems that cannot be assessed or judged from a classic Western foreign correspondent's point of view.

That said, my reporting on India has drawn its fair share of criticism from readers who considered me too cynical about the country, especially in the period when scam after scam erupted during Manmohan Singh's second term. One of them wrote in saying he was convinced that my critical reports must have been prompted by deep-seated fears and insecurities that could only have stemmed from an unhappy childhood.

I responded with a polite note, pointing out that the Indian civilisation was founded on the concept of truth and that, while it is always uncomfortable to see negative news about one's home whilst living abroad, Indians ought to have the depth and resilience to accept their nation's shortcomings. He wrote back immediately, withdrawing his hurtful comments.

I hope this book convinces him that I am not as negative about India as he may have led himself to believe.

Ravi Velloor
Singapore

INDEX